More Praise for *How to Reach and Teach All Children Through Balanced Literacy*

"Sandra Rief and Julie Heimburge detail the complexity of reading and writing difficulties from a balanced view of research and the reality of teaching students who struggle to learn. Teachers will greatly benefit from the thorough coverage of the struggling reader within this text."

—Joyce Wheaton, professor, Frostburg State University, and chair, Balanced Reading Instruction Special Interest Group, International Reading Association

"Is it possible to meet the needs of every student in the upper-grade language arts classroom? This dynamic book details every aspect of a balanced literacy program, as well as provides a wealth of strategies and activities that work! A must for any teacher trying to bridge the gap between slower-progressing and advanced learners."

—Nancy Fetzer, M.A., author, *Writing Connections* and *Reading Connections*

"This book should be on every teacher's desk; it is an invaluable resource for effective reading and writing strategies and helpful classroom ideas! Like a good piece of chocolate cake, it's rich in texture, has many delicious layers, and is chock full of tasty advice."

—Arlyne Skolnik, reading teacher, Long Beach School District, Long Beach, New York

"I enthusiastically endorse Rief and Heimburge's new book, *How to Reach and Teach All Children Through Balanced Literacy*. The volume is comprehensive dealing with important issues about literacy instruction. It provides research-based practice that is reader friendly with strategies perfect for classroom use. It is a pleasure to see topics such as setting up the classroom environment, making oral language a priority, and a thematic approach to literacy instruction as part of a book that deals with children in grades 3 to 8. Most often these important topics are not dealt with in the upper elementary grades. A wealth of information for the new and experienced teacher is provided in this book."

—Lesley Mandel Morrow, Ph.D., professor of literacy, Rutgers, and past president, International Reading Association

"Sandra Rief and Julie Heimburge's years of experience teaching diverse learners have uniquely informed their work on balanced literacy, effectively addressing the ever-widening spectrum of needs in classrooms today. All my staff, both general and special education, will want to read this latest book."

—Dayla Sims, Ed.D., principal, Roosevelt-Carson Elementary School, Lawndale, California

"Teachers and reading specialists interested in providing a truly balanced literacy program in their classroom will benefit from reading *How to Reach and Teach All Children Through Balanced Literacy*. The techniques suggested throughout the book are excellent and provide teachers with proven strategies to maximize student involvement and achievement in reading."

—Patricia Arendt, director, Elementary Education, San Marcos Unified School District

"Brimming with effective approaches to word study, vocabulary, and fluency development. Rief and Heimburge provide a menu of effective word study strategies; each one is instructionally sound and reliable. Collectively, this menu provides a blend of skill practice and challenge, and at the same time allows for the social interaction children and young adolescents need. Offers a wealth of useful tips for teachers."

—Susan Ebbers, reading specialist and author, *Vocabulary Through Morphemes*

"It truly is a pleasure to have a 'how-to' guide to support teachers in implementing the components of the reading and writing workshop. The authors clearly scaffold teachers' learning by describing what each component is and how to provide concrete instructional strategies that will develop independent, life-long readers and writers. *How to Reach and Teach All Children Through Balanced Literacy* is an excellent resource in helping teachers become experts at what they are teaching, what the intended student learning is, and the skills, concepts, and habits we want our children to develop. This is a true must-read for all teachers of literacy."

—Sonia Menendez, New York City Department of Education, local instructional superintendent, Region 1, Bronx, New York

JOSSEY-BASS TEACHER

Jossey-Bass Teacher provides educators with practical knowledge and tools to create a positive and lifelong impact on student learning. We offer classroom-tested and research-based teaching resources for a variety of grade levels and subject areas. Whether you are an aspiring, new, or veteran teacher, we want to help you make every teaching day your best.

From ready-to-use classroom activities to the latest teaching framework, our value-packed books provide insightful, practical, and comprehensive materials on the topics that matter most to K–12 teachers. We hope to become your trusted source for the best ideas from the most experienced and respected experts in the field.

JOSSEY-BASS

HOW TO REACH AND TEACH ALL CHILDREN THROUGH BALANCED LITERACY

User-Friendly Strategies, Tools, Activities, and Ready-to-Use Materials

---

SANDRA F. RIEF • JULIE A. HEIMBURGE

John Wiley & Sons

Published by Jossey-Bass
A Wiley Imprint
989 Market Street, San Francisco, CA 94103-1741 www.josseybass.com

Wiley Bicentennial logo: Richard J. Pacifico

Jossey-Bass books and products are available through most bookstores. To contact Jossey-Bass directly call our Customer Care Department within the U.S. at 800-956-7739, outside the U.S. at 317-572-3986, or fax 317-572-4002.

Jossey-Bass also publishes its books in a variety of electronic formats. Some content that appears in print may not be available in electronic books.

Library of Congress Cataloging-in-Publication Data

Rief, Sandra F.
How to reach and teach all children through balanced literacy : user-friendly strategies, tools, activities, and ready-to-use materials / Sandra F. Rief and Julie A. Heimburge.
p. cm.
Includes bibliographical references and index.
ISBN 978-0-7879-8805-0 (pbk.)
1. Language arts (Elementary)—Activity programs. 2. Literacy—Study and teaching (Elementary) 3. Reading (Elementary) I. Heimburge, Julie A. II. Title.
LB1576.R5195 2007
372.6–dc22

2007010533

Printed in the United States of America
FIRST EDITION
PB Printing 10 9 8 7 6 5 4 3 2 1

ABOUT THIS BOOK

How to Reach and Teach All Children Through Balanced Literacy is a comprehensive resource addressing all key aspects of literacy instruction. It blends practical and motivating classroom activities with research-based guidance and strategies to maximize the achievement of your diverse learners—from those who are advanced to those who are struggling in their literacy development. One of our chief goals is to show you how to effectively balance your literacy instruction and help all of your students become readers and writers who meet or exceed grade-level standards. You will find fourteen chapters describing how to implement strategies and build student success through book clubs and literature circles, thematic teaching, special units of study, nonfiction structures and features, and technology. Other sections address how to strengthen reading comprehension, word knowledge, writing fluency, oral language, and spelling among a range of students. This book is packed with an abundance of engaging, ready-to-use strategies, lessons, tools, and activities that have been proven successful in upper elementary and middle school language arts classrooms.

Some highlights include

Scaffolds, accommodations, and literacy intervention programs to support students with reading and writing challenges

Sixty literacy web sites recommended for teachers and students

A thematic unit of study on survival

Twenty-four motivating literacy stations

Tips on making oral language come alive using quick-talks, commercials, newscasts, and a host of other techniques

A teacher-friendly two-week unit of study on building a literacy community

Advice on putting book clubs into practice, with several management tools and over sixty choices of culminating book club activities

Dozens of reading comprehension strategies for readers of all abilities

Guidance on empowering readers and writers through technology

We hope that you will dog-ear, tab, or sticky-note your favorite parts of this book and find it an invaluable tool in your future instruction! Enjoy!

ABOUT THE AUTHORS

Sandra F. Rief, M.A., is a leading educational consultant, author, and speaker on effective strategies and interventions for helping students with learning, attention, and behavioral challenges. Sandra presents numerous seminars, workshops, and keynotes nationally and internationally on this topic. She received her B.A. and M.A. degrees from the University of Illinois. Sandra is formerly an award-winning teacher (California Resource Specialist of the Year) with over twenty-three years of teaching experience.

Sandra is the author of several popular books, including *How to Reach and Teach All Children in the Inclusive Classroom, Second Edition* (2006, coauthored with Julie Heimburge); *How to Reach and Teach Children with ADD/ADHD, Second Edition* (2005); *The ADHD Book of Lists: A Practical Guide for Helping Children and Teens with Attention Deficit Disorders* (2003); *The ADD/ADHD Checklist: An Easy Reference for Parents and Teachers* (1998); *Alphabet Learning Center Activities Kit* (2000, coauthored with Nancy Fetzer); *Ready . . . Start . . . School* (2001); and other book chapters, articles, and publications.

Sandra also developed and presented these acclaimed educational videos: *ADHD and LD: Powerful Teaching Strategies and Accommodations; How to Help Your Child Succeed in School: Strategies and Guidance for Parents of Children with ADHD and/or Learning Disabilities; ADHD: Inclusive Instruction and Collaborative Practices*, and together with Linda Fisher and Nancy Fetzer, the videos *Successful Classrooms: Effective Teaching Strategies for Raising Achievement in Reading and Writing* and *Successful Schools: How to Raise Achievement and Support "At-Risk" Students.*

Sandra is an instructor for continuing education courses offered through California State University, East Bay, and Seattle Pacific University. For more information, visit her web site at www.sandrarief.com.

Julie A. Heimburge is coauthor of the popular book *How to Reach and Teach All Children in the Inclusive Classroom, Second Edition* (2006, coauthored with Sandra Rief). She is a native San Diegan and earned her B.A. from San Diego State University and her M.A. at United States International University in San Diego. She has been an elementary teacher in the San Diego Unified School District for more than thirty years and is currently a fifth-grade teacher at Benchley-Weinberger Elementary, a California Distinguished School. She has a great deal of experience and expertise teaching diverse learners, from GATE to ELL to students with a range of disabilities and special needs. Julie has served as a mentor teacher, demonstration teacher, guest lecturer, curriculum writer, literacy coach, and a staff developer for her district. She has also been a featured presenter for conferences in other parts of the United States, sharing her creative and innovative instructional practices designed to motivate diverse learners in the general education classroom. Julie is a supervising teacher for student teachers and has been training and coaching new teachers for the California Beginning Teacher Support and Assessment Program (BTSA) for the past several years. Julie is listed in *Who's Who Among America's Teachers* and is a member of the educational sorority Delta Kappa Gamma International.

We dedicate this book to our precious, wonderful daughters —Jackie Skolnik, Jaime Barker, and Sharon Rief—who also happen to be three highly talented, dedicated, and exceptional teachers. We're so very proud of you and your great choice of professions.

ACKNOWLEDGMENTS

Our deepest thanks and appreciation to:

- Our loving, supportive families: our husbands, Neil and Itzik, and our kids, Jaime, Cory, Ariel, Jackie, Jason, Gil, and Sharon.
- Steve Guadarama, for the strategies and helpful feedback he provided us.
- Carolyn Hasselbar, Marian Jacobs, and other colleagues and friends at Benchley-Weinberger Elementary, San Diego.
- Sharon Rief (Sandra's daughter-in-law) for her help and contribution to Chapter Fourteen.
- Jaime Barker (Julie's daughter) for sharing her middle school literacy expertise.
- Our editor, Marjorie McAneny, and the wonderful team at Jossey-Bass.
- Ruth DeCarie, our talented and creative illustrator.
- Our many students (past, present, and future), who inspire and challenge us to keep learning and seeking ways to reach and teach them all.

CONTENTS

Chapter 4
WRITING IN THE LITERACY WORKSHOP—43

Chapter 5
NONFICTION AND ITS PLACE IN BALANCED LITERACY—61

Chapter 7
MAKING ORAL LANGUAGE A PRIORITY—101

Chapter 8
USING A THEMATIC APPROACH: SURVIVAL—123

Reproducibles

Chapter 9
SPECIAL UNITS OF STUDY—145

Chapter 10
BOOK CLUBS AND LITERATURE CIRCLES—173

Chapter 12
READING COMPREHENSION STRATEGIES AND SCAFFOLDS—217

Chapter 13
WRITING STRATEGIES, SCAFFOLDS, AND ACCOMMODATIONS—233

Chapter 14
TEACHING AND ENHANCING LITERACY THROUGH TECHNOLOGY—249

How This Book Maps to Standards

Below are nationally accepted standards for teaching **Language Arts/Writing** from Mid-continent Research for Education and Learning (McREL), along with references to material in this book that helps teachers to meet the standards. For more on McREL standards, go to www.mcrel.org.

	Chapter													
	1	2	3	4	5	6	7	8	9	10	11	12	13	14
Writing														
1. Uses the general skills and strategies of the writing process				x		x							x	
2. Uses the stylistic and rhetorical aspects of writing				x					x				x	
3. Uses grammatical and mechanical conventions in written compositions	x	x				x								
4. Gathers and uses information for research purposes					x								x	x
Reading														
5. Uses the general skills and strategies of the reading process		x	x		x	x				x	x			
6. Uses reading skills and strategies to understand and interpret a variety of literary texts	x	x						x					x	x
7. Uses reading skills and strategies to understand and interpret a variety of informational texts	x			x	x					x		x		
Listening and Speaking														
8. Uses listening and speaking strategies for different purposes							x							
Viewing														
9. Uses viewing skills and strategies to understand and interpret visual media			x					x						
Media														
10. Understands the characteristics and components of the media														x

— Chapter 1 —

BALANCED LITERACY IN THE CLASSROOM

There has been a progression of change during the past several years from a more traditional style of skill-based, directed instruction to a literature-based, holistic approach to teaching reading and writing. Currently there is less controversy among most educators over which is the best way to teach reading and writing because a "balanced approach" to literacy instruction, which is supported by the research, is understood to be what works best. For many of us, this has always made sense. We know that balance in any aspect of life tends to bring the most success. In this book we will look at balanced literacy as encompassing balance in a number of components of the literacy classroom—such as instructional practices, approaches, formats, resources and materials, and other factors.

Our belief is that any literacy program that is going to be successful will incorporate the best of methods and approaches that have been proven effective in teaching students. Children *need* reading material that will captivate their interest, fuel their creative thought, motivate them to think critically, and allow them to make meaningful connections to their lives. The holistic approach, using high-quality literature and other published works, fulfills these needs most effectively. In addition, we know that many students need a more structured, explicit, and systematic approach to learn specific skills fundamental to becoming fluent, competent, independent readers, writers, and speakers. What makes best sense is to find a *balance* in language arts instruction—utilizing a host of strategies and techniques to meet the needs of all learners.

BALANCE AND THE CHALLENGES OF REACHING AND TEACHING DIVERSE READERS AND WRITERS

All students need to be challenged at whatever level they happen to be—pushed beyond their comfort zone while being supported in their learning. High-achieving, advanced readers and writers generally need more choice of assignments and projects, and time to investigate independently, explore their topic of focus at a deeper level, and pursue their passions or interests. They need to be challenged and motivated to work hard and keep growing—sometimes well beyond demonstrating grade-level proficiency in reading and writing standards. Many high-achieving students who are highly competent in some areas of reading and written language will still be average or even have weaknesses in other literacy skills that will require direct teaching and support.

Other students, such as English language learners and those with reading and writing challenges, may require a higher degree of scaffolding and teacher or peer support in order to build their competencies and achieve success. They may also require intervention (from mild to intensive), depending on their needs. Many schools, in their effort to ensure that "no child is left behind," are implementing interventions for students in need of support. These generally involve providing more direct teaching for the struggling student at his or her instructional level (such as extra guided reading and skills instruction). This time for additional instruction and practice may take place during the school day or in before- or after-school programs. Targeted students may also receive more support and intervention through push-in or pull-out services from specialists, and sometimes supplementary reading and writing programs are utilized as well. See Chapter Eleven for a list of some research-validated intervention programs.

COMPONENTS OF BALANCED LITERACY

A balanced literacy program for upper elementary and middle school students includes the following components:

- Explicit teacher modeling for students of effective strategies, skills (general and specific), and metacognitive processes that good readers and writers use
- Opportunities for student modeling and sharing of standard-setting, proficient reading and writing work
- Reading to students (aloud), together with students (shared and guided), and by students (independently), using quality pieces of fiction and nonfiction text
- Oral language development and listening experiences
- Word study instruction and practice to developmentally build students' vocabulary, word recognition, spelling, and fluency skills
- Independent reading and writing to build stamina and fluency and provide for creativity and choice
- Expository and narrative reading and writing experiences throughout the day and threading throughout all the content areas
- Multiple opportunities for engagement, inquiry, and expression through various reading and writing groupings, formats, resources, and projects
- Multiple and varied student assessments to drive instruction

A combination of these strategies works best to enable students to build their communication and meaning-making competencies. In this book, we provide guidance, strategies, and activities and address other essential elements of a balanced literacy classroom.

Balancing Quality Literature and Other Resources in Our Libraries

Through the balanced literacy approach we strive to provide upper graders and middle school students with opportunities to comprehend, appreciate, and respond to a wide variety of pieces of quality literature. Through their reading, writing, speaking, and listening, we hope they will begin to synthesize their understanding of customs and beliefs of different cultures, and they will compare and contrast their own lives to the characters in the books. We want to provide them with opportunities to read other materials besides books, so that they possess the survival reading skills needed in the world of their everyday lives. Classroom textbooks, trade books, magazines, poetry books, newspapers, plays and readers' theater scripts, and digital sources should reflect grade-level standards in both fiction and nonfiction. To accommodate the wide range of reading and writing abilities of upper elementary and middle school students, we need to provide motivating materials at multilevels so that all students can find quality text to access. Each student should have books and resources available that he or she is capable of reading, that address the standards, and support the theme, or "big idea" of the content being taught. See Chapter Two, Setting Up a Balanced Literacy Environment, for ways to incorporate all of these elements.

We must also provide experiences in practical content reading, as well as self-selected, pleasure reading. Through good literature, our students will feel comfortable listening to others, responding in classroom discussions, and transferring their acquired learning into their own writing.

Balancing Reading, Writing, Speaking, Listening, and Word Study

When we look at literacy as a big umbrella (reading, writing, listening, and speaking), although called out separately in the standards, these literacy components really are not separate at all. They are intertwined like strands of a rope held tightly together to form one stronghold. Balanced literacy is much the same.

It allows us to move back and forth and in and out of reading, writing, word study, listening, and speaking to build a strong base in meaning making. For instance, as we read aloud a piece of literature, such as *Donovan's Word Jar* (DeGross, 1994), we might focus on the idea that learning new words can be a very powerful tool. We might front-load or preteach some of the vocabulary such as *orchestral, chortle,* and *definitive* before reading the story aloud at the rug area, where good listening will help us co-create a sequence chart retelling the story. We might gather new words for our personal word jars. We might *turn* and *talk* to our partners about Donovan and how to solve his problem. We might write a response to Donovan about what to do with all of his extra words or write a letter to tell him how we are going to get more knowledge about words. We might reread parts and put a copy of a couple of pages on the overhead or document camera to learn about how good writers structure sentences or use conversation. We might share what we wrote in our response journal with a partner or small group. We might revisit the story to question the author or have a hot-seat character study. There is no end to the conversations, dialogue, word study opportunities, and connections we can make and talk about. We should look at each of these domains as blended experiences that are seamlessly threaded through one or more literacy periods. Looking at a piece of literature provides numerous avenues for us to explore.

Integrating Content in the Literacy Block

Figuring out how to balance everything we have to teach about literacy in the time we have available within the school day is a balancing act in itself. There are only so many minutes, and we have a lot of curriculum to teach. Therefore, it is essential that we prioritize what we teach, when we teach it, and on what day. If you are in a district that has a two- or three-hour literacy block, you must decide how to get more done and be more efficient. Many teachers have begun to double-dip, using their literacy block to integrate content (social studies, science, health, music, or art) into their literacy time. Using content-based literature during the literacy block integrates the curriculum into a thematic unit, helping our students to see the relationships between fiction and nonfiction and how reading, writing, and speaking fit together in the big picture of learning. By integrating this content during literacy, we utilize our multileveled resources. Many of our books and topics address the issues and subjects in our science and social studies content areas and the standards for our specific grade levels.

BALANCING INSTRUCTIONAL APPROACHES

To become proficient in all the domains of literacy, teachers must use and students must be provided with a variety of instructional approaches throughout the day. These approaches move children from the greatest amount of teacher support to the least amount of teacher support. The *gradual release of responsibility* model (Pearson & Fielding, 1991) moves the child from the most teacher support such as through *read-alouds* and *modeled writing*; to *shared and guided* experiences, during which children begin to slowly take more of the responsibility; and finally to the *independent* stage where they take full responsibility for these tasks. If we look at our own childhoods, this gradual release of responsibility is basic to how most of us learned things such as riding a bike, swimming, diving, cooking, building, and even using a computer. Scaffolds were built and then gradually removed as we gained proficiency in learning these new skills. In most cases, we did not have to do these things alone—we were supported by others who made sure that we had a foundation for our learning.

Balancing Learning Style Preferences of Students

Not all students learn the same way. To reach and teach students with diverse learning styles and needs, teachers must employ strategies that will tap into their varied learning strengths and multiple intelligences. This requires using multisensory strategies when instructing, so that all students can receive information through their preferred modalities (auditory, visual, tactile, or kinesthetic) such as graphics and visual displays, demonstrations and hands-on activities, or explanation and discussion. It also means recognition that students are adept in different abilities (such as verbal, mathematical, musical, artistic, or physical) and need learning experiences that let them use and showcase those strengths and talents to their peers. We must provide students options in demonstrating their learning, such as choice in how they will publish their written work and share with an audience or the type of book project they create (for example, a poster or minibook, a summary through song, or a dramatic reenactment of a scene). Some people learn best and are happiest when interacting with others, while others prefer to work and study alone, and this preference, too, needs to be considered when differentiating instruction in the literacy classroom. We must also structure the day or class period taking into account students' need for a mix of high activity level and low, time for lively interaction and for quiet contemplation and reflection, as well.

Balancing Grouping in the Classroom

A literacy classroom involves a mix of grouping formats—whichever is most conducive to the instruction or student practice taking place. Whole-group, heterogeneous grouping is often used to expose all students to the grade-level standards for which they need to demonstrate proficiency. Read-alouds, modeled writing, and shared reading and writing work well for the whole-group format. When students are grouped by interest or ability level or for cooperative group activities, small-group formats are generally used. This instructional format is used for guided reading, guided writing, book clubs or literature circles, and minilessons to teach specific skills and strategies needed for a particular group of students. Collaborative learning experiences such as those that take place in a small group also take place in partner formats. The literacy classroom will frequently involve students paired for partner activities such as for shared reading, providing and receiving feedback and assistance throughout the writing process, comprehension checks, and so forth. Students will also be working alone while they are reading and writing, using the independent format as well. Teachers will meet with students individually for conferencing about their reading and writing and will also provide individual assistance, re-teaching, or other supports, as needed.

It is imperative in the balanced literacy program that students have multiple opportunities to work collaboratively with the teacher and their classmates. No single program works for all children, so it is up to the teacher to modify and adapt lessons into tiered fashion, making instruction multilevel to address the special needs of students with different learning styles, backgrounds, and abilities.

When we *know* our students—their interests, academic abilities, personalities, learning styles, behavioral issues, and home support—we have the knowledge we need to decide what type of group the child needs for a particular task. Most of the time grouping *will* be flexible—it will change for a variety of reasons to address the specific needs of the students and the teacher for that hour, day, week, month, or year.

For instance, if one of our standards is to address homophones in spelling, we have several ways to tackle this subject with students. Through preassessment, a teacher may see that the class needs whole-group instruction, some students may need guided small-group support, others need one-on-one support, and some are ready to embark on their own independent search. Knowing when and how to group or switch groups is an integral part of a focused and effective literacy program. By working in groups of varying size, students see that throughout the year they will be given assistance when needed as they are challenged in a new or renewed learning situation.

Teachers also know that they will sometimes select heterogeneous or homogeneous groups for particular reasons and that students will sometimes be able to select their own groups. Choice is built into the program. There are also times for random groups to be formed. Again, this is part of a balanced literacy program that encompasses teacher expertise. Moving in and out of whole-group, small-group, and one-on-one instruction provides a stable sequence to the literacy block that students learn to feel comfortable with.

Balancing Teacher Talk and Student Talk

Teachers like to talk, and we have a perfect audience: a classroom of students to listen to us. Over the last few decades the amount of teacher *talk* has been curtailed. Experience tells us that students have a lot to say and when children constructively *talk,* there are plenty of peer listeners. Whether it is math, science, reading, or writing, it is time for teachers to become good listeners too. We must allow students to share their ideas and strategic thoughts, their ways of doing things, allow them to be student models for others, and partake in the actual instruction by becoming experts in specific areas. Finding a balance between student and teacher *talk* and active participation builds a safe and comfortable literacy community. Sometimes the classroom is quiet, whereas sometimes it is bustling with engaging discourse and collaborative conversations. Child-centered exploration and inquiry-based instruction put learning back where it belongs—with the kids.

Balancing Teacher-Directed and Student-Directed Activities

Another feature of a literacy classroom that requires balance is the degree of structure built into the learning tasks and the choice students have in assignments and activities. Parts of instruction, assignments, and learning activities are teacher-selected and directed; others give the student freedom to choose and make more decisions. For example, some writing assignments will require students to respond to a specific prompt or use a particular graphic organizer in their planning. Other writing assignments will allow for student choice in topic and planning tools used. Some instruction will involve very explicit, step-by-step teacher instruction, while other tasks will involve an exploratory, discovery approach. There will be some assignments that are very structured. They may, for example, include designated time lines and specific due dates for steps of a project to be accomplished. Other assignments and learning tasks will be more flexible in requirements for completion.

Balancing Formal and Informal Assessments

For most teachers, high-stakes testing has become the reason to teach with such intensity. Their performance is judged by how many of their students scored proficient or above on the tests. Fountas and Pinnell (2001) indicate, "We need to find ways to cope with the demands of the testing environment and still help our students have happy, productive, and satisfying literacy experiences." Although this is a fact of our professional lives, we must be cognizant of other types of assessments that will give us more realistic feedback about our students' successes and challenges.

In the balanced classroom, informal assessments (those done within the same classroom, usually by the classroom teacher) should also hold weight. They tend to be more useful because they are often observational, immediate, and on the spot. Such assessments are helpful for informing instruction and include such methods as teacher, peer- and self-evaluations, reading and writing samples, one-on-one conferences, peer conferences, summaries, interest and attitude surveys, portfolios, spelling tests and inventories, oral presentations, speaking assessments, and checklists.

ESTABLISHING A COMMUNITY OF LEARNERS

The balanced literacy classroom is an engaging environment where students feel comfortable expressing their ideas and learning new things, where thoughts are respected and valued, and where needs, interests, and abilities are honored and attended to. It is a place where children feel successful, challenged, safe, and where they want to be.

It takes a skillful teacher to know how to develop a climate of respect and appreciation for all levels of learning. We must instill in our students the idea that we all have different strengths and weaknesses and that these differences make our classrooms unique. We must set our standards high for all students to achieve, but we must create a safe and trusting environment for even our weakest reader or writer to feel comfortable.

During the first weeks of school, building a sense of community is very important. This can be achieved through the use of specific books that teach about reading, writing, and words. Several of our favorite books for this purpose are *Marianthe's Story: Painted Words and Spoken Memories* (Aliki, 1998), *The Armadillo from Amarillo* (Cherry, 1994), *Donovan's Word Jar* (DeGross, 1994), and *Teammates* (Golenbock, 1990).

To create this literacy community, a two-week unit of study such as the one found in Appendix B can be implemented in the classroom. A detailed first-day lesson plan for this unit is provided below for reading, writing, and word study. The books and standards mentioned in this lesson plan can be substituted with others that are appropriate for your grade level and standards.

GRADE 5 BUILDING COMMUNITY

Read-Aloud Lesson Plan: The Moon and I

Day 1

Focus. Introducing the genre of memoir and making connections to our own lives to make meaning of the story.

Introduction. Authors often take events from their own lives to create all or part of their stories that you and I read. The story that I am going to read to you today is called "Miss Harriet's Room" from *The Moon and I,* by Betsy Byars. You will find a tub of her books in our classroom library. This kind of book is called a memoir, and I'll be sharing other memoirs with you throughout the year. As readers, we connect or relate to these stories in our own special ways depending on our own lives and our own personal experiences. Many times they spark ideas in our own minds and we understand or remember the story better because we personally are linked to it. As you listen today, use your personal connections to help you hold on to the story and understand how Betsy might have been feeling. Think of your first days of school over the years. Were they the same or different from Betsy's?

Text Summary. Betsy has been anxiously awaiting her first day of school in Miss Harriet's room. She has been anticipating the many fun activities that her sister had participated in three years earlier, including the store, painting, and the book called *The Adventures of Mabel,* "the best book in the world." Things do not go as she planned, but her tenacity gets her what she wants in the end.

Questions, Prompts, and Modeling. Have the students clustered near you. This is a real bonding time with your students. Make the most of it. Being prepared is a must. Make sure that you have read the story before you read it to your students. Adding your own personality makes the book come alive. Kids will know that you love the book. Make the story like Miss Harriet did—better than the circus. Engage the students through your voice, your actions, and your delight. You might want to use a highlighter, sticky notes, or notes in the margins to remind you where to stop and question students to make sure they are making meaning. Use a variety of involvement techniques such as volunteers, calling on specific individuals, pairs, triads, and combining two pairs in think-pair-square interactions.

At the very beginning of the year some students are hesitant to risk raising their hands, so you might call on volunteers to get you going. Take it in little steps. Here are a few sample questions that might guide your questioning as you read:

Page 70. What do you think *coveted* means? Is there anything that you have ever coveted in your life? What does Betsy mean that the old shirts and the purse were *sacred*? Is there anything in your house that would be sacred?

Page 71. Were you surprised at what Betsy did? Is it okay for a kindergartener to speak up so boldly about something she wants so badly? How do you think you would have handled the situation? Would it be the same? Different? What does this tell you about Betsy Byars as a person?

Page 72. What do you think made Miss Harriet's room so special? Have you ever felt that way about a teacher? Have you ever had a favorite book that meant as much to you as *The Adventures of Mabel?* Explain your answer. How did Betsy change in the story?

Closure. What kind of connection did you make with Betsy Byars? How did this help you make meaning from the story and understand her character? How do you know that this is a memoir?

Writer's Workshop Connection. Just like Betsy Byars, you might have a special school event or experience that you want to write about today. If not, you may write about another experience or event you have had outside of school.

GRADE 5 BUILDING COMMUNITY

Shared Reading Lesson Plan: "Testing New Waters"

Day 1

Focus. Visualization and introduction to reading poetry for meaning and enjoyment.

Introduction. During shared reading, all students should have easy access to the poem. Having an individual copy of the poem allows students to practice it at a later time independently. The poem may be made into an overhead, but make sure the words are in a font that is easy to read and large enough for all students to see. The poem may also be written on a chart. Make sure that the students are clustered close together and near you so that students can be actively engaged in discussion without distractions.

Since this is our first week of school together, some of you may feel a little scared thinking about what things are going to be like in this class—you are "testing new waters." Sometimes when we are in a new situation, we are hesitant to take risks. In this classroom we will appreciate and respect each other's space and time to grow. Some of you will take longer to warm up while others of you are raring to go. Today I am going to read a selection from *Wham! It's a Poetry Jam* called "Testing New Waters." As we read other poems in this book, I hope you will become actively involved in presenting poetry. We can have lots of fun performing solo and together. Learning seems more enjoyable when we do things together. Reading research finds that proficient readers draw pictures in their minds to see what they read. In poetry, since there are so few words, every word is important. Today, draw a mental picture of a stream with banks along its edge and swirling water passing by. Put yourself in the picture. This will help you "see" the poem "Testing New Waters." As I read it through with you, visualize it and then think about what the poet is trying to say. Think about how that fits into your feelings being in a new classroom with a new teacher and students you might not know. How can we make this a safe environment for people to take risks?

Text Summary. A student is deciding whether to take a risk at something new by taking small steps.

Questions, Prompts, and Modeling. Use a variety of questioning techniques throughout the lesson including TPS (think-pair-share), triads, TPSQ (think-pair-square), volunteers, and calling on individual students.

What do you think the author means by "the bank of what-I-know?" "Unfamiliar water passing in a rush?" "With maybes swirling in my ears?"

What words would you use to describe the author of this poem?

What kinds of fears do you think he or she has?

What makes people have fears about things?

Have you ever felt fearful of something new?

What would be some of the fears people in our classroom might have today, tomorrow, and later in the year?

What can we do to squelch those fears in this classroom?

Have students read the poem in a variety of ways: individually to themselves (quietly whispering the words aloud); to a partner; as a whole class; boys take one stanza, girls another; assign lines; one person reads the whole poem to the class; partners take turns and decide on how to chunk it into segments, and so forth.

Closure. As we become better acquainted this year, we will become more comfortable in taking risks. Some of us love to perform with reading while others of us would prefer not to. We are all members of this team of learners, and as a team everyone is expected to try out new things, however challenging they may seem. We will encourage each person to be an engaged learner. Everyone's input is important to making this an enjoyable place to be.

GRADE 5 BUILDING COMMUNITY

Word Study Lesson Plan: "Testing New Waters"

Day 1

Reading Work. Making meaning in a reading selection when key words in the piece have multiple meanings.

Introduction. When we were reading the selection "Testing New Waters," there were several words that might have been confusing to you as a reader. Many good readers have to reread a piece of work so that they are sure they understand the true meaning of key words. Unlocking the possibilities within the multiple meanings of basic words can be complex. Many words are not one-dimensional. They have several, sometimes many, meanings. If you are reading and it is confusing, slow down the pace of your reading, reread the passage, and try to unlock the correct meaning of the word so that it makes sense. Sometimes when we are confused, discussing the confusion with a friend is helpful. In this classroom we are all teachers. Helping each other is an important part of our reading work.

Text Summary. Use an overhead of the poem "Testing New Waters." Prepare a transparency of the dictionary definition of the word *bank*. Use a simplified children's dictionary to locate word definitions for review. Adult dictionaries are too complicated at this point for easy modeling of basic definitions.

Questions, Prompts, and Modeling. The teacher models the confusion in the word *bank* in the poem. It might mean a place whose business is to keep money safe, a place where a large supply of anything is kept, or the land along the edge of a river or stream. Ask students to think of other types of banks, such as blood bank, donor bank, and word bank. On the overhead, show the enlarged definition of *bank* from the dictionary. Help students determine what kind of word it is (noun, verb, or adjective) from their prior knowledge. Tell students that determining the type of word it is helps them discover the specific meaning the author intended. Elicit which definition makes sense in this selection. The teacher also models thinking about the word *flush* and uses the enlarged definition on the overhead. Which definition fits the author's meaning for the poem? How do you know? What makes you sure? Have students work together with partners, using the definitions for the word *rush*.

Closure. Check student responses. Working together helps us to find the real meaning of an author's word use. Making sure that we understand and question the meaning of a word helps us better comprehend the author's intention for using that specific word. When multiple-meaning words stump us, we can reread, slow down our pace, use a dictionary, and think and talk through the piece with others to become better readers.

See Appendix B for the full two-week unit lesson plan on building community.

— *Chapter 2* —

SETTING UP A BALANCED LITERACY ENVIRONMENT

The new focus on improving literacy makes this an exciting period for educators throughout the United States. The result has been a flood of new and updated books into school and classroom libraries for teachers and students to easily access. Schools and teachers now have opportunities to purchase books for guided reading, independent reading, read-alouds, content reading, and professional growth. Classroom libraries are beginning to flourish, and students at all levels have books in their hands and are reading them. As students gain easier access to books, they become more involved in reading. Especially because many students do not have access to books in their own homes, it is essential that the classroom library is a top priority and focal point in school.

The upper-grade classroom libraries of today look much different than they did a few years ago. As students become more active in the selection, sorting, and leveling of books, they take more ownership in their classroom libraries and become more familiar with the reading process and books in general. Upper graders are a big help in the process. They choose books based on their age, their interests, and their individual comfort levels. Many times, in fact, they are better at selecting books than their teachers because they have insight that adults do not. Often teachers add good pieces of literature to their libraries that students never pick up for reading.

Motivating students to find excellent books keeps them interested in reading. Of course, choosing a book must be a balanced process in order to help students build their interests and stretch their imaginations. Teachers should use their professional judgment during this time to guide students toward books that suit their needs. When students help in the process, they learn how to find books at their own level and where and how to put them back when they are finished.

Primary teachers have had a head start on getting "just right" books, or books that fit the individual reader, into the hands of their students, while upper-grade teachers have been more resistant. It has been a paradigm shift that has not come easily. With the help and guidance of *The Art of Teaching Reading* (2001) by Lucy Calkins, *Guiding Readers and*

Writers (Grades 3–6) (2001) by Fountas and Pinnell, and *Beyond Leveled Books* (2001) by Szymusiah and Sibbersoni, many teachers have made the shift into the twenty-first century with kid-friendly classroom libraries. Some districts, such as San Diego Unified, have provided extensive professional development to help teachers with this transition.

THE LOOK OF THE CLASSROOM LIBRARY TODAY

The library is the focal point of today's classroom. Students can easily navigate through the shelves while having easy access to the books. Books are organized in tubs, bins, or baskets and labeled with appropriate titles by genres, authors, topics, series, and themes. Students can comfortably flip through the books because they are not crowded into the tubs. Books are right at their fingertips and are easy to view and select. In today's libraries, only some books have the bindings facing outward. How delightful to see the entire cover! Even though we are not supposed to choose a book by its cover, children do.

Richard Allington (2006) recommends that classrooms have at least five hundred different books, about half of them narratives and half of them informational. He also states that some books should be on or near grade-level difficulty and some below grade level. Many of the exemplary teachers he studied had more than 1,500 books in their libraries. Getting student's hands on books at their appropriate level is crucial in helping them to become successful readers.

SELECTING BOOKS

Teachers select books according to the needs and interests of their students. The books should reflect the diversity in the classroom, with a large variety of both fiction and nonfiction. Each year, we assess the interests and needs of our students and try to provide new books to our libraries that they want to read. Their input is essential to the success of the library. We continually add favorites, Children's Choice Award books, Newbery Award–winners, and books that are new and updated. Each group of students is unique at the beginning of the school year—no two classes are ever alike. A student interest survey may help in selecting books for your library.

In some schools, teachers rotate into roles as the *gifted and talented teacher* or the *English-language learner (ELL) teacher*. In this case, teachers need to reassess their students' needs each year.

Choosing Quality Books

It is important that classroom libraries be filled with a variety of quality books so that students can expand their thinking in meaningful ways.

Newbery Award Books

Using Newbery Award books is one method of selecting books that will help students learn about what good writers do. The author's book, selected by a committee of fifteen librarians and judged by a strict set of guidelines and rules, is awarded for its distinguished contribution to American literature. This prestigious award-winning book is chosen from over five thousand published children books.

The majority of students do not readily choose these books for independent reading purposes, possibly because of their length, complexity, and challenging vocabulary. They do tend to stretch the student's minds. In general, Newbery Award–winners and Honor Books provide a great foundation for helping students understand literary elements and draw conclusions, make inferences, and analyze and interpret characters and their circumstances. They offer students a foundational point so that throughout the literacy block meaningful conversations about the book may be addressed. Hence, students internalize what good writers do and extend it into their own writing. If there is not time enough to read a whole book, sections can be read as an introduction to the selection.

A complete list of the Newbery Award and Honor Books can be found online at the web site for the American Library Association (www.ala.org/ala/alsc/awardsscholarships/literaryawds/newberymedal/newberywinners/medalwinners.htm). A few of our personal favorites are *Because of Winn Dixie* (DiCamillo, 2000), *The Great Gilly Hopkins* (Paterson, 1978), *Bridge to Terabithia* (Paterson, 1978), *Bud, Not Buddy* (Curtis, 1999), *Number the Stars* (Lowry, 1989), and *Sounder* (Armstrong, 1969).

Picture Books and the Caldecott Award Winners

The American Library Association has granted the Caldecott Award to the artist of the most distinguished American picture book for children since 1937. These books provide enticing stories and illustrations that can hook in our reluctant readers and writers. A complete list of Caldecott Award winners can be found at http://www.fairfaxcounty.gov/library/reading/elem/caldecot.htm. Some of the winners are appropriate for upper-grade students. Among our favorites are *Grandfather's Journey* (Say, 1994), *Snowflake Bentley* (Martin, 1998), *Smoky Night* (Bunting, 1995), *The Polar Express* (Van Allsburg, 1968), *Jumanji* (Van Allsburg, 1982), and *A Chair for My Mother* (Williams, 1983).

Young Readers Choice Awards

This is the oldest children's choice award spanning two nations, Canada and the United States. Harry Hartman, a bookseller in Seattle, established it in 1940. His belief was that every child should have an opportunity to select a book that gave him or her pleasure. Students in grades 4 through12 are allowed to vote on books that have been nominated by children, teachers, parents, and librarians. Occasionally, winners of this award also win the Newbery Award or Honor Book such as *Holes* (Sacher, 1998) and *Maniac McGee* (Spinelli, 1990). Because children have chosen them, they tend to be favorites among most boys and girls and can be a wonderful source for read-alouds. Such books as *Frindle* (Clement, 1999), *Artemis Fowl* (Colfer, 2004), and *The Thief Lord* (Funke, 2005) are some of the award winners. These winners are presented by the Pacific Northwest Library Association and may be accessed online at www.literature-awards.com.

Choosing Books That Are "Just Right"

Children in the upper grades and middle schools are often attracted to books that are too challenging for them to read independently. Therefore, we see the same students repeatedly abandoning books. In the primary grades, students have been exposed to learning about "just right" books. In the upper grades the importance of this idea does not diminish; it still needs to be reinforced and stressed. Although many students are fluent readers by the end of third grade, many others still have difficulty with the reading process. In the upper grades, "just right" books might be referred to as *comfortable,* a *perfect fit,* or *smooth ride* books. Those that are too difficult have been called *challenging, troublesome, frustrating, an uphill drive,* or just plain *hard.* It is the teacher's task to help students distinguish what is a *comfortable ride* for them.

It is essential that upper-grade teachers continue having discussions around choosing books that "fit you as a reader." As Regie Routman (2003) suggests to her students, "Researchers have found that if children read a steady diet of books that are too hard for you, your reading actually gets worse." This should be discussed with students at length. Let them know that you will be checking on them frequently to make sure they are choosing books that fit their individual reading abilities. The one-on-one reading conference is a perfect place to assess their choices.

Using the story of "Goldilocks and the Three Bears" might be helpful for your students. Goldilocks finds out through experimentation that the bowls for porridge are either too hot or too cold, the chairs for sitting in are either too hard or too soft, and the beds for sleeping are either too high at the foot or too high at the head. Only Wee Little Bear's things are just right for her. It is only through trying them out that children find the suitable levels for them, and the teacher should help them at times when they falter or become frustrated.

Children also need to try things out to see if they fit. They may take a book from one level below what they are suppose to read, one that should be just right, and one that is one level above. Because intermediate and upper-grade students are becoming expert in selecting books that meet their needs, they should be pretty good at judging the levels that are right for them.

Struggling readers often have problems choosing books that are appropriate for them. Following is a student-generated chart for selecting a book that feels right. Students should create their own class chart to give them a sense of ownership. Co-created charts are a viable tool for students to reference during independent reading time, when their teacher may not be available to help them in selection. Teachers can use this list during their individual reading conferences to help each student continue to select books that fit him or her as a reader.

SELECTING THAT "PERFECT" BOOK

To find books that fit just right, direct students to

- Skim through the book to see if the book is too easy, too hard, or the perfect fit.
- Look for a book in a series that you have enjoyed before. This book should be about the same level as you need.
- Read the back cover of the book to see if it sounds interesting, enjoyable, or helpful.
- Look for your favorite author.
- Look for a book that has been made into a movie that you have already seen.
- Ask your friends for suggestions.
- Listen to book talks by your classmates or friends.
- Read the inside cover to see if there is other information that will be helpful.
- Read the first page of the book. If there are too many "tricky" words, then the book might be too challenging.

- Read the first page of the book to see if the book is too easy. Everyone needs to challenge himself or herself to do more difficult work.
- Skim through the book and look at the illustrations or special features. If you do not understand the format, ask for help.
- Look for your favorite genres and authors.
- Look for a book or a part of a book that your teacher has read aloud to you.
- Ask yourself if this is a book that your parents would want you to read.
- Read the first few pages of the first chapter.

If the book is too easy . . .

- You read it very fast
- You know all the words
- Your reading flies by
- You don't have to work hard to understand and enjoy it

If the book is just right . . .

- You feel comfortable and it feels like a smooth ride
- You can make sense out of it when you read
- You feel relaxed while you read it
- You have trouble with a few words, but you try to figure them out
- You read a little slower than in an easy book
- You enjoy the story because it seems exciting and you understand it
- You can easily sequence the story or chapter
- You feel comfortable talking about your reading when you are finished with your independent reading
- If there are chapter titles, you can give reasons why it has that title
- You can ask yourself questions about the book and know where to find the answers
- You can make connections to your own life as you read
- You are engaged in your reading
- You laugh in the funny parts
- You say things out loud to yourself like *This doesn't make sense* or *That could never happen to me* or *I wonder what she was thinking here*? or *Why did he do that*? or *Hmmm* or *Huh* out loud or to yourself

When the book is on the hard side . . .

- You find a lot of words you don't know
- You are confused a lot of the time
- You have to read really slowly in order to understand
- You need to reread so that you understand

- You get tired of reading
- You have to stop and think about what you've read
- You forget what you have read
- You don't understand a lot of what you just read
- You read, but you cannot remember what happened
- You feel frustrated
- The print may be smaller and the lines are closer together

One way to test a book to see if it is a good match is by using the Five-Finger Test. Start on the first whole page. Each time you come to a word that you do not know, put up a finger. When you get to the fifth raised finger, you can tell that the book is probably too difficult for you.

Involving Students in Book Selection

The more that students are involved in selecting books for a classroom library, the more interest they have, the more careful they are with the books, and the more buy-in they have in the process of learning to read and reading to learn. That's what we call a chain reaction.

Many book clubs provide catalogs for book selection. These flyers can be sent home for individual purchasing of books. As students purchase their own books, bonus points are accumulated, and the teacher can purchase more books with these coupons. Students who cannot afford to order their own books might be enlisted to order the next set of "free" books with the coupons. When whole classes of students cannot afford to buy individual books, teachers can use book money entitlements to purchase books from these clubs and students can assist in the selection process.

Obtaining More Books for Your Library

Teachers may use many strategies for building a library without making a large investment. Following are some ideas.

Schoolwide Parent Wish List. Request old books, word games, and magazines from parents. Many times, parents keep collections of *Sports Illustrated for Kids, ZooBooks, San Diego, Ranger Ricks, Wild Outdoor World, Muse,* and *Zillions* until their children become older. They sometimes forget that these materials are great supplements for classroom libraries.

Schoolwide Book Fairs. Once or twice a year, the PTA or foundation of your school might have a book fair, where parents and students can come together to select books that are just right for them. Book fairs also encourage parents to come to school and can be coordinated with open houses, back-to-school nights, or another night or afternoon when parents are going to be at the school anyway for a special event. Classroom wish lists generated by students and teacher can be posted.

Letters to Publishers. Have the students write letters to publishers in your city or state letting them know that you are accumulating books for your classroom library. Ask them if they are willing to contribute any of their proof copies to your collection. Who knows what else you might get?

Library Book Sales. Many public libraries have certain days during the month when they sell used books for next to nothing. Ask your public librarian when and if they do.

Garage Sales, Thrift Stores, and Flea Markets. These sources provide a great way for new teachers to start building a library. Most books are sold for a nominal amount. All you need is time to travel and some cash.

Old Anthologies. Once textbooks are deemed antiquated, districts confiscate the books and get rid of them. Try to find out what happens to these old textbooks in your district. If you find out that they will be thrown away or burned, ask for permission to recycle some of your favorite stories. Some of the best stories with the most enticing illustrations have come from old textbooks that have been thrown away. Let students know that there will be a new series the following year, and ask them what stories they liked best. When you find out, use a razor blade or Exacto knife to cut them out of the anthology or textbook, then compile them in construction paper booklets. Write the title and author's name on the front cover for students to enjoy for years to come.

A Classroom Visit to a Bookstore

Once you have received an allocation of money for books, a purchase order, or a procurement card, you can take students on a field trip to a major bookstore to select books for their classroom. If you have $500 allocated for thirty students, you might ask each child to select two books totaling $10. That would still leave you, as teacher, $200 for materials you think are essential to your needs. (Most large bookstores offer a teacher discount.) Before the visit, have your students look closely at what is lacking in the classroom library and decide what books are needed to make a more enticing library. Parameters for the selection process should be set in advance.

If there is no bookstore nearby, have your students choose books from book catalogs or book club catalogs. You can go online to a book company (such as Amazon, Cheapbooks, or Barnes and Noble) and let the students research categories they are interested in reading.

Making Space for Reluctant Readers' Needs

It is important to have a large variety of both fiction and nonfiction books, plus books with illustrations, larger print, and fewer words per page. A survey at the beginning of the year will help establish what your reluctant readers are interested in. Make sure that you have lots of high-interest books with vocabulary that is not too difficult. Offering books on tape is also a successful practice, giving struggling readers access to a text that normally they would have difficulty with. Series and short-story books are important to keep in your library to hook in your reluctant readers.

A good selection of books by a favorite author is also encouraged. For instance, if a reluctant reader likes one Gordon Korman book, whether it was read aloud, recommended by a classmates, or self-selected, the chance is that he or she may be comfortable reading another book by him. An author's subject area or writing style can hook in some of our reluctant readers.

Significant research indicates that boys tend to experience more difficulty in reading than girls. Boys score significantly lower on standardized measures of reading achievement than girls (Donahue, Voelkl, Campbell, & Mazzeo, 1999) and are more likely to be retained at grade level (Byrd & Weitzman, 1994). Providing a lot of short texts with male characters and plots that involve boy adventures will support this gender need. Books like *Guys Write for Guys Read* (Scieszka, 2005), an anthology of stories written by boys' favorite authors about being boys, is a good starting place. Web sites like lazyreaders club and www.guys read.com also provide selections that address reluctant readers' needs.

ORGANIZING THE CLASSROOM LIBRARY

"Spine-out" type libraries require students to constantly look at the shelves without necessarily finding books that seem right for them. There are several other ways you can label your books for easy access, however. The important thing to remember is that the system must work for you and your students. No two classrooms will be exactly alike. The intent here is to give you a few suggestions that might work for you.

In one system, each book might have a colored dot that lets the students know the specific genre of the book. For instance, blue for mystery, yellow for realistic fiction, red for sports, and so on. After the dots are put on the spines of the books, they are placed in plastic tubs. Each genre is discussed thoroughly by the teacher before the tubs are set out for student use. Books may also be labeled by level to help students in their selection. See the section on Labeling Books That Fit later in this chapter. In some classrooms, the library is divided into three sections: leveled, fiction, and nonfiction. Each of these sections is divided into smaller categories, including author studies, theme text sets, genre sets, and student-chosen sets. There are tubs of short stories, comics, picture books, student favorites, magazines, poetry, multicultural stories, and big books. Everything is neatly labeled and easy to find. The students know where to look and where to replace the books they have checked out.

Categorizing Books

Books can be labeled in black permanent marker at the bottom right-hand corner with the initials of a genre. If it is necessary to change the book into another bin or tub, eliminate the black marker label by using nail polish remover. You might start with standard genres such as

- Realistic fiction (RF)
- Fantasy (FAN)
- Science fiction (SF)
- Mystery (MY)
- Biography and autobiography (BIO)
- Adventure (AD)
- Historical fiction (HF)
- Poetry (P)
- Nonfiction (NF)
- Short stories (SS)

Other categories might include teacher and student suggestions and any of the following:

Building a Community of Reader-Writers. Books that deal with characters who are learning to read or write, who have difficulty reading or writing, or who have special relationships with reading and writing.

Books with Special Messages and Literary Elements. Picture books that can be used to introduce literary elements and can sometimes explain a new concept better than a grammar book. Some examples are

Amelia Bedelia series (figurative language)
Merry-Go-Round (nouns); *Up, Up and Away* (adverbs); *Kites Sail High* (verbs)
Fantastic! Wow! and Unreal! by Ruth Heller (interjections and conjunctions)
A Little Pigeon Toad, by Fred Gwynne (homonyms and figures of speech)
Animalia, by Graeme Base (alliteration)
Dictionary of Idioms, by Marvin Terban (idioms and clichés)
Favorite Authors (FA): Paulsen, O'Dell, Jacques, Paterson, Lowry, Avi, Speare, Tolkien, Fleischman, Korman, Colfer, Seuss

Nonfiction (NF)

- Magazines
- Holidays
- Explorers
- Outer space
- Animals
- Oceanography
- Places in the world
- Insects and other bugs
- History
- Music and art
- How-to books
- Food
- Persuasive books
- Informational texts
- Nonfiction mystery
- Geography
- Sports
- Weather
- Natural disasters
- Geography
- Geology
- Biology
- Biography, autobiography, and memoir

Enlisting Student Help for Categorizing

As books become available, students can take ownership of them by assisting in categorizing them for classroom use. Students can take an active part in sorting them into the right genres, reading levels, or themes. When a large allocation of books is received, students sit in small groups of approximately three or four and discuss the books. First they read the back cover of the book and any other information that might give them some insight to what the book is about. As the group discusses the information gathered, they decide where it belongs in the classroom library. If they cannot come to agreement, the teacher gives the book to another group, who also inspects it and offers their opinions about its placement in the library. See Activity 2.1, Independent Reading Books: Selection and Evaluation, at the end of this chapter.

Just when you think your library is the way you want it, the students come up with new ideas. Each year the class may have a new way to arrange the books. This might sound like a nightmare, but if you want to have your library work for your class then you have to accept input from the students. New tubs or baskets show growth in student thinking. Change is good.

Labeling Books That Fit

Having a leveled system in place and an abundance of books at each level within the range of students' needs is part of the ideal classroom environment. To help students find books that are just right for them, teachers can label books by independent levels so that students will know which ones fit their own ability. Letters are written in the bottom right-hand corner. The books may be labeled by Fountas and Pinnell's (1996) letter standards or by *Developmental Reading Assessment* (Beaver, 2002) number levels. Whichever leveling system is used, it should be consistent within the classroom. Some schools have a whole-school leveling system that assists students as they transition into a new classroom; they already know the system because it is standard throughout the rooms. Some teachers post the colors or levels from which the students should make their selection. In some classrooms there are sections of the library labeled by specific levels. We prefer to have leveled books within each basket, bin, or tub, so that all students are able to find a readable level within the genre, author study, theme, or topic. That means that our tubs are filled with a variety of levels.

In the upper grades, a leveling system indicator on books can cause embarrassment for those identified as low readers. For older children, we do not recommend that levels be placed on the books. A book that is easy for one child may be very challenging for another. Older students do not want to read books that are perceived as easy. If not given direction, these students will pretend to read so they do not have the stigma of being "bad readers." With good teacher guidance and instruction and multileveled, stimulating books on a variety of subjects, students will choose books that are at their independent level.

Keeping Books for Yourself

Books that you want to keep special may be put away after you have read them during Reading Workshop, or they can be placed in your own personal tub marked Teacher's Favorites or For Teacher Only. By doing this, however, you should realize that your students will want them even more. The best way to keep a personal selection of books is to explain to the children that there are certain works that you want to keep special, so they will not be out on the shelves. If you decide that there are some books that you do not want to get ruined, you might want to buy two copies—one for you and one for them—or purchase a hardcover copy for you and a paperback copy for them. Another way to protect your picture books is to laminate the paper cover to keep it clean.

Knowing Thy Books

Before any new books are placed in the library, it is essential for the teacher to become familiar with them. This may seem time-consuming, but it is valuable in helping students to choose books that are right for them. The main concern that we hear from other teachers is that there is no time set aside during staff development to become familiar with their books. We hope that you can convince your administrators to build time into your afternoon, morning, or staff development so that you and your grade-level colleagues can hold discussions about your new and old books. Through this process, you will know how to use them in designing effective lessons for your classroom, as well as for conferring with children about their reading. Conversations about strengths of the texts, richness of language, illustrations, vocabulary, and literary elements found inside these covers will lead to rich conversations with students during the conferring segment of Reading Workshop. It will also assist you in creating minilessons that will establish stronger reading skills among your students. In order to assist children in their selections, you must "Know thy books." Of course, you must also "Know thy students," which will help you fit a book to the child.

Displaying Books

The library can be overwhelming to new students who enter the classroom. Therefore, not all books are made available for the children in some classrooms. Some teachers like to start out with fewer books in their tubs, therefore limiting the choices that students have. If this method is used, the teacher usually leaves the additional classroom library books in the cupboards and adds new ones in limited numbers as he or she assesses the needs of the students.

Some teachers leave them in the baskets or on shelves, cover them with butcher paper, and tell the students that the books are not to be used. By keeping books visible but telling the students that they cannot touch them, they create a sense of intrigue and build anticipation and at the same time create a feeling as frustrating as having your mother make chocolate chip cookies and let you smell them but not eat any.

Other teachers display all of their books and explain the contents of the tubs as the year progresses. As the students are introduced to a new genre, author, series, theme, or topic, the books related to these categories are added to the user library. This means that the teacher, or a student who already knows the book, talks about the books and their categories before they are placed on the shelf for student use. The teacher removes books that are not appropriate for the students' needs and interests. What is the use in having high-level books available for independent reading if there are no students who can read them successfully? The importance of knowing your students is paramount to the teacher's choices in the library.

Lending and Keeping Track of Books

If you do not have a copy of *The Librarian from the Black Lagoon* (Thaler, 1997), it is time to get one. This book gives a glance at how a library of the past might have been perceived by a child. The illustrations are priceless and appropriate. One part says, "If you twist your neck and squint, you can read the spines." Another point is that once you are finally in the library, it is difficult to pull out the books to look at them. You cannot actually check out books. In fact, you cannot take them off the shelves. To keep the books in alphabetical order, Mrs. Beamster (the librarian) bolts them together. Isn't that what it must seem like to students who have to select a spine from the tightly fitted bookcase? It is important that we create libraries that make books easily accessible to all students.

Another problem in the past was that book covers were hidden. Children are drawn to book covers. Have you noticed how the grocery stores promote cereal to children? What if all the cereals on the shelf were arranged with the spines out? Would that sell very much cereal? Publishers change the covers of their books over time for a variety of reasons. For one thing, they can update a text so that it captures the interest of its new generation of readers. For another, it might generate new interest in the book if the last cover did not entice boys and girls. These cover changes make for interesting conversation within the Reading Workshop. Publishers know that the covers of books are important, and we need to have those covers clearly visible so that our students can choose a book partially by its cover.

When students take a book from today's library, they place either a paint-stirring stick, a cardboard marker, or a clothespin where the book came from. (Paint-stirring sticks are quite easy to obtain from paint stores. Some stores even give them free of charge when you identify yourself as a teacher.) Print the names of the students on the sticks, markers, or clothespins in permanent marker (you can have the students decorate these markers to personalize them). When they complete a book, they can easily find the right place to return it. Because the student has helped to create this library, he or she has ownership in it and is more apt to return the book to the appropriate place. There are no Dewey decimal numbers to this classroom library, just a tub marked with a genre, author, topic, or theme. Even primary students can use this system of returning books—in fact, many times primary students are more efficient in returning their books than upper graders or middle school students.

Introducing New Books

Sometimes children have difficulty choosing books even when there is an abundance to choose from. You might establish a Book of the Week where one child introduces a new book that he or she feels is worthy of mention. You could also have them fill out a Book Recommendation form that you will find on p. 42, Activity 3.2. These can be placed on a bulletin board for other students to peruse. In one fourth-grade classroom, the teacher placed book recommendations on colored index cards and put them in a chart holder. When someone was having difficulty choosing a book, the child could go over to the chart, look over his peer suggestions, and possibly be motivated to read something new.

Often when bookstores close down, they offer book display rounders for sale to the public. These may be used to showcase books in the classroom. In one classroom, each child and the teacher have a space marked with his or her name for displaying a book that they would like to recommend to others. When students complete books, they place the book in their section of the rounder and attach a book recommendation sheet or card to it with a clothespin. Other children may read the recommendations and find the next book they want to read. This rounder can also have sections for parents to add books, as well as a section for books that are new to the classroom. To begin the year, the teacher has five to ten books that he or she has read during the summer and a book recommendation for each. Guided practice and modeling by the teacher sets the standard for how to write a good book recommendation. Many readers frequently add new recommendations to the rounder, but challenged readers and writers do not. Therefore, it may be necessary to require these students to place at least one recommendation in the rounder each month.

Marking Books

As you are collecting books for your library, make sure that you mark them in permanent marker. Mark your name on the books you buy with your own money. Those purchased with school funding are marked with the grade level and classroom number. This system will help you distinguish between what belongs to you personally and what belongs to the school.

Protecting Books

You can buy double rolls of clear contact paper at home improvement stores at a fairly reasonable cost. As you receive new books, enlist a parent or family member who would like to help. Covering books at home can make family members feel connected to the school and supportive of their children's education. Parents of second-language students can work at home on a nonlanguage task and feel comfortable helping out.

Keeping a Fresh Look to the Library

It is quite impressive to have a large collection of books in the classroom library. The important thing to emphasize, though, is not the number of books you have, but instead having the right books to match the needs of your readers. If there are a lot of books that are old, dirty, faded, damaged, or at inappropriate levels for your class, then it is time to weed some out and do some library spring cleaning! A clean, fresh, kid-friendly library with fewer books is better than a dilapidated collection of many books that students do not pick up to use. Dust off those shelves, clean out the old, unused books, and spiff up that library.

Dealing with a Tired-Looking Library

We know this is a problem in many schools across the nation. So one thing you might try is having the children create new, attractive book covers. Bright, shiny, and clean student-created book covers give new life to old, tired-looking books. After a student has read an older version of a wonderful piece of literature, he or she might personally create or co-create a new cover that attracts other students to the book.

CHECKING UP ON WHAT STUDENTS ARE READING

It is important for teachers and parents to frequently monitor what students are reading to make sure the texts are neither too challenging nor too easy. Through one-on-one conferencing, teachers can assess the reading level that the students are choosing. They can also assess through the use of reading logs. (See Activities 2.2, Reading Log, and 2.3, Home Reading Log, at the end of this chapter.)

Tips for Parents

Encourage parents to keep current with the books their children are reading. With the more mature subject matter in children's literature today, parents need to be careful about some of the selections students are making. The gifted and talented student usually reads about two grade levels higher than his or her peers. It is difficult to find material at an elevated language level with subject matter that is still appropriate for the age.

Having a vast selection of books at home, where children can access them immediately, is ideal. Families should have plenty of books available, so there is no excuse for a child saying, "I have nothing to read" at night when home reading time has started. If there are not a lot of books in the home library, parents may borrow books from the school, classrooms, and local libraries, buy books at a nominal fee at garage sales and flea markets, and borrow books from family, friends, and neighbors. Families should also realize that reading is not just about books—there are also magazines, newspapers, recipes, menus, e-mails, advertisements, notes, and age-appropriate articles of interest from the Internet.

Not So User-Friendly Public Libraries or Bookstores

The teacher supports and scaffolds the students' ability to select a book at their independent reading level. Ultimately, the goal is that all children know how to select a book on their own level. When we provide a lot of practice in the classroom selecting books that are on an appropriate reading level for each child, students will learn how to select books that are just right for them when they go to the public library. In the classroom, the teacher's job is to match books with children and gently wean them from adult assistance and the scaffolding that we have provided. When they go to a bookstore or public library, this guidance will prevail and help them independently navigate through the books.

Activity 2.1

INDEPENDENT READING BOOKS: SELECTION AND EVALUATION

Student's Name______________________________ Date ____________

1. Browse through the book selections in the basket on your desk. Choose two books to look at closely, then answer the questions below. If you have more time, you may evaluate more than two. You should also give some thought to the level (easy, grade-level, challenging) and the cover design and the illustrations, if applicable. You will have approximately 15 minutes for this task. Please work alone.
2. The team leader will hold up a book and those of you who have browsed through it will try to come to consensus about where the book belongs in the library. When you have come to agreement, put a sticky note on the book with the name of the basket it should go into. Put all the books back in the basket when you are completed. If you aren't sure where it goes, put a big ? on the sticky note and your teacher will give the book to another group.
3. After that is done, choose one book to introduce to the class next week. This will help us know what the book is about and who might be interested in investigating it further.

Name of Book 1 ______________________________

Reading Level ______________________________

Genre/Category ______________________________

Cover/Illustrations ______________________________

Summary ______________________________

____

Your opinion ______________________________

____

Name of Book 2 ______________________________

Reading Level ______________________________

Genre/Category ______________________________

Cover/Illustrations ______________________________

Summary ______________________________

____

Your opinion ______________________________

____

Activity 2.2

READING LOG

Reading Log for___________ Room #___________

Write down the name of the book you read. Enter the author, genre, date completed, and how many pages the book has. Evaluate the book with a +, √, or –, depending on your opinion.

Title	Author	Genre	Pages in the Book	Date Comp-leted	Evalu-ation +, √, –

Activity 2.3

HOME READING LOG

Home Reading Log
Week of _______

Day	Minutes Read	Parent Initials
Monday		
Tuesday		
Wednesday		
Thursday		
Friday		
Saturday		
Sunday		
	Student's Signature	
	Parent's Signature	

What did you read?
Books, Magazines, etc.

1. ____________ 4. ____________

2. ____________ 5. ____________

3. ____________ 6. ____________

Home Reading Log
Week of _______

Day	Minutes Read	Parent Initials
Monday		
Tuesday		
Wednesday		
Thursday		
Friday		
Saturday		
Sunday		
	Student's Signature	
	Parent's Signature	

What did you read?
Books, Magazines, etc.

1. ____________ 4. ____________

2. ____________ 5. ____________

3. ____________ 6. ____________

— *Chapter 3* —

READING IN THE LITERACY WORKSHOP

When educators attend a workshop, they expect to get some new ideas and learn how to incorporate them into their own classrooms. We attend workshops to be with skilled experts who impart and model new ideas, guide us in perfecting our own practice, and work with other teachers who have practical experience at all levels of the spectrum. "A workshop is a place where people produce things; a place where people come together to create. Workshops mean that people work together and that there are different skills used and needed by different people" (Frey & Fisher, 2006, p. xxiii). If we look at the literacy workshop model in the same context, children in our classrooms who are involved in the workshop model will be engaged in meaningful learning that will move them forward and give them opportunities to practice their craft with the guidance of a skilled expert.

Throughout this book we focus on capturing the blending of the balanced literacy workshop that incorporates all the domains of literacy instruction. It is our contention that reading and writing are not isolated entities. The workshop provides flexible instruction within a balanced curriculum of reading and writing experiences that include science, mathematics, social studies, and visual and performing arts. The teacher should meet with the whole group, small groups, and individuals for reading and writing instruction. Usually this literacy block of time runs about three hours.

Both parts of the Literacy Workshop (reading and writing) provide the same kinds of structure for instruction. These include a focused lesson, shared instruction, guided instruction, independent reading or writing, and teacher conferring. A variety of materials should be used, including anthologies; guided reading books; trade books; newspapers; digital sources; graphic novels; functional, everyday texts; music; and a myriad of other resources. In this chapter, the focus is on the reading part of the workshop. The next chapter will focus on writing.

SETTING UP THE READING WORKSHOP

It is well known that readers become better readers by reading. The more exposure children have to good stories—whether by being read *to*, read *with*, or by doing the reading themselves—the more likely they will develop as successful readers. As children have more experience with the written word, they will transfer this knowledge and use whatever modeling they have experienced to help themselves become better readers.

Teachers should always first visit a text for reading concerns during Reading Workshop and second revisit the text from a writer's standpoint for shared experience. This can be a powerful instructional strategy.

Setting Goals for Reading

In the upper grades and middle school, students should be setting some standards for themselves. This gives them a purpose and a goal to achieve. During reading and writing conferences, standards provide a conversational starting point for adults and students. Students may be asked to set their goals several times throughout the year, possibly at the beginning of each quarter or trimester. Because some goals are specific and short-term and others are more global and span a larger time frame, students usually write three or four goals. Some goals may carry over into another period of time. Some teachers have students write goals on index cards for the bulletin board and place their pictures next to them. A volunteer or administrator visiting the classroom can then check on how well the goal is being met. Students might brainstorm at the beginning of the year to determine possible goals. These goals might include such things as reading a book from a different genre, reading an extra ten minutes each day, reading a book with a peer and discussing it, stopping and thinking about what has been read by summarizing thoughts on a sticky note, using a sticky note to set a page goal for reading, or using the chapter titles to check comprehension.

Managing the Literacy Workshop

Together, teachers and students establish the guidelines for how the workshop will be laid out. Brainstorming will help establish some basic structures, such as building stamina (how long you stay on task), choosing seats to sustain work, keeping materials in a strategic location, setting goals for work completion, and scheduling possibilities for independent conferencing and peer conversations.

Assessment in the Literacy Workshop

In the balanced literacy classroom, we must use both formal and informal assessment to evaluate where our students are on the educational continuum and to make sure that parents understand their children's developing skills, abilities, and competencies. Through various of types of assessment, including running records, writing samples, DRA (diagnostic reading assessment), observations, and conferring, teachers can determine specific instruction for any given child.

Children must continue to understand and respect the importance of tests in their educational lives, but teachers must also find new and innovative ways to assess students' individual performance to coincide with the freshness of authentic and interesting language, the hands-on approach, and literacy skills instruction. Teachers must use a variety of strategies to assess children's progress, including teacher observation, peer evaluation, student self-evaluation, portfolios, and tests that are appropriate to the child's level of development.

Teachers must become investigators who observe their students and find out how and what they are learning. Discovering a particular student's learning styles and making teaching adjustments so that all children can learn in their own way build stronger character in our teaching skills. It is always a source of fascination to discover a new teaching method that helps more students remember a new concept or skill more fully. Through "kid watching," and recording, teachers can become more aware of how children process information and how creativity enters into their learning.

Observational notes can be taken in several forms. Some teachers keep a notebook with a page for each child's name. As they observe the child in different situations, they make notations on the page and date it. Some teachers have a flip note card system, with each child's name on a card that is stapled or taped together with other student cards on a clipboard. Other teachers have a one-page grid divided into twelve or sixteen squares, where notes may be written under each child's name. (See Activity 3.1 at the end of this chapter.) Yet other teachers carry sticky notes and post them inside student folders at the end of the day.

The method of note taking depends on the individual teacher. Usually the notations focus on reading or writing goals that the child needs to work on, such as *using chapter titles to help check comprehension after reading, rereading conversation or dialogue when meaning breaks down, slowing down at the end of a sentence when you see a period or other punctuation mark, using a question to hook in your reader at the beginning of your piece, using conversation to make a stronger piece of writing, or writing interesting titles to hook in your reader*. When the teacher returns for the next conference, he or she will check to see if the child is making these changes.

There are several methods that teachers use for taking anecdotal records. Some teachers target five or six students per day and watch them specifically. This assures the teacher that there will be a record taken for each child each week. Other teachers watch and record instances as they happen. This is a bit more informal and must be monitored so that every student is covered several times during the reporting period.

Notations are invaluable when teachers are evaluating students for progress reports. They are excellent resources to review before a parent conference and are helpful in showing parents that you truly *know* about their child. Because all notations are dated, you can also track just how far a child has progressed.

Anecdotal records (dated, informal observations and notations that describe development) can be composed of many items such as interview notes and more extensive summaries that are taken during and after reading, writing, and portfolio conferences with the child; comprehension checks during class periods; and observations of group participation, work habits, study skills, and learning styles.

SELECTING QUALITY BOOKS

When choosing books for instruction, teachers need to read the books first and assess whether the level and subject matter are appropriate for their students. Quality books should be selected for read-aloud purposes. Once you find the books you love, you can look at which teaching points you want to bring out to meet your standards. For more about quality books for your classroom, see Chapter Two, Setting Up a Balanced Literacy Environment.

Some books are perfect for selective page read-alouds. For instance, we might choose not to use *To Be a Slave* (Lester, 1968), or *The Slave Dancer* (Fox, 1973) for fifth graders, even though they fit into the U.S. history curriculum. These books contain material that is not considered appropriate for ten- and eleven-year-olds, but may be very palatable to eighth graders when they again study U.S. history. So we may want to use parts of them as a read-aloud or shared reading because they do clarify historical points.

STRATEGIES FOR READING

Reading Workshop is a time when students have a large block of time to read materials that they choose, to interact with authors, read in a relaxed, unhurried way, think about their reading, bounce ideas off of each other, and talk about their reading.

Whole-Class Instruction

It is the current trend to have groups of children read different books at their own level. The teacher selects reading materials that center around a theme, genre, or author. The teacher selects a skill that the students need based on their respective reading abilities and pursues that goal with the students in mind. Students receive differentiated instruction, and their individual needs are met.

Good pieces of literature sometimes need to be taught to a whole class, with everyone developing the same language and knowledge that sets the standard for the entire year's literature study. Through direct teaching, part of a novel may be used for shared reading, another part for independent reading, and another part for a read-aloud. As children begin to develop skills in understanding the author's writing style, literary elements, point of view, genre characteristics, and what makes a great piece of literature, they can be weaned from so much direction from the teacher. Students need to establish common language before they can set out on their own in literature circles or author or genre studies. When they finally have the basic information that allows them to interact with each other and respond to literature as well as informational texts, they have the foundation they need to establish themselves as independent readers and writers.

A Deeper Look at the Read-Aloud

The read-aloud provides the most teacher support. There are several key elements to consider when planning and delivering read alouds to students (Fisher, Flood, Lapp, & Frey, 2004). First, the teacher must select readings appropriate to the grade-level content, the students' emotional and social development, and their interests. It is crucial that the teacher practice the selection before the read-aloud in order to model fluent oral reading at its best. Because the reading is worthy of attention, the students are engaged and actively listen to the text. As the read-aloud progresses, the teacher stops to ask important questions to check understanding, helping students to make connections to their reading and writing and involving students in book discussion through turning and talking to a peer.

The Institute for Learning at the University of Pittsburgh (Resnick, 1995) gives the following guidelines for choosing read-alouds:

1. Choose multiple books by the same author so that students can compare and contrast books to begin to develop a sense of an author's style.
2. Choose some books around a theme so that students can see how different authors address common themes.

3. Choose books that reflect the diversity of the students in the classroom and school community.
4. Honor students' choices by displaying books they recommend or bring from home and, when possible, read aloud these books if they support the teacher's instructional plan.
5. Read aloud books from a wide variety of genres, so that students are exposed to many forms of writing.
6. Read aloud books from a wide variety of authors, so that students build a repertoire of authors with whom they are familiar.

In the upper grade or middle school classroom, it is the teacher's responsibility to locate books that have "meaty" subject matter. Teachers must do their homework by scanning the shelves of bookstores and libraries, talking with co-workers and librarians, and reading book reviews in journals about the plethora of children's literature in today's world. They must keep current with the newest literature and also retain the older, already proven books that have important messages for our present learners. While doing this, the teacher must also take a look at the standards and make sure that the piece of work meets the district or state standards. Pieces of literature provide for quality discussion and higher-order thinking for the students.

When we make good choices in our selections, both the teacher and the students do not mind revisiting the texts and characters again in discussion. Books that pop up again and again are what we refer to as *touchstone* or *mentor* texts. They propel our thinking forward. We connect these characters, settings, and plots with our lives and with the new characters, settings, and plots we investigate, expand, and deepen our discussions.

Sometimes teachers forget the importance and significance of using picture books in upper-level classrooms. During read-alouds, teachers should feel comfortable using picture books to motivate students who may have difficulty staying focused on novels. Mixing a picture book or big book in with a novel breaks up the daily routine and helps students realize that there is a lot to learn from the text and the illustrations. Nonfiction picture books should also be introduced often to bring content into the reading workshop, providing another example of balance. (See Chapter Five, Nonfiction and Its Place in Balanced Literacy.)

In the primary grades students use illustrations to make meaning of the text because the text itself is too difficult for them to access themselves. Offering upper-grade students the opportunities to revisit great picture books for the purpose of reading the text can motivate reluctant and challenged readers to approach more complicated text without being embarrassed to do so. Caldecott Award Winners, for example, are chosen specifically for their illustrations, but many contain beautiful language and description as well. (See Chapter Two, Setting Up a Balanced Literacy Environment.)

A Deeper Look at Shared Reading

Shared reading allows students to access a piece of text even though it may be slightly above what they can read independently (Holdaway, 1979). Through shared reading, students can experience the impact and appeal of high-quality writing and make sense out of texts they may not have been able to access independently. The teacher models fluent reading behaviors so that the students can transfer them into their own independent reading. Shared reading is intended to accomplish several purposes (Allen, 1999): it demonstrates fluent reading so students can experience the "charm, magic, impact, and appeal" of high-quality writing; and it builds bridges between reading and our students' lives and provides guided practice for strategies that make texts understandable. Through shared reading, the modeled fluent reading behaviors will transfer to students' independent reading and will increase knowledge of the language.

This part of the day is enjoyable because the students and teacher take on the reading together. The teacher may read the whole text and the students may read along; the students may have their own texts or they may be reading from an overhead or document camera. Usually the children and the teacher are close together—many times they are on the rug near the projector. Usually the text is a short piece with a skill or strategy focus. The students may read along with the text silently first and then gradually join in. The text may be read in choral verse, boy-girl, whole class, partners, and other configurations. In the upper grades, poetry, songs, and sections of something read in read-aloud the day before, directions for games, cafeteria menus, recipes, and so on can be used while you have a captivated audience. The focus of the lesson should be engagement.

Shared reading should take place every day for approximately fifteen to thirty minutes, using short, relevant texts that are based on students' interests. The lessons are quick, purposeful, and focused. The teacher leads the reading of fiction or nonfiction selections, and the students follow the text from an overhead projector or document camera, a chart with a text written on it, individual student copies, or big books. Samples of standard-setting student pieces can also be used. Students should know the purpose of the reading at the onset of the lesson and know that they may be returning to the text for extended reading, questioning, and analyzing the writer's craft. Keeping a shared reading notebook or file folder of useful pieces is a good idea, so that they are available for future lessons.

Shared reading brings about a sense of group learning because students are gathered together at a focal point where all attention is centered on the piece of text.

Guided Reading

Through informal and formal assessment, teachers discover what strengths and weaknesses students possess. For students who almost have a skill or strategy intact but still need more practice, the guided group is the place for them. If during shared reading you discover that there is a group of children who do not understand the skill, you should form a group for more guided practice. If you are teaching the skill of skimming and you see that several of the students almost have it but still need more assistance, set up a guided group for the next day that will provide guidance and practice of that skill. Each day you quickly glance at your students to see what they have in their toolbox and what they have almost acquired. You assess their understanding and then inform your instruction to scaffold the students who need more guided practice. These groups should be flexible in the upper grades. It is important for teachers to take notes on the reading behaviors that the students are displaying during guided reading. This accountability is valuable for establishing your next set of instructional groupings.

Students who are not proficient readers should have some form of guided reading group three to five times a week, whereas more proficient readers may be seen once or twice a week. The instruction during guided reading should nudge the students forward. Remember that this time frame challenges the reader to tackle a skill or strategy that they are *almost* comfortable with. In this group, the students are doing almost all the work; the teacher is doing the guiding. All students seem to enjoy this personal, small-group instruction. During your work with these small groups, the other students should not be disturbing you for any reason other than an emergency. Questions and concerns should be addressed by asking another student or by waiting patiently until the group is finished.

Guided reading instruction should be balanced in the upper grades with literature groups or book clubs. (See Chapter 10, Book Clubs and Literature Circles.) Challenged readers need opportunities to pursue quality literature in shared groups along with their peers. You may need to make accommodations to support the reluctant readers, but more often than not they will rise to the occasion and become active participants in book clubs.

One of the chief concerns of teachers as they support readers in guided groups is how to keep the rest of the students busy during that time with meaningful activities. During the thirty- to forty-minute independent reading period, the students are reading at their "just right" level of books, while teachers are conferring with individual students, helping them set goals for their reading, jotting down notes about their progress, and checking to see that students are not reading books that are too challenging or too frustrating. Therefore, the thirty- to forty-five-minute guided reading session is another block of time to be filled with literacy opportunities. Many avid readers beg for more independent reading time, but others have difficulty staying focused during another long stretch. Therefore, literacy-related activities are suggested.

LITERACY STATIONS

Literacy stations are a valuable tool during the Literacy Workshop. They provide students with a variety of engaging literacy activities and opportunities to sharpen their skills in reading, writing, word study, listening, and speaking. Students enjoy learning in a more independent way in small groups of peers. Stations seem to work best with three to four students each.

For all literacy stations, the teacher should provide instruction on what the behavior should look like before giving the students access to the activity. What should the students do and how should they behave? Without teacher-directed instruction, the students do not know the expectations.

Children may rotate through the stations. While rotating, one of the groups (or individuals from several groups) is called up to the guided reading or guided writing table for a fifteen- to twenty-minute instructional lesson.

Several literacy stations are described here to help you facilitate meaningful activities in which children can be involved. How many stations to use and how often to use them is a teacher choice depending on the needs of the classroom.

Anthology or Responding to Literature. Students have already read a story from the anthology as a whole or small group. They use this station for a journal response or to finish up their reading of a selection.

Artist's Attic. Students illustrate a story or a poem that they have written or read or a story that a classmate has written. They may research a particular artist (such as Van Gogh, Picasso, or Grandma Moses), a particular art form, or a favorite author-illustrator (such as Roald Dahl, Bill Peet, or Chris Van Allsburg). They may tell what they like about the artist's work and how it enhances a story. They may read a book about art from the art tub or look carefully at the picture books in the Caldecott Book Tub and write why the illustrations are outstanding or how the illustrations help in understanding the story.

Author Study. Offering picture books by a particular author helps students to look carefully at a writer's craft, theme, and possibly even illustrations. Authors like Cynthia Rylant or Jane Yolen give children the chance to look at teacher read-alouds or old-time favorites more carefully for enjoyment or for a written activity.

Big Books. Students peruse the selection of big books for enjoyment. They practice their fluency with a peer or practice reading their book for their kindergarten buddy. Rereading is emphasized. Just as the teacher needs to plan for reading aloud, so should students.

Book Club Preparation. Students plan for their particular role, read their section of the book, fill out a response journal, write sticky notes, or plan questions for their next book club meeting.

Book Recommendation. Students fill out Activity 3.2, Book Recommendation Form, at the end of this chapter, or plan a commercial or book talk about the book to present to the class.

Buddy Reading Practice. Students read a grade-level book together aloud. Reading can be joyful when students are working with a friend on fluency, intonation, and pacing.

Celebrity Writing Station. Students write letters to a celebrity using correct letter writing format. They use creativity to write interesting letters, telling the famous person about themselves and asking questions. Letters may be edited and revised and envelopes addressed.

Choice Reading. Students choose books that are of interest to them—whether fiction or nonfiction. Books may be slightly more challenging or slightly easier than a "just right" book. They may be from home or from the school library. Students might want to update their reading log. (See Activity 2.2, Reading Log.)

Comic Book Corner. Students read graphic novels, joke books, and comic books from the book tub.

Computer Research. Students write down subjects that they are interested in finding out more about. During this period, they work with a partner or alone on investigating their favorite subjects. They write the source of their findings on a sheet of paper or in a folder and mark their sites visited. Students can also write a fact that they learned on a sticky note and file it with other facts that they discover. Students may visit sites that are bookmarked. If an adult is available, he or she may also look for information on a topic the students are studying. The following sites can be bookmarked for fast retrieval: www.kidsreads.com, www.teachnet.com/brainbinders, and www.pbskids.org.

Dictionary and Thesaurus. Special activity sheets and games may be provided at this station so that students become more experienced at using these references.

Functional Reading and Writing Station. On standardized testing, children are expected to be familiar with many types of bulletins, invitations, notices, recipes, game instructions, menus, how-to procedures, and TV guides. Teachers need to make sure that there are multiple opportunities for students to access and understand this information and know the audience that this form of writing is meant to address. At this station children are exposed to all the kinds of information they may be in contact with during their school lives.

How-to Books. Several tubs of books are available for students to learn how to do something new, such as paper folding with dollar bills, folding a tent, taking care of a dog, or making a new food.

Listening Post. Students listen to a novel on CD or cassette with a Walkman or earphones or listen to music that might soothe them while reading.

Magazine Rack. Tubs of magazines such as *Muse, Cricket Magazine, Time for Kids, Sports Illustrated for Kids, Zillion, Kids Discover,* and *Ranger Rick* are available.

Music Station. A tub of music picture books and biographies about famous musicians, as well as bookmarked web sites, are available. Students may read, write, draw, or listen to music on CDs or tapes. They may write about their favorite kinds of music, prepare a musical song, make up a concentration- or Jeopardy-type game with music terms and notation, learn more about famous musicians, or draw instruments and practice musical notations.

Newspaper Nook. This center is filled with a city newspaper, school newspaper, assorted Mini Pages (Universal Press), *Time for Kids, Weekly Reader,* and other social studies and science weekly newspapers. Students may choose activities such as writing an article to the editor with a gripe they have about an issue, cutting out articles of interest and summarizing them, choosing movies they want to see, or choosing a car, house, or other item they would like to buy from the ad section.

Performers' Parlor. At this center students can create a play or reader's theater script from a section of a book that they have read, choose a generic reader's theater script from the collection tub, or write one of their own.

Poetry. Students read silently or aloud for enjoyment, fluency, and intonation. They work alone or with a partner, glancing through poetry books that are in the tubs or that they bring from home. They read into a microphone and tape their poem and play it back to evaluate their reading. They may want to share their poem with the whole class at a later time. They might use sticky notes to mark their favorite poems with their name or have a blue book or folder to record their ideas or use a poetry log.

Researcher Expert. Students choose a subject that they are interested in learning about from the Information genre tub in nonfiction, almanacs, maps, dictionaries, time lines, encyclopedias, web sites, and CDs. With a partner or small group they become an expert and teach their classmates what they have learned.

Science Station. Students read through a variety of experiment books. They choose several experiments that they would like to perform and mark them with a sticky note with their name. A copy of the experiment can be reproduced so they can practice at home and present to the class.

Specialty Books. During a special time frame such as Black History Week, Halloween, Memorial Day, Presidents' Day, Christmas, or Hanukkah, a basket of books on the subject is put out for everyone to enjoy.

Word Study. A variety of word games such as Scrabble, word sorts, crossword puzzles, and word challenges are available. Students also practice personalized spelling words on whiteboards. (See Chapter Six for more information on word study.)

STRATEGIES TO HELP STUDENTS IMPROVE LITERACY

Students and teachers process meaning and assess learning during the Reading Workshop in a number of ways.

Accountable Talking

Lauren Resnick (1995) and her colleagues at the Institute for Learning, University of Pittsburgh, developed and researched the practice of accountable talk, which fosters classroom conversations among partners and in whole-group discussions. It involves high levels of engaging talk and critical thinking among student learners. Accountable talk involves both listening and speaking. Students learn through teacher and student modeling how to speak in acceptable ways, involving both questioning and challenging others' ideas and opinions. They become involved in healthy and courteous exchanges that stretch student thinking with meaningful talk that gets beyond surface thinking into the realm of deeper thinking. Students learn to be respectful of others' ideas, opinions, and thinking. Through this method, they become stronger students, better listeners, and more critical thinkers. Active involvement of all students in discussion is imperative. Teachers guide students into these conversations through partner talks, triads, quads, and small-group and whole-group interaction. Accountable talk involves students in purposeful discourse in language arts and also in the content areas. It is an integral part of the daily instruction.

If accountable talk is established in a classroom, students have little need for raising their hands to respond. It becomes more like adult conversations—students become respectful of each other, wait their turns, and share the responsibility of the conversation. Statements like the ones listed below are examples of how a discussion moves along with established accountable talk:

I agree (or disagree) with you because . . .

I'm not sure what you mean. Could you explain it in another way?

I understand what you are saying, but I see it differently.

I'd like to add on to what you are saying.

This reminds me of . . .

I can relate to that . . .

I don't understand—could you repeat what you said?

I think we are pretty close to having the same idea, but here is my thinking.

Could you give me an example of what you mean?

So you are saying . . .

Graphic Organizers

During a Reading Workshop, students often need more than listening skills to process a piece of text and make meaning from it. Graphic organizers are tools that help students to visually organize information for reading and writing purposes. They are particularly useful for challenged readers and writers in visualizing and processing information from the content areas and in aiding comprehension. Sometimes they are used in a shared environment where the instructor creates the form and students add the information. At other times, students generate their own organizers to help them understand a story or structure a piece of writing. Students sometimes work in pairs or triads to produce larger representations of their thinking.

Graphic organizers can be big or small, individual or group, teacher-directed or student-directed. They may be used for any area of the curriculum. They help students process and hold on to information for future use. Teaching a variety of forms is a wise practice because when children have to perform to a prompt for writing on a statewide test, they need to be able to formulate their ideas into an organized manner before starting to write. Sometimes that is difficult for children to do, unless they have had direct instruction and opportunities to discuss why one kind of organizer would be best to use for a particular assignment.

Graphic organizers are an integral part of the literacy workshop and will provide guidance and assessment possibilities for all students, especially those who are challenged learners.

Several forms of graphic organizers can be found in Chapter Five, Nonfiction and Its Place in Balanced Literacy, and more information in Chapters Twelve and Thirteen.

Conferring with Students

Students should have many opportunities during the week to talk about books. There should be teacher-student talks, student-student talks, and parent-student talks. Through discussion, the child becomes a more active participant in literacy.

One favorite time of the day for both the teacher and the student is individual conference time—conferring with students about their books and setting goals for their future reading. In the upper-grade classes, this time is limited because of the large number of children in a class. Therefore it is important to carve out precious one-on-one minutes with each child. Management of one-on-one time can be tricky. Using a classroom recording sheet with each child's name in a box can be effective. (See Activity 3.1 at the end of this chapter.) Within each square, a child's name and the date is noted. Placing the name of the book the child is reading and any anecdotal records of this conference can become helpful reminders of what was discussed. Setting a reading minigoal with a child is also good so that during the next conference you can talk about it and how the child has grown as a reader by discussing it. A goal may be as simple as "use the chapter titles to refer back to when you are finished." Students may be asked such questions as "see if you can understand why this title was used for this chapter. Why was the chapter titled __________? Can you think of a better title than the one the author used?" Using this strategy helps you to check comprehension and monitor how much meaning a student picked up from the chapter. Sometimes the teacher might ask a child to use sticky notes at the end of the chapter to summarize his or her thinking upon completion of the chapter.

Another goal that the teacher and student might set is "reread the part where your understanding broke down." Some students do not know what to do when meaning gets lost. If the teacher does not feel that the child has grasped meaning, then that child needs to go back and reread—maybe even reading it out loud to him- or herself.

Sometimes in a conference a teacher asks a student to read a passage aloud just to spot-check the fluency and comprehension. If a child is not stopping at the end of the sentences, the goal for the child may be "make a conscious effort to stop at the end of each sentence and think about what you just read."

A teacher can learn so much about his or her students during a three- to five-minute conference. Parents, senior citizens, volunteers, and aides can also be used to confer with children about what they are reading, what they like to read, how they read orally, and if they are comprehending what they are reading. Writing can also be looked at, read aloud, and discussed. Many children do not have the opportunity to spend personal time with their own parents for sharing, reviewing, and reading. The brief conference can, therefore, be very meaningful for the child and for the adult.

Often a parent stops into the classroom and asks if there is anything that he or she can do for a few hours to assist you in the classroom. Having a folder or file for each child is a convenient way to utilize the assistance of a parent when they drop in on the spur of the moment. Use of the reading conference sheet is also suggested for accountability. Some volunteers ask the students to talk about or retell the story. Although this can be helpful in getting students to talk, it should be stressed that students should have more meaningful conversation. It would be best to focus the students on a particular part or a specific skill or strategy and to follow the guidelines that the teacher follows. Questions for parents to use can be found later in this chapter.

Conferring Baskets

There is no way that a teacher can be familiar with every book in the classroom library plus all of the additional books that students in any grade level read. Therefore, the use of the conferring basket can be a helpful aid in assessing students in their choice of books and finding if they are getting meaning from the book that they are reading. The conferring basket idea has grown from the use of "touchstone texts," books that teachers know well and use for many purposes in the teaching of literacy. The more texts a teacher is familiar with, the better he or she can talk to students about their reading. The level of accountable talk is elevated if the teacher is familiar with the book the student is reading. The conferring basket establishes a set of core books that the teacher knows well and can discuss deeply with the students. These books span the reading levels of the children in the classroom. This set becomes the foundation for assessing reading during independent reading time.

A good place to start in the gathering of a few good books for assessing reading is *Guiding Readers and Writers (Grades 3–6)* (Fountas & Pinnell, 2001). There are over a thousand leveled books at the end of this text that will jump-start your conferring basket searches. There are no absolutely correct books to choose: teacher preference is based on the interests, needs, and levels of the students in the classroom. No two teachers' conferring baskets will be the same. Choices should include several books at each level and from both fiction and nonfiction. These books may be kept near the classroom conferring area or they may be carried around the classroom while conferring with students. The procedure for the conferring session may look like this:

- The teacher asks the student to read a short section of the book aloud. An informal running record may be taken to check the child's fluency and miscues.
- The teacher asks the student to complete a few pages of reading on his or her own and asks him or her to return to discuss the pages upon completion.
- The teacher asks key questions about the section that the child should be able to answer. If the child is unable to discuss the key ideas in this section, possibly a longer segment of text should be assigned and another conferring session should be set for the next day. Questions referring to literary elements such as conflict, climax, problem, solution, characterization, setting, plot, use of titles to gain meaning, and what strategies are being used for comprehension should be explored in conversation. Basic questions like "how is your reading going?" or "tell me about your reading" are good lead-ins to get a child started talking about a book.

The teacher and student together assess if this level of text is frustrating, challenging, too easy, or just right. This self-assessment procedure is helpful for making the child aware of the level of books chosen.

Activity 3.1

CONFERRING NOTES FOR READING

Week of____________________ Focus____________________

Student's name______ Book______ Page #______ Discussed______ ______ Goal______ ______ Recheck______			

Activity 3.2

BOOK RECOMMENDATION FORM

This was an A+ book and I think you should read it!

Book Reviewer: ______________________________

Title: ________________________ Author: ______________________

Genre: ___________________

Short Summary: ____

____

____

____

____

____

Why should you read it? ______________________________________

____

____

This was an A+ book and I think you should read it!

Book Reviewer: ______________________________

Title: ________________________ Author: ______________________

Genre: ___________________

Short Summary: ____

____

____

____

____

____

Why should you read it? ______________________________________

____

____

— Chapter 4 —

WRITING IN THE LITERACY WORKSHOP

The last chapter introduced reading in the balanced literacy workshop. But in the upper grades, where children are *reading to learn,* we must also think about writing whenever we think about reading. The two go hand in hand. In this chapter, we explore writing in the Literacy Workshop.

Just as we believe that the more we read the better we read, it is easy to believe that the more we write the better we write. Some teachers, therefore, give students creative prompts and have them write volumes of essays. Certainly we do become more fluent as we write more, but it is unlikely that we learn how to write better just by writing. We now know that to become a better writer, we need to read. When children read good pieces of literature, they see how real authors write; they are exposed to good writing and transfer what they read into improving their own writing skills. When children read good pieces of literature, they interact with fully developed characters, experience the importance of sophisticated, multiple settings, become involved in complicated plots, and are exposed to literary elements that are unique to each author's style. Readers and writers are always centering their attention on texts (Fountas & Pinnell, 2001). The reading and the writing craft are intertwined.

The written word allows us to consider different perspectives. Because everyone comes from a slightly different background, there is no end to the possibilities for writing. But how can we get all students to love writing and feel successful at it? As teachers bring their bag of tricks to the classroom, each bag is filled with unique tools and materials. For some teachers, writing is difficult to teach, and for others it is the perfect avenue for almost everything. Writing should be threaded throughout the day for different purposes. Students might be asked to write a how-to example of a problem in multiplication, write word problems, or explain a graph they clipped from the newspaper for their math journal. They might be asked to write creatively during the Writing Workshop. During science they may be asked to form their own hypothesis and write conclusions to their experiments. In reading they may be asked to respond to a piece of literature, and in social studies they may be asked to write a report about explorers or Native Americans. Through the writing process in the Literacy Workshop, students receive varying levels of support with gradual release of responsibility to reach independence. A good workshop moves the student through the following steps.

Modeled Writing. Students are introduced to the joys of writing. The teacher demonstrates strategies as a proficient adult writer.

Shared Writing. Students have the opportunity to successfully participate in the writing process. Teachers and students share the task of writing.

Guided Writing. Students work in groups or as individuals on effective writing strategies determined through teacher observation of the students' writing behaviors and work.

Independent Writing. Students practice using the writing strategies they have learned during modeled, shared, and guided writing to write on their own.

Just as in the reading workshop, students should set goals in writing and should strive to meet them. Depending on the direction that the class writing program is taking, writing goals can be set to align with instruction. As a class studies good writing craft from mentor authors, they establish some powerful writing goals for themselves. Goals might include such things as reading original writing out loud to hear the way it will sound to others, writing stronger leads to pull the reader into the writing, using a thesaurus to find better words, using similes more often to help the reader better visualize descriptions, or concentrating on a favorite author's craft and trying to use a similar style.

SETTING UP THE WRITING WORKSHOP

Developing readers and writers in today's classroom will feel more successful as they see how the balanced curriculum they have been exposed to is integrated into their lives. The teacher begins to establish an environment and expectation for reading and writing on the very first day of class. Following is an account of the steps Julie Heimburge takes to prepare her students for the year ahead.

A FIRSTHAND ACCOUNT OF JULIE'S CLASSROOM

On the first day of school, I give each of my students a writing journal and ask them to write for fifteen minutes about something that interests them—a situation that happened to them in the past, something that touched them in a personal way, or something they are an expert in. Whatever it is, they need to write for a full fifteen minutes. No talking, and pencils on the paper the entire time. I always find that some students cannot think of anything, and some can write for the full fifteen minutes. This piece of writing becomes my baseline writing assessment for each of the students.

During the first week of school, we launch our writing workshop. We brainstorm lists of things that we might write about and make a chart to hang in the room for topic ideas.

Starting the Year with Personal Narrative

Start with what is familiar to the children. I ask them to write about things that have happened to them, personal stories about their family, friends, vacations, pets, fears, joys, hobbies, things in the real world that they know a lot about, and their interests. We spend one or two months collecting pieces of writing, and as they collect, I teach minilessons on ways that mentor-writers craft their writing, such as use of conversation, descriptive word use, writing good leads, focusing their topics, varying the length of their sentences, and using strong verbs. As a lesson is taught, they try out the skill in their own pieces of writing, drawing from what they have already written in their notebooks. For instance, if we are looking at mentor-authors and how they use conversation in their pieces, the students try using limited conversation in their own pieces—not a new piece, but something they have already started in their notebook during the first month of school.

Establishing a Writing Environment

Writing generally does not begin in the workshop until students have already been reading for a week or two. It is essential to have a myriad of mentor texts that you have already read to inspire students to write and to model author's craft.

I have students sit on the rug close to me when I teach minilessons, read mentor texts, and write and read my own models for instruction. We discuss taking risks in writing and being considerate when students are reading their own writing. We talk about the importance of staying focused on our own personal writing and not disturbing others. We create our own set of rules and guidelines for making a good writing workshop where everyone feels safe about sharing. Student input helps make the workshop run smoothly.

During these first weeks, we have discussions about audience and real-life writing—the kinds of things we write on a daily basis. Through these conversations, the students have multiple opportunities to get to know each other as writers and become more willing to share their own writing. I create abundant opportunities for children to talk *before* and *after* they write and, yes, sometimes even *during* writing for clarification and direction. I have one-on-one and small-group time to talk with students about their writing, and I have a conferring management system that enables me to plan instructional groups, help individual students, and let parents know their child's successes and challenges. Students are encouraged to write daily, publish on a regular basis, and celebrate with other students and parents often. I elevate my own understanding of writing by updating my knowledge through professional books and discussions with my colleagues.

During the workshop, students are expected to stay focused on their writing for fifteen minutes during the first week. This means that there is no talking or sharing during this time. Usually instrumental music is played in the background, which sets the tone for the writing workshop. When the music starts, the writing should start; when the music stops, the writing stops.

Everyone's schedule will look different, but my schedule goes like this:

1. Begin with a minilesson (ten to fifteen minutes)
2. Next have independent writing and student-teacher conferring (twenty to thirty minutes)
3. End by sharing and summarizing the learning (ten to fifteen minutes)

Preassessing Student Writing: What Do They Already Know?

In the first month of school, teachers should be keeping an eye on the writing skills and strategies the students are already using. Very often teachers decide what their writing program is going to be before the students even arrive at the classroom door. Unfortunately this locks teachers into a program without even knowing what the students already know or can almost do on their own. Assign writing tasks to see what they already know about a particular skill such as paragraph indentation or formatting a friendly letter. If you see that a large percentage of them already know about paragraph indentation, a brief reminder might be all that is needed. Students who experience more difficulty should be placed in a small guided writing group to acquire more experience with that skill.

The same holds true with using the correct format for a letter. Most students just need a quick reminder on the letter form. We can overteach a skill. What students already know we can compress into a short, quick reminder, then move on to something else that requires more time and energy.

Modeling the Process

I write a model piece for my students. As they see me write, they write. Together, we talk about what makes a good piece of writing. Sometimes the students make suggestions to make my piece better. They give me new words and new phrases or ways to express ideas that would be easier for the reader to understand. The first piece of writing for the year in my class is a personal narrative. My modeled writing piece that I share with students is about a time when I was a little girl and my mom wouldn't let me leave the table until I finished all of my string beans. I include in this example a hook, conversation, personal voice, organization of thought, a focused topic, word choice, and humor. Because I know the difficulty older students still have with conversation and dialogue form, I spend a lot of time with that. I want the students to know that conversation is broken up into parts with narrative texts. I read, read, read more and more mentor examples so that the students start noticing what it looks like from both a reader's and a writer's viewpoint.

After reading the piece from an overhead or document camera, I ask the students what made it a good piece of writing. After discussing my piece, the students then go back to their seats to start thinking about their own personal narrative topic. I never allow students to leave the rug area until they can tell me what they are going to write about—especially those who are reluctant writers. If someone does not have an idea, I brainstorm with him or her and then give think-time alone *before* giving permission to return to his or her seat. Sometimes peer conferring helps nudge their thinking and gets them started.

Notice that I purposely do not have a title for my piece. I inform the students that I always leave the title until last because I do not want to give my topic away before I have hooked in my reader with my first paragraph. I ask students to help me think of a catchy title that does not let my reader know what I am writing about—I like to sneak into my subject. Although this seems like a perfectly simple lesson for older students, for some it takes an entire reporting period to do three things: focus their topic, write an interesting "hook," and create a suspenseful title. Good modeling by their peers usually moves the other children forward, but not all students.

Throughout the first month of school, we develop our pieces of writing, some finished and some not. Each day we work on a new skill, strategy, or idea, using the mentor texts to thrust us forward. By October we have at least two published pieces—the first day of school writing piece that acts as our baseline writing and our second personal narrative that involves all the lessons that we have studied.

The Six Traits of Writing and How They Help Direct a Writing Program

In her book entitled *6 + 1 Traits of Writing,* Ruth Culham (2003) explains this assessment tool that can become the cornerstone of the classroom writing program. It is not a program per se—it is a form of assessment that is easy to understand and apply. Working as a school is helpful because staff development can be geared toward looking at and assessing student writing with this tool. If instruction is to be meaningful, teachers themselves must understand and plan together. Many teachers are not comfortable with teaching writing because it seems so subjective. The 6 + 1 traits provide us with a valuable tool to help better evaluate and talk to students about their writing.

The 6 +1 Traits of Writing

1. *Ideas:* the content of the piece; the heart of the message
2. *Organization:* the internal structure of the piece; the logical pattern of the ideas
3. *Voice:* the soul of the piece; what makes the writer's style his or her own
4. *Word choice:* rich, colorful, precise language that moves and enlightens the reader
5. *Sentence fluency:* the flow of the language
6. *Convention:* the piece's level of correctness; how the writer uses grammar and mechanics
7. *Presentation:* how pleasing the piece is to the eye (Culham, 2003)

Each of these traits can be taught independently of each other. In some schools, teachers concentrate only on a couple traits during the year. In others, teachers explicitly teach all of the traits.

Through collaboration, teachers can use these traits to talk about student writing across the grade levels. Becoming familiar with the traits takes time. Starting out with one trait at a time and involving the students in an in-depth study instead of a surface study help children to internalize their understanding before moving on to another trait. Teacher modeling is crucial.

Over the course of a year, students will produce incredible pieces of writing. Make copies of these so that you can use them for peer modeling in the future. Culham's book (2003) provides numerous examples that serve as wonderful teaching models and as starting points for instruction and assessment.

Through a combination of observation, discussion, and conferring, the teacher can assess a student's use of the 6 + 1 traits of writing to gain a pretty good idea of where students are in the writing process. Through the understanding of these traits, students can begin to assess their own work more critically and the work of their peers. The traits direct the students' writing and offer them an avenue to becoming more proficient writers.

BALANCING TEACHER-DIRECTED AND CHOICE WRITING

If we truly want children to write, we must provide a balance between guided writing that we assign for specific reasons and choice writing. Children must also have opportunities to write stories with characters, setting, and plot. We need to allow students to experiment and write for themselves or for a different audience. Many times teachers are worried about getting everything in (all the required content and standards) before testing starts, but we must allow time for students to write what they want to write about. Some teachers have a day each week for choice writing. Other teachers allow a certain number of minutes of the writing workshop to choose what to write about.

When a child has a grandparent who dies or a pet that got injured or a scary experience that needs an outlet, writing is the perfect avenue. If we are always concerned about getting more done for testing and not allowing for personal stories to be written, we are doing a great disservice to our students. Making sure that enough time is available for students to write creatively, reflectively, and personally must be valued. By sharing these writings, we will get a deeper look into our students' lives and what makes them tick.

Developing Writing Stamina

It is important to build stamina during the Writing Workshop. Some students enter your classroom able to focus on their writing for less than a minute, while others can stay tuned in for twenty to thirty minutes. Each classroom is unique. Some students come from classrooms where Writing Workshop was quiet and they could write whatever they wanted to, whereas others come from classrooms where everything was teacher-directed. Establishing your standards is paramount at the beginning of the year.

Each day, record the length of time that students have for writing. Start with fifteen minutes and build up through the year to about thirty uninterrupted minutes. You might have a student set a timer. Just like in the Reading Workshop, students need to work on building stamina. It takes practice. Praise students each day they *hold on* to their writing for a longer period of time. Establishing this reflective time is essential for creating a writing climate in your classroom and is well worth your patience.

WRITING ESSENTIALS

The processes of writing were formally identified by Calkins (1994) and others as a series of phases:

Prewriting: brainstorming

Drafting: making a commitment to an idea

Revising: adding to, deleting, or changing what has been written

Editing: making corrections and getting feedback from others

Publishing: sharing the final form with others

For some, these steps are too limited. Writers often weave in and out of these stages simultaneously. The term *recursive* is often used to describe this movement. In reality, writers engage in one or more of these processes at a given time (Frey & Fisher, 2006).

Establishing Audience

Students need to know that their writing always has an audience. The way we write depends on the intent of our audience. Students write for many audiences: their teacher, their classmates, other younger students in the school, a parent or other adult, someone in authority, a manager of a store, an unknown person who is going to read something they write for a competition or contest, the school librarian, a friend, a relative, and sometimes just for themselves. As you confer with students, always make sure that they have a clear understanding of whom they are writing for. Modeling this through your own writing is a quick and efficient way to teach students about your writing audience and how your tone of voice changes with the audience you have in mind. You might not write with the same voice to parents as to students or grown adult children.

Writing in Different Genres

Students need to be afforded experiences in many genres throughout the year. For instance, a schedule might look like this:

September: gathering ideas

October: learning about and writing about personal narratives

November: learning how to write responses to literature

December: poetry

January: learning about memoir, biography, and autobiography

February: writing persuasively

March through April: nonfiction writing through research

May: learning how to write stories and novelettes

Helping Students with Topic Sentences

At the beginning of the year, students need a review on the purpose of topic sentences. Even when they have been taught to start a paragraph with a topic sentence, they forget. So again and again, remind them why they need to do it. As students grow as writers, they learn that a topic sentence does not always come at the beginning of the paragraph, but until the time when they truly internalize that concept, the topic sentence comes at the beginning of the paragraph. So during this writing time, students brainstorm possible topic or thesis sentences as teams, which are then put on charts so that students can refer to them as they are writing.

Sometimes topic sentences are placed on big charts and students move around to the charts with a team and jot ideas down that might go under the topic. This assists students who have difficulty with fluency of ideas.

Usually we take one paragraph at a time. Everyone chooses a topic sentence from the list of brainstormed topics or they choose one of their own. Most students do not need the teacher's help at developing their own, but others do and that is why they are generated collectively, so that everyone has equal access to the curriculum.

Conventions: How Important Are They?

We cannot minimize the importance of conventions—capitalization, punctuation, spelling, grammar, usage, and paragraphing—in writing. Many young people miss having an interview or lose a job possibility because of the way they present themselves on an application. Students need to realize that conventions are important and that they are sometimes the first and only thing that people look at in the real world. Conventions do serve a purpose. They serve as tools to make ideas clear and concise and to let the reader know and understand the intent.

But overemphasizing conventions does not allow students to take risks and be creative. Many times we stifle students' ideas and creativity by focusing too much on the conventions. We need to impress upon our students that we want them to try out new techniques and take some chances, but we also want them to understand the importance of cleaning up their papers to convey the message of pride in their work. Work that is up for display or that is published must be checked for conventions. Students may obtain assistance in this area from their teacher, a family member, a peer, electronically, or a combination of these.

Wall Reading

In many classrooms, the practice of reading aloud has been diminished. For writing purposes, students need to know that reading aloud can be a first step to checking their own work by finding words that have been left out, sentences that are fragments, punctuation errors, or lines that do not make sense. After writing a piece or part of a piece, the child should read the writing to himself or herself. Besides providing an opportunity to *hear* what has been written, it offers a way to practice intonation, speed, and accuracy of their written language. In our classrooms we ask students to read their pieces aloud to the wall—wall reading. Students line the walls at certain points for about three to five minutes when their thoughts are complete. They stand around the perimeter of the room facing a wall or window. Writing needs to be listened to, refined, and adjusted from what has been heard. Many students think that once they finish their last sentence of a rough draft, they are done. For most children, it is the process of reading aloud that helps them to see where mistakes have been made and meaning is lost.

Although most of the time the whole class does wall reading simultaneously, after an independent writing session students do gravitate to the wall to *hear* what they have written at other times. Impress upon your students why they need to read their work orally. This technique can also be used before a writing celebration takes place. Learning how to read their own writing aloud gives writers a new perspective on the importance of their own voice. A combination of wall reading and partner sharing helps throughout the writing process.

Word Banks

The purpose of a word bank is to assist students in using more sophisticated words to describe characters, feelings, thoughts, and ideas. At the beginning of the school year, some students are not ready to write. They may have come from a classroom where very few demands were put on them or they may not like to write or they may not have had good writing experiences in the past. Half of the battle in writing is knowing what is expected and getting ideas formulated. If the child is asked to describe a character both physically and behaviorally, without discussion the reluctant reader or writer will have nothing to say except for surface-type responses.

In the first weeks of school, students are processing your standards—feeling out the expectations you have for them.

After a read-aloud, students can give input about words they have used to describe characters for a class chart or word bank. This can be done during the discussion at the rug area or it can be done at the students' seats. During independent reading, the students can look for words that describe characters—words that are more sophisticated than "happy," "sad," "nice," and "good." This takes some training. Talking about *putting words to rest* because they are overused and not very descriptive is important for children to grapple with. In some classrooms, teachers have *Rest in Peace* signs for tired words like "good," "nice," "big," "little," "happy," and "sad." That is why brainstorming word bank words eases students into using better words for their writing. Looking up on the chart is a scaffold to help reluctant readers and writers to think more deeply about how to describe. Eventually the charts can be taken down, but the image the chart has left in some students' minds will be lasting. New words can be added that children contribute to the chart throughout the year. A child may add a word to the chart with his or her initials after the word. Giving that child an opportunity to talk about the word and why it was chosen to put on the chart builds self-esteem.

Children may establish their own work banks in their writer's notebooks by brainstorming on their own or with the help of teammates or partners.

Spelling Difficulties

Throughout the writing periods, teachers see the types of words that students are spelling incorrectly over and over again. For published pieces of works where the students have gone through the complete writing process including editing, students should have very few spelling mistakes. But if you scan the students' writing journals, you will see certain words written incorrectly again and again. An effective way to zero in on students' spelling error patterns is to scan their writing journals periodically and jot down words that you see are misspelled. This can be very time-consuming, so sometimes a parent who is a good speller can be employed to locate these words for you. Scanning is also done on other types of writing in the content areas. Each word is listed on a personalized word list. Copies of the word lists are made and sent home with the child with a note to parents explaining that the words should be studied. A parent volunteer does periodic checks of the spelling of these words. Over time you can see patterns of difficulties for challenged spellers, which can be addressed in small groups. See Chapter Six, Strengthening Word Knowledge and Fluency, for more on spelling.

DEMONSTRATION OF WRITING

Making sure that all students realize the importance of doing quality work begins early in the year. Student writing pieces should be showcased on bulletin boards and at writing celebrations.

Suggestions for making sure quality work is in place during all times of the year are

- Set your standards high, and model, model, model with your own writing, as well as mentor-authors and standard-setting student work
- Celebrate often with published pieces: polished final drafts
- Make your portfolios extra special
- Make regular portfolio additions and allow the students to share theirs with others
- Use plastic sleeves to protect the children's work

The Writing Conference: The Importance of Talk

Writing starts with conversation. If children can talk about something they are interested in, then they should be able to write about it. Giving students opportunities to talk about their ideas first is a precursor to a successful writing piece. They can talk to partners, in small groups, or in front of the whole class. Talk clarifies our thoughts and helps to formulate ideas. Writing is a way to express thoughts and synthesize thoughts. Writing is a component of linguistic intelligence—one of the eight intelligences that Howard Gardner (1983) talks about in his multiple intelligence theory.

Writing Conference Guidelines

Within the writing conference, we use the research, decide, teach format, but Carl Anderson (2000) divides the writing conference into two parts:

- Conversation about the work the child is doing as a writer
- Conversation about how the child can be become a better writer

As a teacher it is easy to take over in a conference, but that is exactly what not to do. We must act as guides and let the student take us where he or she needs to go. Coming to our conference with our agenda will not be as helpful as creating a plan *with* a child during the conference. By teaching the writer a new skill, strategy, or craft lesson, the student will be able to transfer the learning into his or her next piece of writing.

Teachers must be familiar with the four types of conferences that Calkins (1994) describes:

1. *Content Conference.* Start interesting conversations about the content or topic of the writer's story. What do our students already know?
2. *Design Conference.* What genre is the child writing in? Is it a poem, a letter, or a feature article?
3. *Process Conference.* Where did this idea come from? What problems did you have while writing? How has your writing changed?
4. *Evaluation Conference.* How does this piece of writing compare to others you have written? What did you like about this piece of writing? How would you change this piece of writing to make it better?

Following are some recommendations for writing conferences:

- Hold conferences that are long enough to make a difference in the child's writing. That may mean three minutes, five minutes, or ten minutes. If you have concerns about the child and the new learning, have a short check-in conference later on in the week.
- Interview, decide, and teach: Start by *interviewing* the child about what is going on in his or her writing. Listen long enough to obtain enough information to *decide* what to do with the writer. *Teach* it in an effective way so that the child can take it on (Calkins, 1994).
- Keep a record of your conferences with each child. Choose a recording system that works best for you. (For an example, see the conferring sheet in Activity 4.1 at the end of this chapter.)
- Use the notes you have collected to inform your instruction for specific children, small groups, or for the entire class.
- Form small guided groups when you see several students who are experiencing the same challenges.
- Focus on only *one* teaching point, even though you are tempted to teach more. The conference should be powerful and to the point.
- Make sure that you have the child doing most of the work.

- Decide where you want to do your conferring. Traveling around from desk to desk or from student to student is preferred by some teachers. Other teachers like the students to come to them at a specific location in the room (at a kidney-shaped or round table, for example).

Tips for Volunteers

A perfect conference appears to run smoothly and, for teachers, that natural feeling is what builds trusting relationships between teacher and student. The fact that *we* know each other provides the comfort zone allowing children to learn and to take constructive criticism of their writing. But when a volunteer comes into your classroom to help, the communication can be more awkward and the students can be less comfortable. It is always a good idea to plan ahead for the volunteers who want to help you out during the Writing Workshop.

Keep the following generic plan in a strategic place in the classroom, so that when a volunteer wants to help you with writing, they have guidelines to effectively assist you in the classroom.

1. Select one of the most recent student compositions from a student's Reading or Writing Portfolio, from a writing journal, or one that the teacher has set aside for you to work on.
2. Have the child read the composition to you orally.
3. Respond in a positive way.
   - I really like the part about ...
   - You made me laugh when you said ...
   - One thing I really liked about what you wrote was ...
4. Assist the student in *one* or *two* areas that he or she is experiencing difficulty with, such as:
   - Topic sentences
   - Length of paragraphs: at least five or six sentences
   - Description
   - Spelling
   - Fluency of thought
   - Proper form: indenting, margins, title capitalized, and spacing
   - Agreement of tense
   - Use of dialogue and quotation marks
   - Run-on sentences
5. Ask the writer one of the following questions:
   - What part do you like best in your composition?
   - What part gave you the biggest problem?
   - What prewriting activity did you do?
   - What would you change about your composition now that you have read it again?
   - What did you learn about your writing by having this conference?

Use of the Rubric

Students need to know what your expectations are for their writing. A rubric or scoring guide is given to the child at the beginning of an assignment and will be used to assess the written product when completed. This significantly helps students with writing difficulties because it gives them a visual tool for planning, structuring, and self-monitoring their written work. It also helps parents by explaining from the beginning exactly what the teacher expects in the writing assignment and what is considered proficient performance for the grade level (Rief, 2005).

RUBRIC: PERSONAL NARRATIVE USING CONVERSATION

Student's Name___________________ Due Date__________

- My piece has a catchy title that does not give the subject away.
  1 2 3 4 5
- My piece has a lead that keeps my reader wanting to read.
  1 2 3 4 5
- My piece is well organized and makes sense.
  1 2 3 4 5
- My piece has a strong ending that ties all of my thoughts together.
  1 2 3 4 5
- My piece has conversation in the correct dialogue form, like the form mentor-authors use.
  1 2 3 4 5
- My piece uses conversation and has definite breaks of narrative text to give my reader a rest from too much dialogue.
  1 2 3 4 5
- My piece is an appropriate length, shows _____ grade quality, and has few or no errors in punctuation and grammar.
  1 2 3 4 5

In the two and a half weeks I had to work on this piece of writing, I worked for about __________minutes (or hours).

I used my time wisely in class. Yes/No

I reworked my piece about __________times.

I read my writing out loud to an adult. Yes/No

I read my writing out loud to myself about __________times.

Total Points Given __________

Publishing

Students will write many pieces throughout the year, but will not take them to the publishing stage—the final stage of writing. For some teachers, a goal of one published or polished piece per month is established, but in other classrooms teachers like to publish more often. Each classroom has its own personality and set of writing needs. Looking at your own time frames, your standards, and your own students' needs, you will devise a schedule that works for you. Pieces can be published in many forms, including poster boards, file folders, flip books, PowerPoint, letters, and newspaper articles.

Student Reading and Writing Portfolio

When students understand that a large part of their work will end up in a two-inch white showcase portfolio, their level of expectancy will elevate. As soon as the first piece of writing is completed in final form, place it in a plastic sleeve and put it in the student's portfolio. When you take pride in *their* work, they will take pride in it too! Each time that a piece has been taken through the steps into final form, it should be put in a plastic sleeve and placed in the notebook. As students see their portfolios growing, the pride they feel is monumental.

Have students begin preparing at the beginning of the year to organize their work. Each student will need

- One durable view, 1-1/2-inch to 2-inch three-ring binder
- Five file folder dividers with the following labels:

  Literature Responses

  Informational Writing

  Personal Writing (personal narratives, creative writing)

  Writing About Math (Survival Math and other math projects)

  Miscellaneous (art projects, certificates, awards, and other items that do not fit elsewhere)

- A colorful and *personalized* cover to insert into the view sheet on the binder cover
- A *table of contents* showing all items contained in the portfolio
- A personalized *title page* with the student's name and date
- An *about the author* page with a picture of the child
- Children's work samples accumulated throughout the year

Throughout the year, make sure that most of the pieces you have the students write are formatted on 8-1/2-by-11-inch sheets of paper, or if they are larger, they can be folded into parts that fit into a plastic sleeve or sheet protector. Many of the art projects that the students create are also smaller, instead of big poster projects. With thirty or more students in an upper grade or middle school classroom, smaller projects are more manageable for display and for portfolios.

For each report card period, students receive an updated list of the items that should be inside of their portfolio. They highlight the items that they have evidence of in their portfolio. Those with an asterisk are mandatory; those with no asterisk are optional.

WHAT SHOULD BE INSIDE YOUR PORTFOLIO?

Student's Name ________________

- Title page
- *About the author* page and picture
- Independent reading log
- Reading goal

  Response to Literature section

Reading for Information section
Personal Writing section: personal narratives, creative writing, persuasive writing, and memoir
Math and Literacy Writing section
Miscellaneous

Students who are in their last year of elementary or middle school can give their parents their portfolios at promotion or graduation time. These can be their gifts to their families. For other grade levels, the portfolio can be their end-of-year gift also. Often, the portfolios are two inches thick! Many parents keep their child's portfolio in a special place and look through it regularly. Children love to see their own work and have fun browsing through it for years to come.

Raising the Bar

As the year progresses and more and more skills, strategies, and writer's craft lessons have been taught, students should be encouraged to use the new skills they have learned in their writing. If you spend a week talking about similes, locating similes that mentor-authors use, and figuring out why an author uses them, but you never see students use them in their own writing, you know that they really are not transferring their learning. Good writers use similes to give the reader a visual description and memory of what they want them to keep in their head. When Sharon Creech (1992, p. 2) says "the houses were jammed together like a row of birdhouses," she wants her reader to visualize what the houses looked like by comparing them to birdhouses all jammed together. If you want a child to use a literary element in his or her writing, then make sure the rubric indicates that he or she must include one in the next writing assignment.

KEEPING PARENTS INFORMED

Parents need to be informed about their child's writing experiences. Besides sending out a biweekly newsletter with assignments clearly explained and rubrics included, give a write-up about each writing assignment to the parents at report card periods so they are informed again what the assignment was and how it was assessed. These are placed in the portfolio. Any assignments that are not completed are easy to spot and are then reassigned with the parent's knowledge. Sample write-ups appear in the following box.

RESPONSES TO LITERATURE

Compare-and-Contrast Essay. After reading *Walk Two Moons* by Sharon Creech and *The True Confessions of Charlotte Doyle* by Avi, students were asked to write a compare-and-contrast essay concentrating specifically on the similarities and differences between the two heroines, Charlotte Doyle and Salamantha Hiddleson. Students used a rubric to organize their essay and to clarify the standards to be met.

Extend the Story. Students read the book *The Mysteries of Harris Burdick* by Chris Van Allsburg. They were asked to select one of the black-and-white illustrations created by the author to extend the story and show their understanding of the mystery genre by using some of the mystery elements used in the other mystery pieces of literature that had been developed over the course of the thematic unit.

READING FOR INFORMATION

A Slave's Point of View. Students were asked to write an essay describing the three passages of slavery during the colonial period of time. They were instructed to take the first-person point of view, expressing these ideas through their own eyes. They also used an article on slavery from the *World Book Encyclopedia* and an article from *Encarta* to support their ideas. Students also watched selected parts of the television miniseries *Roots* by Alex Haley and were given ideas through teacher read-alouds.

"Too Much Homework" from the February Issue of Time for Kids. After reading the article "Too Much Homework," students were asked to write an essay showing their understanding of the article by discussing the author's purpose for writing the article and the techniques she used to get her point of view across to her readers. The students interacted with the article by comparing their homework opinions and habits with those of the students featured in the article.

CELEBRATING WRITING

After students have taken their piece of writing to the publication stage, provide an opportunity for them to share their finished products with others, including their classmates, other classes, parents, and possibly an administrator. Students know from the beginning of their writing process that they need to write for a particular audience. Writing celebrations are fun for almost everyone. Because they know they are writing for someone else to hear, the quality is much higher than if they think it is only for the teacher.

During a writing celebration, students read either the whole piece if it is short or a part of a piece if it is long. Students are encouraged to read aloud several times before they read at the celebration so they can feel relaxed and confident in their fluency. Many teachers provide juice and cookies or snacks to make the event more special. These celebrations can become regular monthly events. The motto should be Publish Often—Celebrate Regularly.

Students receive a guideline sheet to inform them of expectations for the writing piece they have chosen to take to the publishing phase.

STUDENT WRITING CELEBRATION

Date ___________

All students will read for at least one minute from their best piece of writing that they have perfected during the last week. The piece should be something that was started in their writing notebook and that has been reworked and perfected. This should be the student's best piece, showing quality writing and incorporating the writing techniques and skills listed below. The piece should be typed, with spelling and grammar checked. If a computer is not available in the home, student work should be submitted to your teacher in neat writing and he or she will type it. These pieces will become part of a booklet that will be put together and handed out to all students.

The writing should have all of the following:

- A strong lead
- A focused topic
- Powerful descriptive verbs and adjectives
- Some conversation, using words other than "said"
- A catchy title that does not give away the topic of the piece right away
- Use of a dash, ellipsis, or other unusual punctuation
- Use of at least one simile
- A strong personal voice conveying feelings, thoughts, opinions, and connections
- Evidence to support the ideas
- Sentences of varied length: short, medium, and long
- Optional use of a question

If the writing is a short story, it must contain character development, setting, problem, solution, and some kind of conflict, as well as the elements above.

HANDWRITING FOR OLDER STUDENTS

As children grow into their adolescent years, parents seem to want an answer to the question, "Shouldn't my child be using cursive writing on his or her papers?" The comment brings to mind the idea that a vast majority of upper-grade and middle school students choose to print or type their work for class work instead of using cursive writing.

Many states have standards for cursive writing in the middle and upper elementary grades, so these standards need to be taught and students still need practice. You may provide guided practice for students in need, possibly by modeling the strokes while talking through the steps of letter formation. Parents should be informed that students need opportunities to use all three forms of writing. For some students, though, cursive writing demands too much fine motor skill and they will never be proficient in cursive writing. It is important that teachers recognize the students who have difficulty with cursive writing and allow them to use printing. In the upper grades, students should have practice with printing, cursive, and typed work. All three forms are useful in today's educational pursuits. The most important point is that the work be readable by the particular audience. Presentation of the work in easy-to-read format is more important than excessive neatness. Some students need to be motivated to write neatly. Use real-life situations to stress the need for legible writing—such as when filling out job applications or writing checks—and explain that most teachers tend to grade neatly written papers higher than sloppy, hard-to-read ones. (See Chapter Eleven for more on support and intervention for writing difficulties.)

Activity 4.1

CONFERRING NOTES FOR WRITING

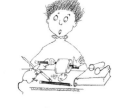

Week of________________ Focus____________

Student's name ______ Writing Project ______ Date ______ Stage of writing process ______ ______ Discussed ______ ______			

— *Chapter 5* —

NONFICTION AND ITS PLACE IN BALANCED LITERACY

The past decade has brought a deluge of research on the importance of teaching nonfiction throughout the grade levels, starting in kindergarten. Studies by Pappas (1991), Sanacore (1991), and Caswell and Duke (1998) note that teaching nonfiction early increases a child's ability to read and write effectively and meet the demands of informational texts in the later grades. Upon entering their formal schooling, children already have a natural curiosity about the world around them, and they have a vast number of questions that they want answers to *now*. With so many questions, parents and preschool teachers have had to answer verbally without a lot of print support. Currently there is a plethora of nonfiction trade books available for children of all ages, including our youngest questioners. As parents and teachers, we must make nonfiction a priority and start to incorporate these informational books into our children's lives as early as possible. In this section, we refer to informational texts as expository and nonfiction synonymously.

WHAT IS NONFICTION?

Nonfiction is a genre that provides ideas, facts, and principles about the world around us. Difficult and complex concepts may be explored, usually organized around a main idea. These texts present information, inform, explain, describe, instruct, persuade, and enlighten the reader. Nonfiction texts must be accurate, current, and include relevant information in order to be effective. They can come in many forms, including essay, journal, letter, picture book, newspaper article, editorial, brochure, map, and poetry, to name a few.

Nonfiction can be very confusing for novice readers because it looks different from what they are already familiar with: narrative. Most upper-grade and middle school students are used to navigating through narrative texts because 80 to 90 percent of their day in the primary years was immersed in fiction (Benson, 2002). They recognize such structures as beginning, middle, end, character development, plot, setting, problem, and solution because this is what they know. For many of us who have been educators for years, this is what we know too.

In the last decade, though, the times have been changing. As adults we are inundated with nonfiction—probably 80 to 90 percent of our reading and writing entails informational or expository pieces (National Geographic School Publishing, 2007). We read newspapers, bulletins, maps, magazines, teacher's guides, the world wide web, biographies, warranties, contract information, instruction manuals, recipes, and labels, to name just a few. If we find time for a good fiction book, it is interspersed with a flood of everyday expository pieces. Therefore it is no wonder that the state and national standards are brimming with nonnarrative goals, beginning as early as kindergarten with locating a table of contents and seeing how it works. In the intermediate grades students are asked to use glossaries and indexes. In upper elementary and middle school, students should understand the text features and structures of informational texts, incorporate them in their own research writing, and be able to analyze public documents and other everyday consumer materials. Seventy to eighty percent of standardized reading tests are nonfiction (Moss, 2004), and statistics show that many of our older children prefer reading nonfiction, especially boys and remedial students (Carter & Abrahamson, 1990).

Why Teach Nonfiction Explicitly?

Nonfiction texts provide challenges for even our strongest readers. Since the primary purpose of expository texts is to provide information, students must learn strategies for *holding on* to that information and comprehending the big ideas. This genre is filled with dense, often unfamiliar material, and sorting out what is important from what is not is a definite challenge. The vocabulary is also taxing—many of the words are new, specialized to the subject matter, and often technical and hard to spell and pronounce. *Holding on* to these words is frustrating, and often the students do not have prior knowledge to help them remember their meaning. And there are so many of them! These texts also demand considerable concentration. A child who is a competent reader in narrative may struggle with the same level of book in nonfiction. Students must know how to read and understand text features such as diagrams, time lines, and charts so that when they see them again in another piece they will be able to unravel the meaning and comprehend the material. They need to know how to maneuver through text structures such as description, cause and effect, and compare and contrast, and know how to transfer this knowledge to another text that is set up in the same way. This understanding will help them use these features and structures in their own nonfiction writing. In order for them to do that, teachers must provide explicit instruction in reading and writing workshops using modeled, shared, guided, and independent practice. Mooney (2001) recommends that "students should first have experience with the various text forms and features through hearing them read, seeing them composed, and through reading and writing them in supported and guided situations before being expected to read or write similar forms on their own."

Entry Points for Nonfiction

There are many entry points for introducing nonfiction in the classroom. Much of what you need is already available or easy to obtain through your resources. Make sure that you have a large variety of materials to hook in your reluctant readers, your gifted and talented students, and everyone in between.

Anthologies. Many states have adopted an anthology, which is a collection of numerous readings covering poetry, short stories, excerpts, and complete works of fiction and nonfiction. Out of the twenty-one works featured in California's state-mandated anthology for fourth grade, three were nonfiction, two were historical fiction, and three were biographies. In other words, about one-third of the content was nonfiction.

Biographies and Autobiographies. These factual accounts of famous persons' lives are enjoyable for most children. They find pleasure in reading about other interesting people and getting to know them in a personal way. There are many levels of biographies that can be accessed by every ability and interest group of students. The sequential structure of this form is predictable and easy to understand for even our most challenged readers.

Picture Books. There are many excellent nonfiction picture books for older readers, many of which act as excellent models for meeting social studies and science standards. Picture books can play a significant role in getting content across to reluctant and challenged readers.

Newspapers. These can be very beneficial for small-group work at relatively low cost. Local papers often participate in the Newspapers in Education Programs that bring newspapers into the classroom at no charge.

Magazines. Articles in magazines such as *Time for Kids* or *Weekly Reader* tend to be short, concise, and student-friendly, with a high interest level that can hook in challenged readers. There are usually personal-interest stories that tap children's curiosity and stories that stimulate ideas for reluctant writers in their own work. Teachers may ask parents for a yearly subscription for the class or may obtain money for magazines through their PTA, school foundation, principal, or other sources.

Functional Texts. School bulletins, bus and trolley schedules, nutrition guides from fast-food restaurants, schedules for the students' soccer and dance performances, recipes, and instructions for playing games are just a few real-life documents that are useful and practical ideas for introducing children to nonfiction.

Big Books. Although the supply of big books for older children is limited, these books can be powerful tools during shared reading. Two nonfiction big books for older students are *Should There Be Zoos?* (Stead, 2002) and *How Your Body Works* (Hindley, 1997).

Poetry. Poets are beginning to see the beauty of nonfiction poetry for drawing in students. Doug Florian has written numerous books of poetry that introduce students to animals and nature through poetry, among them *In the Swim* (1987); *Mammalabilia* (1986); *Insectlopedia* (1998); *and Lizards, Frogs, and Polliwogs* (1989).

Historical Books. Real information is embedded in stories that have memorable, fictionalized characters and plots based on historical events.

Narrative Nonfiction. Many authors capture the interest of children through narrative or story-like texts. Reluctant and struggling readers find this form of nonfiction more palatable than more standard nonfiction. Examples are Jane Yolen's *Letting Swift River Go* (1992) and Lynne Cherry's *A River Ran Wild* (1992). Some publishers have introduced same-topic *paired books* where one text is fiction and the other is nonfiction. These help reluctant readers to see differences in the ways the two genres are formatted around one topic.

Graphic Nonfiction Books. Reluctant and struggling readers can access nonfiction through graphic nonfiction books. These look like comic books and are a fun, motivating format for many reluctant readers. Capstone Publishers has graphic nonfiction books on the *Titanic,* Salem Witch Trials, King Tut, and the Boston Tea Party. Students can replicate this format easily in their own writing.

The Mini Page. This syndicated four-page nonfiction tabloid appears in over five hundred newspapers (via Universal Press Syndicate). It is perfect for most third-grade readers and for the more challenged readers in grades 4, 5, and 6. It usually presents a major topic for the week or for several weeks, such as the president, elections, the Olympics, Black History Month, or other current events. The content is concise, easy to read, and full of current photos and activities for children to use. To obtain additional copies of *The Mini Page,* ask parents to send them to you from their local newspaper. It is a good idea to laminate them or put them in plastic sleeves for protection. (For more information on this resource, see Newspapers in Education at www.nieonline.com.)

Songs from History. The Voices of America series is a package of CDs or tapes with a reproducible book of songs for children to sing from different historical periods and informational narration that explains the era and makes history come alive. The series contains *Pre-colonial Times Through the Revolutionary War, The Young Nation Through the Civil War,* and *The Westward Expansion of the United States.* Students enjoy singing these songs and learning history through them.

Historical Scripts. Commercial historical plays are written for students to perform. This provides oral language opportunities to break down complicated concepts through acting out the parts. Students internalize nonfiction when it comes in different forms.

LEARNING ABOUT TEXT STRUCTURES

A good writer of nonfiction organizes or structures information in special ways. When complex ideas are well organized, readers are much more likely to retain them. Text structures are essential in constructing meaning. Children must have exposure to and experience with these text structures in order to be successful nonfiction readers and writers. They must be explicitly taught through isolation and with simple texts that the children can easily remember.

What Are Common Text Structures?

Educators generally agree as to the five most common nonfiction text structures (First Steps, 1994; Fountas & Pinnell, 2001).

Compare-and-contrast structures look at two or more items simultaneously to show similarities and differences.

Problem-and-solution structures describe a problem and give a solution.

Cause-and-effect structures give a reason and an explanation for events.

Description structures help the reader to form images or visualize processes.

Sequence or time order structures present ideas or events in the order in which they occur.

Other text structures that children like to point out are *lists, question-and-answer, how-to,* and *persuasive.* Question-and-answer and persuasive texts are recognized as subsets of the descriptive structure. How-to texts fall under sequence or time order.

Certain graphic organizers are also aligned with the structures, as shown in Figure 5.1. These help children see relationships and assist them in organizing for their own writing. Offering an abundance of opportunities to use mapping, charting, and webbing activities throughout the year will help children see the relationships of texts and structures.

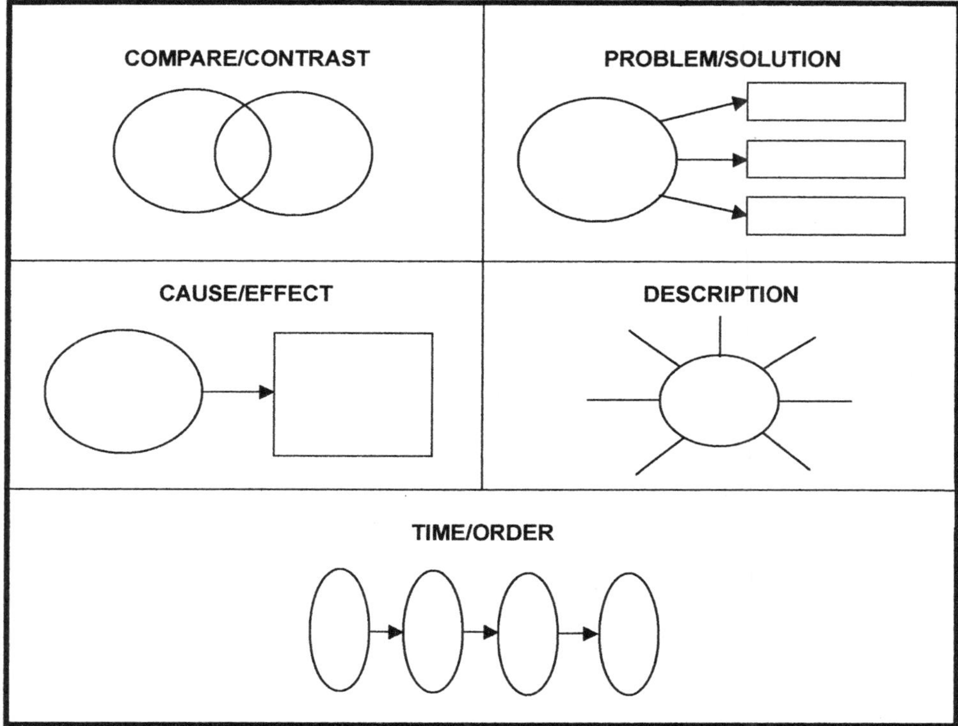

Figure 5.1. The Five Graphic Organizers for Text Structures.

Teaching Text Structures

Text structures need to be taught intentionally and individually. Each of the structures should be modeled by the teacher using good pieces of nonfiction. Usually it is a good idea to start this text structure study with a picture book several grade levels below the level of instruction. After the students have grasped the idea of the structure using isolated pieces, then they will be able to pull out the structure in the paragraphs of a more complex grade-level piece of writing.

Text structures should be taught to older children for a variety of reasons, such as the following:

- Seeing patterns in texts gives students a comfort zone that strengthens their comprehension.
- Knowing how authors structure their writing helps students navigate through a more challenging text with confidence.
- It helps students anticipate content and make predictions.
- It helps students make connections with other similarly constructed books. When connections are made, students hold on to the content more easily.
- Students will transfer these structures into their own writing.
- The reader is trained to see clue words that signal a particular structure making what is read easier to remember.
- It allows students to work with specific graphic organizers that match up with a particular structure.

- Most upper-grade books contain more than one structure, and they become more difficult to distinguish in high-level books.

Providing students with practice in recognizing the features and structures of nonfiction is of key importance. See Activities 5.1 through 5.4 at the end of this chapter.

A Deeper Look at Description

The most common structure used in nonfiction is description. Books by Gail Gibbons such as *The Moon Book* (1997) and *Caves and Caverns* (1993) can be used to ease students into a study of the descriptive structure. Although these books are very simple picture books, they have many text features and a fairly straightforward descriptive text to inform the reader about the main subjects. Although the pictures are very telling, the words and phrases help students visualize even when the pictures are not shown.

Seymour Simon's books such as *Storms* (1989) and *Wildfires* (1996) are also written in the descriptive structure. The photographs are the true beauty of these books, but the text is quite dense and contains very few, if any, text features to help students get through the text. Simon's books are excellent for developing strategies for visualizing from words. A good exercise using them is to ask children how the books could be more fully understood if other text features like highlighting, captions, headings, special fonts, or diagrams had been used. The conversation might also include reasons Simon did not include more text features to support the descriptive structure.

A subset of this structure is question-and-answer. It is a favorite of many children because it is clear-cut and uncomplicated and can be replicated in their own writing at a later date. Books such as *If You Were at the First Thanksgiving* (Kamma, 2001) and other books in this series and *What Do Sharks Eat for Dinner?* (Berger & Berger, 2000), part of the Scholastic Question and Answer Series, are all wonderful examples of this structure.

The other subset of this structure is persuasive texts. A book that is perfect for persuasive instruction is *Should There Be Zoos?* (Stead, 2002). For more information about this structure, see Chapter Thirteen.

Sequence or Time Order Through Biographies

Although they are usually told in a narrative form, biographies fall under the nonfiction umbrella. This form of literature usually is told in sequential order, from childhood through the stages of adulthood. Students like to read biographies because they are about real people, and they are told in a narrative format. Offering many opportunities for children to hear and read biographies will store this structure in their memory banks for use when they take to writing their own autobiographies.

USING BIOGRAPHY TO TEACH TIME-ORDER STRUCTURE

Book used: Jump by Floyd Cooper (2004)
Focus: Structure (time order)
Author's Message
Note to the Reader (text feature)

Time: One or two class periods
Graphic Organizer: Web, using three different colors or pens
Class Arrangement: Close to teacher and the book, either on the rug or in chairs

Reading Workshop Procedure

- Ask students what they already know about Michael Jordan and chart that information in *blue pen.* (Place student initials next to the information they contribute.)
- Ask them to start thinking about how the author organized the book and what his big ideas were for writing it.
- Read the book, asking about one-third of the way through if anyone has figured out which type of organization this book uses.
- When someone is able to tell you what it is and why the author might have chosen that structure (time order or sequential), talk about other books that use the same structure.
- Have students *turn and talk* about *new* information they have learned about Michael Jordan. Chart any new information. Use *red pen.* (Place student initials next to the information they contribute this time.)
- Complete the book and ask the students what they think the author's message was. Chart any ideas in *green pen.*
- Read the *Note to the Reader.* (Do not read it before you read the book because it tells the big idea and you want the students to practice figuring it out on their own.)
- Ask how many students usually skip that part when they read. (Most students admit they do not read the *Note to the Reader* because it is not important.) Pointing out this text feature makes the students aware that it is important and why they should not skip it when they see one in a book. Add any new thoughts gleaned from the *Note to the Reader* to the green section of the web.
- Have students review the web. Ask why the author, Floyd Cooper, might have used a sequential structure.

> Maybe he wanted us to see how Michael Jordan's youth affected him as an adult. Michael Jordan had to work hard to become what he is today.
>
> He wanted us to see how the competition with his brother pushed him harder to do things.
>
> He wanted us to see that Michael Jordan had challenges throughout his childhood that made him work harder.
>
> Maybe he wanted us to know that in order to be good at something, you have to be determined from a very early age and keep working at it.

- *Word Study.* determin<u>ation</u>, persever<u>ance</u>, persist<u>ence</u> (suffixes, root words, and meaning).

- *Writing Workshop*. Choose something that you love to do and that you are willing to spend a lot of time doing so that you can just keep getting better and better like Michael Jordan and basketball.
- Share a piece of your writing about your passion. Discuss how you hooked in your reader before you started the main part of your writing.
- As students become ready to tell you what they are going to write about, excuse them from the floor to go back to their seats and get started.
- Talk about building writing stamina: being able to stay focused on the writing for an extended amount of time.
- Give the students fifteen to twenty minutes of writing time. Impress upon them that they should write for the full amount of time.
- When the writing time is up, students practice reading what they wrote using the wall reading wall method (where they practice what they wrote, reading with expression, facing the wall). Students usually discover that they have left out something or need to rewrite a portion of their piece by using this method.
- Have the students work on their own "hooks."
- Confer with a few children on writing their hooks while the others are working on theirs at their seats. Put sample hooks on transparencies or on paper to use with an overhead projector or document camera for the next day's Writing Workshop minilesson. Hand the papers back and have the student elaborate on their interests with more detail. Have the students read their papers to one another.

Having a biography genre study helps students understand this structure. All students are asked to read a biography during the month. During read-aloud the teacher shares a variety of biographies using picture books, short excerpts from longer biographies, and articles about famous people. The students are asked to report about their subject in a number of ways. They may create poster boards, use a dramatic format by *becoming* the person, or create a PowerPoint presentation.

Producing time lines about a person's life is also a useful activity. As a child is reading a biography or autobiography, he or she can keep track of the major events in the person's life, giving a linear perspective of time order. After being exposed to a number of time lines from their textbooks and other sources, children can create their own personalized ones based on their own lives. For a formal outline, students must use rulers and divide lines into equal segments.

The Structure of Cause and Effect

In Carolyn's upper-grade classroom, Lynne Cherry's book *A River Ran Wild* (1992), a narrative form of nonfiction, was read aloud. She prefaced the reading with these instructions: "Listen carefully to figure out how the author wrote the book." She restated the question for more clarity: "How is the story organized?" As she read a section of the book aloud, she started a chart, asking the boys and girls to summarize the events as she added their comments to the chart. She read a little bit more and repeated the same procedure. As she solicited student comments, she reminded the students to think of how the author structured the story. Several students responded with "time line order," "chain reaction," and "cause and effect" and showed their thinking with circular and linear drawings. Carolyn explained that there is usually a graphic representation that can accompany a specific structure in nonfiction. The important thing they learned on this particular day was that authors organize their books in different ways. They surmised that this helped the reader to predict the next step in the piece and retain the information.

Ultimately the children created their own text structure books for younger children, using books and online resources. See Activity 5.4, Text Structure or Text Feature for a Children's Book.

TEXT FEATURES

Text features help readers locate information in the text. They work together with the text structures to assist the reader in gaining more information and making meaning from the text. Without text features, the student could still make sense of the text, but not as easily. Features include such supports as sidebars, headings and subheadings, inset sections, glossaries, tables of contents, charts, epilogues, maps, graphs, time lines, diagrams, illustrations, and photographs.

Fountas and Pinnell (2001) divide the features of information texts into four categories:

Print features, such as font, bold print, and colored print headings

Graphic aids, such as diagrams, graphs, maps, charts, and time lines

Organizational aids, such as table of contents, preface, glossary, and index

Illustrations, such as color or black-and-white photographs and labeled drawings

Delving into Text Features

Text features may be introduced on the first day of study, with a discussion of the differences between fiction and nonfiction. Partners or triads fold a piece of twelve-by-eighteen-inch construction paper into halves. They use marking pens to write their thoughts. On one side, they mark *fiction* and on the other side they mark *nonfiction.* With their peer group, they brainstorm the differences between fiction and nonfiction. After five minutes, they share their charts with other groups. In most cases, the preassessment activity has shown that almost everyone understands the difference between fiction and nonfiction. Preassessment activities let you move on if your students already understand a concept.

Ask the class, "How does the author of a book support you in your reading to help you understand the page in nonfiction?" Have the students *turn and talk* with a partner. As they are talking, walk around to listen to the conversations. Dialogue might concern photographs, maps, color prints, and so on. Use an overhead projector or document camera to show a social studies textbook page that has all the special text features masked with sticky notes so that only the text itself showed. Ask, "What is wrong with this page?" The students might respond that the page looks too plain, not very interesting, and needs pictures or photographs. One by one, pull off cover-ups to disclose a text feature—a map, a color print, a graph, or a photograph with a caption. As each feature is uncovered, discuss the support it gives the reader. Ask, "How is the page different now?" Students might respond, "It is colorful. It has pictures to help us understand when we read."

Ultimately the students should understand that the text and the features work in harmony with each other to give greater understanding of the content material. Students should understand that you can eliminate all the features and still get meaning from the page, but the additional text feature information that supports the text helps give a fuller and more in-depth understanding and helps us retain the material better.

Instructional Activities to Ensure Understanding of Text Features

The following activities are fun to do and show whether children understand what a text feature is and how it is used:

Activity 1. Give the class a piece of informational text with words only. Let the students work with partners to try adding other features that would help the reader understand the written part.

Activity 2. Show a sheet with some features on a particular subject, such as the rain forest. There may be a map, a photograph with a caption, a diagram about the different layers of the forest, a glossary, a description of a particular animal that lives there, some key words in bold letters, and a time line. Have partners write down appropriate text that would accompany the features.

Activity 3. Place a basket containing about ten nonfiction books on a table of four students. Children should look through the books, locating as many text features as they can within a fifteen-minute time frame, and marking each with a sticky note as they converse about the feature.

Activity 4. Have students list on a chart the text features found in several nonfiction books. Hold a scavenger hunt to locate the features in other books.

Activity 5. Make copies of as many features as possible from different texts. Put them all together on one or two sheets, with a number next to each one. Provide another sheet with the names of all the features for students to cut out. Have partners cut out the picture and the feature name and glue them together on a piece of construction paper.

Activity 6. Have students cut out examples of features from magazines and glue them onto pieces of paper with the name of each feature and a brief explanation of what it is and how it is used.

Activity 7. When plenty of time has passed and the students have a pretty good handle on text features and how they work with the text, have them create their own text feature booklet showing the features they know and how those features help them as readers.

After discussion about the types of features we find in nonfiction pieces, the students come up with a list of features that they are familiar with and we place this list, along with a brief reminder of its purpose, on a classroom chart that may be referred to later in our study. Find examples in texts of any features not mentioned through class brainstorming, such as epilogue, appendixes, afterword, inset, and cutaway, and introduce them during the year in whole-class or guided group instruction. Revisit text features often with older children so that these aids take hold and become automatic in navigating the maze of information to come.

SKILLS AND STRATEGIES FOR ACCESSING NONFICTION

The following sections help students to access nonfiction.

Vocabulary in Nonfiction

One of the stumbling blocks in nonfiction is the difficulty of the vocabulary. The words are not used very frequently in children's everyday language, so struggling readers have difficulty hanging on to them. As you are studying a particular concept in social studies or science, you can keep a section of the Word Wall or chart for the purpose of these content words. Once students reach the intermediate grades, they meet approximately ten thousand new words—words never before encountered in print—in their school reading each year (Nagy & Anderson, 1984). Many of these words come from textbooks and the content areas. A large number of them are multisyllabic and troublesome to pronounce, let alone remember.

Cooper (1993) suggested that the direct teaching of vocabulary can help improve comprehension when we follow certain guidelines:

- A few critical words are taught: limit the number of words to five or six at a time.
- The words are taught in meaningful context.
- Students relate the words to their background knowledge.
- Students are exposed to the words multiple times.

Other ideas include the following:

- The children should have lots of practice using the words in classroom conversation and with partners in turn-and-talk situations. Word games can be helpful and fun ways for students to learn new content or nonfiction words.
- *I am thinking of a word that means* _________.
- Place words on your back: a word is pinned to Partner A's back and Partner B gives clues to the word's meaning.
- Keep topic word boards for things like space words, words about explorers, and words about weather.
- Use cluster organizers to group specific words such as words we hear for the Olympics, words about biology, or words to describe the Spanish missions.
- Have fun with harder words—let the students use whiteboards to write them down.
- Plan a word scramble activity. Partner A scrambles up the letters of a word and Partner B tries to unscramble them using the Word Wall for help (taqicosrdoun = conquistadors).
- Create word jars of social studies or science words. Excuse tables for recess or lunch if they can give you the definition of a word you pull out of the jar.
- Have table competitions. Say a content word and have the table write a brief definition on a whiteboard. Tables get points if they give accurate definitions of the word.
- Give special recognition or a small reward if a student correctly uses the word in class discussions or in his or her writing.

See other vocabulary building activities in Chapter Six.

The goal in word study is to have children start using the word in their everyday speech and writing. Content word walls can be taken down after a unit or concept is completed and words in the word jar can keep growing so that they become embedded in long-term memory.

Skimming and Scanning

Results from standardized tests and research show that children experience difficulty searching for information in nonfiction texts (Pearson & Fielding, 1991). Therefore, children need a lot of guided practice searching for information in a variety of expository texts.

Skimming and scanning are two techniques that students need as they acquire knowledge in nonfiction. Most adults use these techniques for a good portion of their day. They do not read every piece of paper with a critical eye or with the intent of remembering it all. Depending on their purpose, they use different styles of reading to gain information.

Skimming When we skim an article, we quickly look over it to identify the main ideas and some of the details. We read very quickly and leave out parts that are not essential to the main ideas. Because we are not reading every word, our comprehension is lower. Fifty percent is a good average comprehension score for skimming (Fry, 2000). In many texts, the first and last sentences of each paragraph are important because they contain key ideas or summary statements, so students must be reminded to concentrate on them a little more carefully.

When we are looking at a newspaper, we are actually skimming. We do not read every word—instead we skim it to get a general idea of what the main articles are about. We might use the headlines, photographs, and captions to help us decide if we want to delve further into a particular article or skip it and search further.

Scanning When we scan, we are looking for a specific word or bit of information, again not reading every single word. We use scanning when we are looking in the telephone book, the dictionary, or a television guide. Our eyes are quickly moving down a page searching for special words and clues that will give us a reference point for finding our exact information. The material we are using has some form of logical arrangement. For instance, a dictionary or a telephone book is alphabetical, so we use the guide words to help us locate the answer we are seeking. In a television guide, the arrangement is by channel and time. One hundred percent accuracy is the goal of scanning (Fry, 2000).

Children need a great deal of practice with these two techniques. A teacher should assess who is having difficulty with skimming and scanning by giving them short practice sessions and then forming guided groups to assist those who need more help. These two techniques are essential in both fiction and nonfiction because locating material is a useful lifetime skill and helps make a person a better reader.

Highlighting and Using Sticky Notes

It is always a good idea to show students a book you are using for your own professional growth to demonstrate how you manage to remember the expository information for future use. You might also borrow a colleague's book to show the differences in how you approach remembering the content in comparison to another teacher. Whatever your personal style—whether it be highlighting, underlining, circling words or phrases, making comments in the margins of the book, attaching sticky notes, or taking notes—students will become familiar with an adult's way of selecting information for easy retrieval. Your modeling will be the visual that a child will take away in his or her memory.

Try this preassessment experiment with your older children. Give them a piece of expository text and ask them to highlight the important information. You will see anywhere from one or two lines to almost every single line highlighted. Some of the students definitely need direction on determining importance in nonfiction texts.

To model the technique of highlighting important parts, take another text and put it on the overhead projector or document camera. Demonstrate how you think through marking text to remind you about what you have read. What do you do when you are highlighting? Why do you highlight information? Pass this on to your students. Many students have difficulty with this skill, but through interactive modeling of students and teacher, the class will learn about highlighting the main points and leaving out the interesting details. A good rule of thumb for upper graders is that no more than one-third to one-half of a piece should be highlighted.

The use of sticky notes must also be modeled. Since a textbook cannot be marked up, students need to see how sticky notes can be used for retaining information. This is discussed in Chapter Ten.

Technology: Benefits and Challenges

Technology creates possibilities for nonfiction access. The Internet, CD-ROMs, and DVDs open up research possibilities for students to access new information, but they must understand that limitations and frustrations can accompany their learning. Stephanie Harvey (1998) lists some of the challenges students face using the Internet:

- Accessibility
- Search difficulty
- Validity
- Supervision
- Transient web sites
- Typing errors
- Cyberspace gridlock

In general, students are not proficient in researching materials on the computer. The Internet is complicated, and students become easily frustrated when a basic search turns up hundreds of web sites. Learning how to specify search vocabulary takes skill and practice. Matching a knowledgeable web surfer with a challenged learner as computer buddies makes for good cooperative pairing during Internet research.

Although many students think the only place to find material for their inquiries is on the computer, they should be cautioned about what they find there. Many articles are undocumented and invalid. As in any type of reading, a person has to be cautious and careful not to believe everything on the page. Minilessons and discussion from both parents and teachers help students understand the web's limitations.

Also, material displayed on a computer screen is more challenging to read than print. Students must learn how to read and take notes from a screen. This can be very frustrating for researchers because they tend to lose their places easily while frequently looking up and down. Teaching students to copy and highlight the text helps limit these challenges, as do a few lessons in note taking during read-alouds.

Using both online and print texts helps students thoroughly delve into their interests, passions, and assignments.

SUPPORTING STRUGGLING READERS AND WRITERS DURING THIS STUDY

There are many things you can do to support your challenged readers in a nonfiction study:

- Assess their understanding using flexible groupings for guided reading groups.
- Use a book at a lower reading level.

- Use lots of charting to support learning.
- Provide opportunities every day for reading nonfiction to build stamina (the length of time they stay focused on independent reading) by using a stopwatch or timer.
- Use multiple sources at a variety of levels.
- Preteach words that might cause students trouble.
- Teach and reteach text features and structures.
- Model reading nonfiction.
- Reread.
- Teach skimming and scanning.
- Talk about dipping in and dipping out in nonfiction.
- Teach them how to use the index and table of contents.
- Revisit text that students have heard as read-alouds.

NONFICTION ASSESSMENT PRACTICES: BASELINE AND FINALE

Observe students as they begin their early experiences reading nonfiction with you the first week of school. This observation becomes your baseline assessment for student needs and instructional practices. Try to distinguish those who seem to know less about reading nonfiction. You will see that some students are really confused, some students read the whole page, just the captions, or just the incidental parts, and do not look for the main points. In general, students read nonfiction more slowly than narrative. During nonfiction study, teachers should spend a significant amount of time watching kids and conferencing individually and in small groups.

Formal and informal student assessment measures understanding of nonfiction. Teachers should encourage creativity and choice when selecting nonfiction writing and other assignments such as postcards, field guides, brochures, accordion books, poetry, or newspapers; drama assignments such as role plays, readers' theater, scripts written from textbook content, how-to demonstrations, mock trials, hot seat, or radio or talk shows; art assignments such as poster boards, cartoons, and picture books; and projects like song writing or dance performance.

Because of the major role they play in our lives, nonfiction and informational texts must be analyzed and studied using both reading and writing.

Activity 5.1

TEXT FEATURE ACTIVITY

Student's Name__________________

- Using one or more of the nonfiction books that you have chosen on one subject, create a text feature booklet.
- Select eight to ten features of nonfiction text and create a booklet showing each feature.
- Underneath each feature, write a reason why this feature has helped you to get greater meaning out of the text that you are reading.
- You may work alone or with a partner.
- You should select features from the chart that we made together in the classroom.
- Remember that a feature gives you more support in understanding the text.
- You may draw your own pictures by hand, you may make copies of these features, you may use items from the Internet, or you may use combinations of any of the above. You may cut samples out from magazines or newspapers if they apply to your subject.
- You may use colored pencils to color in your pictures.
- Please proofread your writing.
- Ask a classmate for help if you are confused.
- Include the names of the people who helped you.
- Have fun with this activity.

Activity 5.2

DO YOU KNOW YOUR TEXT STRUCTURES?

Student's Name ______________

- In the basket you will find eight to ten primary- and middle-level picture books, each with a different text structure.
- With a partner you are to look through the books and try to discover what particular text structure the author used to help you have greater understanding of the book.
- Remember that some of the texts may have a *combination* of structures.
- Using the small piece of paper provided in the basket, talk with your partner and write down the title of the book, the structure you think the author used in writing the book, and then defend your choice by telling how that structure will help you to better comprehend what you are reading.
- Keep your choices with you so that you can share them with your classmates during the share-out session.
- Identify at least five of the structures used in the books.

  The structures you are looking for are
  Cause and effect
  Compare and contrast
  Description
  Problem and solution
  Question and answer
  Sequential order
- Have fun.

Activity 5.3

FEATURE AND STRUCTURE SEARCH

Look carefully at the books in your basket. Decide what text structure the author has chosen; then search further for any text features the author has used. Put a check mark (✔) next to the items you find and indicate the page number for each one.

Book Title ☞								
Text Structure								
Cause and effect								
Compare and contrast								
Descriptive								
How-to								
List								
Persuasive								
Problem and solution								
Question and answer								
Sequential order								
Text Features								
Bold print								
Bullets								
Captions								

Activity 5.3

FEATURE AND STRUCTURE SEARCH (*Continued*)

Charts								
Color print								
Cross-section or cutaway								
Diagrams								
Fact box								
Glossary								
Headings								
Index								
Introduction								
Italics								
Labels								
Magnifications								
Maps								
Photographs or drawings								
Pronunciation guide								
Sidebars								
Size comparisons								
Supplemental information								
Table of contents								
Tables								
Time lines								
Titles								

Student's Name(s) ______________________ Date ________________

Activity 5.4

TEXT STRUCTURE OR TEXT FEATURE FOR A CHILDREN'S BOOK

You will have the opportunity to create a children's book based on one of the text structures of nonfiction texts. The structures you may use are

Cause and effect
Compare and contrast
Description
Problem and solution
Question and answer
Time order, sequential, or chronological

- You will also try to incorporate some of the text features we have studied such as illustrations, pictures, maps, diagrams, bold print, colored print, bullets, captions, fact boxes, glossaries, graphs, headings, indexes, italic print, labels, pronunciation guides, sidebars, table of contents, tables, charts, time lines, and titles.
- You will need to thoroughly research an animal, a place, or a thing of importance to you such as the *Titanic,* fish, rabbits, caves, frogs, the desert, the rain forest, deer, insects, electricity, San Diego, Australia, and so on.
- Now that we have studied the features and structures of nonfiction texts, you will be transferring these ideas into a book of your own, which you will make for a younger brother, sister, relative, or your kindergarten buddy.
- Remember that your text should be simple, but it should also be rich in the special features that will help the younger child make sense out of your topic.
- You will select a graphic organizer to do your initial planning and thinking.
- Your text will be typed. You may draw your own text features by hand or on a computer.
- Your work should be of grade-level quality.
- Your work should be proofread.

— *Chapter 6* —

STRENGTHENING WORD KNOWLEDGE AND FLUENCY

In any classroom there is a tremendous range in students' word knowledge—their vocabulary, ability to decode (read) and encode (write), and their ability to employ strategies to "solve" or figure out unknown words as they read and spell. This chapter will focus on what we know from current research about how children develop through predictable stages in these word knowledge skills and recommended instructional practices and strategies in the areas of *word study:* word recognition, spelling, and vocabulary. These are important skills that must continue to be taught in the upper elementary and middle school grades in a balanced literacy classroom. We must ensure that students acquire sufficient knowledge of how the English language works to become competent and fluent readers and writers. One of the key components and building blocks of reading identified in the research is *fluency,* which depends on ease and speed of applying word knowledge skills (National Institute of Child Health and Human Development, 2000). Research-based fluency strategies and techniques will be addressed in this chapter as well.

WHAT IS WORD STUDY?

Word study is defined as an instructional process involving the learner in an investigation of words that results in "word solving" in reading and writing (Marten, 2003). Word study occurs through hands-on activities analyzing words and word elements. During word study, words are sorted in routines that require children to examine, discriminate, and make critical judgments about speech sounds, word structures, spelling patterns, and meanings (Bear, Invernizzi, Templeton, & Johnston, 2004). To become proficient at breaking the code in word recognition and spelling, students need knowledge and skill in four areas identified by Tompkins (2001): *phonetic analysis* (sound-symbol relationships), *analogy* (deducing the pronunciation or spelling of an unfamiliar word by associating with words they already know), *syllable analysis* (awareness of the types of syllables and how to break multisyllabic words into syllable parts), and *morphemic analysis* (applying knowledge of root words, prefixes, and suffixes to read and spell unfamiliar words). "The purpose of word study is twofold: (1) for students to actively explore and examine words—in order to discover consistencies within our written language system (the regularities, patterns, and conventions of English orthography needed to read and spell); (2) to help students master the recognition, spelling, and meaning of specific words" (Bear et al., 2004, p. 4).

Cindy Marten (2003) refers to word study as "word crafting." With this approach teachers carefully orchestrate and design lessons and word activities that are appropriate to students' developmental stages.

THE TEACHER'S ROLE IN WORD STUDY

Begin with Assessment. Knowing individual students' specific stage of development enables teachers to appropriately group and make instructional decisions. We know what to teach based on what students already know and are ready to learn. There are various means for assessing students' individual stages of spelling and other aspects of written language development, such as observation, administering inventories, analyzing writing samples, individual conferencing, or other means.

Spelling inventories are recommended for preassessment to determine each student's development stage and later to assess his or her learning and progress. The goal of an inventory is to get an overall sense of word knowledge and to tell us the stage at which the student's linguistic knowledge begins to break down (Marten, 2003). There are various inventories available, such as those by Bear et al. (2004) and the Developmental Spelling Analysis in Ganske's *Word Journeys* (2000).

Select the Right Words. Teachers choose words for study based on the individual student's word knowledge development. The focus is on words that students are able to read and are currently using, but are sometimes confusing. The word study instruction will involve manipulating, examining, and categorizing words by word patterns and features that students are confusing (Feldman, 2000).

Guide Students with Questions. Good teaching involves guiding students through our questioning and prompting as they think and make their own discoveries. Following are examples of some questions and prompts we may ask students as they struggle with unknown, misspelled, or misread words.

- How else might that word be spelled? What other ways can you spell the sounds in that word?
- There's a tricky part in this word. Can you find that part on our chart to help you?
- That's like what word on our word wall?
- Write the part that you know.
- Let's count out (or tap out) the syllables. Did you remember a vowel sound in each syllable?

- Stretch out the sounds and say the word slowly. What do you hear first? Next? At the end?
- Listen for the vowel. What are the different ways you can spell that vowel sound?

Note: Also prompt with any mnemonics, associations, or tactile-kinesthetic cues for letter sounds that may have been taught.

SPELLING

Spelling is a functional skill necessary for expressing ourselves and accurately communicating in writing. Some children seem to be natural spellers. These students may be very adept at visualizing and recalling the correct letter sequences, patterns, and configurations of words they see in print and have well-developed phonemic awareness and phonetic skills. They are able to sound out and spell words with ease and automaticity. Other children struggle with spelling and get frustrated. We must help each child develop his or her spelling and "word solving" competency and build this important communication skill.

Developmental Stages of Spelling

Children pass through predictable developmental stages on their way to becoming proficient spellers. Various authors call these stages by different names. It is widely recognized that these are stages that *all* students pass through as they gain knowledge and competence in the English orthographic system and how words work (Invernizzi & Worthy, 1989; Zutell, 1998). Students with learning challenges progress along this same continuum, often at a slower pace, encountering many difficulties along the way (Bender & Larkin, 2003).

The following five developmental stages are described by several authors, along with the focus of word study instruction at each stage (Marten, 2003; Bear et al., 2004; Bender & Larkin, 2003; Tompkins, 2001; Feldman, 2000).

1. Prephonemic or Preliterate: Emergent Stage
   The child knows the names of some letters and can write some letters, but generally scribbles, makes drawings, has no sound-symbol relationship, and often pairs a random mix of letters with a picture. They are learning the concept of print, letter names and forms, phonemic awareness, and a few letter sounds.
2. Letter Name: Alphabetic Stage
   The student knows the names of letters, experiments with letter sounds, may spell words with consonants only (leaving out vowels), and writes some words with correct use of short vowels. He or she is learning single consonants, short vowel patterns, consonant digraphs, and clusters.

3. WITHIN-WORD PATTERN STAGE
Students spell most single-syllable short vowel words and beginning and ending consonant blends and digraphs correctly. They recognize and use patterns and word families. Students are learning common long-vowel patterns, r- and l-controlled vowels, complex consonant patterns, compound words, common inflections and diphthongs, and homophones.
4. SYLLABLES AND AFFIXES STAGE
Students spell most one-syllable short- and long-vowel words correctly. They make errors at the syllable juncture and in unaccented syllables. They are learning less frequent vowel patterns, multisyllabic words and syllable patterns, inflectional endings, and more complex prefixes and suffixes.
5. DERIVATIONAL PATTERNS STAGE
Most words are spelled conventionally. Misspellings show errors in morphology (the internal structure and forms of words) and etymology (the origin and development of words). Students are learning the spelling, meaning, and connection of words derived from the same roots or bases and those of Greek and Latin origins.

Most third graders have reached the within-word pattern stage, and upper elementary students are generally at the syllable and affixes stage. However, there is wide variation in a diverse population. A child with learning disabilities, for example, may remain in an earlier developmental stage much longer than the average student of his or her grade, and a student with advanced phonological and word recognition ability may move to a higher stage much earlier than his or her grade level peers. Also, students will continue to need review and practice of skills learned earlier.

Characteristics of Proficient Spellers

Following are competencies and characteristics of proficient spellers or word solvers (Marten, 2003; Pinnell & Fountas, 1998). These students

- Understand the orthography of English—how words are formed based on sounds, patterns, and meaning
- Know strategically what do when attempting to spell an unfamiliar word or when recognizing and correcting a misspelled word
- Have spelling consciousness—are aware of and care about work being spelled correctly
- Write a large number of known whole words quickly and easily
- Listen for and use word parts to construct words
- Look for patterns
- Use knowledge of known words to write new words
- Check on words they have written to be sure they look right and represent accurate letter-sound relationships

- Use partial information along with references and resources such as word lists and dictionaries
- Use the structure of words and their meaning to spell or pronounce a word
- Use the largest chunks of information possible
- Constantly search for connections between what they know about words and what they are trying to figure out

According to Pinnell and Fountas (1998), to become a proficient speller students must develop understanding of

- Consonants, vowels, and vowel combinations
- Word patterns
- Phonograms, which are also called *rimes* or word families (for example, **-ike, -ot,** and **-ump**)
- Open and closed syllables
- Base words and root words, prefixes and suffixes, and plurals and possessives
- Syllabication
- Contractions
- Compound words
- Synonyms and antonyms
- Homophones
- The origin of words (such as Anglo-Saxon, Greek, or Latin)

High-Frequency and Commonly Misspelled Words

One specific set of words represents a high percentage of all words typically found in written language. Students benefit greatly from knowing these words with automaticity and accuracy.

In many classes, teachers call the high-frequency words focused on for that grade level No Excuse Words (Marten, 2003); others call them Fast as a Snap words (Fisher, Fetzer, & Rief, 1999) or other such nicknames. These are words that students need to read with automaticity and spell correctly in their written work. They are generally posted on charts or the word wall in the classroom, and students may have their own notebook or desk copy. These are also words that throughout the year students are encouraged to memorize so they can be written quickly and accurately.

A variety of multisensory techniques is available to help teach high-frequency words, such as using manipulatives to form the words; typing them several times in different colors, sizes, and fonts; tracing and writing the words several times in motivating formats and mediums (in color and texture). Chanting the letters rhythmically is another powerful auditory strategy for learning and recalling the spelling of these words. It is recommended you apply mnemonic strategies whenever possible to help recall the letters and sequence of the irregularly spelled high-frequency words.

Cunningham and Hall (1998) identify ninety commonly misspelled words that are recommended for upper-grade word walls. They include such words as *beautiful, because, through, favorite,* and *enough.* Selecting a few of these words each week from a published list or through students' individual common misspellings in their own writing is recommended.

Those few words can be practiced the same way as above. Some of the commonly misspelled words are among the high-frequency words; others are not.

Pinnell and Fountas (1998) recommend that students be given a pretest of high-frequency words, highlighting on a personal list which ones they know. A few words each week from those words that were not highlighted can be selected for study.

Students frequently ask adults how to spell a word while they are writing. Rather than automatically spelling a word for the student, encourage the use of self-help strategies: locating the word on the word wall, word chart, looking up the word, or sounding it out as well as possible and circling it to check the correct spelling later.

Instructional Activities

Marten (2003), Pinnell and Fountas (1998), and Ganske (2000) suggest the following activities and features as part of a word study program:

- Teach students spelling strategies such as how to look for patterns and word parts, remembering words that sound or look the same, and trying several ways to write a word and checking to see which one looks right.
- Study, practice, and test on high-frequency words and personal words.
- Teach students to actively explore words with word sorts and to generalize spelling patterns and rules through their discoveries.
- Keep word study and word-crafting notebooks throughout the year to include the generalizations they have learned and as a record of their growing linguistic knowledge.
- Use word charts and word walls as resources and references.
- Make words with letters and letter clusters.
- Make word webs.
- Participate in cooperative learning activities that center on words and their sounds, visual features, and meaning.
- Provide minilessons and conferences in Writing Workshop focusing on spelling.
- Use student-centered, interactive, inquiry-based approaches to word exploration.
- Have word hunts.
- Use games.
- Use dictionaries and other word references.

Of the many possible word study activities, some are described below. The key is that students are actively engaged in focusing on word elements, patterns, and features, thereby making discoveries on their own.

Word Sorts. Generally word sorts begin with teacher-directed "closed sorts." The teacher selects the word features for a group of students at a particular developmental level to study. This is an excellent way to differentiate instruction and enable students to compare, contrast, and analyze words at their own stage or level of understanding. First, the teacher models the sorting procedure, and facilitates discussion of why the words are being sorted into the particular categories. Next, students engage in "open sorts"—classifying the given set of words according to features they discover themselves.

In a word sort activity, the headings at the top of each category column are indicated by either a sound/spelling (such as **ane /_ain**), or by key words (cane/rain). Students then sort a stack of word cards under the appropriate category heading.

Words Their Way (Bear, Invernizzi, Templeton, & Johnston, 2004, 3rd edition) is a wonderful source for word sorts at varying developmental stages and is designed for easy teacher use.

At the Syllable and Affixes Stage, appropriate sorts might include

- Plurals spelled differently (**s** versus **es**), such as schools/churches
- Words that drop the final **y** and change to **i** before adding the ending (**ed**); and words that do not drop the final **y** and change to **i** (fried/played)
- Words with single or double consonants before **ing** (hopping/hoping; pinning/pining)
- Words with multiple syllables (two-, three-, and four-syllable words)
- Words whose **ed** endings are pronounced differently, such as:

Want**ed**	stopp**ed**	fool**ed**
Needed	licked	posed
Busted	stretched	raised
Hated	cooked	joined

In this sort, students attend to the fact that words with an **ed** ending make either the */ed/* sound, */t/* sound, or */d/* sound. Once sorted, they make and share their observations about why words make the various sounds.

With word sort activities, students can be given a page of words to cut apart. They store the manipulative words they have cut apart for that particular sort and use them again during the week. They can be stored in an envelope or ziplock bag for future practice and use.

After students do the hands-on task of sorting words, they might record words in categories in a word study notebook or log. Students use their notebook to record words and information they are learning about words. This includes any of their discoveries and generalizations. The word study notebook also serves to document their individual growth and progress throughout the year and can be part of their literacy portfolio for the school year.

Word Creation. In this activity (also called "making words") children are given some letter cards or strips of paper or cardboard containing the letters used for that lesson. Students cut apart their letter cards and use them as manipulatives for building words from those letters. Students are to use the letter cards to make words of three letters, then four letters, five letters, and more until they make the last word, which includes all of the letters from the lesson of that day. Cunningham and Hall (1997) have wonderful materials for these activities. For example, in Lesson 119 of their book, given the eleven letters **e, e, i, o, b, l, n, p, r, s,** and **s,** students are to form four-letter words (such as *lion, boss,* or *bone*), five-letter words (such as *bless, rebel,* or *sense*), six-letter words (*relies* or *reopen*), seven-letter words (*replies* or *lioness*), eight-letter words (*ripeness, sensible,* or *response*), and the challenge word using all eleven letters (*responsible*). They are also guided to find word relatives among the words they have formed, such as lion/lioness, sense/sensible. Teachers can also give clues in guiding students to change specific letters to form new words by adding, deleting, or moving them around. For example, "Can you add a letter to the beginning of that word (*less*) to make a new word (*bless*)? "

Sound and Pattern Activities. The following phonics and spelling activities involve sounds, patterns, and attention to features and letter sequences in words.

Little-Word Search. Students are to look for as many little words as possible within a given word without changing the sequence of letters within the word. Examples: **great:** eat, at; **stubborn:** stub, tub, born; **lieutenant:** lie, ten, an, ant, tenant.

Word Hunt. Challenge students to find words containing a phonogram being studied, such as **ind, ank,** or **ight.** As they locate words in books or other sources, they add them to a chart of that phonogram or spelling pattern or to the appropriate column in their word study notebooks.

Clothespin Words. Cut strips of tag or card stock about two to three inches wide. Down each strip write the rime or base word that will become a complete word or new word once the beginning letter cluster or prefix is added to the front of the word. On a clothespin write the beginning blend, digraph, or prefix that will be used for that word strip. As students slide the clothespin down the side of the strip, they read the full words. The same can be done with clothespins placed on the right side of the word strip, adding suffixes or forming words with a final consonant blend or digraph. It is recommended that students practice reading their strip of words and, when ready, do so with a partner. Then, if the partner says the words were read correctly, the student reads the words to the teacher. If all words were read accurately and fluently, the student writes his or her name on the back of that word strip.

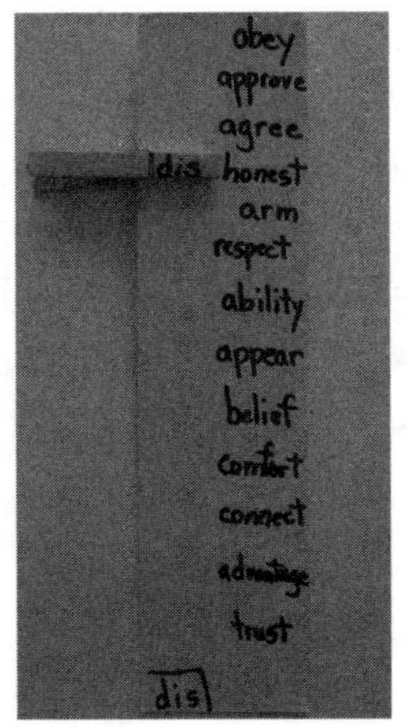

Figure 6.1. Clothespin Words That Begin with *dis-*

Scrambled Words. Give scrambled words and about six to eight correctly spelled words in a word bank box. Given clues, the student is to unscramble the letters to find the word from the box that completes each sentence or clue. Example: "Maria and I don't know each other well. She is just an uaacetcaqinn. _ _ _ _ _ _ _ _ _ _ _ _" One possible answer from the word bank box is "acquaintance" (Glassman & Einhorn, 2004).

Word Detective. Using the given words in the word bank box, students select words and use the clues to fill in the blanks. Glassman and Einhorn (2004) offer these examples: "What do you do when you admire a mansion? You _______ an ______." (You appreciate an estate.) "What do you do to make your situation better? You ______ your _________." (You enhance your circumstance.)

Fun Web Sites. Some excellent web sites, such as PBS Kids, teach and reinforce phonics and build word knowledge through song lyrics and animated video clips and are appropriate for elementary students (http://pbskids.org/lions/songs).

Figure 6.2. Clothespin Words That Begin with *gl-*

Missing Letters. Provide first and last letters of a word with blanks in between. Challenge students to generate a list of as many words as possible in a given time frame (and the words must be spelled correctly). For example, from "w_ _ _ e," some possible answers are *where, whose,* and *white.*

Homophones and Homographs. Play games and various activities with homophones (also called *homonyms*). These are words that sound the same but have different meanings (such as bear/bare, board/bored, not/knot, and bury/berry). Do the same with *homographs,* which are words that are spelled the same but have different pronunciations, often with an accent on a different syllable (content'/con'tent, pres'ent/present'). Activity 6.1 at the end of this chapter shows multiple homophone activities.

Mnemonic (or Memory) Strategies. Help students learn tricky spelling words through mnemonics (memory aids) such as "a **pie**ce of **pie**" or "keep qu**iet** about my d**iet**." Use an acrostic sentence to help students remember various spelling patterns, rules, or exceptions to rules. For example, the sentence "The n**aught**y d**augh**ter was t**aught** a lesson when she got **caught**" contains all words spelled with **aught,** while all others have the **-ought** spelling (such as **bought, fought, brought, sought,** and **thought**).

Word Lists and Charts. Generate lists of words to chart that are examples of various language features. For example, make charts of words with a particular vowel sound, phonogram or rime, prefix, suffix, silent consonant, and so forth.

Word Walls. Word walls have become very popular in classes of all grade levels. When used appropriately (not just posting the words but actively using the wall instructionally), they serve as a valuable tool and reference for students. Teachers often use a word wall in the upper grades for commonly misspelled words in writing, high-frequency words for the grade level, and exemplar words containing a phonetic pattern or spelling (for example, **ea**gle, with a picture as well, to attend to the **ea** spelling for long *e* words).

The word wall must be in an easily visible and accessible location for it to be useful. Words posted on the wall are typically written in large letters on word cards, and many teachers frame the configuration of the word (and often cut out the words along the configuration). Words are added gradually, perhaps a few per week.

Wagstaff (1999) describes the use of a "chunking wall." This is made up of key words containing common spelling patterns, or chunks. These chunks, such as the rimes **-ike** in bike and **-ool** in school, help students read and write unknown words by analogy to known words, rather than sounding them out letter by letter or using phonetic rules. *Note:* a rime is the vowel and what comes after it in a syllable (such as **-ank, -ent,** and **-ote**). As the chunking wall continues to grow, another category can be added for chunks such as prefixes and suffixes.

Words Meaning (Roots, Affixes, Origins). For more advanced decoding and spelling, students at the syllable and affixes and derivational stages need to be taught and have practice working with words in morpheme and word structure analysis, and understanding of words derived from Latin and Greek. In addition to the word sorts, charting, and other activities described above, we also offer the following tips:

- Teach students word origins, such as the Latin **bene,** which means "good" or "well" and is the root of the words **benefit** (something that is good for a person), **benevolent** (having a wish to do good), and **beneficial** (being of help).
- Using a root word, have students form as many words related in meaning as possible. For example, from **social** we link to **antisocial, sociable, socially, socialite, unsociable, society,** and **socialist.** Word webs can be created stemming from the root word.
- Teach prefixes and then create a list or chart or have students record in their word study notebooks words that contain that prefix. For example, from **ambi** and **amphi** (meaning "both") we get **ambidextrous,** meaning skilled with both hands, and **amphibious,** meaning living on both land and water. Record those examples and definitions, along with an illustration, if possible.

Teach the meaning of suffixes (a letter or letters added to the end of a word) such as **-al** (having characteristics of), **-er** (person connected with), **-tion** (act, process), **-ant** (one who does), **-ly** (characteristic of), **-en** (having the characteristics of), and **-ance** (state of being). Then give sentences in which students must add correct suffixes to the base word. For example, "Some say ignore is bliss. (ignorance)" "The swing set may be old, but it is function. (functional)" (Glassman & Einhorn, 2004).

Puzzles and Games. Crossword puzzles and games such as Hangman or commercial games such as Scrabble and Up Words (Hasbro), Word Yahtzee (E. S. Lowe), Boggle (Parker Brothers), and Jumble Word Game (Cadaco) are other great ways for having fun spelling and working with words.

VOCABULARY

There is a strong relationship between one's vocabulary and one's background knowledge, comprehension, and academic achievement (Marzano, 2004). According to the research, one of the key contributors to the acquisition of vocabulary is wide reading. Research has shown that past the fourth grade, the number of words a person knows depends primarily on how much time he or she spends reading (Wren, 2003c). Many poor readers who do not read much therefore have a huge vocabulary deficit to overcome. Nagy and Anderson (1984) estimated that the average student in the middle grades and beyond must acquire approximately three thousand new words yearly to stay current with each succeeding grade level. So clearly every effort to increase students' reading during the day and to motivate them to read outside of school are important strategies for increasing students' vocabulary.

Research also shows the importance of direct vocabulary instruction for improving students' background knowledge and the comprehension of academic content. Marzano (2004) emphasizes the importance of directly teaching students the specific vocabulary terms and phrases that they will encounter in their academic subjects based on the standards and provides word lists across the content areas to help schools and individual teachers wishing to target those words (Marzano & Pickering, 2005).

Instruction: The Big Picture

According to Allen in *Words, Words, Words* (1999), shared and guided reading provides multiple opportunities to teach new words and word learning strategies, such as

- Using context to figure out meanings
- Creating visuals, webs, or organizers to develop memory links for words
- Showing why some words require deeper understanding than other words
- Demonstrating how to use resources (dictionaries and thesauruses)
- Connecting individual words to a larger concept
- Highlighting the importance of specialized vocabulary

Kinsella (2005) recommends that students repeat new words to be learned multiple times, at first repeating the word in a choral response. After defining the word and giving students many examples, provide opportunities for students to repeat the word and use total physical response (*showing* you what the word means) when possible.

The teaching of vocabulary should be infused throughout the entire curriculum, providing students with numerous opportunities to learn and use new words. Teachers should also seek "teachable moments" to motivate students to learn vocabulary relevant and meaningful to them. For example, high-profile trials in the news provide wonderful opportunities to teach words such as *defendant, prosecutor, indictment, conviction, attorney, evidence, bail,* and so forth.

It is important to check regularly for understanding when instructing and reading with students. Over the years we have been amazed at how many words and terms native English speakers did not know—words we assumed they must already know—including words critical to academic task directions such as *analyze, interpret,* and *eliminate.* Academic language and content-specific words need to be directly taught to accelerate students' acquisition of the vocabulary knowledge necessary for school success.

Strategies, Activities, and Scaffolds

Numerous activities are available to build vocabulary and support students in their understanding of words. Following are some activities and techniques.

Sentence Expansion. Start with a basic, simple "bare bones" sentence written on the board, overhead, or chart. Model and guide students in answering questions such as: how? when? where? why? to expand and add "meat" to the sentence. For example: *The girl worked.* (How?) The girl worked *frantically. Note:* diligently, steadily, and other possible responses are recorded. (When?) *late through the night* (Why?) *in order to complete her assignment on time.* To build a more powerful sentence, generate other verbs that might be used instead of "worked" (labored) and nouns that could be used instead of "girl" (fifth grader, Amanda). Make a list of possible adjectives that could be added (exhausted, nervous, determined). The modifiers (when, where, why, how) can be moved around, such as to the beginning of the sentence to add variety to sentence structure.

Vocabulary Detective Work. Using the Vocabulary Detective Work form shown in Figure 6.3 and Activity 6.2, students record an unknown word from their reading, as well as

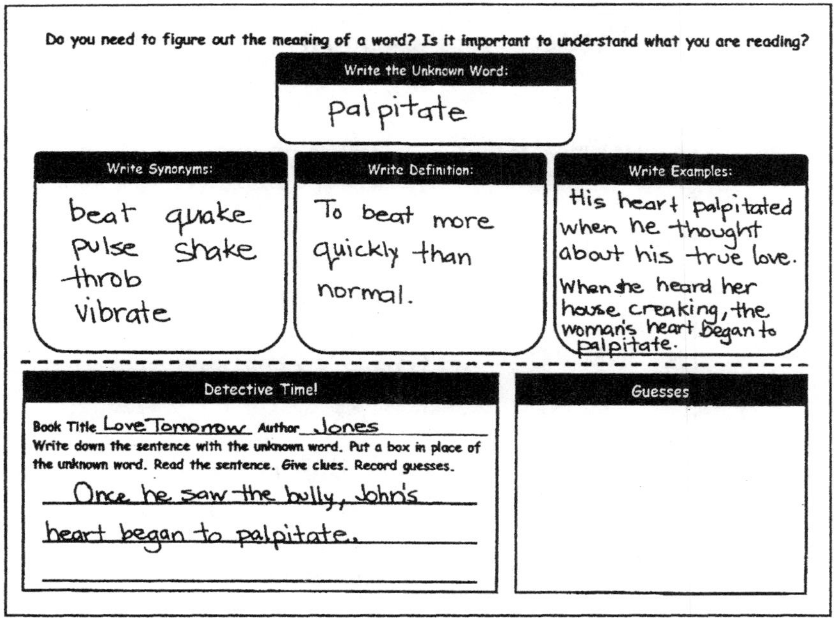

Do you need to figure out the meaning of a word? Is it important to understand what you are reading?

Write the Unknown Word: palpitate

Write Synonyms: beat quake pulse shake throb vibrate

Write Definition: To beat more quickly than normal.

Write Examples: His heart palpitated when he thought about his true love. When she heard her house creaking, the woman's heart began to palpitate.

Detective Time!

Book Title Love Tomorrow Author Jones

Write down the sentence with the unknown word. Put a box in place of the unknown word. Read the sentence. Give clues. Record guesses.

Once he saw the bully, John's heart began to palpitate.

Guesses

Figure 6.3. Vocabulary Detective Work
Source: N. Fetzer. (2006). *Reading Connections.* Murrieta, CA: Nancy Fetzer's Literacy Connections. www.nancyfetzer.com. Used with permission.

the other information on the organizer using available resources such as a thesaurus, glossary, or dictionary. When confident that the student knows the word's meaning, he or she then challenges other students to try some vocabulary detective work. The organizer is folded on the dotted line to show only the bottom section to classmates. The student reads the sentence in the Detective Time box and points out the unknown word (*palpitate*) to the other student(s). They are to guess the word's meaning from the context clue. Then the student reads more of the clues: first the example, then the definition, and then synonyms. Classmates can continue to guess during the process as clues are revealed (Fetzer, 2006).

Front-Loading Vocabulary Prior to Reading. Nancy Fetzer (2003, 2006) has developed very creative and powerful scaffolds and techniques for teaching students key vocabulary prior to their reading of the text. A few of her techniques are highlighted here, and more detailed information can be found in her books and web site (www.nancyfetzer.com). One such technique, Lecture Notes, is described in Chapter Thirteen of this book. Following is another prereading activity for front-loading vocabulary.

Two-Minute Vocabulary Run. The teacher lists vocabulary words on the board in the order they will appear in the story or text. Students are divided into small groups and are assigned one of the vocabulary words to define within two minutes. They are also given one sticky note. The teacher states, "You have two minutes to find your word meaning. Ready, set, go!" The groups are to use any of the resources available (dictionary, glossary, thesaurus, or other students) and record the definition, synonym, or illustration of the word on the sticky note. Next, in the order that the words are listed on the board, a representative from each group stands and tells the class the word meaning and adheres the sticky note next to their word on the board. Once the words have all been defined, the teacher guides students in locating each word in their text and highlighting it with a piece of removable highlighting tape.

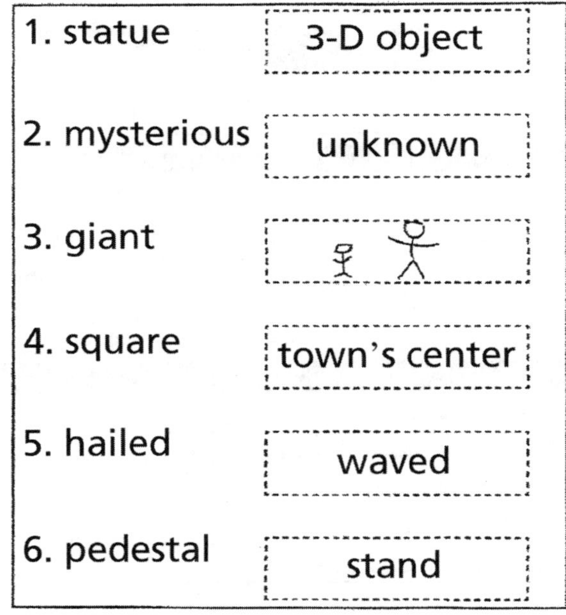

Figure 6.4. Two-Minute Vocabulary Run
Source: N. Fetzer. (2006). *Reading Connections.* Murrieta, CA: Nancy Fetzer's Literacy Connections. www.nancyfetzer.com. Used with permission.

The teacher then models how to refer to the word meanings on the board and use contextual clues to understand the story or text at a higher level (Fetzer, 2006).

Vocabulary Charts and Lists

Generate lists of words that are charted and posted, adding to them throughout the year. Such lists might include the following categories:

- Character traits or descriptions, such as *inquisitive, stubborn, ambitious, mischievous, greedy, adventurous, resourceful, generous,* and *sincere*
- Feelings, such as *suspicious, elated, optimistic, perplexed,* and *discouraged*
- Connecting and transition words, such as *however, consequently, therefore,* and *nevertheless*
- Overly used words, such as *happy, said,* and *went*
- Verbs or action words, such as *ambled* or *hiked:* a list of verbs that are more descriptive and specific than the typical *went, walked,* and so on
- Topical or thematic words pertaining to the theme or topic being studied in various content areas (see Chapter Five for more strategies to teach content area vocabulary)
- Contractions, compound words, and homophones (or homographs)
- Latin derivatives and Greek derivatives

Dictionary and Thesaurus Skills. Teach, model, and practice how to use these reference materials, including the electronic versions in computer word processing programs. Also, provide online access to web sites such as www.dictionary.com or www.thesaurus.com.

Mnemonics. In the wonderful book *Vocabulary Cartoons*™ (Burchers, Burchers, & Burchers, 1998), vocabulary words are taught through a keyword technique. A cartoon incorporating a funny visual of a word that *sounds like* the target vocabulary word is drawn, engaged in some action, with associations to make it memorable. For example, the target word, **encumber** (which sounds like *cucumber,* and means "to weigh down unnecessarily"), is presented through a cartoon showing a cucumber sweating as it runs to catch a train with several suitcases in its arms. It is an "encumbered cucumber." The cartoon and associations make it memorable and easy to recall the word and meaning. Sources for words taught through this technique can be found at www.vocabularycartoons.com (New Monic Books).

Vocabulary Notebooks. Students maintain a notebook divided into academic subject areas (Marzano, 2004). As students are presented with new vocabulary terms in the content areas, they record them in the appropriate section. Each page is divided into three columns labeled My Description, Representation, and New Insight.

Other Strategies

- Define words for students by paraphrasing and using simple explanations and synonyms. If possible to explain using antonyms (opposites), do this as well.
- When teaching new vocabulary, give examples and nonexamples. Try this strategy: "This is a ____." "This is not a _____." "Is this a ______? How do you know?"
- Do *semantic webbing* for vocabulary development. Write a specific vocabulary word in the center of the web, with synonyms for that word or phrases related to that central word stemming away from the center.

- Have students make flash cards with their vocabulary words written on one side and definitions on the other. Then they should practice with a partner.
- Crossword puzzles are a wonderful means of developing vocabulary, spelling, and language skills from childhood through adulthood. Incorporate age-appropriate crossword puzzle activities (for individuals, partners, or small groups) whenever possible.
- Have students create their own crossword puzzles and word matches using new vocabulary words.
- Play concentration games matching vocabulary words with definitions.
- As students are dismissed, enter the room, and so forth, have them say a new vocabulary word and tell what it means or use it in a sentence. This might be the students' "ticket out the door" at the end of the day or the period.
- Play commercial games that enhance vocabulary and language skills, such as Password, Jeopardy, One Minute Wonders, Taboo, Scattergories, and Outburst.

READING FLUENCY

Fluency is the ability to recognize words and read with ease, speed, accuracy, and expression (good phrasing and intonation). Meyer and Felton (1999) describe fluency as the ability to read connected text rapidly, smoothly, effortlessly, and automatically, with little conscious attention to the mechanics of reading, such as decoding. As fluent readers do not need to put forth a lot of mental energy trying to figure out the words on the page, it frees them to focus their attention on comprehension and makes reading far more enjoyable and rewarding than it is for readers who labor to read word by word (Armbruster, Lehr, & Osborn, 2001; Allington, 2006).

Maryanne Wolf (2006a, 2006b) reconceptualizes the definition of fluency as a lengthy developmental process involving multiple linguistic systems (phonological, orthographic, morphological, syntactic, and semantic) that contribute to it. She suggests that to achieve fluency as a goal, we must help students build automaticity from the level of letter and word identification through the connected-text level, and this involves building decoding skills, vocabulary knowledge, and other linguistic skills.

The National Reading Panel identified fluency as one of the key building blocks to reading. The research clearly shows a strong correlation between reading fluency and comprehension, and that struggling readers often have fluency problems. By third grade, most students have become fluent readers (Tompkins, 2001), but unfortunately some continue to read slowly, haltingly, and without expression.

Factors That Contribute to Fluency

Word Recognition. One aspect of becoming a fluent reader is accuracy in word recognition. So solid and effective decoding instruction is important, particularly in the lower grades. Struggling readers of all ages with poor word recognition need more intensive instruction and practice working with and analyzing words (Feldman, 2000), as described earlier in this chapter. Some will benefit from a more intensive intervention such as through one of the research-based programs designed to build these skills in Chapter Eleven.

Reading Volume. Lots of reading practice with appropriate leveled text (not too easy and not too hard) is also key to developing fluency. Providing students enough practice to gain fluency requires *choosing* to read independently both during and outside of school. Allington

(2006) points out that for this to take place we need to ensure students have access to books and reading material of interest to them at their level.

Reading Rate. Children should be able to read about 110 words per minute (wpm) by the third grade (Wolf, 2006a). Allington (2006) also notes that reading rate is related to reading volume, because children with slower rates simply read fewer words than faster readers do in the same amount of time. He cites the following general range of adequate reading rates by grade level identified by Harris and Sipay (1990):

Grade 3: 115–140 wpm
Grade 4: 140–170 wpm
Grade 5: 170–195 wpm
Grade 6: 195–220 wpm
Grade 7: 215–245 wpm
Grade 8: 235–270 wpm

Prosody. To increase fluency, we need to provide modeling and practice reading so that it sounds like talking: reading in phrases or clusters of words (not word by word) and with appropriate melody, intonation, and expression. This is referred to as "prosody."

Strategies to Build Fluency

Research shows that fluency can be developed through a variety of techniques, particularly through repeated and monitored oral reading, with students rereading passages as they receive guidance and feedback. Armbruster, Lehr, and Osborn (2001) say that for fluency practice, the text used should be at the students' independent reading level (can be read with 95 percent accuracy or misreading only about one of every twenty words). Others recommend between 90 and 95 percent accuracy level as appropriate for fluency practice, using text that is of student interest. Following are strategies and techniques suggested in the literature to be appropriate and helpful for building reading fluency (Allington, 2006: Armbruster, Lehr, & Osborn, 2001; Feldman, 2000; Tompkins, 2001; Rief & Heimburge, 2006).

Student-Adult Reading. The student reads one on one with an adult. The adult reads first, providing a model of fluent reading. The student rereads the same passage with adult feedback and coaching as needed until the reading is fluent.

Choral Reading. Students read in unison with a fluent adult reader. This is best done in upper elementary and middle school classrooms by projecting text on the screen (via an overhead projector or document camera) or reading together from individual copies of a text. Generally the teacher models and reads the text with fluency first, and then the students join in for the choral reading, with everyone reading the text in unison a few times. *Echo reading* is a variation: the teacher reads a line or short amount of text and then the students reread (echo read) the same in unison. Poetry and song lyrics work very well for fluency practice in this format.

Partner Reading. This technique can be done in two ways. In the first variation, a stronger reader and a less fluent reader are paired. The stronger reader reads the page or passage aloud first while the partner follows along. Then the less fluent reader rereads the same passage, while the stronger partner provides coaching and assistance. In the second variation, partners at the same reading level are paired to reread a passage or story that they are familiar with already: for example, orally rereading text (chorally) after having read a piece in a guided reading group.

Tape-Assisted Reading. The student reads along with a book on tape or digital recording read by a fluent reader. After hearing the book read, the student reads aloud along with the recording. This is practiced until the student can read the text independently.

Practicing to Perform. Readers' theater, puppet shows, and plays offer wonderful and motivating opportunities for students to practice fluency by rehearsing their parts in preparation to perform for an audience.

Cross-Age Tutoring, or Buddy Reading. Upper-grade students often have lower-grade reading buddies. Practicing reading a book several times provides good fluency practice in preparation for reading a selected book to a lower-grade buddy.

Predetermined Standard or Goal. Students practice reading and rereading to reach a goal or standard (for example, number of words read with accuracy in a one-minute read of a passage). The reader charts his or her progress. Students are motivated to time and graph themselves as they strive to reach a speed, rate, or accuracy goal.

Software. Technology such as talking software is another means of practicing fluency by reading aloud along with the digitized text, provided the reading rate and prosody from the computer sounds fluent.

Fluency Resources. Excellent resources are available for building fluency skills that incorporate some of the recommended techniques above. See Reader's Theater for Fluency and Comprehension, by Benchmark (www.benchmarkeducation.com); The Fluency Formula™ Program, by Scholastic (www.scholastic.com); Quick Reads, by E. F. Hiebert, published by Modern Curriculum Press (www.quickreads.org); Read Naturally, by Ihnot & Ihnot (www.readnaturally.com); Reading Assistant: The Fluency Solution, by Soliloquy (www.soliloquylearning.com); and Insights Reading Fluency,® by Charlesbridge (www.charlesbridge-fluency.com).

INTERVENTIONS

Students who have word-level reading and writing weaknesses and are significantly below grade level in their knowledge of how words work need much more intensive instruction and practice to build their skills. Children with these difficulties require more time and instruction than is typically provided for word study, particularly at the upper elementary and middle school levels. We need to increase the systematic, multisensory instruction and guided practice these struggling students need to accelerate their reading and writing progress and provide research-based interventions. See Chapter Eleven for information on intervention programs with proven efficacy and results in building these literacy skills.

Activity 6.1

A STUDY IN HOMOPHONES

Student's Name ______________ Due Date ______________

Words that sound the same but have different meanings are called *homophones* (also called *homonyms*). The name comes from the Ancient Greek words *homos* (same) and *phone* (sound).

> Dear (Deer) students,
> During the course (coarse) of the week (weak), you (ewe) are to (too) go on a search in (inn) your life for (fore) other homophones that exist in (inn) the English language. Read (reed) through (threw) your books with a careful eye (I). You may work in (inn) pairs (pears) or alone. Be (bee) sure to (two) do (due) all (awl) the lesson (lessen) activities. Don't wait (weight) until the last minute because you (yew) might (mite) get into a jam (jamb). You (yew) know (no) that it is not (knot) a good idea to moan (mown) and groan (grown). Don't pull your hair (hare) out or sit and be (bee) bored (board). You do (due) not (knot) want it to (two) be (bee) overdue (overdo). Have a great (grate) time doing this study.

1. With a partner, brainstorm as many homophones as you can in five minutes. Write them in your Word Study notebook.
2. While you are independently reading, skim your books for homophones. You will need to keep a list of them in your *Word Study notebook*. Try to locate at least twenty-five different words. Jot down the name of the book you are looking through and the page number you find them on. Do not repeat words. You will be astounded at how many words are homophones.
3. Create a minimum of two homophone riddles similar to the ones found in *Eight Ate: A Feast of Homonym Riddles* (1982) by Marvin Terban. Here are some examples:

   Q: What do you call the totally uninterested directors of a company?
   A: A bored board.
   Q: If four couples went to a restaurant, how many people dined?
   A: Eight ate.

   Write the riddle and draw a picture to illustrate it on a piece of paper or a three-by-five-inch index card (on the plain side).
4. Using the list of homophones that you were given, select ten words that you are not familiar with, such as bizarre/bazaar, foul/fowl, capital/capitol, weigh/whey, and carat/caret, and use the dictionary to find out their meaning. Write down what they mean. Circle the words that you use on your homophone list.

Activity 6.1

A STUDY IN HOMOPHONES (*Continued*)

5. Select any ten homophone pairs from *your* list or from the homonym sheet. Put the words on index cards of the same color. Write a definition on the opposite side. Be neat. With the definition side up, play Concentration with a partner. When you find a pair, use the words in sentences to show their meaning.
6. Read the Jack Prelutsky poem entitled "If" from the book *A Pizza the Size of the Sun* (Prelutsky, 1996). Try to think about why he might have written this poem and what his message is. Turn and talk with your partner about the poem and how it fits into this homophone word study.
7. Create a story similar to the one written at the top of the first page. Make it at least twenty-five to fifty words in length. Use the correct spelling of the homophone and underline the word in the story. When yours is complete, we will display it on the overhead and try to figure out the matching word in the pair and what it means.
8. Be sure that you study the meanings of the following words that have been misused most often by upper grade/middle school students. You will be expected to know how to spell and use each of these words correctly. Write each of these in sentences that show you know the meaning. You may need to use a dictionary or other resource.

Their, there, they're	Here, hear	Steel, steal	Through, threw
Too, to, two	Know, no	Waste, waist	Piece, peace
Which, witch	Meet, meat	Whose, who's	Whole, hole
Desert, dessert	Right, write	Where, wear	Break, brake

9. Create a word search or crossword puzzle using any of the words you worked with this week. Use graph paper or create one on your computer. (*Optional.*)
10. Cross off all of the words you worked with this week from your homophone list. If you worked with words that aren't on the list, add them.
11. Write a summary statement in your Word Study notebook about your homophone learning. How will you be more focused on these words now that you have concentrated on them for an entire week?

Activity 6.2

VOCABULARY DETECTIVE WORK

Do you need to understand the meaning of a word? Is it important to understand what you are reading?

Write the Unknown Word:

Write Synonyms:	Write Definition:	Write Examples:

Detective Time!	Guesses:
Title:____________________ Author:____________ Write down the sentence with the unknown word. Read the sentence. Record guesses for the word meaning in the next box.	

Source: N. Fetzer. (2006). *Reading Connections.* Murrieta, CA: Nancy Fetzer's Literacy Connections. www.nancyfetzer.com. Used with permission.

— *Chapter 7* —

MAKING ORAL LANGUAGE A PRIORITY

At a recent discussion among teachers about preparation for back-to-school night, the first meeting of the year with parents to explain the instructional program for each classroom, the level of apprehension in several of the teachers' voices about having to stand up in front of a classroom full of parents was amazing. One teacher said, "I'm just fine in front of the kids, but the fact that these are adults makes my stomach nauseated!" Another teacher said, "I can interact with the parents on a one-to-one basis every day, but when they all get together and they're all looking at me, I get so nervous I just want to get it over with." Several teachers confessed to having the same feelings and said that they learned to compensate for their discomfort by playing a video of their class in progress during the day or showing a picture presentation or by taking lots of pictures to put on the document camera—anything to take the attention off of them. If our teachers are talking about these fears, think of our students, who are asked each day to speak in front of their classmates. They too must experience fear when speaking in their daily classroom activities.

Fear of speaking in public (glossophobia) is documented as the number-one fear in America. According to Richmond and McCroskey (1995a), 95 percent of the population reports some degree of anxiety about communicating with a person or in groups. The good news is that although some nervousness is normal, proper preparation and rehearsal can help reduce the fear by 75 percent (Laskowski, 1996). In the twenty-first century, good verbal communication is highly valued. Silence is no longer golden and children *should* be *seen* and *heard,* contrary to the beliefs of past generations. Teachers must make sure that all children have multiple opportunities to communicate to one another (both speaking and listening) throughout the day in a variety of ways and with a number of purposes. These opportunities should include talking and listening using social and academic and formal and informal language—with peers and adults and in one-on-one, small-group, and whole-group settings.

SPEAKING AND LISTENING: NATURAL SKILLS?

As you listen to young children, there seems to be no end to the amount of social conversation they use each day. Talk *seems* to be a natural process. But as they mature into the upper grades and middle school years, although they still like to talk socially outside the classroom, some become very hesitant to speak in front of their peers in academic settings. While we must respect the child's personality, cultural background, and learning style, we must also strive to actively engage all students in the oral language process. Of course, the trust that a teacher nurtures within the classroom from the first day of school is what makes or breaks the oral language community. Respect for each other's thoughts and ways of doing things is a major part of a teacher's responsibility in extending the flow of communication that occurs in his or her classroom.

So it seems that listening and speaking are *learned* skills and may not be as natural as we once thought them to be. "Students must study and practice communication in order to achieve competence: it does not come naturally" (National Communication Association, 2007).

Communication Skills as Part of the Core Curriculum

The language arts domains of reading, writing, listening, and speaking must be taught in conjunction with each other, not independently. Although specific skills can be taught in each of the domains, it makes better sense for children to experience communication threaded through the day within a rich and engaging core curriculum. For instance, students need to move back and forth within a speaking mode and a listening mode during math conversations and explanations, during reading and writing one-on-one conferences, and during science presentations and experiments. Reading, writing, listening, and speaking are skills that improve with study and practice. Through steady practice, children learn to reduce their anxiety and to increase their skills in speaking and listening.

In the National Communication Association (NCA)'s *Speaking, Listening, and Media Literacy Standards for K Through 12 Education* (2007), Vangelisti and Daly were quoted in 1989 saying, "Nearly 20 percent of the nation's young people cannot accomplish any of the simplest communication tasks, including relaying specific information, giving instructions, recounting details, defending personal opinions, and developing a persuasive argument; 63 percent cannot give clear oral directions." If this trend still holds true today, teachers indeed have their work cut out for them.

While many states have written standards for listening and speaking, the National Communication Association (NCA), the largest international association of communication scholars and teachers, also has established standards for grades K–12. Besides listening and speaking standards, they have pointed out the relationship between visual and media literacy and language development. These twenty standards include the fundamentals of effective communication and what competent speakers, listeners, and media-literate communicators demonstrate. These can be viewed at http://www.natcom.org/Instruction/ceri/Index.html#K-12%20FILES.

The Whole Group: A Scary Place

Often students enter the classroom and are asked to say something about themselves on the first day of school. This can be disconcerting for reluctant or challenged speakers. An opening get-acquainted icebreaker activity can run something like this: first students write down responses on an activity sheet with spaces for *favorite music group, favorite movie, favorite book, favorite place to travel, favorite pet,* and so on to introduce themselves. Then the teacher asks them to choose one or two ideas that they would like to share with the whole group. A ball of yarn is held, beginning with the teacher, who tells a few things about him- or herself and then it is gently thrown to another student who tells something about him- or herself. This continues until all students have introduced themselves in some way. Each student holds the yarn in place until everyone is finished and it crisscrosses the group becoming somewhat tangled. As in the classroom, everyone is interconnected and what one person does affects everyone else. All the lives, like the yarn, touch others in some ways, so everyone needs to trust and respect each other. This allows everyone to feel comfortable taking risks in the learning environment because it is a safe place to talk and share ideas.

The Magnificent Seven

In many classes, there are six to seven students who tend to control conversations. They have their hands up ready to answer questions, to expound on thinking about literature, social studies, and science, to read their writing aloud, to go first presenting their science experiment or oral language presentation. They are not hesitant to talk about any subject. They are sometimes referred to as the Magnificent Seven. Most often they are the leaders in the class who happen to be comfortable with conversing. Sometimes, though, they are students who just like to hear themselves talk and who really do not have the correct responses or those that are just impulsive talkers.

Start Small, with Opportunities for Students to Speak

Every child needs the opportunity to speak—to share ideas and thoughts—with others. With the exception of the Magnificent Seven, upper-grade and middle school students seem to become progressively less interested in telling what they know. They do not want to appear to be too knowledgeable or too smart; they want to blend in. Teachers need to pull in students who are not participating in conversations through a variety of approaches.

The least intimidating way to get everyone to talk is to have children discuss the problems or questions provided to them with partners. Students form partnerships early in the year when the teacher asks them to buddy up with the person next to them at their desks or on the floor. Triads sometimes have to be formed. After reading a story, presenting a math problem, or asking students to read their writing aloud, the teacher asks students to *turn and talk* or *turn and share* with their partner(s). Most students do not have difficulty with this strategy, although some prefer not to talk or share with anyone. Careful seating placement or one-on-one conferring with these especially hesitant students might encourage oral involvement.

To ensure that each child is encouraged to speak, teachers may try one of the following methods:

Use seating chart tally marks. Add a tally mark on the seating chart to show child responses. When teachers know who is doing the active speaking and who is not, they can easily adjust their instructional practices.

Use a deck of card or tongue depressors. Write each student's name on a playing card, an index card, or a popsicle stick or tongue depressor. Randomly draw one card at a time to ensure that every child participates.

Set patterns. Establish a set pattern of asking for responses by, for instance, calling on Tables 1, 2, and 3, then proceeding clockwise around each table to chairs A, B, C, and D, so that no student is left out.

Ask for a ticket out. Have students respond with answers to your questions as they are leaving the room. This technique is referred to as their *ticket out* the door. You may include questions or ideas such as "Name the three states of matter." "Tell me one describing word." "Tell me one thing you learned today about the Revolutionary War." "Name one preposition." This is not only a way to spur each child to respond but also an assessment tool.

STRATEGIES FOR PRACTICING ORAL LANGUAGE

Myriad oral language experiences will enable students to hone their communication skills and prepare for their future education and their personal and professional lives.

Quick Talks

A *quick-talk* warm-up first thing in the morning gets everyone's brain rolling. In this partner exercise, each child is asked to speak without stopping for fifteen, thirty, or forty-five seconds about something he or she did yesterday, over the weekend, or on a holiday. Either the teacher or a verbally comfortable student models this exercise first. Students must continue actively talking for the full amount of time. This technique can be used before a writing period to get the brain warmed up and as a springboard for a writing idea. Note that most students will use one long run-on sentence connected, of course, with "and." This habit sets the groundwork for a future lesson on run-on sentences and sentence fragments during a language period.

Another idea is to have a quick talk where the child cannot use the word "and" for the entire time. Doing this is much more difficult and slows the talk down considerably. For another variation, students can be asked to speak for the entire time without using "uh" or "um."

Content material can be added to this exercise. After reading a section in the science textbook, for example, the teacher might ask students to talk for a minute about magnets, hurricanes, or the solar system. In social studies, students may be asked to talk for one to two minutes about the pyramids or the Civil War. In addition to providing a nonintimidating opportunity to share with others, it becomes an assessment tool. Short, informal book talks can also be handled this way.

Each verbal adventure is difficult at first, but children build up their skill quickly. Challenged speakers find these exercises enjoyable and not too risky.

Prompts for Talking with Partners or in Small Groups

With partners or in triads, students explore open-ended, thought-provoking questions or prompts that the teacher writes on the board, usually with more than one position that can be taken. Discussion can be sparked with *The Kids' Book of Questions* (Stock, 2004). The book is set up with 268 questions that are easy for students to respond to. Following are two examples:

#48. What things do you think kids should be punished for, and how should it be done? Is there an age when people are too old to be punished for the mistakes they make? If so, what age and why?

#197. If you could e-mail any famous person and be sure they'd read and answer your note, whom would you write to and what would you say?

One-on-One Conferencing

In the upper-grade and middle school classrooms, class size often exceeds thirty to thirty-five students. It is difficult to find time to listen attentively to each child in a one-on-one conference, but the benefits of these exchanges are abundant. Whether it is during reading, writing, or the content areas, a teacher-student conference is where we learn the most about each child's thinking and learning. Looking over problems missed on a math test with a child gives us great insight into a child's thinking and how he or she derived the answer: this individual information cannot be attained in the whole classroom situation.

Accountable Talk

Partner and whole-group discussions are fostered in the Balanced Literacy Workshop. High levels of engagement in creative and critical thinking among learners involve both speaking and listening. Accountable talk involves staying on topic, using accurate information, and thinking deeply about what is being discussed (Resnick, 1995).

Accountable talk develops over time in a safe environment. Children are released from teacher interference and questioning and are able to have meaningful conversation on their own. Students learn through teacher and peer modeling that they are capable of asking their own questions and guiding their own conversations. It is essential that students think the books that they are asked to talk about are important and worthy of deep conversation. Accountable talk may involve exchanges such as

I agree (or disagree) with _________ because . . .

I like what ____ said because . . .

I have a slightly different slant on your idea.

I can connect with what you are saying because . . .

I see what you are saying, but . . .

My thoughts are very similar to what you are saying, but my idea is a little bit different . . .

At the beginning of accountable talk instruction and practice, students sound very stilted in their delivery, but as the year progresses they begin to transfer the modeled language into their own ways.

Listening carefully to each other, extending the thinking that has been heard, creating new thoughts out of the ideas that have been previously stated, asking for clarification of ideas, politely questioning the speaker, and agreeing and disagreeing push learning forward and provide a natural, respectful discussion. This level requires extensive teacher modeling, management, time, and patience to develop.

Book Talks and Book Clubs

A book talk is short, concise, and often informal. All students should have opportunities to participate in this experience as often as three or four times a week. After independent reading, students might turn and talk with a partner about what they read, focusing on the characters, setting, plot, or other teacher-modeled strategies. Orally apprehensive students can be paired up with a stronger orator who will take the lead and model the talk. Sometimes the teacher may want to pair up with the reluctant speaker, first modeling the book talk with a book he or she has read and then letting the child proceed.

Students may also be asked to speak about their books alone, with partners, or other small-group configurations. Book talks act as catalysts for motivating peers to read these spotlighted books.

In classes where many students are reluctant speakers, a teacher may use the wall-speaking strategy where students speak to the wall about their reading before they speak to a larger group. This allows for planning and organization *before* being asked to speak to others. This form of gathering ideas on one's own first provides a supportive environment where a child can think things through before being asked to share in front of peers. In wall speaking, children find a wall, cabinet, or window to softly speak to in a low voice for approximately two or three minutes. This technique may be used with a few children at a time or with all students at the same time. During this activity, the teacher should walk around and listen in on the conversations, making all students accountable.

Book Clubs also provide small peer-group opportunities for children to talk about the common books they have read. (See Chapter Ten for more on book clubs and literature circles.)

Commercials

Students are captivated by television commercials that use persuasive techniques and propaganda to grip their thinking by appealing to their visual and auditory senses. The commercial format can be used in many ways for oral language. A child may try to sell his or her classmates a book that has been read, a product that is already manufactured, or a new product that the child creates on his or her own. Book or product commercials should be kept to thirty-, forty-five-, or sixty-second time limits. See Activity 7.1, Cereal Box Book Report and Persuasive Commercial, at the end of this chapter.

Fishbowl for Peer Modeling

Use the fishbowl activity to model conversation. As you walk around listening, notice a smart or important conversation that is going on either in pairs, triads, or small-group discourse. Call out "fishbowl" to the rest of the class, and all the students will quickly form a circle around the group, listening intently to the conversation that is going on. Through listening and observing, others can see what should be going on and go back into their own groups, enhancing and extending their own thinking. Peer modeling is an excellent strategy to use to elevate the conversations in any classroom.

Talking Before, During *and* After *Writing*

Many students have difficulty thinking of ideas to write during Writing Workshop. The practice of talking *before* writing is essential for good organization and planning. Brainstorming ideas in pairs, triads, or quads is a helpful strategy to get students off and running. Formulating what they will write about often gives reluctant writers the boost they need to be successful.

Students often need to clarify or read a part of their writing to see if it sounds right. Writing Workshop is not always quiet. When a child writes something, he or she often needs to bounce the phrase, paragraph, or word off of a peer. This helps students stop, regenerate themselves, and nudge forward to the next part of their writing.

Reading aloud to each other after a writing experience is also an essential part of the oral language process. When children are enthusiastic about what they have written, they want others to hear it. Reading a personal writing piece aloud enhances the specific skills required for good presentation in speaking.

Use of a Microphone in the Classroom

In today's large upper elementary and middle school classes, there is a lot of interest in the use of microphones and sound systems to assist the students in hearing their teachers over background noises such as heating and cooling systems, hard floors, and other outside interference. These electronic devices can enhance student listening and speaking in many ways. In some classrooms, writing celebrations involve the students reading their pieces with a microphone to a group of parents. Students love amplifying their voices and when given the opportunity to use a microphone, they readily speak out. A 1993 to 1995 study done in Florida found that children in amplified classrooms paid attention longer, completed their assignments in reading and math, and generally maintained an academic edge over their peers in nonamplified rooms (Rosenberg, 2000). It seems that allowing students to amplify their voices for reading, writing, and other academic presentations may also enhance their peers' listening skills.

Some teachers hold an open-mike session one day a month where children who are interested perform a song, musical instrument, poem, dance, reader's theater, or any type of creative performance. Children sign up ahead for a block of time. Usually it takes a few moments to get everybody warmed up for the event. Some students are confident of their abilities to stand in front of an audience and show their talent. As time passes and the students get to know each other better, the performances grow in numbers and sophistication. By the end of the year, everyone seems to have something to perform. Open mike can be extended to an evening performance, and parents may serve as both observers and performers. Although this experience can be intensified with a real microphone, it is not absolutely necessary.

Writer's, Author's, or Reader's Chair

Writers need opportunities to share their writing with their peers. This strategy allows students to read in front of a small audience, possibly seated on a special piece of furniture such as a rocking chair, teacher's chair, or a stool. Some teachers allow their students to wear a special hat or Harry Potter glasses or hold a stuffed animal. These props help the reluctant speaker to feel more comfortable. In this speaking exercise, intonation, speed of delivery, and emphasis of certain words can be assessed.

Storytelling or Acting Out a Scene

Storytelling is a very powerful form of communication and a gift that many teachers recognize as a helpful tool for developing good listening skills. It encourages visualization, the use of active imagination, story sense, and vocabulary. It is an excellent vehicle for motivating distractible, hard-to-reach students. Whaley (2002) notes that storytelling is also an excellent way to engage students in speaking in front of their peers because it fosters narrative discourse. After students complete a book, they are asked to retell the story through drama and storytelling. For instance, a group might read the book *Tales of Despereaux* (DiCamillo, 2003), create a script with narrators and key characters, and re-create the story by acting out the main parts. The rest of the class can feel the excitement as the performers provide this storytelling experience to the delight of their classmates. This retelling can be prepared and formal or impromptu and informal.

Hot Seat

In this role-playing situation, one child plays the main character from a book or a real figure from a biography or autobiography. Attempting to think as the character, the child fields a number of questions from the audience. The audience can write questions before the role-play begins or ask questions on the spot to get into the mind of the main character.

Tongue Twisters

Tongue twisters are phrases or sentences that are difficult to say because most of the words begin with the same letter or sound (alliteration). Some examples include *three free throws, a noisy noise annoys an oyster, friendly Frank flips fine flapjacks,* and *fat frogs flying past fast.* Tongue twisters are used to help develop speech skills, for speech therapy, to help get rid of an accent, and for those who just have fun with the challenge of saying them. They can be fun for oral language possibilities in any classroom. Some teachers place a daily or weekly tongue twister on the board for students to practice and learn. Later, students are asked to either say the twister in front of the class or say it privately to another adult or their peers.

Web sites provide an abundance of fun tongue twisters for your students to attempt. Here are two to get you started:

http://www.geocities.com/Athens/8136/tonguetwisters.html

http://www.indianchild.com/tongue_twisters.htm

Children should be encouraged to write and recite their own. They enjoy writing their own alliteration twisters with their names such as *Carolyn caught crispy caterpillars, Jamie jumped jubilantly in January, Madison made mud pies in Minnesota,* or *Jason jabbered joyously.* Several books written in alliterative format, such as *A Walk in the Rainforest* (Pratt, 1992) and *Animalia* (Base, 1993), also provide models for read-aloud or independent study.

Performing Poems

Poetry entices students to participate more enthusiastically. The poems of Shel Silverstein and Jack Prelutsky work wonderfully for early oral language experiences. Children who have inhibitions about oral presentation tend to lose them fairly quickly when humorous poetry is used. Poems such as "The Turkey Shot Out of the Oven" (1984), "Homework" (1984), and "Suzanna Socked Me" (1984) by Jack Prelutsky and "Messy Room" by Shel Silverstein (1991) are examples of poetry that students relate to and feel at ease presenting.

Through these two poets, children learn that oral language encounters can be fun. Each child receives a copy of a poem that he or she must memorize and recite in front of the class. The teacher can be selective in giving students who have difficulty shorter poems to memorize and present. The children can be encouraged to dress up as a character in the poem or bring a visual aid to enhance the recitation. Multiple periods should be given for the children to practice with another peer or at the wall. For wall reading, like wall speaking, the children stand alone and read in a soft voice to the wall, a window, a cabinet, or a bulletin board. All of the students in the class can read at the same time, providing a hum as children check their fluency, intonation, speed, and personal voice. Children learn quickly that practice improves the presentation. The outcome is a videotaped student presentation that serves as an assessment tool for the students themselves and their peers. After looking at all the presentations, students are able to evaluate their own presentations effectively and honestly by asking themselves, "How does my presentation compare with those of the my peers?" Three other students plus the teacher evaluate each classmate's presentation.

Some teachers have regular poetry parties throughout the year to spotlight their students' oral language skills. The more practice the students get, the more confident they become. Each student is responsible for sharing a poem of his or her choice. Memorization of the poem is optional, but strongly encouraged. In Michele's third-grade classroom, parents also take part in this poetry party. Each parent or family member also presents a poem, and some families present a poem together in choral verse. Other family members create their own poems and read them. Some parents need help selecting a poem, so Michele offers a list of poems for parents to choose from. If weather permits, these poetry parties are held outside on blankets or carpet squares and refreshments are served.

Some students prefer to read more serious selections by famous poets such as Edgar Allan Poe, Alfred Tennyson, Henry Wadsworth Longfellow, or Robert Louis Stevenson. One or two book baskets filled with all kinds of poetry geared to a class's cultural backgrounds, gender preferences, and personal interests encourages poetry reading and writing.

Poetry experiences in fiction and nonfiction should be provided throughout the year, not just for a few weeks during an isolated unit of study. During the Balanced Literacy Workshop, some teachers provide weekly exposure to a poetry center where students can read, recite, perform, memorize, dramatize, tape and listen to their reading, and write poetry on their own.

When the classroom is richly supplied with a large variety of poetry books for the students to use and enjoy and the teacher gives instruction in basic poetry, students readily use poetry to express themselves.

Guidelines for Performing a Poem

Students need to have good teacher and peer modeling for performing their own poems aloud. First, students must be aware of who their audience is. The way a poem is prepared for peers is uniquely different from how it is performed for adults. Next, students should look through a variety of books and anthologies or from their own personally written poems to find a poem that interests them. Poems with lots of action are easiest to perform. If one poem is not long enough for the presentation time allotted, two poems should be chosen. After that, the poem should be read aloud many times to oneself, peers, or parents for practice. Upper-grade and middle school students should know not to overemphasize the beat, making the poem sound too primary and sing-songy. Finally, simple body gestures, humor, props, different voices for selected parts (ranging from soft to loud volume and from low to high pitch), artwork, sound effects, and music can be added for special enhancement.

Group Poetry

Performing poetry as a group or team is more fun than performing alone. The poem can be divided into individual parts and into sections where voices are combined in choral fashion in pairs, triads, quads, or the whole group. The mix of voices adds variety.

Paul Fleischman has contributed two books that are helpful in enticing children to read poetry aloud. His books *Joyful Noise* (1988) and *I Am Phoenix* (1985) are created for children to read together, sometimes simultaneously and sometimes with alternating voices. These books support reluctant speakers well, because students do not have to present the poem alone. The needs of second-language students are also met because the poems are short and concise and provide scaffolding.

Newscast Creation

Newscasting is another means to inspire oral language. The class should be encouraged to watch a newscast on a local news station for the week preceding the activity or, if that is not possible for most students, the teacher might record a newscast and let the students watch it during class time. The first fifteen minutes are the most crucial. Students should evaluate and note the responsibilities of the anchorperson. They should also notice how the news team works together to report the news. How do they dress? What does the background look like? How do they present the news? Is the newscast relaxed or more formal? The students then meet in news teams that the teacher has formed. Usually heterogeneous groupings of about five people work best. Together they decide on the responsibilities that each member of the group will have, such as

- Anchorpersons
- Weather reporter
- Traffic reporter
- "Staying Healthy" reporter
- Restaurant reviewer
- Sports reporter
- Troubleshooter for consumers
- School reporter

Teams will enjoy deciding on props and attire that the anchorpersons will wear. Weather reporters might want to use sticky notes on the map to show weather conditions in other parts of the country and the world.

The process will take about a week of class time and some at-home research and practice. Most newscasts last approximately five to ten minutes. Students enjoy creating their own name for their television station, with a logo and a slogan to represent it. They may discuss and evaluate their presentations after viewing the videotapes.

Interviews to Build Confidence in Speaking

Throughout the year, students should be given opportunities to interview another person. One option that always seems successful is interviewing the oldest member of one's family. Besides offering an avenue for bridging the generation gap, it also inspires students' compassion and sensitivity for older people. Students might also interview a World War II survivor, a person who served in another war or lived during these wars, or someone who has survived another circumstance, such as being lost in the mountains, being lost at sea, being in a car accident, or having a particular health issue like diabetes, knee surgery, or cancer.

Interviewing experiences take some advanced thinking and planning and can offer cross-generational discourse. Students need to understand that they do not want to waste their subject's time, so should prepare key questions before the interview. The Interview Planning Sheet in Activity 7.2 provides a framework for this preparation. They should try to think of meaningful, sensitive questions that bring out the best in the person they are interviewing and make the subject feel comfortable. Students should be reminded in advance to thank the person for the help after completing the interview. Students might conduct a talk-show scene, interviewing a famous person from history that they have read about such as Christopher Columbus or a living person who survived a historical event such as World War II or Desert Storm.

Oral Language with Puppetry

Most children like to get involved in puppet shows. Whether the puppets are created commercially or made by the children, oral language seems natural with a puppet in hand. Students who are hesitant to speak up in class can have a miraculous surge of confidence when they can hide behind a puppet or a puppet theater. It can be fun to create scripts during Writing Workshop and then use uncomplicated puppets to convey the words of the scripts for oral interpretation. Simple how-to books kept in a basket give directions on creating puppets from socks, tongue depressors, paper, felt, paper bags, paper plates, Styrofoam, drinking straws, and other materials. Students enjoy making their own puppets for book sharing, culmination activities for book clubs, and biographical figures in the present and in historical settings.

Reader's Theater for Literature and History Presentations

During reader's theater, students improve their reading fluency by performing a script from a poem, play, or piece of literature for performance. In its original form, the reader's voice is the important tool, conveying the meaning of the text. In a modified state, good readers learn their parts so well that the parts seem spoken instead of read. In reader's theater original form, costumes and other props are not used. Although not necessary, many confident readers like to add their own flair to the script by adding a simple prop or costume such as a hat, illustrations, and gestures, making the script more interesting and engaging for the audience. An engaged actor cannot help but add facial and other body gestures to make the character or narrator more believable.

Students can participate in reading, writing, and presenting reader's theater scripts by writing their own, using commercial scripts for both fiction and nonfiction pieces of literature and content, writing variations of pieces of literature that they have read in class, and by participating in a literacy station with previous scripts that have been written. (See the section on literacy stations in Chapter Three.)

Writing scripts for reader's theater presentations is one way to bring literature alive. Students read a piece of literature together and then divide the book into sections or more manageable parts. They select one small part or chapter to re-create and adapt the section into their own words. Character parts as well as narrator parts are written.

Writers must prepare well for their presentation by reading it multiple times orally until they are fluent, conveying the voice and dialect of the character and feeling comfortable with the part. Both individual and group practice solidify the presentation.

As an oral assessment tool, reader's theater presentations can help teachers learn a lot about their students. The student should make characters come alive, use expression while speaking, understand the character fully, show creativity, and add some of his own personal voice, use gestures in the correct places, slow down or speed up as needed, speak loud enough to be heard by the audience, look at the audience, practice enough to be a fluent speaker, show confidence in his or her delivery, and become familiar with the script for a good comfort level in the presentation.

Fun with Role Playing

In role playing, children imagine themselves as a historical or fictionalized character or in a different role such as a reporter or a senior citizen looking in on a situation. Acting out a scene is usually done impromptu and allows children a chance to show what they know through drama and creativity. Many opportunities for students to show what they know through acting can be offered during the week. Some students are more adept at using the dramatic form to show their understanding, while others must be nudged into it.

Both fiction and nonfiction role-playing situations can be provided. In Gary Paulsen's *Hatchet* (1987), role-playing situations can be set up using the scene when the pilot is talking to Brian about operating the airplane or when Brian is trying to converse with someone on the other end of his radio as the plane is flying out of control. Little practice time is given—the role is taken quickly and on the spot. Teachers can easily assess comprehension of a section of the book through this strategy.

Teaching Board Games to Peers

Another oral language experience that helps students become more adept at speaking clearly is that of presenting a game to their peers. The purpose is to give clear, concise directions that all students agree are the correct set of rules that will be accepted by all students. Students are broken up into groups of two to four and become experts in how to play a particular game. It is their responsibility to impart their expertise and explain how to play the game to their peers. (It is always a good idea to start learning a game in its most standard form, with no substitutions, variations, or new rules—just those in the printed directions.) Game days provide a more relaxed environment for children to interact orally with other students they might not normally converse with.

Demonstrating Science Experiments

After observing several science experiments modeled by the teacher, students are asked to choose a simple experiment to demonstrate a scientific principle. They can find experiments on the Internet, from a tub of science investigation books, or in the school or public library. They may perform the experiment with another student or alone. Science demonstration allows students who are sometimes hesitant to speak in front of others to shine. There's something about science experiments that brings out the best in children. See Activity 7.3, the Science Experiment Planning Sheet, at the end of this chapter.

FORMAL SPEECHES

Past oral experiences provide the foundation that fosters confidence in a child's presentation skills. As the year progresses, you may want to provide information and training about how to make more formal speeches. Upper-grade and middle school students should have the opportunity to present each of the three following basic types of speeches:

Inform: give information

Demonstrate: show how to do something

Persuade: present facts to change people's minds

Use the following guidelines to set expectations or create your own:

- Model each type of speech for your students. Let them know your standards.
- Give a specific time allotment, maybe one to two minutes at the beginning of the year and three to five minutes later on, as students become more relaxed.
- Encourage the use of visual aids to enhance the presentation.
- Make sure that students know the importance of preparation in the presentation process.
- Provide a planning sheet like the Speech Plan Sheet in Activity 7.4 at the end of this chapter for students to use to prepare a brief written plan to follow when delivering their speech.
- Allow students to glance at but not to read from notes.
- Provide opportunities for students to do wall reading or wall speaking, practice in front of a mirror, or practice with a peer.
- Provide parents and students with a rubric (a set of guidelines) outlining your expectations for the presentation.
- Provide a list of expected oral language experiences for the year to help students plan for future events.

In *Writer's Express* (1995), Dave Kemper, Patrick Sebranek, and Ruth Nathan lay out the following steps for preparing a formal speech. Careful consideration should be given to each step, especially in the planning stages.

Pick the topic carefully

Narrow your topic

Gather enough information

Prepare an exciting introduction

Write an outline

Write your speech

Practice your delivery

Present your speech

Just as in writing, good leads *hook* our listeners into presentations. Hooks can take various forms, whether a famous quote, an interesting question, a brief story, a striking statement, a reference to a recent incident or a personal story or experience, use of figurative language (such as simile, metaphor, personification, or hyperbole), a sound effect (onomatopoeia), or descriptive language.

Older students might benefit from monthly opportunities to be video or digitally recorded giving formal oral presentations. Video or digital recordings can help track the child's oral language development over the course of a year. See Activity 7.5, Monthly Oral Language Presentations, the end of this chapter, for types of speeches that might engage students, starting with the least difficult form, and Activity 7.6, Oral Language Presentation: A How-to Speech, for instructions that a student might follow to prepare one of the easiest forms of formal speech, the how-to. Always encourage students to choose topics of particular interest to them.

ACCOMMODATIONS FOR RELUCTANT SPEAKERS

Students who are reluctant to stand in front of an audience might prefer to give their presentation to the teacher individually. Sometimes teachers allow reluctant speakers to come in during recess or lunch to give their performance without other class members in the room. Other teachers allow them to choose two or three friends to be their audience. It is important to be cognizant of the fear that some students have in expressing themselves in front of a large group. Accommodations should be made to ensure that they feel comfortable speaking, but they must also be encouraged to take risks, develop their speaking abilities, and meet the standards each year.

ORAL LANGUAGE ASSESSMENT

Because of the complexity of oral language assessment, teachers should seek direction from their local state or district standards. Formal and informal assessments, along with anecdotal records, teacher observation, and active listening are among the main assessment tools. Every teacher needs to be an active observer and an active listener. Video cameras and tape recorders are other tools for keeping records of student performance. Teachers may keep a record with tally marks when a child responds or raises his or her hand to share an idea. Teachers must observe and take records on the fly as students participate in small-group and independent activities, making sure that everyone is actively involved.

Students should also be involved in the evaluation process, using a student or teacher rubric to evaluate their own and other students' presentations. See Activity 7.7 at the end of this chapter for a form that can be used for teacher and peer evaluations.

AN AFTER-SCHOOL SPEAKERS' CLUB OR DRAMA CLUB

In some schools, a teacher becomes the sponsor of a speakers' club or a drama club. Identifying students who would benefit from and enjoy a club setting to experiment with oral language activities will build confidence and poise in those individuals. Both of these clubs would be beneficial to the school and provide an enjoyable forum for communication. Inviting guest visitors to assist in the process will liven up the club. If you know a member of the Toastmasters Club or a drama club from the local high school, college, or university, you can possibly set up a partnership that should be advantageous to both the school and the organization. Tapping the many resources in the community will help build confidence and bring intrinsic rewards to both the participants and the volunteers, as well as adding a new dimension of knowledge and instruction.

Activity 7.1

CEREAL BOX BOOK REPORT AND PERSUASIVE COMMERCIAL

Student's Name ________________ Due Date __________

This month you will be responsible for persuading your classmates to read a new book—one that you just finished. You will create your own visual aid that will help with your persuasive oral presentation. You might want to use some of the propaganda techniques that we have talked about such as glittering generalities, bandwagon, transfer, descriptive and emotional words, repetition, humor, and testimonial. These will help you "sell" your book.

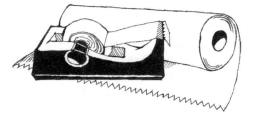

Here is what you need:

- A cereal box covered with butcher paper
- A light piece of construction paper to create the front cover of the book, which should include the title of the book, the author, the illustrator, and your name at the bottom.
- On the spine of the book, tell about the main character, including what he or she looks like and acts like. Give an example of the worst thing the character did and the best thing the character did. Tell how you related or connected to the character and how you might have done things differently.
- On the back of the book, write a one-paragraph summary of the book, including the major problem that the characters faced. Tell the solution to the problem.
- On the bottom panel of the book, tell how the story ends. Create a better ending of your own for the book.
- On the top panel of the book, tell about the funniest part or the saddest part or your favorite part and tell why you think so.

For your oral presentation:

- You will prepare a thirty-, forty-five- or sixty-second commercial to sell your book to others.
- You may use props to support the commercial.
- You may invite other students to assist you, but they will not be getting the grade—you will, so make sure your participants are responsible.
- You may videotape your commercial at home if you like.
- Come prepared on the day you are assigned.
- Have fun.

Activity 7.2

INTERVIEW PLANNING SHEET

Sometimes when you do research, you will want to get a more personal look at your subject. For instance, if you are trying to find out something about World War II, you might find out a lot by reading a book or an article in a magazine or online. For a more personal touch, you also might want to interview a person who lived during that period of time.

A good interview takes some thinking. Because you do not want to waste your subject's time, you should always be prepared *BEFORE* you start the interview.

Try to think of some meaningful questions that bring out the best in the person you are interviewing. These questions should make your subject feel comfortable. Make sure the questions are appropriate and show sensitivity. When you are finished with the interview, thank the person for helping you.

Interviewer's Name: ____________________ Date of interview: ____________________

Person being interviewed: ____________________ Place of interview: ____________________

How do you know this person? ____

QUESTION 1: ____

ANSWER: ____

____

QUESTION 2: ____

ANSWER: ____

____

QUESTION 3: ____

ANSWER: ____

____

QUESTION 4: ____

ANSWER: ____

____

QUESTION 5: ____

ANSWER: ____

____

Activity 7.3

SCIENCE EXPERIMENT PLANNING SHEET: ORAL PRESENTATION

Names of students: ______________________

Briefly describe your experiment: ______________________

____

____

What will your **question** be? ______________________

Hypotheses: Predict what you think will happen.

I think that ______________________

____

____

Procedure:

Step 1 ______________________

Step 2 ______________________

Step 3 ______________________

Step 4 ______________________

Step 5 ______________________

Scientific principle behind the experiment: ______________________

____

Materials needed: ______________________

____

Conclusions (Findings): ______________________

____

Activity 7.4

SPEECH PLAN SHEET

Presenter ________________________ Date _________________

Title of Presentation: _______________________________________

Materials and equipment I will need:

1. ____
2. ____
3. ____

Main points of my speech:

1. ____
2. ____
3. ____
4. ____
5. ____
6. ____

Answer the following questions:

1. I practiced my speech about ____________ times.
2. I practiced my speech with __________________________________.
3. I feel prepared for my speech. YES NO
4. I could do better by __________________________________.
5. I feel I have really done my best. YES NO
6. I deserve a (an) __________________________________ on this speech because

____

____

Activity 7.5

MONTHLY ORAL LANGUAGE PRESENTATIONS

MONTH	PRESENTATION TYPE
SEPTEMBER	Magazine or newspaper article (1 minute—alone)
OCTOBER	Hobby or special interest (1 to 2 minutes—alone)
NOVEMBER	Mystery person, place, or thing (3 to 5 minutes—alone or pairs)
DECEMBER	Teach a Game (5 to 10 minutes—cooperative groups)
JANUARY	Biography book report (2 to 3 minutes—alone)
FEBRUARY	Demonstration speech (how-to) (3 to 5 minutes—alone)
MARCH	Science experiment (3 to 5 minutes—alone or pairs)
APRIL	News team (5 to 10 minutes—team project)
MAY	Persuasive speech (3 to 5 minutes—partner debate or alone)
JUNE	Poetry (1 to 2 minutes—memorization)

Activity 7.6

ORAL LANGUAGE PRESENTATION: A HOW-TO SPEECH

For the month of ________________

What to Do:

You are to become an instructor. You will choose a subject that you are truly interested in. Remember the KIS rule (keep it simple). You will be expected to speak for one to three minutes. You may use an outline while you are presenting, but do not write the speech out word for word.

Here are a few examples to get you started:

1. How to French-braid hair
2. How to set up a two-man tent
3. How to apply makeup
4. How to draw a person's face
5. How to make an origami frog
6. How to throw a football correctly
7. How to draw a cartoon character
8. How to eat an Oreo cookie
9. How to make finger Jell-O
10. How to make basic knots with rope

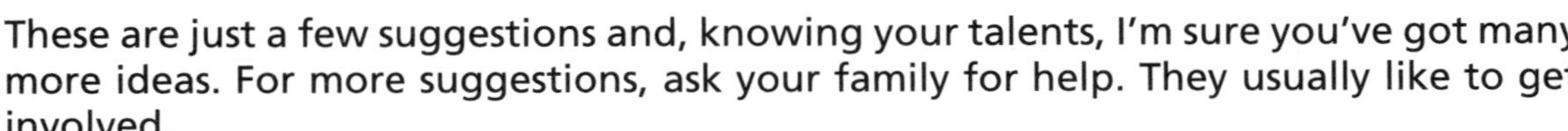

These are just a few suggestions and, knowing your talents, I'm sure you've got many more ideas. For more suggestions, ask your family for help. They usually like to get involved.

Requirements:

1. Hand in your plan sheet to have it approved by the teacher.
2. Gather your materials together and come prepared on your assigned day.
3. Practice your speech at home and come prepared.
4. Speak for one to three minutes. You will be timed. If you need extra time, you may request it *before* your presentation.
5. You must use a visual aid.
6. You may have an assistant, but everyone must do his or her own speech.

Activity 7.6

ORAL LANGUAGE PRESENTATION: A HOW-TO SPEECH (*Continued*)

Grading:

You will be evaluated on the following elements:

1. Your visual aid
2. Eye contact
3. Evident preparation
4. Speed of your delivery
5. Loudness of your voice
6. Enthusiasm
7. Content and information
8. Posture and poise

Note: There will be a sign-up sheet on the door with presentation dates and times. Sign up early. It's easier to get it over with and not have to worry.

Activity 7.7

ORAL LANGUAGE TEACHER EVALUATION

Presenter's name: ______________________________

Evaluator: ______________________________

Evaluate with a +, $\surd$, or — :

Time taken: ______________________________+______

Visual aid: ______________________________

Eye contact: ______________________________

Evident preparation: ______________________________

Speed of delivery: ______________________________

Loudness of voice: ______________________________

Enthusiasm: ______________________________

Content and information: ______________________________

Posture and poise: ______________________________

Comments: ______________________________

Note to the teacher: Before the presentations begin, the class should discuss how the presentations will be evaluated. A list of positive comments and constructive suggestions can be formulated by the students, so that negative comments do not become overwhelming.

The teacher should fill out one copy of this form for each speaker. Students may also use this form to evaluate peers. At least five classmates in addition to the teacher should evaluate each presenter. After the presentation, the evaluators' copies are given to the presenter.

— *Chapter 8* —

USING A THEMATIC APPROACH: SURVIVAL

Thematic teaching makes sense within the classroom setting because it enables students to see how major ideas and subject areas connect in meaningful ways to their own lives. The big idea transcends the limits of one subject and allows students to realize that all learning is connected. The focus in a thematic unit is seeing the big idea and all the related parts as one. Research shows that we learn best from whole to part. Meaningful learning activities generate greater understanding of the subject and allow students to search for creative ideas that overlap and interrelate.

ESTABLISHING A THEME

A thematic unit is a way of organizing time, resources, and materials around a central topic, allowing the teacher to integrate curriculum from all the content areas. Students participate in a variety of activities that involve reading, writing, speaking, listening, and thinking in all subjects and disciplines. A thematic unit may take a few weeks, a month, a semester, or even an entire year. A classroom, several classrooms, or even an entire school can teach around a central theme. Each teacher may choose a different approach to the theme, or students might create the thematic learning path.

Teachers sometimes mistake small topics for themes. Topics like bears, pumpkins, apples, or clowns do not have the substance to allow integrated subject areas throughout the curriculum and are very limited in terms of content and interconnections. With older children, it is wise to consider using broader areas of study. Some universal themes to consider are patterns, mystery, marvels, connections, frontiers, structures, discoveries, communities, families, exploration, or survival.

Getting Help from Other Teachers

On school days we are often confined within our own classroom walls. Pulling a theme together is always easier when you share the workload. Looking for materials, resources, technology opportunities, references, books of all reading levels, visuals, and core literature to support the theme is a monumental task. Share the work with colleagues through creative brainstorming sessions. Thematic teaching brings teachers together to share the wealth. Everyone *gives* something and everyone *gets* something.

Involving Parents

Parents can be part of the supportive process of a theme. Ask them to watch for educational programs that can enhance your unit and provide visuals, so that all students have access to the concepts being developed. The History Channel has many excellent programs that can support your theme, and the TV guide contains program schedules for recording. It is essential to obtain enough materials to bring the total theme experience to those students who do not have resources in their homes, and this approach is ideal for parents who cannot offer to help in the classroom.

Modifying to Meet the Needs of Students

After a theme is developed, it can be adjusted, modified, or extended to meet diverse classroom needs. Teachers can use school, district, and public libraries to develop a unit.

Most students have access to online information at home, but many need ample classroom time to locate materials. Students who are academically challenged will need teacher or peer assistance to locate level appropriate materials.

High-achieving students can conduct in-depth research using resources in the classroom, library, and at home. Accessing multiple resources stimulates higher-order thinking and challenges them to think beyond just the basic ideas.

Thematic teaching helps you focus on gathering materials that support the curriculum, whether you teach third grade, move up to fifth grade, or even to seventh grade. Identifying key concepts in the unit will help in developing and modifying it to reach any grade level. Consider these concepts when purchasing supplies for the unit.

Getting Started

The easiest way to set up a thematic unit is by looking through good pieces of literature that encourage shared, independent, and guided reading activities. Begin with whole-group instruction to core literature. For instance, if the theme is exploration, the class begins with Avi's (1990) book *The True Confessions of Charlotte Doyle,* which contains suspense, adventure, character change and development, an abundance of literary elements, and plenty of descriptive language. At the beginning of the year, use a directive approach to guide students through basic skills. Find a piece of grade-level literature that all students can read together. Students learn the process of literary analysis and delve into character, plot, setting, and literary elements together. This sets the stage for the rest of the year, before book clubs, book chats, and independent study can take place.

SURVIVAL AS A THEME

In this chapter, you will learn how to use the survival theme in your classroom setting. Within this theme, curriculum is interrelated so that learning becomes more meaningful.

Why Survival?

Present-day television programs such as *Survivor* and *Lost* have great appeal to our older children and their families. They have become a phenomenon, because they are based on people trying to survive the elements. We put ourselves in their places and think, "Oh, I could never do that" or "I would die before I ever ate that." We watch these programs but subconsciously believe that nothing like that could ever happen to us.

Upper-grade novels are abundant with clues, suggestions, and ideas for character survival. In fact, in almost every book, a character must use strategy in order to survive or succeed. Through books, children learn to cope with daily realities like unpleasant situations, unkind behaviors, bullying, loss, discomfort, divorce, and adaptation. During content lessons, students recognize how plants, animals, and people survive in different environments. For instance, different plants have developed certain characteristics to survive in the desert, the ocean, or the mountains. Many life forms have had to adapt in order to survive. As they read, students transfer these coping skills into their own lives.

Fitting Survival into the Curriculum

Thematic teaching shows students that literacy, content, and fine arts are all interrelated. Starting the unit with discussions about daily survival tactics helps students make relevant connections to their own lives. The theme of survival encompasses all areas of the curriculum. Activities and projects help students observe their surroundings and reflect on how they might react in unforeseeable situations.

Getting Started with Grade-Level Novels

Many novels deal with survival in the wilderness. Our favorites are *Hatchet* (1987) and *The River* (1991) by Gary Paulsen. (*Brian's Winter* [1996] can also be used.) In *Hatchet,* Brian is involved in a plane crash and spends fifty-four days in the Canadian wilderness, learning to survive with only the aid of a hatchet given to him by his mother and also learning to survive his parents' divorce. In the sequel to that story, *The River,* Brian is asked by a government survival school to return to the site of his first experience. They want to use his experience to help train others who might find themselves in similar situations. Both novels provide a number of opportunities to link research and personal involvement into the theme.

Hatchet is best introduced when read aloud by the teacher and also on audiotape or CD. Allowing the children to listen to the text in two different voices provides a change of pace. Children may also consult their own books to follow along, and plot development can be discussed as a class or in small groups. Charting helps students focus on challenging parts of the story.

The River also begins well as a read-aloud, but as the story progresses it works better as an independent reading assignment. Students mark their books with sticky notes to help them remember the plot. After small groups discuss the book each day, follow up with whole-group discussion and charting.

After the books are completed, students work at centers or independently to complete a survival activity. Following are a few possibilities, with curriculum categories noted in parentheses:

- Create a class newspaper about Brian Robeson's adventure in *Hatchet* and *The River*. (See Activity 8.1 at the end of this chapter.)
- Invite your school nurse or a doctor into the class to discuss the causes of heart attacks (health).
- List the warning signs of a heart attack (health).
- Locate where Brian's plane crashed and label the provinces of Canada (geography).
- Purchase a cow heart and dissect it to show students the structure of a heart (science).
- Find videos, CDs, or DVDs about hearts, such as *I Am Joe's Heart* (Wright, 1987) (health and science).
- Do simple exercises to show how the heart speeds up from resting state to active state (science).
- Brainstorm ways to protect your heart (science).
- Look at menus that show nutrition guides and plan a healthy heart meal (health).
- Obtain a model of the brain to show which areas are affected by a coma (science and health).
- Provide several books and videos that show the devastation that a tornado can cause (science).
- Have the students look for amazing survival stories in the newspaper and post the clippings on bulletin boards (language arts).
- Locate nature words, animals, and places that crop up in Paulsen's books, such as altimeter, turbulence, camouflage (word study).
- Look for other books that use divorce as one of their main themes (social science).
- Make a list of all the animals mentioned in the book and research some of them (science).

COMPARING BOOKS TO MOVIES

A Cry in the Wild (Griffiths, 1990) is a movie based on the story *Hatchet*. Students enjoy the movie as either a culmination of their reading at the end of the book or in segments as each part of the book is completed. The class may chart the similarities and differences between the movie and the book using a Venn diagram (two overlapping circles showing similarities and differences of two sets of information). There is an example of one in Chapter Five.

Children should be able to learn that movies and books have slight differences. Other opportunities to compare and contrast the two genres in pairings are *Because of Winn Dixie* (DiCamillo, 2000), *Holes* (Sacher, 1998), *The Chronicles of Narnia: The Lion, The Witch and The Wardrobe* (Lewis, 1950), *Charlie and the Chocolate Factory* (Dahl, 1964), *Harry Potter* series (Rowling), *A Series of Unfortunate Events* series (Snicket), *Tuck Everlasting* (Babbitt, 1975), *Charlotte's Web* (White, 1952), *Bridge to Terabithia* (Paterson, 1978), and *Matilda* (Dahl, 1988). When students see that movies are formatted to loosely parallel the books, great conversations follow as to why they are not exactly alike. The opportunity to compare and contrast with peers develops critical thinking and observation skills necessary for understanding the two genres of storytelling.

ISLAND SURVIVAL: A SAMPLE PLAN

The Cay (1969) and *Timothy of the Cay* (1993) by Theodore Taylor are also about survival. The language and historical background of *The Cay* requires a lot of teacher direction. After the students listen to the first part of the story, they are prepared to study the book independently, with small-group discussion for low-achieving students and daily whole-class discussions.

Timothy of the Cay is a much more complicated read because of its back-and-forth prequel-sequel format and should be entirely read aloud. Navigating through this unique format together helps students develop strategies to eventually do it on their own. A sample lesson plan to introduce a prequel-sequel unit follows.

SAMPLE LESSON PLAN: PREQUEL AND SEQUEL IN *TIMOTHY OF THE CAY*

Objective. The students will be able to distinguish between the unique writing styles for sequel and prequel used by Theodore Taylor in the story *Timothy of the Cay.* They will demonstrate understanding of both forms by predicting five events that might have taken place in the life of Timothy before he met Phillip, and five events that might take place with Phillip after his rescue. They will then extend their events into paragraph form, starting in class and completing at home.

Performance Standard (California)

5.3.1. The student responds to fiction using interpretive, critical, and evaluative processes. The student identifies and analyzes the characteristics of fiction as forms chosen by an author for a literary purpose.

5.6.1. The student writes works in specific genres that incorporate appropriate literary features.

5.6.2. The student produces a response to literature in which he or she demonstrates an understanding of literary work.

Room Setup

Cooperative groups in close proximity to place of instruction

Students

Thirty-three fifth-grade students heterogeneously grouped, including gifted and talented (GATE) students, resource students, and English-language learners (ELLs). Students will be in A and B pairings.

Connecting Link. Students complete reading two stories—*Hatchet* (1987) and *The River* (1991) by Gary Paulsen—and should understand what a sequel is. Most recently the students have read *The Cay* by Theodore Taylor.

Introductory Discussion: Access Prior Knowledge

- Discuss other books that have unusual writing styles—like *Walk Two Moons,* with several stories going on at the same time, by Sharon Creech (1994)—and *The Fighting Ground* (1984) by Avi*:* a twenty-four-hour period broken down into smaller segments of time.
- Establish purpose: Why is this important to know? This book is written in an unusual way that might be confusing to those who read it. So today for our shared reading experience, we're all going to take a look at this unique literary form.
- Give a brief background of Theodore Taylor and possible reasons for writing a prequel or a sequel.
- Elicit the definition of a *sequel* by discussing *Hatchet* and *The River.* What other books might have a sequel?
- Chart students' definitions of the word. Discuss how this is different from an *epilogue.* (This text feature has already been introduced from other books. Display the definition from previous lessons.)
- Elicit the definition of a *prequel* and chart the students' responses. Ask if the students know other books or movies that have a prequel. Discuss the *Star Wars* and *Batman* series. Discuss how a prequel is different from a *prologue.* (Students should already know this word. Display the definition from previous lessons.)

Shared Reading Experience

- Display overhead of *USS Sedgewick* (sequel) (Taylor, 1993, p. 1). Read aloud as students follow, or they can read their own copies.
- Elicit responses:

  What do you notice about the date and the point of view?

  How is this different from a flashback?

  Highlight the words that tell you it is in first person.

- Display overhead of Looking for Work (prequel) (Taylor, 1993, p. 8). Students can read aloud as others follow or they can read silently. (Students will need individual copies of this page.)
- Elicit responses:

  What do you notice about the date and the point of view?

  How can you tell that this is a different writing form?

  Why do you think Theodore Taylor wrote this story in this way?

  Why do you think it might be confusing to read?

How is this different from the epilogue in *Hatchet?*

Highlight the words that tell you that it is in third person.

Guided Practice: Brainstorming Chart

- Ask: What might have happened to Timothy before he met Phillip? What did he do before he was stationed on the *Hato* in 1942? Think of his childhood, schooling, family, jobs, and experiences. Students turn and talk about their thinking.
- Ask: What might happen to Phillip in the future? Students turn and talk about their thinking.

Writing Workshop and At-Home Paragraph Completion

- Students return to their own seats and jot down notes about the two questions.
- They begin to write their paragraphs, which will be completed at home tonight.

Evaluation and Closure

- Students share their ideas with a partner and then as a class.
- Students discuss the difference between a prequel and a sequel.

Students will share their finished paragraphs the following day.

Supplementary Activities

To add interest, choose one of the following activities or another:

- Ask a person who is blind to visit the classroom to talk about his or her life as a blind person.
- Ask a visitor who has a Caribbean accent to read Timothy's parts in the book to give the authentic feel of the part.
- Ask someone who has lived in the Caribbean to talk with the class about the animals, plants, and weather of the region.
- Locate Curacao on a map and discuss its importance during World War II.
- Discuss U-boats.
- Discuss the process of oil refining.
- Discuss what a *cay* is.
- Research hurricanes.
- Do a simulation of being blind. Students work in pairs, one blindfolded and one as leader. They can walk around the school and experience what it is like to be blind.
- Research information about telegrams.

After students have read *Hatchet, The River, The Cay,* and *Timothy of the Cay,* they should be able to compare and contrast the two boys and the survival techniques they used to save their own lives. In Activity 8.2 at the end of this chapter, students can use the letter format to show their understanding of the main characters in these books. For more options, see Activity 8.3, Prejudice and Discrimination Based on *The Cay*; and Activity 8.4, The Perfect Island.

Using Fact Cards

One outstanding resource for this survival unit is the Wildlife Explorer® (available from IMP Publishing, at www.imp-usa.com or 800-444-9270). It contains over a thousand cards on such subjects as mammals, birds, reptiles, fish, insects, and spiders, which are perfect for challenged readers because they are well formatted, easy to understand, and illustrated. More advanced learners can use them as a starting point and pursue in-depth research methods later on.

Organizing a Survival Book Club

Together, students and teacher should gather copies of books they think would be appropriate for the unit, covering different aspects of survival through the main characters in different settings. After the books are selected and introduced to the class, students pick their first, second, and third choices for reading. The teacher decides which books are suitable for each group of readers. For more information on book clubs, see Chapter Ten.

The following books provide a variety of survival reading opportunities for older students:

The Black Pearl (O'Dell, 1977): survival on the ocean
Bridge to Terabithia (Paterson, 1978): survival in a new place and death
Bud, Not Buddy (Curtis, 1999): survival during the Depression
Call of the Wild (London, 1903/1963): survival in the Arctic
Esperanza Rising (Ryan, 2000): survival in a new country
The Great Gilly Hopkins (Paterson, 1978): emotional survival
Holes (Sacher, 1998): survival in the desert
Maniac McGee (Spinelli, 1990): emotional survival
My Side of the Mountain (George, 1959): survival in the mountains
Number the Stars (Lowry, 1989): survival during war
Sounder (Armstrong, 1969): survival because of prejudice
Surviving the Applewhites (Tolan, 2002): survival in a new family
Witch of Blackbird Pond (Speare, 1959): survival in Colonial America

KEEPING A RESPONSE JOURNAL

Students should routinely write entries into literature response journals. During this theme study, use a college blue book. The small size of these books helps reluctant readers and writers feel less intimidated than with a regular composition book that has lots of pages to fill. After completing the unit, students can revisit their responses and draw conclusions about survival. Blue books fit nicely into plastic sleeves that can be placed in a portfolio for students to keep.

Journals can be reviewed for assessment. Because journals contain individual reflections and thoughts, it is imperative that teachers read responses, check understanding, and offer clear, objective feedback.

INCORPORATING NONFICTION

Publishers now recognize the newfound interest in survival. *The Worst-Case Scenario Survival Handbook* (1999) and *The Worst-Case Survival Handbook: Holidays* (2002), both by Piven and Borgenicht, are among many updated survival books that fascinate students and teachers. They help to establish a foundation for survival.

During the month of December, teachers read aloud or share-read through *The Worst-Case Survival Handbook: Holidays,* which explains how to extinguish a burning turkey, how to treat mistletoe poisoning, how to make an emergency menorah, and how to fit into clothing that is too tight.

The *Worst-Case Scenario Handbook* has many appropriate lessons for students to connect to *The Cay* and *Hatchet,* such as how to escape from a bear, how to escape from a mountain lion, how to treat frostbite, how to survive when lost in the mountains, how to make a fire without matches, and how to avoid being struck by lightning.

USING AUDIOBOOKS AND COMPACT DISCS

Many books have audio counterparts that can enhance sharing these books with students. Reluctant readers can take them home to review the story before a writing assignment. Listening to a tape or CD for a second reading can be effective; it can be listened to as a family in the car on the way to school or on a trip. These media may also be set up at the listening center for all students to enjoy while they are involved in literacy activities. Some of the audio titles that can be used for this study on survival are *Hatchet; Bud, Not Buddy; Holes; Shiloh; Rascal; The Lion, the Witch and the Wardrobe; Call of the Wild; Walk Two Moons; Tales of Despereaux;* and *A Series of Unfortunate Events.*

In the World War II project, students read *Number the Stars* (Lowry, 1989) and, if time permits, *The Upstairs Room* (Reiss, 1973). With the information provided in these two books about the war and its effect on the people of Europe, the students begin to understand this period of history. Discussion is held in class about the fear people had of Adolph Hitler and the German soldiers, and what life was like living with this fear.

The World War II activities found at the end of this chapter offer twenty-three possibilities involving music, interviewing, writing, researching, drawing, reflecting, and observing. See Activities 8.5 and 8.6 in particular. Other books about war that fit nicely into this unit of study include *Journey to America* (1970) by Sonia Levitin, *The Devil's Arithmetic* (1990) by Jane Yolen, and *The Fighting Ground* (1984) by Avi.

TYING IN OTHER SUBJECT AREAS

The content areas can be integrated throughout the survival study through activities and projects such as Survival Math found in *How to Reach and Teach All Students in the Inclusive Classroom* (Rief & Heimburge, 2006).

At the end of this unit, choose one or more projects to enhance the theme study. For example, students might choose a news story from a newspaper or a magazine or interview someone who has survived an illness, injury, accident, or other exceptional life experience and write about it. (See Activity 8.7 at the end of this chapter.) Following are some other possible individual, group, or station activities to use, or you can design your own final project.

- Write a newspaper article about Brian (from *Hatchet*) or Phillip (from *The Cay*) being lost.
- Explain how to make a fire without a match.
- Invite a forest ranger or rescue official to speak to your classmates.
- Watch a movie at home where the main character has shifted to survival mode.
- Write a missing person's feature story for the newspaper. Include a hand-drawn picture of Brian or Phillip. Include the five parts of a newspaper story: who, what, where, when, and how.
- Take a portion of the book *Hatchet* or *The Cay* and write a reader's theater script. You might use any of the following passages: at the beginning when the pilot and Brain are talking, when Brian is talking with his mother, when Brian is talking to a controller after the pilot has had his heart attack, when Brian gets rescued, when Brian gets home, when Phillip first meets Timothy, when Phillip gets rescued, when Timothy's accent has to be translated in his conversation with Phillip, or when Phillip tries to tell his parents about Timothy for the first time.
- Find examples of animals tracks or scat. Make a chart to show to other classmates.
- Consult several survival books to research a survival topic.
- Learn more about latitude and longitude.
- Make a compass.
- Choose a worst-case scenario procedure and make a presentation to the class.
- Create a file folder entry using the Wildlife Fact File.
- Research one of the poisonous plants found in the wilderness. Give a report to your class and show a picture of it.
- Research a poisonous fish or sea creature that lives in the Caribbean area. Give a review of your learning to your peers and show a picture of it drawn by you or copied from a book.
- Write a postcard from Brian to his mother.
- Design a T-shirt that either of the boys should receive upon their rescue.
- Reread the epilogue at the end of the story. Search for other epilogues in new stories.
- Scan your book and make a list of all the animals that Brian encountered.
- Make a list of eight items you would want to have with you if you were Brian or Phillip. They must all fit on your body or be small enough to carry in your hands or arms. Compare your lists with several other students.
- Give some ideas of how you would protect yourself in the wilderness or in the Caribbean. Use the lessons you learned from the four books.
- Explain what you would do differently from Brian or Phillip if you were lost in an unfamiliar place.
- Research one of the following topics: mosquitoes, food drying, foolbirds, langosta, fresh water versus salt water, protective clothing, navigating by the stars or position of the sun, or the difference between tornados and hurricanes.
- Develop your own survival kit.

- Write a letter to Gary Paulsen or the relatives of Theodore Taylor telling them about your feelings about the book.
- Look at the book on knot tying. Practice a few knots and then teach someone else how to make them.
- Read the Kids Discover magazine *Shelter*. Read about the different kinds of shelter: shelter from the cold, shelter from the heat, houses on the move, and shelters on the move. Read about one of them and make a list of the important features of that particular shelter.
- Research more online about shelters and protecting yourself from the elements. Make a report on your findings. Add pictures and share it with your class.
- If you are in scouting, find out and share your knowledge about survival with your peers.

OTHER RESOURCES FOR A SURVIVAL THEME STUDY

There are several survival book series available that you may want to add to your collection, including Rory Storm's *Survival Guides* (Scholastic), dealing with the desert, the jungle, and islands; the *How Would You Survive in . . . ?* series; *Survival Series* by Duey and Bale, dealing with earthquakes, blizzards, fires, floods, hurricanes, and cave-ins.

Activity 8.1

A GROUP NEWSPAPER ABOUT BRIAN ROBESON'S ADVENTURE IN *HATCHET* AND *THE RIVER*

Student's Name ____________________ Due Date ____________

You have just finished *Hatchet* and *The River* by Gary Paulsen. Now it is time to show that you have comprehended what you have read by thinking like a journalist. This report will be in newspaper form. You will be working in groups of six writers and illustrators. Each of you will cover Brian's story by writing a particular type of article and covering the story thoroughly. You must cover all the stories, so some members of your group will have to write more than one article. Additional bonus activities are suggested for fast workers or for those who would like extra credit.

Instructions:

- Select a title for your newspaper. It should relate to Brian's story in some way.
- Assign the article(s) to be written by each member of your group.

Reporter 1. Write an article about Brian's disappearance. Make sure that you include the who, what, where, when, and why of the story. Include a headline such as "Boy Missing in Canadian Wilderness."

Reporter 2. Write a want ad from Brian's parents with a title such as "Help Needed in Finding Missing Boy" to help them find their son. Also include a picture of Brian as seen through your eyes.

Reporter 3. Tell how Brian changed over the course of the book physically as well as mentally. Write it as if you were Gary Paulsen, the author of the book. Title this article "Note from the Author."

Reporter 4. Write a letter from Brian to his parents explaining what is happening to him. Your headline should be something like "Letter from a Survivor."

Reporter 5. Write a book review explaining your likes and dislikes of this book. To whom would you recommend this book? Why? Create a headline entitled "Book Blurb."

Reporter 6. Pretend that Brian has written you a letter asking for your advice on how to survive in the wilderness. Based on what you have read, respond to him in our advice column. Tell how a person should act if he or she were lost in the wilderness. Write a headline for your article titled "Adventure Advice."

Activity 8.1

A GROUP NEWSPAPER ABOUT BRIAN ROBESON'S ADVENTURE IN *HATCHET* AND *THE RIVER* (*Continued*)

Reporter 7. Write a weather section that describes the kinds of weather conditions that a person in Brian's situation would have to watch out for. Make a headline called "Weather Wise."

Reporter 8. Make an advertisement for something needed or wanted by Brian during his experience. Put the headline "Want Ad" on it and draw an illustration to accompany it.

Reporter 9. Write a section called "Making Connections" where you discuss the ways that you and Brian are alike and compare him to different characters that you have read about this year.

Bonus Activities:

- Write an article titled "Animal Watch." In the article write information about one of the animals found in *Hatchet* or *The River,* such as porcupines, bears, or turtles.
- Write a column about heart attacks based on the information in the book and any other research information you find. The headline should read "Health Alert."
- Choose an issue related to these books and take a position on it. Write a "Letter to the Editor" describing how you feel about the issue. Think carefully and honestly about what you want to say. Write an editorial about one of the following concerns that Brian had:

  Why people should not fly in small planes with only one pilot

  Why parents should always fly with their children

  Why people should not get a divorce

  Why people should not eat food that is high in cholesterol

  Why every child should be required to learn how to use a hatchet when he or she reach twelve years old

  Why every child should have survival training before his or her twelfth birthday

- In this book the major conflict is between man and nature. Explain in an article titled "Man Versus Nature" what this means and how Brian fought against nature to survive.

Activity 8.2

A LETTER FROM CHARACTER TO CHARACTER

Phillip Enright (*The Cay*) and Brian Robeson (*Hatchet*)

You have just completed two books with male characters who survived in environments that they were not accustomed to. Compare and contrast the two boys and the survival techniques they used to save their lives. Think of their ages, the time, the setting, their problems, and the circumstances that got them into the survival mode. Plan out your thoughts in an organized way. Then you will write a letter from Phillip Enright to Brian Robeson. Even though they lived almost fifty years apart, they would certainly have a lot to say to each other about their circumstances. You may write from the voice of either boy. Remember this is in first person, so you will be using *I, my,* and *me.*

Use this organizer to help you think through both boys' experiences.

Circumstance	Phillip Enright	Brian Robeson
Setting		
Length of time lost		
Age and family		
Circumstances of disaster		
Problems faced		
Other people involved		
Thoughts, concerns, and emotions		
Rescue		
Survival techniques used		

Activity 8.3

PREJUDICE AND DISCRIMINATION BASED ON *THE CAY*

Student's Name ________________ Due Date ____________

You have just finished a book by Theodore Taylor entitled *The Cay.* Think about Phillip Enright and how he felt about and treated Timothy before he really got to know him. Reflect on our discussions in class over the year on prejudice. Synthesize the information that you have learned from other sources, including your social studies textbook and novels you have read. Then develop an essay that explains your own feelings and ideas.

Paragraph 1: The world is filled with prejudice. Explain what you think prejudice is and give at least two examples from today's world.

Paragraph 2: Phillip Enright was prejudiced in the beginning of the book. Explain why you think he was prejudiced against Timothy and give at least two examples of how you know he was prejudiced against Timothy. Cite evidence from the book.

Paragraph 3: Explain how Phillip's feelings toward Timothy changed in *The Cay.* Give at least three examples that prove that Phillip's opinions of black people had changed, specifically his opinions of Timothy. Tell why you think Phillip was able to be more accepting at the end of the book.

Paragraph 4: Think of other examples of prejudice and discrimination that you have read about this year. For example, revisit the characters in *Walk Two Moons, The True Confessions of Charlotte Doyle, Number the Stars,* another in-class novel, or one of your independent reading books. Try to find similarities and differences between the ways that the characters dealt with prejudice and discrimination. Think of how they learned these ideas and how they developed their feelings and behaviors. See if you can make any connections.

- Make sure you include some type of graphic organizer with your rough draft to show that your thoughts were organized before you got started.
- Read your rough draft to someone at home and also to a fellow classmate. Ask them both for a brief oral critique.
- People I read my essay to: ________________________

Activity 8.4

THE PERFECT ISLAND

Student's Name ___________________ Due Date___________________

You have just completed *The Cay* by Theodore Taylor. Phillip and Timothy had no choice as to which island they would be forced to live on. You, on the other hand, will have a choice. In the following assignment you will be asked to create a perfect island: one that you could survive on very easily. Be creative and have fun.

All paragraphs will be written on three-by-five-inch index cards, and illustrations such as the flag and the island itself will be drawn on the blank side of the card. Make sure that each of your cards has a topic sentence. Let the questions guide your thinking. Don't just answer the questions. Incorporate the question in your answer.

You may type or print your cards for easy readability.

Paragraph 1: What is the name of your island? Why did you give it that name? Who will be allowed to live there? Make a name card separate from your paragraph. This will be the heading of your project.

Paragraph 2: Since you are the leader of your island, describe the kind of person that you are. What qualities will make you a good leader?

Paragraph 3: What does your island look like? Describe it in words. Use descriptive imagery like the mentor-authors that you have read this year use.

Illustration 1: Draw a picture of your island. Use colors, and label places clearly.

Paragraph 4: What rules do you have on your island? How will the rules be enforced? Will there be rewards and punishments for those who do and do not follow the rules?

Paragraph 5: Describe your flag or banner. What do the symbols mean? What do the colors mean?

Illustration 2: Draw a picture of your flag or banner.

Paragraph 6: What kinds of clothes do the people of your island wear? Describe them.

Illustration 3: Draw the clothing that a female and a male would wear.

Paragraph 7: What kinds of games, sports, activities, music, and art are part of the lives of your island's inhabitants?

Paragraph 8: If you had visitors from other islands, what would you serve them for dinner? Plan a breakfast, lunch, and dinner menu.

Activity 8.4

THE PERFECT ISLAND (*Continued*)

Paragraph 9: How will your island be protected from intruders? Will you have a police force? An army? A navy? An FBI? A fire department?

Paragraph 10: How is your island different from the world you live in now? What will be some of your fears, concerns, and survival techniques? Sum up all of your thoughts in this concluding paragraph.

Criteria:

Your paragraphs are high-quality work.

Each paragraph has a topic sentence.

Your illustrations are neatly drawn and colored.

Your paragraphs are written neatly, either in handwriting or on the computer.

You have a heading on each card written in black fine-point marker to make it stand out.

Your name is clearly written on the project.

Note to the Teacher: You may modify this assignment to accompany your study of *Bridge to Terabithia* by Katherine Paterson. Instead of an island, this assignment would take on the title of *The Perfect Kingdom.*

Activity 8.5

WORLD WAR II PROJECT BASED ON *NUMBER THE STARS* BY LOIS LOWRY

Student's Name ____________________ Due Date ____________________

You have just read a piece of core literature that dealt with World War II and the fear that the main characters had about concentration camps and the German soldiers. In order to understand this period of history better, you are to choose **at least one** of the following activities and research the topic thoroughly.

1. Interview a person who lived during World War II (WW II). Use the Interview Planning Sheet to plan out what you will ask. Interview your person. Find out how he or she was influenced by the war and how his or her life changed during that time. Then write up a report to tell what you learned. Include a picture of the person you interviewed, if possible. *Note to teacher:* the Interview Planning Sheet is Activity 7.6, in Chapter Three.
2. Who were the leaders of the major countries that were most active in the war? Tell who they were and what country they represented.
3. Write a report about the attack on Pearl Harbor and why the United States became involved in the war.
4. Draw pictures of the flags of the major countries fighting in WW II. Tell something about how and why each country became involved in the war.
5. Which countries were the Axis Powers and which countries were the Allied Powers? Make a chart.
6. Draw pictures of the uniforms of the Americans in WW II. Label each and explain something important about each one.
7. Locate some information about Adolf Hitler in a book or encyclopedia and tell why you think such a cruel man could become so powerful with the German people. What did he hope to accomplish by his cruelty to the Jews? Summarize your views in written form.
8. Draw pictures of the American air or sea craft used in WW II. Explain something about each of them. Label each.
9. Draw a map of Europe and show the countries that Adolf Hitler took control of during this period.
10. Read about and write a report about the role of women in WW II. Show how military women and civilian women dressed. You may want to watch the movie *A League of Their Own to* give you some ideas.

Activity 8.5

WORLD WAR II PROJECT BASED ON *NUMBER THE STARS* BY LOIS LOWRY (*Continued*)

11. Research the Hitler Youth organization. Tell how German children became part of the war.
12. Review a movie about WW II, such as *The Diary of Anne Frank; The Sound of Music; Tora! Tora! Tora!; Schindler's List; The Hiding Place; Burma Road; The Dirty Dozen; South Pacific; Anchors Away; Midway; Patton; Enola Gay;* or *Bridge on the River Kwai.* If you can think of others, check them out with your teacher first. Write up a review of the movie.
13. Read a book about WW II, such as *The Diary of Anne Frank, Journey Back, Don't Fence Me In, Farewell to Manzanar, The Upstairs Room,* or *Frederick.* Write a summary of the book. Bring the book into class and give an oral presentation to the class. If you find other related books, let your teacher know which one you will be reading.
14. Locate some songs that were popular during WW II. Write down the lyrics by hand or on the computer. Tell how popular music was different then. Compare the songs to the music of today. Sing or play something from that period of time for the class.
15. Create your own activity. Check it out with your teacher first.
16. Watch a documentary on television that covers WW II. Write a summary of it. *Victory at Sea* is one possibility and has twenty-six episodes to choose from.
17. Research what life in your home town was like during WW II. Make a list or write a report telling about it.
18. Locate photographs taken in the era from 1940 to 1945. Arrange the pictures together in an artful way on a poster, with a brief description in your own words under each one. Make sure that you space them out neatly and that you do not leave too much background showing. The poster should be no larger than eighteen-by-twenty-four inches. Neatly label the photos in straight lines, and remember to title the poster.
19. Watch a movie that was made during the period from 1940 to 1945. Give attention to the clothes, cars, hairstyles, makeup, and so on. Make a poster to advertise the movie showing some of these features. Include a title and the names of the major stars.
20. Make a list of at least ten important people who lived during the years 1940 to 1945 who should be remembered for their contributions. Tell why each was important to the world, including film stars, politicians, musicians, people in medicine, and so forth.
21. If you have visited a place that deals with WW II—such as the Holocaust Museum, Pearl Harbor, or Manzanar—write up a summary of your visit and share some of the mementos you purchased or snapshots you took.

Activity 8.5

WORLD WAR II PROJECT BASED ON *NUMBER THE STARS* BY LOIS LOWRY (*Continued*)

22. Write a report about the Japanese Relocation in the United States after the attack on Pearl Harbor.

Requirements:

1. All projects must be neat—in pen or cursive writing or typed.
2. If items are drawn with pencil first, make sure to finalize them in thin black marker. Then erase all excess pencil marks.
3. All projects should be done on regular size paper (8-½ by 11 inches).
4. Maps and illustrations should be in colored pencil or marker.

Activity 8.6

WORLD WAR II PROJECT
TEACHER OR STUDENT EVALUATION

Teacher Evaluation

Student's Name ______________________

Comments

Content ________ ______________________________

Quality ________ ______________________________

Neatness ________ ______________________________

Effort ________ ______________________________

****

Student Evaluation

Student's Name ______________________________

1. What did you like about doing this project?

____

2. Where did you obtain the information for this project?

____

3. Who helped you with your work?

____

4. How much time do you think this took you to finish?

____

5. What grade would you give yourself? Explain.

____

Activity 8.7

SURVIVAL THEME: CRITICAL READING AND INTERVIEWING

Student's Name ______________________________ Due Date ______________

Circle your choice(s): option A or option B.
Choose either option A or option B below. You can do both if you want.

A. *Choose a news story from the newspaper or a magazine.*

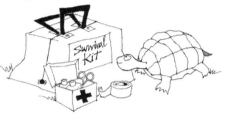

- Locate the who, what, when, where, and why of the story.
- Identify the survival techniques used and tell whether they are *tangible* (such as heat, matches, hammer, shelter, food, or other touchable things) or *intangible* (such as courage, inner strength, resourcefulness, initiative, innovation, love of family, faith, a positive attitude, confidence, or other qualities).

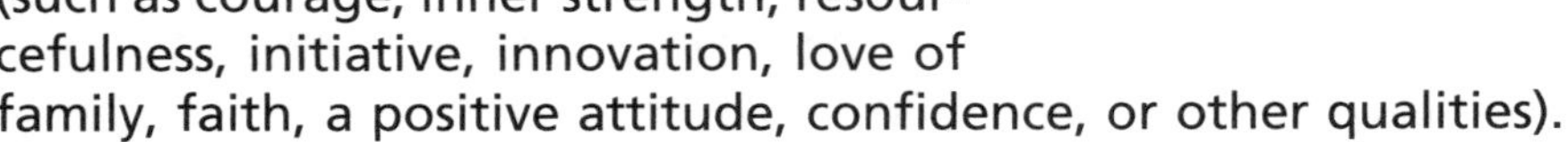

- Write up a summary of your findings.
- Include the article, where you found it, and a picture, if possible.
- Be prepared to share with the class.

B. *Interview someone you know who has survived an illness, injury, accident, or other exceptional life experience.*

- Before the interview, write down eight to ten questions to find out the who, what, when, where, and why of this experience.
- Think of questions that also include what survival techniques were used to help this person get through the event or situation.
- Ask your parents to review your questions to make sure that you have been sensitive to the person's feelings that you are interviewing.
- Include your interview questions, a picture of the person, and, if possible, a picture of you with the person being interviewed.
- Write a summary about your interview including all of your findings.
- Be prepared to share with the class.

— Chapter 9 —

SPECIAL UNITS OF STUDY

There is great value in developing in-depth units centering around authors, story elements, and genres. They provide wonderful opportunities for student involvement and interaction by enriching the basic literacy program and providing stimulating talk that challenges readers to go beyond the surface of understanding. They propel thinking and wondering forward.

AUTHOR STUDIES TO PRODUCE STRONGER READERS AND WRITERS

Author studies are important motivators for all readers and writers. When a child likes a particular author's topics, voice, writing style, or word choice, he or she develops a personal connection with the author. As he sees that he can have success reading these books, the child becomes less intimidated and more confident, seeking more books by that author and anticipating the next book that the author will write. When a child actively reads books by one author, he or she is motivated to read other informational books that explain things discussed in those books. A chain reaction occurs when Gary Paulsen prompts children to look for more details about survival techniques, heart attacks, comas, the environment, tornados, animals of the forests, plants found in the wilderness, and the like. Finally, when a child internalizes some of the characteristics of a special author's craft, it motivates him or her to try these techniques in his or her own writing.

Following we discuss three different authors and offer suggestions for featuring them in author studies.

Chris Van Allsburg, Author and Illustrator

As part of a mystery genre study unit, Chris Van Allsburg is introduced. There is no better book to get kids thinking creatively about mystery than *The Mysteries of Harris Burdick* (1984). His illustrations are truly inspirational writing *hooks* for enchanting, haunting, mystical, and mysterious ideas. Kids love to delve into these creative stories that the book beckons them to write.

The book is read aloud to the children, and discussion ensues. Quality talk about the illustrations, the writer's mood, purpose, theme, voice, and other elements is fostered. Creative thought is encouraged as the illustrations unfold.

With the trend towards more expository writing in other units, little time is left to pursue the art of creative writing. We are convinced that we must continue to allow time for creative thinking in order to develop creative problem solvers and innovators for the world of the future. By encouraging and allowing time for creative writing in the classroom, the teacher can balance the writing periods so that students realize that writing can be fun and is a viable outlet for the stresses of school and growing up.

After using the illustrations as prompts from Chris Van Allsburg's *The Mysteries of Harris Burdick*, one sixth-grade student said, "This is the best thing that I have ever written!" What a profound statement! Besides building self-esteem, we have a child who has opened up a whole new world of possibilities.

By exploring books by the same author in an author study, students begin to see similarities in the writing style. Sometimes an author's language is repeated, using lots of descriptive words, similes, and metaphors, for example. The students become familiar with the forms of language that the author uses.

Other Books by Chris Van Allsburg for Read-Aloud Chris Van Allsburg has written and illustrated a large number of picture books that provide mystery and intrigue. Never discount the power of a picture book, even for upper-grade and middle school students. The following list shows only a few from his collection:

The Garden of Abdul Gasazi (1979)
Jumanji (1981)
Ben's Dream (1982)
The Wreck of the Zephyr (1983)
The Polar Express (1985)
The Z Was Zapped (1987)
Just a Dream (1990)
The Wretched Stone (1991)
The Widow's Broom (1992)
The Sweetest Fig (1993)

Directions for a Student Literary Center or an Independent Study of Chris Van Allsburg You have just completed a read-aloud author's study of Chris Van Allsburg. He has exceptional talent for not only writing but also illustrating. Most people work as either a writer or an illustrator, but Van Allsburg is highly skillful at both. He uses both the right and left sides of his brain to create each story in verbal and graphic form. What a gift! When you are at the Author Study Station, carefully read the instructions, look through the books, plan your thoughts, and then write.

- Look through the books that you have heard in read-alouds over the past two weeks.
- Choose your favorite book and explain why you chose it. Tell about the pictures and the story. Try to think of both the writing and illustration styles of Chris Van Allsburg as you describe the book.

- Use a separate sheet of paper to create a planning chart with headings like the one below.

PLOT	STORY: WHAT YOU LIKED ABOUT IT	ILLUSTRATION STYLE	FAVORITE PART (AND WHY CHOSEN)

- Choose two of Van Allsburg's books that you would like to compare and contrast. How are they similar and how are they different? For instance, you might compare two black-and-white illustrated books and tell how the illustrations in this form help create a certain feel or mood to the story. Use the Venn diagram below to help you organize your thoughts. Write a paragraph on a separate sheet of paper explaining what you know now about Van Allsburg's overall writing and illustration style and why his stories are mysterious and eerie. In your opinion, why he is so successful as a writer and an illustrator?

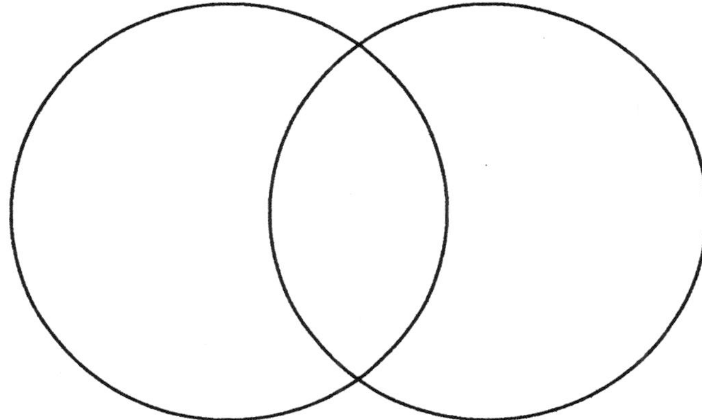

Figure 9.1. Venn Diagram of Two Overlapping Circles

Avi: A Versatile Writer

Avi has a gift for writing, and he has created a great number of exceptional books for older readers. His craft is unique because he can write with such versatility. He is not stuck in one time frame or genre. Sometimes the reader cannot tell that Avi is the author of the book, because his subjects are so varied: in one book he writes about a mouse and in another he writes about a young boy in the Revolutionary War or a girl on an ocean voyage without any parents. Studying an author like Avi inspires good upper-grade and middle school conversation about how one writer can know so much about so many subjects. Avi is a mentor-author who can definitely be appreciated by the older child. When an Avi book is read aloud, the boys and girls need to listen carefully for clues that open up Avi's writing characteristics. Critical listening reveals little nuances that show how masterful an author Avi is. *The True Confessions of Charlotte Doyle* (1990), *Poppy* (1995), *Ragweed* (1999), and *The Fighting Ground* (1984) are used as read-alouds to show Avi's versatility as an author.

The students research other books by Avi and select books for book club study. The books cover a range of reading abilities: *Night Journeys* (1979), *Encounter at Easton* (1980), *Wolf Rider* (1986), *Ereth's Birthday* (2000), *Who Was That Masked Man, Anyway?* (1971), *Windcatcher* (1991), and *The Secret School* (2001).

After the students have had three or four opportunities to be involved in Avi book clubs—some with a great deal of teacher support—they will produce a culminating activity for the entire unit of author study. For this type of study, the activities will focus on a broader spectrum about Avi: his writing craft, themes, settings, and characters and how they can be compared from book to book. We want students to realize that one author can be prolific and that sometimes we can draw conclusions from the way he or she writes. (See Chapter Ten for book club culminating projects in Activity 10.7.)

Students can work on several different kinds of writing activities to show their understanding of Avi's works. (See Activities 9.1, 9.2, and 9.3 at the end of this chapter.)

Katherine Paterson: Comparing and Contrasting

The Great Gilly Hopkins (1978) and *Bridge to Terabithia* (1978) by Katherine Paterson provide another opportunity to compare two books that are Newbery Award–Winning or Honor books. Students can see how one author's style permeates his or her books.

Because there are so many exciting types of reading materials available to "fire up" our most reluctant readers, we must continue to search for the ones that inspire them to read. Although certain children may not feel comfortable with an upper-grade chapter book, we must offer a large variety of reading materials like these two by Paterson that children can pick up and read successfully. No matter how short or simple the reading material is, we know that the more a child reads, the better a reader he or she becomes.

Reading two books by the same author helps struggling readers to recognize patterns, writing styles, or similarities in theme. As students read independently or have these books read aloud to them, they will begin to pick up likenesses of style. If a reluctant reader likes one book by a specific author, chances are the author has written other books that he or she will be willing to try. Active writers produce many books, and teachers in particular can appreciate the abundance of options one author can create for all readers.

In both *The Great Gilly Hopkins* and *Bridge to Terabithia*, the characters have personal struggles that they need to overcome. Survival is key to both of these characters. Gilly is a foster child who has been dragged from home to home. She has developed a big chip on her shoulder, but for good reason—she does not have a caring, loving family to take care of her. She has learned some defensive mechanisms to help her survive being hurt even further. In *Bridge to Terabithia*, Leslie and Jess form a strong friendship and through it they both change. Leslie meets up with an unexpected tragedy and Jess must survive this loss.

Author studies can be approached through read-alouds, shared reading, or book clubs. Powerful conversations about survival techniques and personal struggles should be threaded though the study.

DIGGING DEEPER INTO STORY ELEMENTS

As older children interact with narrative reading, they should be developing a more sophisticated understanding of story elements of not only character, plot, and setting, but also other elements such as symbolism, conflict, and flashbacks, which can make a major impact in a story. In the following section, you will find special units that develop beyond the surface level as mentor pieces of literature are explored. Teachers should look carefully for those examples of literature with literary elements that children can hold on to as their educational experience progresses. Provide students with a copy of Activity 9.4 and ask them to keep those reading and writing terms on hand for reference. After they learn about a story element and how authors use it to make stories more interesting and complicated, students ideally will begin to use the element in their own writing as they mature. A fully developed lesson on character development is explored here. Similar units of study on plot and setting may be pursued.

Character Study

During the year, older children should be exposed to an in-depth study of characters. The standards in all grade levels expect students to continuously develop their understanding of the importance of characters in literature. Students love to write their own short stories with their own original characters, so this study is practical preparation for their own writing.

As teachers choose touchstone and mentor texts with rich characters where a lot of discussion can develop, they must look for strong characters who reach the diversity of the classroom. They need to strive for balance in the gender of the characters chosen. An abundance of boy characters can hook in the male students, but can leave out the females. What we want to see in story element study is students expanding their ability to relate to the characters and unravel what makes the characters tick.

Following are a number of ways that teachers can help students during a study of character:

- Co-create purposeful charts to scaffold students' understanding.
- Use graphic organizers as learning progresses.
- Provide talking and thinking sessions during Reading Workshop.
- Model thinking by using sticky notes.
- Encourage accountable talk that goes deep into the character's thoughts, feelings, and actions.
- Provide books with strong characters in a variety of genres.
- Read and reread memorable character books as read-alouds.
- Provide shared reading experiences that help children become more familiar with the characters.
- Let the students act out the moods, behaviors, and dialogue of the characters.
- Have students complete the character chart in Activity 9.5.

Using Picture Books That Students Already Know to Initiate the Study of Characters Having a few familiar picture book texts available for students to revisit is a great entry point for the study of character. Most students love to hear the primary mentor texts read aloud again as older children. They begin to realize that picture books have more complicated text and that when we gain deeper understanding of the characters, the books take on new life. Older students are able to look beyond what they see in the pictures and infer from the text. A few books that offer an introduction to characters can provide a brief assessment of what the students already know about characters. Second-language students can be introduced to shorter stories so that they can be reintroduced to character study. A few of our favorite character study books for older children are *The Ballad of Lucy Whipple* (Cushman, 1996), *Stone Fox* (Gardiner, 1996), *Island of the Blue Dolphins* (O'Dell, 1960),

The Sign of the Beaver (Speare, 1983), *Maniac McGee* (Spinelli, 1999), and *Anastasia Krupnik* (Lowry, 1979).

Getting to the Depth of Character Kindergartners quickly learn what a character is and the part it plays in a story. As students develop in the middle and upper grades and even further in middle school, their conversations about characters have to deepen to challenge and stretch their thinking about how they impact the story. Knowing about characters is not enough. Teachers need to push student thinking forward, broadening their base of understanding to keep up with their development. Older students should dig deeper into character development as they become more sophisticated themselves. If the students are still on the surface level of thinking, it is time to set the standards higher for conversation. If you are asking questions in the upper grades such as *Who is the main character? What does he look like? How does he behave?* try adding a few of the questions below during book talks, read-alouds, and shared reading. You can lift the talk and the thinking for all your students, which will transfer into their book clubs and writing responses. When you model with interesting questions, discussions become richer.

- Who is the main character in this story and how does he or she impact the plot and the setting?
- How do the characters talk, interact, look, feel, and act?
- How do others react to this character?
- How is dialogue used to reveal the character?
- What motive does the character have?
- How do you think the character is feeling? Back it up with evidence.
- How does one character compare to another? Can you show it on a Venn diagram?
- Can you predict the character's actions?
- Can you tell what might happen next by what the character says or does?
- What are primary, secondary, flat, and round characters?
- How do the secondary characters contribute to the story or theme?
- How do you find out about the characters? What does the author tell you? What do you have to infer? What do the other characters tell you about this character? What actions and behavior do the characters show? What do the characters look like?
- Are you using character words such as *protagonist*, *antagonist*, *motivation*, and *conflict* when you discuss stories?
- In what ways are the characters in different stories the same (or different)? Are you comparing the characters from different books by the same author?
- Can you compare two characters from two books of the same genre? Do these characters act or think alike?
- What types of conflict does the character encounter? Character versus nature? Versus self? Versus society? Versus another character?
- How does the character change over time? Give evidence.
- How do you feel about the character at the beginning of the story? At the end?
- Do you know anyone in your life who is like this character?

- How do you relate to this character? How are you alike or different?
- Why did the author choose to tell the story through this character?
- If you could change this character, how would you do it? Why?
- What qualities did you like dislike in this character?
- How would you deal with this character if you met him or her?
- What kinds of things would you want him or her to share with you?
- Is there a difference in the way you view real human characters versus animal characters who can talk?
- How does an author give believability to personified animal characters?
- How do the characters differ when you compare them across genres, such as the classics, fantasy, and realistic fiction?
- How does the author convince you that these characters could be real?
- What purpose do strong characters have in the development of the story?
- What relationship do the characters have to the setting of the story?
- What ideas from the characters you have been introduced to can you use to develop the characters in your own stories?

During the study of characters, children will develop a relationship with the main character and be able to express empathy, make connections to their own lives, and give them advice through reading, writing, or speaking.

Developing Character Word Banks In Chapter Four, supporting reluctant readers and writers through word banks was discussed. During character study, the students generate word banks such as those shown below to assist them in talking and writing about characters.

Feelings That Characters Can Have

amazed	eager	humble
agitated	edgy	ignored
angry	elated	jealous
ashamed	embarrassed	lonely
astonished	enthusiastic	moody
bored	excited	mortified
calm	frazzled	meek
cheerful	frightened	mischievous
concerned	glad	overwhelmed
content	grateful	pleased
courageous	happy	proud
daring	hopeful	regretful
depressed	inspired	relieved
disappointed	high-spirited	safe

secure
shocked
shy
smothered
solemn
surprised
terrified
thankful
tired
unhappy
upset
weary
wild
worried

How Can We Describe Characters? Personality Traits

annoying
apprehensive
arrogant
bold
bratty
brave
bubbly
callous
caring
cold-hearted
competitive
conceited
concerned
conscientious
courageous
courteous
cruel
curious
disobedient
determined
disrespectful
energetic
extroverted
fierce
flexible
foolish
friendly
generous
greedy
happy-go-lucky
helpful
hateful
hopeful
ignorant
inconsiderate
jealous
kind
kind-hearted
ignorant
imaginative
immature
intelligent
introverted
lady-like
lively
loyal
mature
mean-spirited
mischievous
mysterious
nosy
obedient
obnoxious
outgoing
popular
quiet
respectful
responsible
rigid
rude
self-centered
selfish
scatter-brained
smart-aleck
spirited
spoiled
social
sophisticated
strong
stubborn
superficial
suspicious
talkative
tense
thorough
tough
trusting
ungrateful
unpleasant

Developing Character Sketch Cards

In this activity, students must be instructed on the differences between a physical characteristic and a personality trait. Children find the physical characteristics quite easy to identify, but the personality traits are more difficult. Keeping a personality trait word bank on a chart in the classroom assists those students who experience difficulty in this search. An ongoing list can always be available for students who need extra support when starting to write. On the back of the card, students may draw a picture of the main character. The two sides can be pasted together, paper-punched and hung on a string, or displayed on a board. (See the character sketch cards in Activities 9.6 and 9.7 at the end of this chapter.)

SYMBOLISM IN *BECAUSE OF WINN-DIXIE*

In *Because of Winn-Dixie* (DiCamillo, 2000), the story element of symbolism is strongly developed. Most children are able to understand how well DiCamillo worked a litmus lozenge into a story that symbolized the sweet and sour experiences of everyday life. Because this book is short, simple, and can be read quickly, reluctant readers relate to it well. If it is read aloud, the students become very cognizant of the importance the lozenge plays in the story. It becomes apparent in Chapter Fifteen and on that the lozenge is important to the lives of all the characters in this small community. In this uncomplicated story, a simple piece of candy lets students unwrap a sometimes hard-to-understand literary device and tuck it away until they meet up with symbolism again.

This book is also a perfect study for the theme unit on survival and writer's craft and can be paired up with *Tales of Despereaux* (DiCamillo, 2003) for an author study.

LITERACY LESSON PLAN ON SYMBOLISM

1. *Literacy Framework Element. Because of Winn-Dixie* by Kate DiCamillo read-aloud.
2. *Language Arts Standard 3.5.* Describe the function and effect of common literacy devices.

Understanding the element of symbolism and how it helps us better comprehend the author's message is not an easy task for students. By exposing students to the strong examples of symbolism used in *Because of Winn-Dixie*, you help students better understand its use and how it can be transferred to their own writing.

Lesson Focus. Knowing what symbolism is and how the author uses it in the text helps us understand the story better.

QUESTIONS

- What is a symbol?
- What other examples of symbolism have you seen in *Winn-Dixie*?
- What does the litmus lozenge stand for? How does the author let you know?
- How does the writer's use of symbolism make for a better story?
- How could DiCamillo have said the same thing without using a symbol?

- Why do you think she decided to use a piece of candy as a symbol of sadness and loneliness?
- How did DiCamillo introduce the candy symbol?
- Was she effective in getting her point across by using this piece of candy?
- Was the story better because she used this symbolism in it?
- Do you think younger children would understand the idea of symbolism in this and other stories?

Instruction, Modeling, and Teaching Points

Students will access prior knowledge from other books and will be able to remember how symbolism was used earlier in the book. They will make connections to their own world and the symbols around them. During a first reading of this story, readers might become so engrossed in the story that they completely miss the symbolism of the litmus lozenge. Glossing over this literary element would make the story lack the substance of a more sophisticated reader.

Students will work in pairs and triads to respond to the level of questioning orally. Together teacher and students will create a chart for their ideas about the significance of the litmus lozenge in the story.

Guided Practice

Over the next few days students will find examples of symbolism in their own independent reading and mark them with sticky notes. Students will share their findings and place their sticky notes on a teacher-prepared chart for that purpose. Throughout the remainder of the year students will find examples of symbolism in their own reading and listen for examples in read-alouds and shared reading and be encouraged to share them with their classmates.

Student Achievement

The teacher assesses how well students understand the focus of the lesson by conferring with them during the next week of independent reading, by listening carefully to their responses during class discussions, and by watching to see if any of them use the idea of symbolism in their own writing.

Follow-Up

After completing the book, students watch the movie version. They compare the book and movie using a Venn diagram. (Each child has one in hand, and there is a lot of sharing of information.)

The students are then ready to write a response to this piece of literature. We co-create a basic rubric to guide our writing and I model one paragraph each day on the overhead or document camera. I have the students talk about the things they would put in their paragraph and I write their thoughts on a chart. They write their paragraph in class, read what they wrote to a classmate, and take it home to finish their ideas. The following day, we start the next paragraph on the rubric using modeling first, talk, and then write and share.

To celebrate our completion of the book and our writing pieces, we reenact the *Winn-Dixie* party episode with punch, dill pickles, litmus lozenges, and egg salad sandwiches with no crusts on the bread, then display plenty of pictures of dogs around the room. One child in my class decided to make litmus paper for a science experiment, so the class was able to see what litmus paper was all about and got another look at what symbolism was. The experiment was found in *Science Experiments You Can Eat* (Cobb, 1994). Another child decided to try out a recipe for candy, creating her own flavor of litmus lozenge, wrapping the candy in special paper, and writing "Litmus Lozenge" on each. Some books just lend themselves to having fun.

SIMILES IN *THE THIRTEENTH FLOOR*

The Thirteenth Floor (Fleischman, 1995) is a perfect introduction to the New England colonies and the witch trials in America. It contains an abundance of similes. When hearing the book read aloud, the students pick out the similes easily and see how effectively Fleischman uses them as part of his writing craft. Sometimes they become so apparent that the students make a game of calling out *simile* when one appears in the story. This opens up a whole new understanding of how authors use similes in their writing to help readers draw pictures in their minds, so that they better remember the text. Similes are of little significance unless students know how and why authors use them. By doing a simile search throughout the book and in their own independent reading books, students begin to embrace the idea that they can use similes in their own writing. Other literary devices such as hyperbole, imagery, and metaphor can be addressed through a story element unit of study. See Activity 9.8 at the end of this chapter.

GENRE STUDIES

For students to fully understand the characteristics of a particular genre, occasionally teachers should go in-depth to explore a genre-specific study. During this time, all or most read-alouds, shared reading, guided reading, and independent reading experiences focus on that particular genre. As children are fully immersed in the study, they will be guided into the special features of the particular genre and build understanding of how the particular genre works so that when they pick it up to read alone, they can comprehend their reading and predict how the genre is written. When reading a mystery story, students can expect to find particular vocabulary and story elements, such as *clues, motive, suspect, evidence*, and *victim*. They discover through classroom discussions that mystery stories are solved through a series of clues that lead us to a solution. They also find out that mystery stories have protagonists and antagonists, and there is conflict that leads to resolution. As the story unravels, the clues make sense, and the mystery is solved. See Activities 9.9 and 9.10 at the end of this chapter for a sample schedule of genre studies and a book response idea.

It is fun to take a break from pictureless texts and gather together Caldecott books that older children can review to enjoy the beauty of their illustrations. Assemble a Caldecott collection from primary-grade colleagues, school libraries, and the children's personal home libraries. See Activity 9.11 at the end of this chapter.

Activity 9.1

CREATING A FLIP BOOK: STORY ELEMENTS

Student's Name ________________ Due Date ___________

You have just finished a study of space. Your job now is to show what you have learned by developing a flip book with the categories listed on the sample below. If you want to make it more extensive, you can add other subjects to write about by adding additional pages. Take four sheets of 8-1/2-by-11-inch paper and stagger the bottom of each page a half inch up from each other. With the pages still layered, fold the paper at the top gently over to form four more layered sections at the bottom. They too should be a half inch apart. You now will have seven areas to write on and seven labeling sections to write headings on. Put two staples at the top to hold the flip book together. Create an interesting top section with a title and some illustrations.

[Title, student name, date, and illustration here]
Setting
Avi's Writing Style
Zachariah
Captain Jaggery
Charlotte Doyle
Charlotte Doyle's Parents
Plot

Activity 9.2

FLIP BOOK FOR CHARLOTTE DOYLE: STORY ELEMENT RESPONSE TO LITERATURE

Sample Topic Sentences to Get You Started

Topic Sentence #1. *The setting of The True Confessions of Charlotte Doyle is a very important element in the story.* (Tell how the characters are affected by the setting. Title this section *Setting*.)

Topic Sentence #2. *Avi has a very unique writing style. He uses a lot of descriptive language to make the reader feel that he or she was really there and pushes us to want to read more.* (Title this section *Avi's Writing Style*.)

Topic Sentence #3. *Zachariah is a black galley mate on the Seahawk. He is Charlotte's only real friend.* (Explain what you know about Zachariah, including physical appearance and personal qualities. Title this section *Zachariah*.)

Topic Sentence #4. *Captain Jaggery is a very strong, cruel, and controlling person who commands his ship and crew by intimidating them.* (Write a character study of him and title it *Captain Jaggery*.)

Topic Sentence #5. *Charlotte Doyle changes drastically from the beginning of the book to the end. In the beginning she was . . .* (Tell how Charlotte changes and title this section *Charlotte Doyle*.)

Topic Sentence #6. *I was surprised at Mr. and Mrs. Doyle's response to Charlotte when they were reunited. Mr. Doyle did not believe Charlotte's story and took action. Let me tell you how he responded and how I feel about the treatment he gave Charlotte.* (Title this section *Charlotte Doyle's Parents*.)

Topic Sentence #7. *The plot of the story was very complicated, but filled with lots of suspense. First . . . Second . . . Then . . . After that . . . Later on . . . Near the end . . . Finally* . . . (Title this section *Plot*.)

Activity 9.3

COMPARE AND CONTRAST TWO BOOKS BY THE SAME AUTHOR

Student's Name ___________________ Due Date _______________

***Poppy* and *The True Confessions of Charlotte Doyle* by Avi**

1. The first paragraph introduces the idea that the books have both similarities and differences.

   1 2 3 4 5

2. The second paragraph tells about the similarities between the two books.

   1 2 3 4 5

3. The third paragraph tells about the differences between the two books.

   1 2 3 4 5

4. Evidence and supporting details are given in paragraphs 2 and 3.

   1 2 3 4 5

5. The last paragraph draws the writing together and restates the main ideas of the paper.

   1 2 3 4 5

6. The paper displays quality grade-level work.

   1 2 3 4 5

The paper shows the reader's connections or interactions with the stories and shows that the reader related in some way to the main character, plot, setting, or a combination of these elements.

Activity 9.4

JUST A FEW READING AND WRITING TERMS YOU SHOULD KNOW

Student's Name ___________________

Note to the Student: Keep these terms in your reading or writing folder so that you can refer to them as needed.

Alliteration: The repetition of the same sound in two or more words that are next to or near each other. These sounds may appear at the beginning of words or within words. This sets a rhythm or mood to sentences and phrases. It is fun and pleasing to the ear and calls attention to certain words or phrases. (*Some smug slug slithered across the sand.*)

Anecdote: A brief story used to make a point. The story of Abe Lincoln walking two miles to return pennies to a customer is an anecdote that shows Abe's honesty.

Characterization: The techniques a writer uses to let the reader know about the characters. Characterization may let readers in on the traits of a character's personality or behavior. These techniques may reveal the character's opinions, thoughts, or feelings, or they may let the reader see the reaction of other characters to that character.

Four methods of characterization:

1. Describe the character's physical traits and personality
2. Report the character's speech and behavior
3. Give other characters' opinions of and reactions to this individual
4. Reveal the character's thoughts and feelings

Conflict: Conflict occurs when the main character struggles with another character or other force. There are four types of conflict: person against person, person against him- or herself, person against society, and person against nature.

Cliché: A familiar word or phrase that has been used so often that it is no longer an interesting way of saying something, such as *good as gold* or *bright as the sun*.

Climax: The most exciting or suspenseful point in the story, which occurs toward the end of the story.

Activity 9.4

JUST A FEW READING AND WRITING TERMS YOU SHOULD KNOW (*Continued*)

Description: Writing that paints a picture of a person, place, thing, or idea using specific details.

Dialect: Speech patterns of a certain locale or region.

Dialogue: Conversational element: when characters talk with one another.

Diction: A writer's choice of words. In a story about everyday life, a writer may use very informal, everyday language. For a business letter, a writer will use more formal or proper language.

Exaggeration: Words that stretch the truth. Exaggeration is used in tall tales. (*The mosquito is so big it needs a runway to land.*)

Expository Writing: Writing that explains, such as in report or research paper.

Figurative Language: A special way of writing to create an effective word picture. This is a way of using language that expands the literal meaning of words to give a new look at the topic. Similes and metaphors are two common types of figurative language. Both compare a word to something else in order to embellish the meaning of the word.

Flashback: An interruption in the action of a story to show an event that happened at an earlier time.

Focus or Main Idea: Concentrating on a specific part of a subject. When writing about a favorite person, you might focus on his or her sense of humor.

Foreshadowing: A technique for plot development where an author gives clues that suggest events that might come later in the story.

Humor: Laughable incidents.

Hyperbole: A big exaggeration. *(I'm so hungry I could eat a horse! I'm the happiest person in the whole world.*)

Idiom: An expression with a different meaning from the meaning of the individual words joined together. (*I'm tickled pink. It's raining cats and dogs. Don't burst my bubble.*)

Imagery: Details that appeal to the senses. Use of descriptive words to give a clear mental picture or suggest a sensation of sound, smell, taste, or touch. (*This pie is to die for!*)

Activity 9.4

JUST A FEW READING AND WRITING TERMS YOU SHOULD KNOW (*Continued*)

Irony: Using a word or phrase to mean the exact opposite of its normal meaning. (Having the flu is *so much fun,* don't you think?)

Metaphor: A figure of speech that compares two different things without using a word of comparison such as *like* or *as*. (*The flashlight was my friend. The vacant field was a desert. Her eyes were two deep pools.*) Often used to clarify an idea. (*The ship plows the sea.*)

Mood: A feeling or atmosphere in a piece of writing that is created with descriptive terms. Mood may give a feeling of beauty, honesty, silliness, darkness, fear, or happiness.

Motive: This is *why* characters behave or act the way they do.

Objective: The type of writing that includes facts, with no opinions or personal feelings.

Onomatopoeia: The use of words such as *buzz, hiss, moo, knock knock, kerplunk, choo choo,* or *splash* that vocally imitate the sound they are trying to describe. The word actually makes the sound of what it is or does.

Personal Narrative: Writing that tells a story from the writer's life—a personal memory of something that made you laugh, shudder, feel angry, sad, excited, or happy, for example.

Personification: Giving human characteristics to things that are not human. Representation of an animal or object as having human characteristics. (*The rock jumped up and hit me. The trees whispered in the wind.*)

Plot: A series of events that the author uses to build a story. It usually involves a situation, problem, or conflict followed by a climax and a resolution.

Persuasion: Writing that is meant to change the way a reader thinks or acts.

Point of View: The writer's chosen narrator for the story. Following are two possible ways of telling a story:

First Person: The narrator tells the story using "*I.*"

Omniscient (or All-Knowing) Point of View: The narrator is an outsider who describes the situation. (*He, she,* or *they* is used to refer to the characters.)

Activity 9.4

JUST A FEW READING AND WRITING TERMS YOU SHOULD KNOW (*Continued*)

Pun: A word or phrase—usually a homophone—with a funny double meaning. (*That story about rabbits is a real hair raiser.*)

Purpose: The main reason a person has for writing something—to entertain, persuade, inform, and so on.

Rhyme: The repeating of sounds. These may occur within lines of writing or at the ends of the lines.

Sarcasm: A comment that actually means the opposite and is often meant to put someone down. (Your hair looks *absolutely beautiful* today.)

Setting: The time, place, and atmosphere in which a story occurs.

Simile: A figure of speech that makes a comparison between two unlike things that are essentially different but share some common factor. This comparison uses either *like* or *as*. (*I'm as quick as a cricket. Her eyes sparkled like two diamonds.*)

Slang: Special words and phrases used by friends when they are talking to each other. (*Chill out. It's a bomb!*)

Style: A writer's choice of words, phrases, and sentences. For instance, Gary Paulsen uses short, simple sentences.

Subjective: Writing that includes personal feelings.

Symbol: A person, object, event, or place that has its own meaning but suggests one or more other meaning as well. (*A seagull is a symbol of freedom. A dove is a symbol of peace.*)

Theme or Author's Message: The central idea or message in a piece of writing that the writer wants to convey to the reader. Often a chapter book has more than one theme, and the reader figures it out without being explicitly told.

Tone: The approach or attitude that the writer takes toward the subject of the writing. The tone may be hostile, amusing, serious, argumentative, or playful, for example.

Topic Sentence: The sentence that contains the main idea of a paragraph.

Transitions: Words that help tie ideas together. (*For this reason, for example, along with, otherwise, on the other hand, in the same way, therefore, finally,* and *in conclusion.*)

Activity 9.5

CHARACTER CHART

Title of Book ______________________

Name of Character ______________________

Words (what he or she says) :

(Draw the character here)

Actions (what he or she does):

Thoughts and Feelings:

Appearance:

What others say, think, or feel about the character:

How the character changes in the story:

Student's Name ______________________

Activity 9.6

CHARACTER SKETCH CARD (FRONT)

Student's Name: ________________	Student's Name: ________________
Book title: ____________________	Book title: ____________________
Character's name: ______________	Character's name: ______________
Physical characteristics: __________	Physical characteristics: __________
______________________________	______________________________
______________________________	______________________________
Personality traits: ______________	Personality traits: ______________
______________________________	______________________________
______________________________	______________________________
Where he or she lives: ____________	Where he or she lives: ____________
Student's Name: ________________	Student's Name: ________________
Book title: ____________________	Book title: ____________________
Character's name: ______________	Character's name: ______________
Physical characteristics: __________	Physical characteristics: __________
______________________________	______________________________
______________________________	______________________________
Personality traits: ______________	Personality traits: ______________
______________________________	______________________________
______________________________	______________________________
Where he or she lives: ____________	Where he or she lives: ____________

Activity 9.7

CHARACTER SKETCH CARD (BACK)

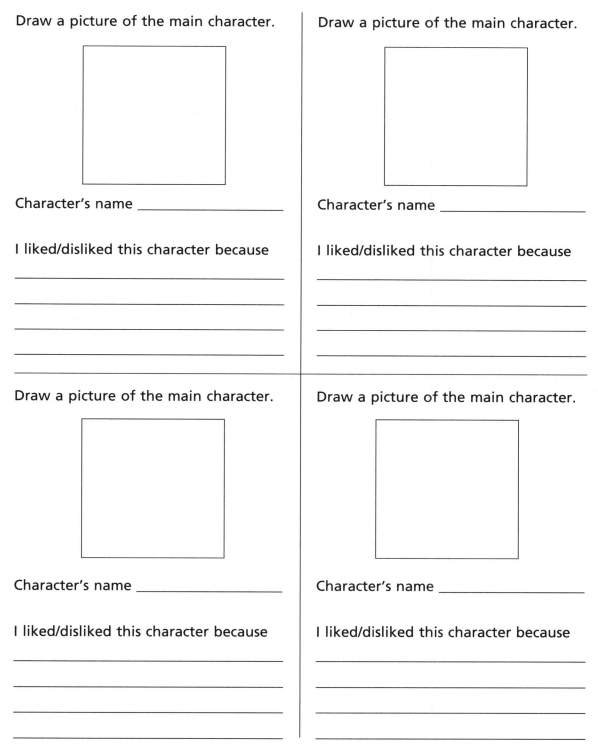

Draw a picture of the main character.

Character's name ____________________

I liked/disliked this character because

____
____
____
____

Draw a picture of the main character.

Character's name ____________________

I liked/disliked this character because

____
____
____
____

Draw a picture of the main character.

Character's name ____________________

I liked/disliked this character because

____
____
____
____

Draw a picture of the main character.

Character's name ____________________

I liked/disliked this character because

____
____
____
____

Activity 9.8

AUTHOR'S WRITING TOOLS AND STORY ELEMENTS

Student's Name ____________________

Chapters Sixteen, Seventeen, and Eighteen of *The Thirteenth Floor* Skim the chapters that you have just read and look for the following writer's tools. Locate the indicated phrase or sentence on the page noted in parentheses and tell whether you found it at the top, middle, or bottom of the page. Also tell which kind of tool it is: imagery, simile, metaphor, or hyperbole.

"A wind was charging along the street." (page 100) ____________________

____

"splintery ship" (page 101) ____________________

____

"narrow, black hull" (page 101) ____________________

____

"a name in fancy gold letters" (page 101) ____________________

____

"fragile as an eggshell" (page 101) ____________________

____

"fast as a mosquito" (page 101) ____________________

____

"fabulous, show-stopping performance as an attorney-in-fact" (page 102) ____________________

____

"A large flag of England fluttered at our stern, almost touching the sea." (page 103)

____

Activity 9.8

AUTHOR'S WRITING TOOLS AND STORY ELEMENTS (*Continued*)

"wing-flapping chicken" (page 104) ________________________

____

"I do like to rest my head on a cloud of feathers." (page 104) ____________

____

"I found it less scary to squirrel my way up the ratlines." (page 105) ________

____

"I let out a gasp of surprise that must have carried all the way to the twentieth century." (page 105) ________________________

____

"The chicken had been reduced to bones." (page 106) ______________

____

"The man-o'-war's following us like a seabird." (page 107)______________

____

"For the rest of the day the sea words bounced around in my head." (page 107) ____

____

"her sails cracking like rifle shots" (page 108) ____________________

____

Points Earned ________

Activity 9.9

MONTHLY GENRE STUDY SCHEDULE

Month	*Book Type*	*Project Suggestion*
September	Fiction	Sequence chart
October	Biography	Poster board
November	Nonfiction	Informational report
December	Sports	Sell-a-book oral presentation
January	Newbery book club	Sharing with a small group
February	Five Caldecott books	Create your own big book
March	Fantasy or science fiction	Book jacket
April	Mystery	Flow chart
May	Realistic fiction	Written report
June	Poetry	Poetry recording sheet

Activity 9.10

BOOK JACKET

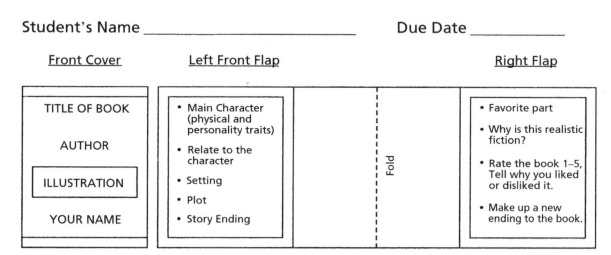

Student's Name ______________________________ Due Date ____________

Front Cover	Left Front Flap		Right Flap
TITLE OF BOOK AUTHOR ILLUSTRATION YOUR NAME	• Main Character (physical and personality traits) • Relate to the character • Setting • Plot • Story Ending	Fold	• Favorite part • Why is this realistic fiction? • Rate the book 1–5, Tell why you liked or disliked it. • Make up a new ending to the book.

Begin Each Paragraph with a Topic or Thesis Statement

1. **Main Character.** Discuss the physical and personality traits of the main character. Give evidence or proof from the story. Mention his or her name. Tell how he or she changes from the beginning of the book to the end. (Three to five sentences)
2. **Connection to the Main Character.** Explain how you and this character are the same and how you are different. Bring in some of your personal experiences and past knowledge. (Three to five sentences)
3. **Setting.** Tell where and when this story takes place. How is this different from the setting of your own life? (One to two sentences)
4. **Plot.** Summarize the main event in this story. Discuss the problems the characters face and how the problems are solved. Make sure you tell about events in the beginning of the story, in the middle, and at the end. (Six to ten sentences)
5. **Ending.** Summarize how the story ends. Give details. (Three to five sentences)
6. **Favorite Part.** Tell about your favorite part of the book. Give details. (Three to five sentences)
7. **Genre.** Consider why this book is considered realistic, historical, or science fiction. (One to two sentences)

Activity 9.11

PICTURE BOOK STUDY: CALDECOTT BOOKS RECORDING AND INFORMATION SHEET

Student's Name__________________________

In the spaces below you are to preview three to five Caldecott Award–winning books. Your teacher will set your guidelines. Pay careful attention to the illustrations, the text, the story itself, and the appeal it would have for younger children. Try to decide why the book earned this most distinguished award. Enjoy.

1. Name of book: ________________________________Author:__________________

   Summary:____

   ____

   ____

   ____

   What do the illustrations look like? (Include colors, size, modern, old-fashioned, and so on.) What medium was used to create them? (Paper collage, block print, watercolor, pen, photographs, or other?) How did they relate to the story? What did they add to the appeal of the story? Do you think younger kids would appreciate these illustrations? Why or why not?
   Illustrations: ____

   ____

   ____

   ____

2. Name of book:_________________________________Author:__________________

   Summary of book:____

   ____

   ____

   ____

   Illustrations:____

   ____

   ____

   ____

Activity 9.11

PICTURE BOOK STUDY: CALDECOTT BOOKS RECORDING AND INFORMATION SHEET (*Continued*)

3. Name of book:________________________________Author:_______________________

   Summary of book:____

   Illustrations:____

4. Name of book:________________________________Author:_______________________

   Summary of book:____

   Illustrations:____

5. Name of book:________________________________Author:_______________________

   Summary of book:____

   Illustrations:____

— *Chapter 10* —

BOOK CLUBS AND LITERATURE CIRCLES

The grouping of children for literature discussions has been viewed extensively over the years by many researchers, including Daniels (1994, 2002), Calkins (2001), Fountas and Pinnell (2001), and Raphael and McMahon (1994), all of whom help inform our own classroom perspectives and everyday trials and errors. In the beginning of the year, we size up our classes and decide how we can use the structure to fit our students. We have preassessed our students' skill levels and their knowledge of talk, observed their levels of independence, and adjusted our concept to fit our students' needs. Every teacher needs to configure his or her book clubs or literature circles to fit the current year's unique set of students. What experiences have these students had selecting books? What kind of behavior does the class present during independent work sessions? Were the book clubs in their previous experiences structured or more informal? All of these questions need to be addressed before the classroom teacher can plan for book clubs in the individual classroom.

"LITERATURE CIRCLES" OR "BOOK CLUBS": WHAT SHALL WE CALL THEM?

The term *club* gives a member a sense of *belonging*, and belonging invites socialization and interaction. It connotes the sense that we are part of something important. For this reason, and because our students prefer the term, we have chosen to refer to literature discussion groups as *book clubs* in our classrooms. For the purpose of our discussion in this book, the terms *literature circles* (Daniels, 1994, 2002), *literature discussion groups* (Routman, 1996), and *book clubs* (Raphael & McMahon, 1994; Calkins, 2001) are synonymous.

Regardless of the name, book discussion groups have some critical features in common (Raphael & McMahon, 1994):

Enhanced student talk about text

High-quality literature in the form of trade books

Opportunities for all students to participate through interaction with their peers

Acceptance and valuing of personal responses as highly as traditional displays of comprehension

A natural approach to how students structure conversation about text and determine discussion topics

What Is a Book Club?

A book club is an instructional format or strategy in which small groups of students talk and think about a common book as they are reading. During and after reading a section of the book, the students prepare formally or informally for discussion. Some book clubs assign roles or responsibilities in a more formal manner, whereas others follow a natural flow of conversation with more informal planning. Students prepare for discussion by taking notes, writing journal entries, drawing illustrations, and reflecting on the book before the group meets. The children have regular meetings where they listen to the other members discuss their parts and then come to consensus as to how many pages should be read and by when. At the end of the book, the club members prepare a culmination activity as a way of sharing highlights of the book with the rest of their classmates. After the culmination activity, students select new reading and move into a new cycle.

The Benefits of Book Clubs

There are many advantages to starting up book clubs in the classroom. First, children seem to read *more* when they are independent of the teacher. Because they are making choices by themselves, offering input as to what they want to read, and pursuing their own reading interests, they enjoy reading more. The added element is the conversation that ensues, giving students the ability to bounce ideas off of each other and to question and wonder about the characters, plot, and setting in fiction, or events and information in nonfiction books.

Another benefit is that students work harder when they are pacing themselves, while assuming responsibility for scheduling and accountability. Because they are making their own decisions about how much they read as a group, often times they do not allow lax behavior—they like having a self-selected schedule of the number of pages to read and when it has to be finished. A piece of quality literature allows no slackers!

Book clubs teach students how to work together and how to be independent of the teacher. This collaboration gives them a feeling of responsibility and success: they are guiding the reading behaviors that they have put in place themselves.

Most students do not like to let their peers down, so they do what is expected of them. When the group agrees on an assignment, each member has to do his or her part. It might mean that everyone is pushed a little bit more than normal and there is a feeling of urgency to finish the assignment. A real camaraderie develops. Students who are falling behind are encouraged and motivated by their teammates. Often they are assisted in finishing their part.

Because book clubs are child-oriented and child-driven, students share responsibility for their learning and are actively engaged in purposeful and relevant learning. They begin to take risks, experiment with their independence, and feel successful when they receive positive feedback. Book clubs are filled with learning possibilities.

PUTTING BOOK CLUBS INTO PRACTICE

The size of the group depends on how many books are available as well as on the interests and needs of students. Book clubs may pair up as few as two students and as many as eight, but a group of three to five is ideal because it is small enough to be manageable and just right for personal interaction. All students have opportunities to talk and offer input to the discussion. The students feel comfortable talking and have less trouble coming to consensus about reading decisions. Students are not overwhelmed with too many members, and they can all have a voice in the group. The group may branch off into pairs for some of the reading work and come back together for a portion of the period. Challenged readers may glean new understanding by listening to conversations from other stronger readers and more articulate members of the group. The smaller size adds a comfortable and personal element to the club.

Although you may have a reason to place only two students in a book club, it probably is not the best configuration due to its lack of opportunity for rich conversation. Occasionally it is wise to place only two students together to push or challenge those who have difficulty taking an active part in a larger group. In this situation, the teacher may intervene more often. The paired book club may also be implemented if students have difficulty with independent behavior, as some students may still need help working toward personal management. The smaller the group, however, the less interaction takes place. This also causes difficulty when the group has someone absent. How can you have a discussion when a member of a paired group or triad is out of class, absent, or late to school?

Timing for Book Clubs

Discussions provide the foundation for the book club, and without a solid baseline book clubs can be flat, with only surface types of interaction. Rich, in-depth conversations need to be established before book clubs can begin. Even when previous teachers have had them, the students still need to know your style and your expectations for what this year's book clubs should look and sound like. Several months of daily interaction provide demonstration on how book clubs will work this year. We need to raise the bar each year, starting in third grade and progressing to middle school and above. If a book club in third grade looks and sounds the same as a book club in eighth grade, the teacher needs to do more modeling to lift the discussion.

Students stay in a book club for a set amount of time, possibly two or three weeks. Some teachers keep book clubs together for a long segment of time, whereas other teachers reconfigure groups with the change of books.

Ideas for Grouping

How well the students work together and what works best for them are most important. Heterogeneous or homogeneous ability–level groups may be formed, depending on the goal for students during a particular book club session. Advanced readers need times when they are grouped with similar readers, while at other times they may be grouped by interest with less able readers and act as positive models for the group. Sometimes there are advantages to mixing a variety of reading abilities in a group. Opportunities for both types of interactions are rewarding and necessary for building comprehension, cooperation, and collaboration. Often students are grouped by interest in particular subjects, themes, genres, or authors. For instance, when a Newbery Award study is being planned, the teacher can bring in a list of award-winning books and give the students a survey to see which books might be their favorites. Students can then rank their first, second, and third choices for books they would most like to read. The teacher then weighs the possibilities and does the best that he or she can to form groups that will work based on the choices, needs, and behaviors of the students. As other examples, teachers may have students choose from several works by a particular author, such as Avi, or from among a genre, like mysteries.

A special interest club can be formed to meet the needs of culturally diverse groups. In one classroom, a mixed group was formed for the purpose of building an appreciation for cultural backgrounds by using *Esperanza Rising* (Ryan, 2000). Capitalizing on the author's use of Spanish words in the book, a group of five proficient readers and one almost-proficient reader were placed together, including two English-only students and three others whose native language was Spanish. The club functioned at a very high level, but one Spanish speaker needed additional assistance to keep her reading going. Because she was a slower reader, the group supported her learning by calling her at home and providing comprehension checks to make sure that she understood her reading. The group utilized the Spanish words in the book by first making a list and then helping the English-only readers in their pronunciation. The group chose a radio talk show as their culminating activity. They wrote and presented the show in both English and Spanish. The enjoyable exchange of teaching and learning made a big impact on the rest of the class and set the stage for motivating another mixed-gender, multicultural group to choose this book for their next reading.

Groups may also be heterogeneous or homogeneous in terms of gender. Boys tend to resist stories about girls and are more inclined to read informational texts (Smith & Wilhelm, 2002). When studying Native Americans, for example, girls can be asked to read *Sing Down the Moon* (1970) by Scott O'Dell, with a girl as the main character, and the boys can read *Sign of the Beaver* (1983) by Elizabeth Speare, with a boy as the main character. Each group can look at history through its own gender perspective and then compare their lives now with the character's life in the book. Of course, there are always students who are anxious to read both books, and that approach can work out well. In addition, gender mixing is sometimes necessary to balance thinking, and boys need to be nudged into areas they try to avoid.

Choosing Materials to Read

In order to start book clubs, you will need quality books that are well written and meaningful to the students in your class. Newbery Award–winners are just that: award-winning books. They are filled with deep characters in rich settings, with complicated problems and solutions that twist and turn along the way to often unexpected endings. Newbery books have conflict that has to be resolved and surmountable obstacles for the characters to get through. The characters in Newbery books are ones that we can connect with; they help us to transfer their problems and solutions to our own lives. (See the section on Newbery Award–winning books in Chapter Two.)

Quality books come in nonfiction, too. As discussed in Chapter Five, navigating through nonfiction is complicated because of all the special features and vocabulary. For fifth graders, having a Jean Fritz author study in book clubs is a great starting point. Her books on famous people are small and filled with interesting information about such people as Ben Franklin, Patrick Henry, King George, and George Washington. She writes at a variety of levels to accommodate all of our learners. Besides using short nonfiction texts, you can use magazines that fit with your social studies or science standards such as *Kids Discover; Zillions: Consumer*

Reports for Kids; or *Cobblestone: The History Magazine for Kids*. This is an opportunity for upper-grade teachers to put some content into the literacy segment and read a more complicated genre with the support of group discussion.

Getting Started

One way to begin working with book clubs is by using short stories. Each small group is given a short story taken from a collection such as *Hey World, Here I Am!* (Little, 1986), *Seedfolks* (Fleischman, 1997), or *It's Fine to Be Nine* (MacLachlan, 1998). Start with one short story for the whole class and proceed to independent short stories for book clubs. If you are using roles such as summarizer, illustrator, or connector, start with one story and teach all the students about one role. Have them practice the role and then proceed with the whole class to teach another role. The teacher models the roles until each child can fill them independently. Everyone learns the different roles and is prepared for them during their first independent books. Other ideas include

- Start with only one or two groups at a time and gradually move the others into book clubs.
- Start with the most competent readers and conversationalists first, then build up the rest of the class.
- Hold only one or two book clubs at a time, while guided groups and independent reading continue on.
- Start with nonfiction book clubs, like a Jean Fritz author study.
- Start with a genre study such as mystery. While you are doing a mystery read-aloud and building knowledge of the genre, start groups independently reading mystery books for book clubs.
- Start with a narrative author study such as Gary Paulsen. For a read-aloud, read *Hatchet* (1987). Have numerous copies of Paulsen's books and let students choose groups by interest.
- Start with a theme like survival. As you read a book aloud such as *The Cay* (Taylor, 1969), ask students to suggest other books that fall under the survival theme. Form book clubs based on the students' suggestions.
- Ask a group of adults (who will all be available when you start) to form their own book club of children's literature that will be read by the students during the year. They can meet occasionally to review the books through discussion. Then when the class begins book clubs, you will have a few parent helpers who can assist groups as needed.
- Start with the whole class at the same time—just jump in!

Setting the Schedule

Schedules vary, but often groups meet every other day and take a break on the other days to catch up with their new assignment, take notes, and write in journals. On the days of meetings, the schedule may look like this:

- Ten-minute minilesson for modeling or refining elements needed for successful book clubs
- Fifteen- to twenty-minute discussion by members
- Five to ten minutes for paperwork and scheduling reading
- Twenty-minute reading of book club book or reflective journaling

Students may choose to read and complete some of their responsibilities as homework.

Student Roles in Book Clubs

Individual members of the book club may assume specific roles (Bender & Larkin, 2003; Daniels, 1994: Vacca et al., 2003). Activity 10.2 at the end of this chapter describes several possibilities.

The assignment of roles depends on teacher preference and any role choices children may already have in place. Role sheets provide the support that younger children need to give them ideas for things to talk about. Sometimes these roles make conversations seem stilted and artificial, but it is a foundational point that will move forward with modeling. In third grade, the use of role sheets is important because this is probably students' first exposure to literature groups. Third-grade conversations are often unsophisticated and need a lot of teacher direction and facilitating, whereas middle school students should be able to work with only minimal teacher intervention. Moving children quickly from role sheets into their own authentic conversations about books is preferable, but role sheet modeling is a scaffold that many students still need.

In schools with lots of second-language learners, the talk must be modeled and demonstrated, and everything is taken slowly. In this type of situation, wait until accountable talk is firmly planted and then attempt short story book clubs first as a whole class. As the year progresses, the students can be given opportunities to work independently.

MANAGING BOOK CLUBS

Managing book clubs takes some thought and projection. Good planning and organization will pay off in the end.

Rules of Etiquette

Upper-grade students cocreated the following chart to guide the book club sessions. The chart had a prominent place in the classroom throughout the year and was revisited often.

BOOK CLUB ETIQUETTE: RULES TO GUIDE YOUR CONVERSATIONS AND BEHAVIOR

Everyone must

- Participate in the conversation
- Show evidence of reading and thinking with sticky notes
- Sit at the same level and close together
- Stay focused on reading talk, not social talk
- Bring your own book
- Stay with your own group for the entire discussion time; discussion between groups is not appropriate

- Be a polite listener
- Use an inside voice so other groups can hear each other
- Come to consensus about what the next assignment will be

Book Club Folders

Every member of the club should have a notebook to keep his or her book club activities and responses to literature pieces. A notebook with two pockets works well, with one side for book club management information and the other side for a response journal and a good supply of sticky notes. As the group progresses to the culminating activity, the students will want to keep their work-in-progress notes.

Inside the folder the following sheets can be kept (see Activities 10.1 through 10.9 at the end of this chapter):

- Book Club Reading Schedule
- Book Club Roles
- Book Club Daily Evaluation
- Book Club Discussion Notes
- Book Club Planning Sheet
- "Fat Questions" to Keep Your Book Club Conversation Going
- Book Club Culminating Activities
- Rubric for Book Club Presentation and Project
- Book Club End-of-Unit Student Evaluation

Questions to Bring Out the Voices

When students are not experienced at creating questions on their own, this too must be modeled over and over in the minilesson section of the book club. Many students have become familiar with the ideas of *skinny* and *fat questions*. Fat questions have depth and complexity, offer more than one way to respond, and once you have answered them your way someone else might answer them completely differently. These types of questions are open-ended and allow others to feed off of them. The words "how," why," or "if" can be used to start out these questions.

- How did you relate to the story? Explain your ideas.
- Why did the main character act the way that he did?
- If you could add on a new chapter to this story, what would happen in it?
  What do you think the author was trying to say to the reader in this book?

Skinny questions can be answered with one word, and the respondent either knows the answer or does not. Once the question is answered, there is really nothing more to be said or discussed. Steer students away from these questions.

- What was the main character's last name?
- Who was the first person to arrive at the park?

- Who received the most money for working—John or Paul?

Besides eliciting one- or two-word answers, the questions themselves are weak and unnecessary. They really do nothing to help students make meaning from the text. Developing questions to make student dig into their brains, look for evidence in the text, and spur new thinking from their team members is what book club discussions are all about.

Through demonstration, setting expectations, and through practicing verbally and in written form, students can elevate the level of questioning in the room. In book clubs, *all* questions should be fat questions.

Keeping the Discussion Moving

When students are just getting started with book clubs, sometimes discussion lags. It takes time and practice to maintain a free flow of discussion that does not break down occasionally. For that reason, a list of things to talk about is placed in the students' folders or can be placed in a visible location in the classroom for reference. This list is also helpful for visitors who are helping with book clubs, such as substitute teachers, volunteers, student teachers, and administrators. See Activity 10.6 at the end of this chapter for some questions to keep the book club conversation going.

Using Sticky Notes

As adult readers, we sometimes underline or write notes in the margins of the pages as reminders of our reading. Children can use sticky notes to track their thinking. Children do not know how sticky note taking works until they are shown how to do it. The best process is to take a piece of your own reading, place it on the overhead or document camera, and model the way you mark your books. This strategy encourages stopping and thinking along the way, making connections, and actively processing the text.

Examples of things to briefly write on sticky notes might include

- Questions to the author—what was he thinking?
- Questions to the characters—what made you act that way?
- Questions about the setting
- Things that are confusing to you
- Things you think are interesting to share with your group members
- Things that surprised you
- Things that you connected with
- Places that are good examples of writer's craft
- Sections that make you ponder
- Passages that have great conversation, interesting words, or beautiful description

Response Journals and Literature Logs

Students need chances to be more reflective in their reading by completing longer writing pieces. Nancie Atwell (1987) found that among adolescents "written responses of books would go deeper than their talk, that writing would give them time to consider their thinking and their thoughts captured would spark new insight." The reading response journal is a perfect place to jot down more complete thoughts every few days, whereas the sticky notes provide brief, short comments on a daily basis. Responding to literature should be an ongoing process in the upper-grade classroom, allowing students to record their responses and reactions to all kinds of literature including read-alouds, shared reading, independent reading selections, and even textbooks. Students may summarize, give opinions, express feelings, make connections, or write questions. Journal writing must be modeled by the teacher and also by other students to ensure that the quality level meets your particular standards. Using student models on the overhead or document camera lifts the level of responses, and so does the occasional exchange of journals with other classmates.

Students in Shira's upper-grade class assembled the following list of possible journal topics for the times when they could not think of topics on their own.

- A favorite segment, situation, event, or chapter
- A summary of what was read
- Pictures, drawings, or illustrations with written descriptions of what is going on
- A description of a character's appearance, feelings, or actions
- Personal connections with the book
- Something noticed about the author's craft or literary elements
- Letters to the characters or the author: something of concern
- Confusions about the characters or plot
- Concerns, questions, opinions, solutions to problems, or descriptions of settings
- Graphic organizers to arrange personal thoughts
- Something a character should have done instead of what he actually did
- Feelings about the section or chapter read

Teachers should read students' journal entries to gain insight into the children's processing and comprehension of the pieces that they have read. Responding to their entries provides valuable feedback to students—at least for some of them. Management of the journals may be on a rotational basis, taking five or six journals to read on a certain day.

Charting

Students may occasionally be asked to chart or write down three to five key ideas that their group discussed in their book club meeting. (See the book club discussion notes in Activity 10.4 at the end of this chapter.) This activity sheet can be assigned to a particular member of the group who records the major discussion topics so that the teacher can review them at a later time.

Troubleshooting

Management concerns will need to be addressed during book clubs. Students can easily stray off topic and get distracted, so we must make sure that our book clubs are grounded in text focus, organization, accountable and authentic talk, respectful behavior, time management, and consequences for those who do not complete their assignments. We must work hard to train children in the appropriate behaviors and model them through minilessons and demonstrations so that the book club process runs smoothly.

Accommodations for Special Needs

Book clubs must be accessible to all of our students. Therefore, it is important to plan effectively for all of our special needs.

For Struggling Readers Struggling readers sometimes need special assistance to make their book club experiences more successful. Following are recommended ways to modify your instruction:

- Have an adult read to or with the child.
- Have the child read with a buddy.
- Use shorter stories that are less complicated and less complex.
- Use texts that are supported with pictures or illustrations.
- Make books on tapes available for listening at home or at the listening post.
- Provide a book that they can relate to or that interests them.
- Have parent helpers who have read the book come in to work with students who are struggling.
- Form a homogeneous group that receives additional teacher support on a daily basis.
- Inform the parents that additional reading will need to be done at home.
- Vary the makeup of book clubs so that struggling readers are not always with other struggling readers.
- Modify the management sheets.
- Break the reading into smaller chunks.
- Support the reading with a sequence chart of main events. Occasionally provide opportunities for book clubs centered around graphic novels or comic books.
- Look for selections that have humor in them.

For Advanced Readers

- Make sure there are ample books available to capture the interest of advanced learners.
- Use homogeneous groupings of kids who love to read and will push each other's thinking.
- Use Newbery Award books.
- Give them more independent time without teacher oversight.
- Keep students together for longer periods of time.
- Keep the expectations high.

- Provide opportunities to integrate students from several classes so that they have times to meet with new people they do not know as well.
- Use them as models for other classrooms to introduce the idea of book clubs to younger children.
- Videotape them for modeling purposes.
- Push them with books that they would normally not read.

Culminating Activities and Assessment

Students need to understand from the onset of this literature experience that they will be expected to make a book club presentation to the rest of the class and sometimes for their parents and other classes too. As groups finish their books, the team may start thinking about the activities they wish to complete.

The list in Activity 10.7 at the end of this chapter comes from several sources including Harvey Daniels (1994, 2002), but mostly from activities that third- through eighth-grade students have initiated themselves over the years of classroom application of book clubs. Keeping a notebook of photos, overheads, copies, and actual projects and ideas that have been produced by former students is a very effective way of demonstrating the standard of quality that is expected.

Some activities can be worked on independently, whereas others can be done in pairs, triads, or the entire group. The presentation itself may be completed independently or combined with the individual parts as one group. Students may choose one or more than one activity.

Through observation, informal note taking, looking over sticky notes and journal entries, and listening to discussions, teachers have a good chance to make sure students are developing better reading skills and understanding through the book club process. The teacher is the facilitator and must gradually release the responsibility of reading into the hands of the students. Assessment must be continuous in the reading and writing workshop. Students are part of the assessment process. Through self- and peer-evaluation, students learn how they measure up on a daily basis. High standards of personal behavior and reading behaviors must be maintained throughout the book club sessions, and students must be held accountable.

VARIATIONS OF BOOK CLUBS

Many special kinds of book clubs can also be formed throughout the school. These make the school community more connected and further develop the idea of communication on a wider scale of understanding. Following are a few types.

Schoolwide Book Clubs. Schoolwide book clubs are beneficial for students and provide common language and cross-age interactions to talk about common books.

Professional Book Clubs. Some schools provide professional reading opportunities for staff to learn new and current theories in education. The teachers read a book like *Reading Essentials* (2003) by Regie Routman. They chunk the book into smaller segments for reading purposes, discuss the segments in small groups, reflect in their personal reading journals, and respond to the whole group on things they have gleaned from their reading. At the end of the reading, teachers are asked to reflect on their thinking and what has helped them become better teachers as a result.

Writing Book Clubs. At some schools, small groups of teachers form a writing book club on their own. A middle or upper-grade group can form to read *The 6 + 1 Traits of Writing,* the primary team could read *Creating Young Writers* (Spandel, 2004), and the kindergarten team might read *Teaching Young Writers Strategies That Work* (Schaefer, 2001). Periodic meetings are held to support each other's learning, and new ideas are implemented in their classrooms.

Parent Book Clubs. A school might experiment with forming a parent book club to preread children's novels that support the standards, teacher instruction, and struggling readers' needs in a particular grade level.

After- or Before-School Reading Clubs. Some schools allow students to form their own book clubs around a book that they are all interested in reading. This can be monitored by a volunteer teacher who is willing to sponsor an after-school or before-school reading club.

Grade-Level Book Clubs. Grade-level book clubs can be formed to get everyone reading the same novel or hearing it read to them. This approach gives students something to talk about during recess and lunch periods. The sharing of a book evokes great conversations. Students can also be mixed during class book club sessions so that children who are interested in a particular book that will not be covered in their classrooms are able to join another classroom's book club. Management of this approach requires flexibility from several teachers, but it can be very successful.

BUILDING A SCHOOLWIDE READING COMMUNITY

With the excitement of reading permeating the classroom environment through extended reading time and flourishing classroom libraries, it is a perfect time to have a schoolwide reading experience. This may be done two or three times throughout the year or, for some schools, on a more regular basis. A committee representing the staff and the community may determine the selection of the book(s) related to a genre, author, or theme to consider the interests, needs, and culture of the school. This common reading of a book as a school seems to unite teachers, administrators, students, and parents and develops a sense that everyone is a member of a reading team. Usually the book is presented as a read-aloud or a shared reading experience. Related activities and accountable talk provide opportunities for the teacher to assess student understanding. Individual classrooms create a myriad of activities in reading, writing, art, music, and drama to show that the students "own" the book. For a period of several weeks or a month, there is confirmation around the school that everyone is "into" this special book. A display in the cafeteria, media center, or even in the hallways suggests that there is true collaboration going on at the site.

With hectic schedules and standardized testing weighing heavily on our minds, it is always difficult to find time to add one more thing to the day. For a first-year attempt, it might be good to start small and try one book each semester.

At Gage Elementary School, three literary categories were selected for a schoolwide read to touch everyone in some positive way. In January, a book was chosen from the sports genre, which provided a nice segue into February's Winter Olympics. The selection committee decided to focus on the book *Wilma Unlimited* by Kathleen Krull (1996). Although it is about a summer Olympic gold medalist, it allows the reader see the true heart and soul of an Olympian and the challenges that a champion must overcome. It was decided that this book would be perfect for grades K–5, building the sports genre interest while motivating students to meet their own challenges as they grow up. According to teacher's preferences, this unit could be taught as a theme or genre study.

WILMA UNLIMITED: ACTIVITIES AND PROJECTS

- Brainstorm a list of words that describe Wilma and other Olympic champions. Take the letters in her name and create strong phrases and words to describe her.
- Write paragraphs showing what you think it would be like to walk in Wilma's track shoes. Use running shoes to frame your paragraphs.
- Write a point-of-view paragraph taking the view of Wilma's track shoes. What would your life be like?
- Choose another great athlete and compare his or her life with Wilma's success.
- Read another story about your sports hero and explain his or her successes, physical and personal characteristics, and tell why he or she is your hero.
- Write a personal narrative telling who is your favorite sports hero and why.
- Create a song or poem depicting Wilma's life.
- Write an essay explaining how Wilma overcame the odds.
- Create a time line about Wilma's life.
- Create a poster or collage showing and explaining what kinds of foods Olympic champions would most likely eat. Make sure you include all of the basic food groups.
- Write a letter to Wilma as if she were still alive. Explain who you are and what you admire about her.
- Research polio. Find out the names of other famous people who also had it.
- Invite a trainer, doctor, physical therapist, or physical education teacher to speak to your class. Have this guest talk about keeping your bodies in good shape and the importance of eating right and exercising. Take pictures and write up what you learned.
- Interview someone you know who had polio. Write down questions that you would like to ask him or her before the visit. Write down the responses.
- Take photos of kids in warm-up activities that Wilma might have done. Explain the exercise.
- Write letters to other famous sports heroes using *The Kids' Address Book* (Levine, 2001). Have everyone read a book about a sports hero. Create book jackets to go along with their own books.
- Create a class poem.
- Present a class shared reading about Wilma on video.
- Create a storyboard about Wilma.
- Create a videotape dramatizing events in Wilma's life.
- Have students prepare a group report on Wilma.
- Create a life-size representation of Wilma stuffed with crumpled-up paper.
- Make a list of Wilma Rudolph web sites to visit. Mark them on a computer under favorites. Set them up for all to use.

For February, more than one book was selected. All classrooms were invited to take part in Read Across America's Dr. Seuss celebration. The schoolwide read would be an author study that would coincide with Dr. Seuss's birthday. Units of study were written up by a committee of teachers for both the primary and the upper-grade teachers with certain titles designated as more appropriate for grades 3 through 5.

At the end of the year, *Ordinary Mary's Extraordinary Deed* (Pearson, 2002) was selected to call students to action and encourage them to see that one person can change the world. All classes provided a display project for the auditorium.

In summary, a schoolwide read is an excellent way to allow everyone to contribute to a larger community: the school. So often in today's world, teachers and students feel very isolated from each other. Through these kinds of collaborative school efforts, conversations about books will open up and the schoolwide community will be more solidified.

Buddy Classes

Many elementary classes and K–8 schools pair an upper-grade room with a primary room for literacy activities. For the schoolwide read, this collaborative effort is a perfect fit. Primary students and their upper-grade buddies are able to have beneficial discussions about a book and the elements that are specified in the standards, such as character, plot, and setting. Sometimes younger children are more comfortable discussing a selection with an older child than they are in classroom sessions with the teacher or their own peers. A deeper, more meaningful discussion that bridges ages and grades is beneficial for both groups. This cross-age literacy exchange is a building block for deeper academic discussion and provides access to stronger communication. When the older children initiate the conversation with their buddies, the teacher can assess whether they are learning what is being taught in the Reading Workshop in their own classroom.

One Big Book Club

This experience provides students across the grade levels with their first book club discussion and collaboration. There is chatter around the school about a book that all students, teachers, office staff, custodians, and administration have read. You cannot escape the enjoyment of students sharing a piece of literature. The school community unifies into one big all-encompassing book club.

Activity 10.1

BOOK CLUB READING SCHEDULE

Name of the Book

____

Book Club Members: ______________________________

____

____

Date	From Page	To Page
________	________	________
________	________	________
________	________	________
________	________	________
________	________	________
________	________	________

Date	From Page	To Page
________	________	________
________	________	________
________	________	________
________	________	________
________	________	________
________	________	________
________	________	________
________	________	________
________	________	________

Culmination Activity ______________________________

____

____

Due Date: ________

Activity 10.2

BOOK CLUB ROLES

Basic Roles All group members keep a record of their findings on sticky notes or other paper. This written account should be neat and contain few errors in spelling or grammar. All sticky notes should be completed on your scheduled meeting date. Group members may assist each other in finding pertinent evidence to support your points. The roles marked with an asterisk (*) are required, whereas the other roles may be assigned as needed or when ideas for more conversation are needed.

***Discussion Director** Your responsibility is to think of good questions to ask during the discussion of the chapters that you just read. The questions should be "fat questions"—in other words, they should be open-ended. Each person should be able to add on to the discussion. It is a good idea to have each person talk about something that they have marked in their book such as a question, wondering, response back to the author, confusion, or a favorite or interesting part. If the discussion is not going well, you might use the "Fat Questions" sheet in Activity 10.6.

***Illustrator** You are responsible for creating a visual picture of three different scenes from the reading selection and illustrating one on the sticky note provided. Prepare an illustration and write a brief summary of what you have drawn and why you drew it. What events led up to this picture and what happened afterwards? Ask your group to guess what your picture is about before you tell them. Help your group members talk about the event.

***Connector** You will use sticky notes to save places in the story that you or other members of the group can connect with or relate to. Think of things that you have in common with the main character. What do other characters from books you have already read this year have in common with this character? You should look for text-to-text, text-to-self, and text-to-world connections that are important to you as a reader and will help you hold on to the gist of the story and make meaning.

***Summarizer** You are responsible for briefly summarizing what the group has just read. Make sure you share the key or main events from the reading. Use bullets to identify the main events. Ask your group members to agree or disagree with your account.

Conflict Connector Conflict is the main struggle that takes place in the story. Most stories center around four basic types of conflict.

- Character versus character
- Character versus nature (storms, forest fires, or tornadoes)

Activity 10.2

BOOK CLUB ROLES (*Continued*)

- Character versus himself or herself (being afraid, lonely, unhappy, or angry)
- Character versus the laws or customs of society

In your job, you are to decide which conflict was the dominant one in the story. Identify three different ways the main character tried to resolve the conflict. If you were the main character, would you have tried to resolve the conflict the same way or in a different way? Explain your answer.

Literary Element Locator You are to mark places in the chapter where the author has used story elements such as similes, metaphors, flashbacks, foreshadowing, conflict, writing style, voice, point of view, and so on. Page numbers should be marked with sticky notes. Other elements such as italics, conversation, chapter titles, themes, and special writing techniques may also be discussed. Your group should be encouraged to locate these elements within the story too. You might ask them to find the element on page ___. When someone finds it, ask him or her to tell the rest of the group if it is at the top, middle, or bottom of the page. You might ask someone else to read it back to the group. You can also take the group back into the story where there is descriptive language or other memorable parts. Refer to Activity 10.6, "Fat Questions" to Keep Your Book Club Conversation Going.

*__Word Wizard__ Your job is to look for special words in the story that are difficult, unfamiliar, funny, or unusual. The words should be marked with sticky notes, defined by looking them up in the dictionary, and used correctly in a sentence. You might ask the group to locate the word on the page you found it and have someone read the sentence aloud to the group. Have one group member try to define the word and use it in a sentence. Use sentence strips so that all of your group members can see the word. Put the word on the word wall when you are finished with your group.

*__Character Investigator__ Your role is to help your group better understand the characters in the book. You should be watching for any changes in personal growth in the characters. Think of at least three characteristics of the main character. Look for ways that the character reveals himself or herself to you. Support these character traits with an example or evidence from the text. Consider what might happen to the character as the story progresses.

Passage Picker Your job is to pick parts of the story that you want to read aloud to your group. You can choose parts that are funny, scary, interesting, powerful, sad, or engaging. Have your group follow along as you read the section to them. Then ask your group questions about their feelings about those passages. You might want to try different voices for each of the characters and read with the voice that you think the character would really use. You should practice your reading several times aloud so that you are fluent in your delivery.

Note to the Student: These are examples of roles you might be asked to assume during book clubs. Read through each role and discover which kinds of things you might prefer to do. Of course, you might think of more innovative ways to perform your role.

Activity 10.3

BOOK CLUB DAILY EVALUATION

Week of: ______________________

Book Title: ______________________

Author: ______________________

Student's Name ______________________

1. Completed reading on time
2. Brought the book to discussion
3. Showed evidence of reading (sticky notes, notes on paper, and so on)
4. Prepared for discussion (with summary and questions)
5. Participated in discussion
6. Listened politely
7. Responded to others in group
8. Wrote in Literature Log and shared out

Leader Initials: ________

Note to Group Leader: Evaluate each group member with a +, $\surd$, or – on each day you meet. Place your initials at the bottom of the column you evaluated.

Activity 10.4

BOOK CLUB DISCUSSION NOTES

Names ______________________ Date of Meeting ______________

Book ____

Name five *important things* that your group talked about today in your book club.

1. ____

____

2. ____

____

3. ____

____

4. ____

____

5. ____

____

Activity 10.5

BOOK CLUB PLANNING SHEET

Group Members ______________________________

Book Name ______________________________

How do you think you will pace yourself on this book? ______________________________

What challenges do you think you will have, both with the book and as a group?

How do you think you will prepare for a conversation about this book? ______________________________

How will you support members of your group who have difficulty completing their reading and responses? ______________________________

What help will you need from the teacher? ______________________________

What guidelines will you set for your group members in order to make sure everyone completes his or her reading and discussion preparation? ______________________________

Activity 10.6

"FAT QUESTIONS" TO KEEP YOUR BOOK CLUB CONVERSATION GOING

"Oh, she's preparing her 'Fat Questions.'"

- Why do you think the author wrote this chapter or book?
- What do you think was the author's big idea or message?
- What did you wonder about as you read this chapter or book?
- If you had a chance to talk with this author, what would you ask him or her?
- Why do you suppose the author titled the chapter or book the way he or she did?
- Does this chapter or book remind you of other books we have read in this class or that you have read in your independent reading? Which ones? Give evidence for your answer.
- Did you connect with any of the characters? Explain.
- Who in this class do you think would like this book? What makes you think so?
- Do you think this is an important chapter or book? Explain your idea.
- How does the main character change in the chapter or book?
- Where did you see the change begin?
- Is there any part of the chapter or book that really had an impact on you? Explain that part. If a part didn't impact you, explain your favorite part.
- Do you think the title fits the chapter or book? Explain your thinking.
- Do you have another name for this chapter or story? Why would you call it that?
- Are there chapter titles in this book? If so, how did they help you understand the story?
- Explain the setting of the story. How did the location and period of time affect the characters and the plot?
- Can you think of any stories with the same or similar settings?
- Find a part in the story that is important to you in some way. Read the part aloud and explain its importance.
- What questions do you have to ask the main character about his or her behavior? What parts of the chapter or story were confusing to you? Ask your book club members to help you understand the part.
- Find examples of literary elements such as *foreshadowing, flashbacks, comic relief, satire, sarcasm, mood, theme, dialect, informal language, conflict, rising action, climax, point of view, and so forth*. As you find them, mark them in your book with sticky notes.
- How would you shorten this book? Or lengthen it?

Activity 10.7

BOOK CLUB CULMINATING ACTIVITIES

Due Date ______________________

When your book club finishes reading its selected book, your group will select one project to present during our culminating activities. Final evaluation will be based on the quality of this project and your written self-evaluation.

Following is a list of possible projects.

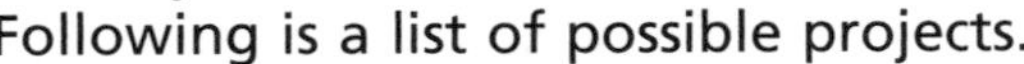

Writing Activities

- Create a ***new ending, another chapter***, or a ***new experience*** for the main character.
- Make a ***chart*** or ***poster*** telling what messages the author was trying to convey.
- Write a ***letter to the author*** or ***to a character.***
- Write a ***book review*** for the school newspaper.
- Write a ***Reader's Digest version*** of the story for a younger person, including a few pictures.
- Produce a ***choral verse*** about the story with your whole book club group taking a part.
- Do some ***research about the author***, referring to books or the Internet.
- Write ***letters to school*** or ***public librarians*** telling them why they should purchase the book for others to read.
- Write ***a letter to a friend*** or ***relative*** convincing him or her to read the book using persuasive arguments.
- Create a ***comic-type spreadsheet*** retelling the story with talk bubbles and simple comic illustrations on plain white paper.
- Advertise ***the book*** using the propaganda techniques that real commercials use.
- Make a ***literary scrapbook*** about a character in the book with postcards, pictures, award certificates, report cards, and so on.
- Write a ***prequel*** or ***sequel*** for the book.
- Make an enlarged ***report card*** for the main character.
- Create a ***diary*** for the main character, with five entries in it as if you were the character.

Reading Activities

- Have your ***whole family read the book.*** Discuss the differences between your feelings about the book and the feelings of your family members. (You could videotape the book talk.)
- Read ***another book by the same author*** and use a Venn diagram to compare the two books.

Activity 10.7

BOOK CLUB CULMINATING ACTIVITIES (*Continued*)

Read aloud ***key passages*** using the voice of the character and your voice as the reader and tell why you chose those parts.

Oral Language Activities

- Develop a ***book talk***.
- Make a tape recording of your group members reading different parts of the book. Use ***different voices for the characters*** you choose.
- Choose ***ten things from your houses*** that represent the story. Bring them in a special box. Pull one out at a time and explain why the item is important to the story. Display the items on a table and label each one.
- ***Impersonate the characters*** in costume with props.
- Present a ***newscast*** reporting the events that happened in the book.
- Present a ***debate*** about one of the issues in the book.
- Put one of the characters in the book on the ***trail of a crime.*** Prepare your case, giving all your arguments and supporting them with facts.
- Pretend you are a ***TV or radio interviewer.*** Prepare an audio- or videotape interview with a character in the book.
- Have a ***group discussion*** about why the author might have written this book. Did he or she have something that he or she wanted children to think about more deeply? If so, what was the message he or she was trying to convey?

Word Study

- Create a ***word challenge.*** Find eight to ten words that might cause someone to have difficulty.
- Find ***ten new words*** from the text that you might be able to teach to others. Write them on sentence strips and put them on a chart. Read the word from the text. See if classmates can figure out the meaning.
- Create a ***word game*** to challenge your classmates to learn several new words or create a Word of the Day section for the word wall, bulletin board, or classroom whiteboard based on the new words that you encountered in your book.
- If you are reading a book with ***foreign words*** in it, such as ***Esperanza Rising***, make a chart of at least ten of these words. Put the foreign word in one column, the pronunciation in another column, and the meaning in the last column. Make sure you know how to pronounce the words and practice them with the help of the class.
- Prepare a ***crossword puzzle*** using questions from the book.

Activity 10.7

BOOK CLUB CULMINATING ACTIVITIES (*Continued*)

Performance Activities

- Create a ***radio show on tape or a talk show*** interviewing people about their feelings about the book, interviewing the characters, or interviewing the author about reasons for writing the book. Make sure you prepare eight to ten questions ***before*** the show.
- Compose a ***skit*** based on a part of the book.
- Create a ***reader's theater*** script and act it out.
- Perform ***hotseat:*** one member of the group poses as the character. The other members ask the character meaningful questions about his or her behavior, actions, feelings, reasons for doing things, and so on.
- Create a ***video*** of one of the scenes. Bring it to school for your classmates to enjoy.
- Produce a ***live performance*** using props and costumes.
- Role-play a ***phone conversation*** or ***conference call*** between two or more characters.
- Write and act out an ***advertisement or commercial*** for the book using a video camera.

Music and Art Activities

- Create a ***song or a dance*** about the book.
- Create a ***scene in the book*** inside a cereal box, shoebox, or other type of box. Include a written paragraph to explain what is going on in the scene you have chosen.
- Use a camera to shoot ***photographs*** that retell the story.
- Create a ***piece of art*** to represent the book using painting, photography, collage, or other art media.
- Create a ***set of puppets*** or ***character sticks*** and perform one of the scenes from the book.
- Make up a ***board game*** to represent a part of the story or all of it.
- Create a ***poster board***.
- Create a ***musical representation*** of the book. It might be a song, chant, or jingle. You might also have musical accompaniment.
- Make a ***banner or mural.*** You might want to divide it into sections.

Research Activities

- Look up information in books or on the Internet about the ***history of the period or the setting*** of the book. Inform your classmates about your findings.
- Research the author of the book. Inform your class about your discoveries.

Activity 10.7

BOOK CLUB CULMINATING ACTIVITIES (*Continued*)

Games

- Create a ***twenty questions game*** about the book.
- With your group, plan a ***Jeopardy-type game*** with $10, $20, $30, $40, and $50 questions. Also include a Daily Double.

Miscellaneous Activities

- Present a ***book talk*** in your native language.
- Create a ***memory basket*** with items representing events or themes in the story.

Activities Using Graphic Organizers, Diagrams, or Charts

- Make a list of the ***major and minor problems*** faced by the characters in this book. Talk about the solutions.
- Make a ***sequence chart*** with sentence strips to show the main events in the story. Paste them onto a large piece of paper.
- Create a ***time line*** of the events in the story. Consult your social studies book for the correct form.
- Create a ***Top Ten chart*** of what you should know about this book.
- If your book is in movie form, ***see the movie or watch the video*** with your group. Discuss how it resembled and how it differed from the book. Make a Venn diagram poster showing your thinking.
- Use two different ***graphic organizers*** to retell, sequence, or compare the story with another one.

Activity 10.8

RUBRIC FOR BOOK CLUB PRESENTATION AND PROJECT

Group Names: ____

______ Planning for our project is evident.

______ We worked as a team on this project.

______ We have evidence showing that we each played a part.

______ Our work is grade-level quality.

Explain what part you played in this presentation. ______________________

____

____

____

Tell me anything I should know about how your other group members participated in your presentation. ____

____

____

____

I think my group should receive a/an ____ on this book club project.

I think I should personally receive a/an ____ on this book club project.

My opinions about this book are: ____________________________________

____

____

____

____

____

The next book I would like to read for book club is: ______________________

____

Group Grade: _______ Personal Grade: ____________

Activity 10.9

BOOK CLUB END-OF-UNIT STUDENT EVALUATION SHEET

Student's Name: ______________________________

Book: ______________________________

Members in my book club: ______________________________

____

List the things that you did to help your book club during reading, discussing, and presenting segments: ______________________________

____

____

____

What grade do you think you should receive overall? ______________

Why do you think you should get that grade? ______________________________

____

What grade would you give to the whole group? ______________________________

Give reasons for this opinion. ______________________________

What would you like your teacher to know about your team members' participation and how you worked together? (confidential) ______________________________

____

____

Book Club Grade: ______________ Teacher Comments: ______________

____

____

____

— Chapter 11 —

READING AND WRITING DIFFICULTIES IN STUDENTS

Note: In preparing this chapter, the authors relied on two of their previous publications: *How to Reach and Teach Children with ADD/ADHD* (2nd ed.), by S. Rief, 2005, San Francisco: Jossey-Bass. Copyright 2005 by Sandra R. Rief; and *How to Reach and Teach All Children in the Inclusive Classroom* (2nd ed.), by S. Rief and J. Heimburge, 2006, San Francisco: Jossey-Bass. Copyright 2006 by Sandra R. Rief and Julie A. Heimburge.

The past decade has brought to the forefront the science of teaching reading. The research has taught us much about how children learn to read and why some struggle in doing so, and it now guides literacy instruction in schools across the United States. The National Institute of Child Health and Human Development (NICHD), provided much of the research that has advanced our understanding of reading and how to prevent reading problems. NICHD developed a research network consisting of forty-one research sites in North America (and other parts of the world) that conducted numerous studies on thousands of children over a period of decades. The evidence from this wealth of research first came to light when it was presented by G. Reid Lyon to the U.S. Senate (Lyon, 1998). More research findings on this topic were revealed at around the same time by the Committee on the Prevention of Reading Difficulties in Young Children, in the National Research Council. These results can be found in *Preventing Reading Difficulties in Young Children* (Snow, Burns, & Griffin, 1998).

In response to a request from Congress, an expert panel—the National Reading Panel (NRP)—was formed and charged with the task of reviewing the research to identify the best ways of teaching children to read. The panel found that a combination of techniques was effective (NRP, 2000), but five key areas identified in this report have become the focus for reading instruction: phonemic awareness, phonics, fluency, vocabulary, and text comprehension.

The No Child Left Behind legislation signed by President Bush in December 2001, and the Reading First initiative that followed, both highlighted these five areas, explicitly mandating that they form a central part of any reading initiative funded by federal money (Wren, 2003a).

Why is it so important to raise reading achievement and prevent reading failure? Following are just some of the statistics that indicate the urgency:

- Ten million children, or 17.6 percent, have significant reading difficulties (Hall & Moats, 1999; Schwab Learning, 2002).
- According to the National Assessment of Educational Progress, approximately one in four students in the twelfth grade (who have not already dropped out of school) are still reading at below basic levels, while only one student in twenty reads at an advanced level (Wren, 2003b).
- The percentage of fourth graders reading at or above proficient was 31 percent in 2002 and has remained steady since then. Seventy-three percent of eighth graders were at or above basic (indicating partial mastery of fundamental skills) and 31 percent were at or above proficient in 2005 (National Center for Education Statistics, 2006).
- In some schools, as much as 70 to 80 percent of inner-city students and 30 percent of suburban students are reaching upper elementary levels unable to read and understand grade-appropriate material (Honig, 1999).
- In some communities, the proportion of students beyond third grade who cannot read well enough to participate in grade-level work is between 60 and 70 percent, depending on the grade and year of assessment (Moats, 2001).

READING PROBLEMS AND RESEARCH

As a result of this abundance of research (Lyon, 1998; Snow, Burns, & Griffin, 1998; NRP, 2000) we now know much about underlying causes of reading failure, what is necessary to prevent reading problems from occurring, the importance of early intervention, and what happens to students who do not receive the help they need. We know that children who are most at risk for reading failure enter kindergarten limited in their awareness of sound structure and language pattern, phonemic sensitivity, letter knowledge, the purposes of reading, and have had little exposure to books and print. Approximately 50 percent of reading difficulties can be prevented if students are provided effective language development in preschool and kindergarten and effective reading instruction in the primary grades.

"We learned that for 90 percent to 95 percent of poor readers, prevention and early intervention programs that combine instruction in phoneme awareness, phonics, fluency development, and reading comprehension strategies, provided by well-trained teachers, can increase reading skills to average levels. We have also learned that if we delay intervention until nine years of age (the time that most children with reading difficulties receive services), approximately 75 percent of the children will continue to have difficulties learning to read throughout high school" (Lyon, 1998).

Failure to read proficiently is the most common reason that students drop out, get retained, or are referred to special education. In fact, as many as 80 percent of referrals to special education involve reading difficulties. The most frequent characteristic observed among children and adults with reading disabilities is a slow, labored approach to decoding, or sounding out, unknown or unfamiliar words and frequent misidentification of familiar words.

According to Lyon (1998), research points to at least four factors that hinder reading development among children irrespective of their socioeconomic level and ethnicity:

(1) deficits in phoneme awareness and development of the alphabetic principle (and the accurate, fluent application of these skills to reading text), (2) deficits in acquiring comprehension strategies and applying them to the reading of text, (3) lack of the development and maintenance of motivation to learn to read, and (4) inadequate preparation of teachers.

Struggling Older Readers

Many poor readers in the third through eighth grades were simply never taught in the earlier grades the skills that we now know are so important for reading success. Phonemic awareness was not something that most teachers had ever heard of or directly taught, and many whole language classrooms provided minimal instruction in phonics and decoding skills. Some students are poor readers because they have been insufficiently taught. However, many struggling readers have a brain-based, neurobiological reason for their difficulty learning to read. Regardless of why students are lacking in some of the five building blocks for reading (phonemic awareness, phonics, fluency, vocabulary, and text comprehension), if weakness in a particular area is holding them back in their reading progress, that weakness needs to be addressed.

Kevin Feldman (2001), director of reading and early intervention in the Sonoma County Office of Education (in Santa Rosa, California), believes that older struggling readers must fill in the holes and build the literacy foundations they have missed, such as

- Phonological and phonemic awareness
- Grapheme and phoneme matching
- Decoding of single and polysyllabic words
- Reading fluency
- Word structure (for example, syllable complexity and morphology)
- Word study and layers of the English language
- Comprehension and text-handling strategies
- Study skills, habits, and strategies in content-area reading and writing

For upper elementary and middle school teachers, it is too late to implement that valuable early intervention that research shows can *prevent* a high percentage of reading failure. But it is never too late to intervene. In fact, we must do so. We need to identify the specific reading difficulties of readers who are struggling in order to provide the appropriate intervention. Assessment is necessary to identify those "holes" in their particular reading skills and then to provide the targeted instruction and intervention to boost those particular skills. There are numerous strategies and suggestions throughout this book to help classroom teachers provide a rich curriculum and accelerate students' reading growth. For those students whose reading skills are significantly below grade level, additional, more intensive intervention will be needed to expedite growth and get through the barrier of avoidance, poor self-concept, and other issues that will have developed from years of reading failure.

As Moats (2001) describes the challenge of teaching older students who are poor readers, "They cannot read, so they do not like to read; reading is labored and unsatisfying, so they have little reading experience; and, because they have not read much, they are not familiar with the vocabulary, sentence structure, text organization and concepts of academic 'book' language. Over time, their comprehension skills decline because they do not read, and they also become poor spellers and poor writers. What usually begins as a core phonological and word recognition deficit, often associated with other language weaknesses, becomes a diffuse, debilitating problem with language—spoken and written."

Learning Disabilities and Other Brain-Based Reading Problems

Learning disabilities is a term used to describe a neurobiological disorder and set of conditions that interfere with the ability to receive, process, store, respond to, or produce information. These disabilities affect somewhere in the range of 5 to 15 percent of the population. They can cause difficulty with language, memory, listening, conceptualization, speaking, reading, writing, spelling, math, and motor skills—in various combinations and degrees. Each individual is unique in the combination of strengths and weaknesses and the degree of impairment. Learning disabilities (LDs) may affect any combination of the reception or input of information into the brain (visual or auditory perception), the integration of that information in the brain (processing, sequencing, and organizing), the retrieval from storage (auditory or visual memory), and the output or expression of that information (communicating through motor skills or through oral or written language) (Rief & Heimburge, 2006).

Dyslexia

Most children with LDs have deficits in their language-based skills: reading, writing, spelling, listening, and word retrieval and use. This is the type of LD known as *dyslexia*. Individuals with dyslexia have a language-based learning disorder predominantly affecting their reading, but generally other language skills as well. Of the population with a reading disability, 85 percent have dyslexia (International Dyslexia Association, 2000).

Some characteristics you might see in children with dyslexia include the following (Currie & Wadlington, 2000):

- Poor phonemic awareness, phonological processing, and decoding
- Lack of fluency or automaticity when reading orally
- Adding or deleting letters, sounds, or syllables from words
- Poor reading comprehension
- Very poor spelling
- Poor written composition
- Problems recalling names of events, people, places, and objects
- Difficulty sequencing, scrambling, or reversing letters, words, and/or numbers
- Problems with directionality
- Difficulty expressing ideas orally
- Delay in verbal response
- Difficulty following oral directions, often needing information repeated
- Very literal interpretation of slang or figurative language
- Great difficulty learning a foreign language
- Problems with math related to language, sequencing, or directionality
- Slow at completing tasks involving reading and/or writing

- Frustration, anxiety, and avoidance when faced with language tasks
- Achievement that lags behind intellectual ability

For students with reading disabilities who do not have phonologically based problems (the core problem for most), orthographic processing may be the key deficit. These children have weakness in the visual processing areas. These learners typically have difficulty recognizing letters and words, recognizing and recalling the sequence of letters within words, and using productive cues to help them visually distinguish word patterns (Stanovich & West, 1989; McCormick, 2003).

When teaching reading to learning disabled/dyslexic students, Feldman (2000, p. 102) recommends "the same things as with any other student, but provided with more and better instruction . . . that is to say, more systematic, more explicit, more precise, more time spent in modeling, practicing skills and strategies, etc. 'LD/Dyslexic' students do not need different . . . they need *better* and *more*!" Feldman (2000) also identifies these five factors as necessary for improving reading achievement for any student:

Continuous assessment—teaching driven by data and results

Time—increasing the amount of time children spend reading and writing

Teaching—explicit modeling and practice of useful reading strategies

Differentiation of instruction—teach 'em where they are

Motivation and ownership of literacy activities—involving students in choices, interests, and connections they care about

Determining if a child or teen has an LD impairing reading requires a psychoeducational evaluation. It is important for upper elementary and middle school teachers to advocate for struggling readers who may have LDs impeding their reading. Discuss these issues with your school's student support team (SST). Talk to your reading specialists, administrators, and special education staff. Seek any support and intervention that you feel is needed for a student's success. You may need to be persistent in advocating for an evaluation.

Attention Deficit/Hyperactivity Disorder (AD/HD)

Another common neurobiological disorder that may cause some students to have difficulty in reading is AD/HD. Students with AD/HD may have some reading problems, despite generally having average or strong skills in decoding and word recognition (if they don't have a coexisting LD). Although they may read fluently, their distractibility and poor executive functioning skills can cause problems focusing on their reading, recalling what they have read, and effectively using their metacognitive skills. This often results in "spotty comprehension" of the reading material.

Inattention can cause the child difficulty maintaining his or her train of thought while reading, thereby missing words and important details. Distractibility can interfere with his or her processing of the information and comprehension of the text, which is particularly common when reading material the child finds boring or difficult (Rief, 2005).

Many students with AD/HD, LDs, or some combination of these fail to use the metacognitive strategy of self-monitoring comprehension while reading the text by addressing errors in comprehension as soon as they arise. They are not actively engaging while reading (for example, predicting, making connections, and self-questioning). They aren't realizing as they read that they are not comprehending the text and applying the fix-up strategies to correct this when it occurs. These students need to be taught how to become strategic, active readers and thinkers. They need explicit instruction and practice in strategies such as paraphrasing, summarizing, and reciprocal teaching through the use of techniques that require active involvement in thinking about and responding to what is being read. They need to learn to read a portion of the material and then do something with that information, such as sharing with a partner, recording a few words on a graphic organizer, or answering a question. See Chapters Three and Twelve for more on teaching students to become strategic, active readers.

The Gender Gap in Reading

Boys are known to be more at risk for poor reading achievement than girls. William Brozo (2004) cites some of the research with regard to this gender discrepancy. Studies show that boys in elementary through high school score significantly lower than girls on standardized measures of reading achievement (Donahue, Voelkl, Campbell, & Mazzeo, 1999). Because boys of all ages fail in reading more often than girls, they are more numerous in corrective and remedial reading programs (National Center for Education Statistics, 2000). In addition, boys are far more likely to be retained at grade level (Byrd & Weitzman, 1994) and are three to five times more likely than girls to have a learning or reading disability placement (National Center for Education Statistics, 2000).

Other statistics, such as those reported in *Newsweek* magazine (Tyre, 2006), show that boys are 60 percent more likely than girls to have repeated at least one grade and 33 percent more likely than girls to drop out of high school. Fourth-grade girls score 12 percent higher on writing tests than boys. Eighth-grade girls score on average 11 points higher than boys on standardized reading tests and 21 points higher on standardized writing tests.

Brozo (2004) points out that in order to address the needs of failing boys and reverse the trend of their lower reading achievement, creative programs and instruction such as book clubs are needed. See Chapter Ten for information and guidance on book clubs. It is important for schools to address the gender discrepancy in reading and increase motivation and support for boys. For example, classrooms should offer a wealth of reading materials tapping into boys' interests. Effective ways to increase motivation include offering choices in activities and assignments and using mentoring programs that match boys with positive male role models who encourage reading. As discussed earlier, *practice* is key to becoming a stronger reader. To motivate boys to read during and outside of school hours, we need to provide books, magazines, and other reading materials at the appropriate reading level that will interest and excite them. For more on this topic, see the many strategies for hooking in reluctant and struggling readers in *How to Reach and Teach All Children in the Inclusive Classroom* (Rief & Heimburge, 2006).

Strategies for Working with Struggling Readers

Joseph Torgeson (2003), professor at Florida State University, has identified the following instructional features necessary to provide effective intervention for children with reading disabilities:

- Systematic and explicit instruction for the component skills that are deficient
- A significant increase in the intensity of instruction

- Ample opportunity for guided practice of new skills in meaningful contexts
- Appropriate levels of scaffolding as students learn new skills
- Systematic cueing of appropriate strategies in context
- Teachers who are relentless in their efforts to build students' reading competency

In his book *What Really Matters for Struggling Readers: Designing Research-Based Programs* (2006), Richard Allington notes that there is no single best method, material, or program that will deliver appropriate strategies and interventions for struggling readers. All effective intervention designs must vary based on reader needs, and these needs must be based on analysis of the type of reading difficulties the student is struggling with. Intensive, expert instruction is another important factor for those students who have significant reading difficulties. The research clearly demonstrates that reading volume and practice make a huge difference. For that to take place, students must have access to instructional texts that they can read accurately, fluently, and with good comprehension. Unfortunately, many struggling readers in the upper grades have very limited access to text at their level and thus no opportunity for steady practice.

Allington cites a study by Guthrie and Humenick (2004) that found four classroom factors that were strongly related to student success. Ensuring students had easy access to interesting texts was the most influential factor. Allowing students more latitude in choosing what to read, who to read with, and where to read produced an effect nearly as large as access to interesting texts. Fostering pupil collaboration during reading and writing and focusing more on student effort than outcomes both produced moderate effects on achievement. Several strategies throughout this book address these factors.

STRUGGLES WITH WRITING

Many students—particularly those with neurobiological disorders such as LDs and AD/HD—struggle significantly with written language. These children are often knowledgeable about a topic, but unable to communicate on paper what they know (Rief, 2003, 2005).

Research has paved the way toward prevention and interventions for writing difficulties among students with LDs. Graham, Harris, and Larsen (2001) recommend six principles to prevent writing difficulties and build writing skills:

1. Provide effective writing instruction
2. Tailor writing instruction to meet individual needs
3. Intervene early
4. Expect that each child will learn to write
5. Identify and address academic and nonacademic roadblocks to writing
6. Employ technologies

Graham, Harris, and Larsen also describe some of the components of effective writing instruction, such as integrating reading and writing around thematic units; teacher modeling, discussion, and guided practice in planning and revising procedures; numerous opportunities to engage in meaningful writing; providing students with temporary supports that scaffold their learning; activities involving student collaboration and sharing; and explicit and systematic conventional skills instruction. Many such strategies for effective writing instruction are found throughout this book.

They also point out that a critical aspect of tailoring instruction to meet the needs of students with LD is finding the right balance between formal and informal instruction, as well as between meaning, process, and form. Each of these factors should be emphasized when developing a writing program, but teachers should adjust the emphasis placed on each to meet an individual child's needs.

Written language is a common area of difficulty because the process of writing involves the integration and often simultaneous use of several skills and brain functions: planning and organization, memory, language processing, graphomotor skills (handwriting and fine-motor skills), spelling and other mechanics, self-monitoring, and speed of processing. To produce written compositions, all of these skills must be integrated. Students who have challenges in any of the language areas—whether in planning, organization, memory, or attention—can easily have difficulty with written expression and production and thus may struggle to meet grade-level writing standards.

Writing difficulties are often manifested in one or more of the following areas (Rief, 2003, 2005).

Planning and Organization

The ability to generate, plan, and organize ideas is often the most challenging (and neglected) stage of the writing process, especially for those who experience difficulties with written expression. When given a written assignment, students with LDs or AD/HD often get stuck here. They do not know what to write about, how to organize and begin, or how to narrow down and focus on a topic that will be motivating for them to write about.

Memory

Working memory is necessary in order to juggle the many different thoughts that one might want to transcribe onto paper. It involves

- Keeping ideas in mind long enough to remember what one wants to say
- Maintaining focus on the train of thought so the flow of writing does not veer off course
- Keeping in mind the big picture of the piece while also manipulating the ideas, details, and wording

The process of writing also requires retrieval of assorted facts and experiences from long-term memory about the writing topic, as well as recall of vocabulary words, spelling, mechanics, and grammar (Public Broadcasting Service, 2002).

Language Processing

Writing requires the ability to express thoughts in a logical, cohesive, and coherent manner. Individuals with LDs frequently have some kind of language disorder, whether phonological, morphological, syntactical, or semantic. Impairments in one or more of these areas can significantly affect writing ability. Good writers generally have facility with the language, from vocabulary to word use, sentence structure, and mechanics. They are able to use a wide vocabulary to express themselves and write descriptive sentences while maintaining proper sentence and paragraph structure. Each writing genre—whether persuasive, response to literature, or personal narrative—has its own structural components. The writer must know the structure and specific language and vocabulary to use to persuade an audience or compare and contrast, for example. Students with LDs and English-language learners often have difficulty with some of the following three aspects of language.

- *Syntax*. This is the structure of language: the grammar or order of words in a sentence. It is common for students with delays in their awareness and understanding of syntax to write many run-on sentences, use too many conjunctions (such as *and*), make errors in verb and pronoun use, and become confused by structurally complex sentences (Mercer & Mercer, 1993; Mather & Roberts, 1995).
- *Morphology*. A morpheme is the smallest meaningful unit of language. Morphology has to do with the understanding and use of root words and affixes (prefixes and suffixes), verb tense, regular and irregular verbs, possessions, plurals, compound words, and rules for word formation.
- *Semantics*. This concerns the meaning of words and the way words are used to convey meaning. It involves knowledge and use of vocabulary and the subtleties of language such as idioms, similes, metaphors, and words with multiple meanings. Individuals who lack facility with precise and colorful vocabulary are hampered in their writing.

Graphomotor Skills

Many children with AD/HD, LDs, and other neurobiological disorders have impairments in graphomotor skills that affect the physical task of handwriting and organization of print on the page. Such impairment interferes with their written production and their ability to "show you what they know."

They often have trouble

- Forming letters correctly
- Writing neatly on or within the lines
- Spacing and organizing their writing on the page
- Copying from the board or book onto paper
- Executing print or cursive with precision or speed

Many struggle with handwriting due to poor fine motor coordination, slow processing speed, and inability to remember with automaticity the sequence of fine motor movements needed to form letters. The physical act of handwriting is inefficient, fatiguing, and a great source of frustration. When the result of their efforts are messy and illegible, it is no wonder that these students often hate writing and resist doing so. Children with these difficulties often have "dysgraphia" and may exhibit some of the following tendencies as well (Jones, 2003; International Dyslexia Association, 2000):

- Inconsistent mixtures of print and cursive, upper and lower case, and irregular sizes, shapes, or slants of letters
- Cramped or unusual pencil grip
- Strange wrist, body, or paper position

- Slow or labored copying or writing (though the result may be neat and legible)
- Content that does not reflect the student's other language skills

Spelling

Children with LDs are typically weak in spelling because of one or more of the following problems:

- Deficiencies in phonemic awareness and phonological processing (for example, learning letter-sound correspondence, discriminating between sounds, and having the ability to segment and blend sounds into words).
- Auditory-sequential memory deficits, which cause much difficulty in remembering and writing the sounds of a word in the correct order. Sounds are often written out of sequence, and sounds within a word are often inserted or deleted.
- Difficulty comprehending spelling rules, patterns, and structures (Currie & Wadlington, 2000).
- Difficulties with orthographic processing. Visual-sequential memory deficits may cause difficulty recalling the way a word looks and getting it down in the correct order or sequence. This results in misspelling common high-frequency words (such as *said, they, where, does, of,* and *because)* that cannot be sounded out phonetically and must be recalled by sight.

The International Dyslexia Association (2000) points out that "the visual memory problems of poor spellers are specific to memory for letters and words. A person may be a very poor speller, but be a very good artist, navigator, or mechanic; those professions require a different kind of visual memory."

Students with LDs generally progress through the same series of stages in the acquisition of spelling as other children, but at a slower rate than their peers without LDs (Weiner, 1994; Rhodes & Dudley-Marling, 1988; Mather & Roberts, 1995; Moats, 1995).

The spelling difficulties of children and teens with AD/HD may not be due to a processing problem but instead to inattention—not noticing or paying attention to the specific letters, sequence, or visual patterns within words—or to impulsivity, which causes many careless mistakes (Rief, 2005).

Other Mechanics

The accurate use of capitalization and punctuation is an area of weakness for many students, particularly those with LDs and AD/HD. Some children lack the skills and awareness to apply proper capitalization and punctuation. Others are inattentive to details such as these mechanics and do not notice their errors in use.

Editing

Students who find the writing process very difficult and laborious may exhibit resistant, even oppositional, behavior when asked to revise and edit their work. They should be provided with assistive technology and other supports. It is unrealistic to expect these students to proofread, revise, or edit their work without direct help.

Self-Monitoring

Written expression requires thinking and planning ahead, keeping the intended audience in mind, and writing with a clear purpose. The writer must attend to and follow the specific structure of the particular writing genre (for example, steps of a complete paragraph, narrative account, persuasive essay, or a friendly letter) and recognize when their work needs revising or the ideas need more thorough development. Some students, particularly those with learning or attention difficulties, do not effectively self-monitor during the writing process.

Speed of Processing

Some students rush through writing assignments, often leading to illegible work with many careless errors. Others write excruciatingly slowly. For example, many students with LDs or AD/HD may know the correct answers and be able to verbally express their thoughts and ideas articulately, yet be unable to put more than a few words or sentences down on paper. This frustrates both the child and the teacher. Part of the problem with the rate of output may be slow processing speed, impairments in impulsivity and inhibition, difficulty sustaining attention to task and maintaining the mental energy required in written expression, or graphomotor dysfunction.

The Teacher's Role

Observation and assessment inform teachers about students' learning and performance, and guide instruction. With awareness of the particular difficulties students experience in their writing, teachers are better able to differentiate instruction accordingly. It is important for teachers to observe students with a "diagnostic" eye, identifying their learning strengths, weaknesses, and developmental stages. Then it is possible to provide the targeted instruction and practice individual students need to progress in their writing competency and build deficient skills. Understanding LDs and the types of processing problems that can affect writing can also help teachers recognize the signs of a possible brain-based disorder impairing a child's writing development.

One of the principles that Graham, Harris, and Larsen (2001) identify for preventing writing difficulties and building writing skills is early intervention. For students in third through eighth grade, the opportunity for early intervention has already passed them by. However, it is not too late to significantly build their writing skills or to get these students the help they need. If you suspect a student may have a disability or disorder causing him or her to struggle, it is important to bring the issue to the attention of your school team. A referral may be needed for evaluation in order to determine and obtain appropriate support, interventions, and accommodations.

STRATEGIES FOR BYPASSING AND ACCOMMODATING WRITING DIFFICULTIES

It will often be necessary to provide accommodations or modifications to enable struggling writers to work at grade-level standards. Following are possible accommodations and ways to help students bypass some of the obstacles they face in writing. Consider the following when writing individualized educational programs (IEPs) and 504 Accommodation Plans to support children and teens who struggle with writing.

Reduce Writing Demands

- Stress the quality of the writing, not the volume.
- Reduce the need to copy from the board or book.
- Remember that it generally takes students such as those with AD/HD and/or LDs significantly longer to produce written work (often two to three times longer than their peers, if not more). Assign reasonable amounts of homework and writing assignments. Be willing to make adjustments if written output is a struggle and accept modified homework and reduced written tasks.
- Set realistic, mutually agreed-on expectations for handwriting and neatness.

Substitute Other Modality Strengths and Provide Direct Assistance

- Substitute nonwritten projects for written assignments, such as oral reports and demonstrations.
- Give students options and choices that do not require writing, such as through hands-on, project-oriented assignments, and other means of drawing on their strengths and learning styles.
- Follow written exams with oral exams and average the grades for those students.
- Allow oral responses in assignments and tests when appropriate.
- Permit students to dictate their responses while someone else transcribes for them.
- Provide note-taking assistance by assigning a buddy who will take notes, share, and compare with the struggling student.
- Provide assistance for the typing or printing final drafts of papers.
- Help students get started writing by sitting with them and talking or prompting them through the first few sentences.

Make Specific Accommodations

- Provide worksheets with extra space and enlarge the space for doing written work (on math papers and tests, for instance).
- Give in-class time to get started on assignments.
- Provide note-taking assistance. Students with AD/HD and LDs should still take their own notes in class, but be allowed to *supplement* them with the more detailed and organized copies from a buddy or designated note-taker.
- Increase the time allotted for completing written tasks.
- Extend time for testing, particularly written assessments such as essay questions.
- Permit subvocalizing or quietly talking out loud while writing, as auditory feedback often helps these students stay focused and self-monitor.
- Permit these students to write in either print or cursive, whichever is easier and most legible.
- Increase the amount of guided practice of handwriting, keyboarding, and other writing skills.
- Grade content separately from spelling and mechanics.

Use Tools and Assistive Technology

- Encourage use of highlighting tape and experimenting with various types of writing utensils and aids such as mechanical pencils and pencil grips.
- Allow students to use a tape or digital recorder instead of writing to summarize learning, respond to questions, plan, and record ideas.
- Allow the use of a hand-held electronic spell-checker.
- Help children learn proper keyboarding and typing skills and provide many practice opportunities. See recommended keyboard software in Chapter Fourteen.
- Help children learn word processing skills, including the use of editing options such as cut and paste, spell check, and grammar check, and various format options.
- Provide struggling writers training in and access to assistive technologies, as discussed in Chapter Fourteen.

RESEARCH-BASED LITERACY INTERVENTION PROGRAMS

Most students are able to accelerate their reading and writing performance through a classroom instructional program of balanced literacy and good teaching. This book is intended to provide guidance, strategies, and activities to incorporate such a program. Struggling readers and writers in the third- through eighth-grade level (whether or not they have an identified disability) may need additional support and intervention. The intensity of the intervention depends upon their level of need. In response to the No Child Left Behind Act, schools are providing a wide range of interventions to students making insufficient academic progress in reading. This includes extra instruction before, during, and after standard school hours and supplemental literacy programs, as well as other types of student supports. Some schools are doing an excellent job of implementing intervention programs for students in need, both in general and special education. Many others are not. As with any program or approach, when the research shows it to be effective, that means results have been good for a group of children *as a whole*—not necessarily for a specific student. The program may have been found to raise scores on average, but it does not mean the program is guaranteed to be effective for each individual student (Allington, 2006). So we need to tailor our interventions to address the identified needs of the individual student and not use a one-size-fits-all approach to intervention programs.

The Reading First Initiative requires that interventions for kindergarten through third-grade students in schools receiving federal funds must be research-validated programs. The University of Oregon has evaluated several adoptions and curriculum material, including supplemental reading programs for evidence of their effectiveness. See their web site for a very comprehensive listing of programs (http://oregonreadingfirst.uoregon.edu). Some are geared for kindergarten through second grade, others include third grade, and some are geared specifically for third grade, such as Accelerated Vocabulary, Great Leaps, Lexia SOS: Strategies for Older Students, Soar to Success, Rewards, and Kaleidoscope: Level B.

Some research-based programs are designed for and used most commonly with students who have reading, writing, and language disabilities or for other reasons are functioning two or more years below grade level in literacy skills. Many of these programs are used with students through special education, as part of a schoolwide three-tiered approach to intervention, or may be provided privately. Most are multisensory, systematic and explicit, and provide for a high rate of feedback and practice. Following are just some such programs that may be used with third- through eighth-grade students needing more intensive intervention, or as a different approach to reach and teach struggling readers and writers. These programs are designed for different purposes—some as a total language arts program and complete curriculum, others to target and build certain skills (such as Read Naturally for fluency and Fast ForWord for phonemic awareness development). Detailed information about each program is available on the web site given below.

Arbogast, A., Bruner, E., Davis, K. L., Englemann, O., Englemann, S., Hanner, S., Osborn, J., Osborn, S., & Zoraf, L. (2002). *Reading mastery plus*. New York: SRA McGraw-Hill. www.sra4kids.com.

Archer, A. L., Gleason, M. M., & Vachon, V. (2006). *Rewards—Reading excellence: Word attack and rate development strategies*. Longmont, CO: Sopris West. www.sopriswest.com.

Enfield, M., & Greene, V. (2005). *Project Read: Language circle*. Bloomington, MN: Language Circle Enterprise. www.projectread.com.

Fast track reading. (2004). DeSoto, TX: Wright Group/McGraw-Hill. www.wrightgroup.com.

Fell, J. (2007). *Language! The comprehensive literacy curriculum*. Longmont, CO: Sopris West. www.sopriswest.com.

Hasselbring, T., Kinsella, K., & Feldman, K. *Read 180 reading intervention program*. New York: Scholastic. http://teacher.scholastic.com/products/read180.

Herman, R. (2007). *The Sopris West Herman Method for reversing reading failure*. Herman Method Reading Institute. Longmont, CO: Sopris West Educational Services. www.sopriswest.com.

Ihnot, C., & Ihnot, T. *Read naturally*. St. Paul, MN: Read Naturally. www.readnaturally.com.

Johnson, G., & Engleman, Z. (1999). *Corrective reading*. New York: SRA/McGraw-Hill. www.sra4kids.com.

Lindamood, P., & Bell, N. *Lindamood-Bell learning processes*. San Luis Obispo, CA: Lindamood-Bell Learning Processes. http://www.lindamoodbell.com.

Orton-Gillingham failure free reading program. (2002). Birmingham, MI: Institute for Multi-Sensory Education. www.ortongillingham.com.

Reach system. (2002). New York: SRA-McGraw-Hill. www.sraonline.com.

Schifini, A., Short, D., & Villamil Tinajero, J. (2000). *High point*. Carmel, CA: Hampton-Brown. www.hbhighpoint.com.

Slingerland multisensory structured language instructional approach®. Bellevue, WA: Slingerland Institute for Literacy. www.slingerland.org.

Tallal, P., & Merzenich, D. *Fast ForWord reading program*[(r)]. Oakland, CA: Scientific Learning. www.scilearn.com.

Wilson, B. *Wilson reading system*. Millbury, MA: Wilson Language Training. www.wilsonlanguage.com.

Peer-Assisted Learning Strategies (PALS), which increases student opportunities to practice reading and boosts reading fluency and comprehension, is another research-based intervention for students in general education classrooms. (For information about PALS, which was developed by Fuchs, Mathes, and Fuchs, go to http://kc.vanderbilt.edu/pals.) The Richard Allington and Kevin Feldman interventions described earlier in this chapter—such as more expert instruction and time and opportunities for practicing skills with support and feedback—are important as well. In addition, Chapter Fourteen includes information about the use of assistive technology as support and intervention for struggling readers and writers. Many more research-based strategies and interventions to build literacy skills and support struggling readers and writers are suggested in other chapters of this book. Schools need to get creative in finding ways to supply the time, opportunities, and expert instruction needed by struggling readers and writers.

For issues with handwriting, one recommended program developed by an occupational therapist is *Handwriting Without Tears*™. The author, Jan Olsen, uses numerous multisensory techniques and mnemonic cues for helping children learn proper letter formation. Developed at Vanderbilt University, the *CASL Handwriting Program* is validated by research and is successful with disabled children (Graham & Harris, 2000).

— Chapter 12 —

READING COMPREHENSION STRATEGIES AND SCAFFOLDS

For reading comprehension to occur, one must be actively engaged throughout the reading process in constructing meaning from the text. Many activities throughout this book involve students in deep processing of the material—before, during, and after the reading. This chapter will introduce an array of additional reading strategies and supports to strengthen comprehension among readers of all abilities.

Fielding and Pearson (1994) suggest the following four components as critical for a successful comprehension program: (1) large amounts of time for actual text reading, (2) teacher-directed instruction in comprehension strategies, (3) opportunities for peer and collaborative learning, and (4) occasions for students to talk to a teacher and peers about their responses to reading. These components will be embedded within many of the instructional and metacognitive comprehension strategies described throughout this chapter (as well as the other reading chapters).

CHARACTERISTICS OF GOOD READERS

In order to boost reading abilities in all students, it is important to understand what is required to be a reader with strong comprehension skills—one who is adept and confident in his or her ability to construct meaning from the text. Skilled readers do the following (Rief, 2003, 2005; Harvey & Goudvis, 2000):

- Read for a specific purpose
- Draw on their background or prior knowledge (schemata) as they are reading
- Make connections to other books previously read (text-to-text), to their own life and experiences (text-to-self), and to other information and concepts they know (text-to-world)
- Reflect as they read

- Use metacognitive strategies to think about what they are reading and self-monitor their comprehension and understanding
- Use self-correction or "fix-up" strategies when confused
- Constantly predict and either confirm or change their predictions as they read
- Understand organization and structure for different types of text (literary and expository)
- Visualize while they are reading, making mental images
- Distinguish the main ideas and important information from details and less important information in the text
- Engage in many kinds of thinking processes while reading (such as questioning, analyzing, synthesizing, interpreting, evaluating, and reflecting)
- Apply and monitor a host of strategies, knowing which strategies to use for various reading tasks and types of material
- Read strategically and actively for meaning

According to Harvey and Goudvis (2000), proficient readers also draw inferences by taking what they know, adding the clues from the text, thinking ahead to make a judgment about what will happen next, and then synthesizing information. Good readers combine new information with existing knowledge to form an original idea or interpretation.

METACOGNITIVE READERS

According to Gerald Grow (1996), strategic readers read with purpose, meaning, and goals. They exercise conscious control over what and how they read, are flexible and able to adjust to different types of reading material, are confident and efficient in monitoring their comprehension, and make good use of metacognitive strategies.

What does it mean to be a metacognitive reader? Metacognition is the explicit awareness or self-knowledge a person has of his or her own unique mental processes (Townend & Turner, 2000). The term refers to the control or regulation individuals have over their own thinking (Baker and Brown, 1984). Metacognitive skills necessary for being a good reader include the following (Baker & Brown, 1984; McCormick, 2003, Townend & Turner, 2000):

- Planning: thinking about the purpose and determining what is important or most relevant and what is not; organizing and planning in advance how to go about a learning task, such as read a textbook chapter and answer the questions.
- Monitoring comprehension: when aware that they "get it" and understand the material they continue reading, but when aware that something doesn't make sense they apply a fix-up strategy to clear up the confusion.
- Deciding to utilize specific strategies to aid in comprehension, such as selecting and implementing one of the pre-, during-, or after-reading strategies discussed in this chapter.
- Monitoring the time or degree of focused attention needed for different types of material—whether textbooks, test questions, books for pleasure, or magazines—and for different purposes and adjusting accordingly.
- Questioning throughout reading of the text, for example, *Does this make sense? Do these ideas fit in with previous information?*

PREREADING COMPREHENSION STRATEGIES

To read for meaning and to gain comprehension, a number of strategies are helpful and effective *prior to* reading, *during* reading, and *after* completing the reading assignment. *Prereading strategies* are important for several reasons. They help prepare the reader mentally through techniques that establish the purpose or goal for the reading task. They also activate the reader's prior knowledge about the topic and prime the brain to make connections while reading the text. Students with diverse reading abilities and learning styles benefit from prereading strategies to motivate and "hook them in" for the actual reading of the text.

Prereading Instructional Strategies

Use these strategies and techniques whenever possible *before* the actual reading of the text (Rief, 2003, 2005):

- Relate the story or informational text to the students' experience and background knowledge through class discussions, brainstorming, and charting prior knowledge ("What do we already know about . . . ?").
- Set the stage and establish the purpose for what students are about to read ("As you read, think about what you would do if . . .").
- Lead the class through making or listing predictions prior to reading.
- Generate interest and increase students' background knowledge and frame of reference before reading by using concrete objects and audiovisuals related to the topic of study (such as maps, photos, DVDs, or videos).
- Give time to students to survey and preview the key information in the text—illustrations, captions, headings, and chapter questions—before reading.
- Preview passages by reading them aloud first before students reread and study them independently.
- To activate prior knowledge, have students write down everything they know about the topic in their "learning log."
- Link prior knowledge to new concepts and information that will be studied using advanced organizers, anticipation guides, and other strategies such as K-W-L and semantic maps.
- Preteach, rehearse, and discuss selected vocabulary that may be challenging for students.
- Encourage students to think of some questions they would like answered by the reading selection.

Prereading Metacognitive Strategies

The following metacognitive strategies, supported by research, are beneficial for use during the pre-reading stage.

Anticipation Guide. Students receive a list of teacher-generated statements about a topic in advance of the reading of informational text. They individually respond to the statements (true or false; agree or disagree) and then discuss their choices briefly with partners or small groups prior to reading the text. After reading the material, students discuss whether their beliefs have changed (Head & Readence, 1986).

K-W-L. This strategy begins prior to reading but continues during and after the process (Ogle, 1986). It involves a chart divided into three columns:

- The first column (K) indicates what is already *known* about the subject or topic. This step activates students' prior knowledge. Ideas are recorded during a class brainstorm.
- The middle column (W) is *what* the students want to learn or find out about the subject. This column sets the purpose for reading: to find the answers to those questions.
- The third column (L) is filled in on the chart as new information is *learned* from the reading or other teaching. This column is for recording "what we learned."

Directed Reading-Thinking Activity (DR-TA). The first part of this DR-TA takes place at the prereading stage. Students are guided to make predictions about a passage or story and set a purpose for reading. Then the passage is read (orally or silently) and at predetermined points students are asked to summarize the reading. At these points students are asked to confirm or revise their predictions and to give reasons for their decisions using evidence located and cited from the text. After a certain number of passages or pages read, the process starts again, cycling through predicting, reading, confirming, or rejecting via discussion throughout the reading of the material (Stauffer, 1975).

Advanced Organizers. These tools provide students with the basic organization of the material to be learned prior to actually studying the material. Graphic organizers of various types and study guides are examples of advance organizers. The organizers can help students focus on the task at hand both prior to and during reading (Bender, 2002). See examples of graphic organizers later in this chapter.

Lecture Notes. Nancy Fetzer's lecture note technique (2003, 2006), described in Chapter Thirteen, is very beneficial as a prereading whole-class strategy designed to front-load difficult concepts and vocabulary prior to reading the text. It involves the students in processing the information through multiple modalities: verbal presentation, with student chanting and repetition; visual presentation and imagery, by drawing and writing down key words and graphics; and physical body motions to enhance engagement, recall, and comprehension. Fetzer's strategy incorporates several research-based approaches such as preteaching vocabulary and providing an advanced schema to organize thinking, visualization, and collaborative learning.

DURING-READING COMPREHENSION STRATEGIES

These strategies should be explicitly taught in order to engage students in thinking about and interacting with the reading material. This interaction is crucial for comprehension, maintaining focus, and actively applying metacognition throughout reading of the text. Modeling, guided instruction, and practice in the classroom are key to teaching students how to become competent, strategic readers.

During-Reading Instructional Strategies

The following instructional strategies are recommended for use *during* the reading process:

- Teach students how to paraphrase and put into their own words the main idea and significant details of text. Paraphrasing each paragraph, passage, or section and recording it on cassette or tape digitally is also a very helpful study technique.

- Teach how to find the subject, main ideas, and sift out the key facts and important details from the irrelevant and redundant words and text.
- Give a few stopping points at strategic locations throughout the text for students to interact with the material in some manner—to question, react, discuss, summarize, predict, clarify, or record.
- Provide students with a pad of sticky notes. As they are reading they can jot down notes, vocabulary words (to clarify), and questions near items they do not understand. The sticky notes can be placed directly next to key points and main ideas for easy reference.
- Use any of the instructional strategies involving students with collaborative reading and analysis of the material, such as reciprocal teaching, book clubs, and buddy or partner reading. Learning and recall are greatly enhanced by the act of talking about the text. These collaborative formats are ideal for working together to summarize, discuss, and clarify points in the reading.
- Teach and model "fix-up" strategies for resolving difficulties when comprehension breaks down—for example, slowing down, going back and rereading, reading ahead to see if their questions are clarified later on, talking with someone about their understanding or confusion, or jotting down questions to check later.
- Enlarge a page of the book and make a transparency or directly project the page with a document camera if you are fortunate enough to have this wonderful instructional tool in your classroom. Have individual students come up to the overhead or document camera to locate and point out (via highlighting, underlining, or circling) important information in the text.
- Provide study guides to aid in looking for key information in the text and graphic organizers such as those discussed later in this chapter.
- Audio-record textbooks with a digital voice recorder or traditional tape recorder for individual use or group listening at a listening post. For ease in following text, have clear signals on the recording for when to turn the page or include page numbers periodically on the recording. Pages can be marked with the track number at the beginning of each chapter.
- Use Activity 12.1, Mapping What I Read, at the end of this chapter. Provide comprehension checkpoints, such as the end of a chapter or section. At that point, students are asked to make predictions, make connections, list the main events in the section, sketch a picture to help remember a main event, or think of a title that would help them remember what they read of that section.
- Teach students to make text-to-text, text-to-world, and text-to-self connections (see Figure 12.1). Have students verbally share those connections with their partner or a small group, record them while reading, or both.

DURING-READING METACOGNITIVE STRATEGIES

Research supports the use of the following metacognitive strategies for strengthening reading comprehension during the reading process. They benefit students with diverse learning abilities and should be part of instruction in a balanced literacy classroom.

Figure 12.1

Imagery and Visualization. This technique aids comprehension by creating mental pictures of what is being read. Students are encouraged to create an image in their mind as they read. This skill can be taught through a series of guided questioning techniques that elicit from the child vivid detailed pictures as he or she moves through the passage. Examples of guided questions include "What do you see?" "Where is he sitting?" "How does it feel?" Discuss and illustrate how to make the words come alive and mentally picture characters, settings, and actions.

Think Aloud. This approach (Paris, 1986) basically involves externalizing and making overt the thinking processes used when reading, thereby demonstrating what efficient thinking sounds like. Students have a model of what it might sound like to internally grapple with the text.

- The teacher orally reads to the students as they generally follow along with the text.
- The teacher models the process of interacting with the text—for example, stopping to make predictions or guess what will happen next, asking questions of self or author, describing what is visualized, working through problems to figure out unknown vocabulary, or making connections.
- The teacher clearly models how to self-monitor his or her own comprehension by stopping periodically and asking: "Is this making sense to me?"

Students can then practice some of these strategies with partners.

Guided Reading. In this instructional strategy, students of approximately the same reading level gather in reading groups (usually no more than six per group). The teacher selects books for each group to read together that are new to them, using strategies that those students specifically need to practice. Usually "leveled" books are used for guided reading groups in the lower grades and any selection at the students' instructional level in upper grades. See Chapter Three for more on guided reading.

GIST (Generating Interaction between Schemata and Text). This is a strategy used for comprehending informational text and determining the "gist" of the reading material (Swanson & DeLaPaz, 1998):

1. In cooperative groups, students read sections silently.
2. When done reading a short section, the members of the group work together to write a one-sentence summary.
3. All group members then record that summary sentence.
4. Students continue in this fashion, reading a segment, stopping at logical points, jointly deciding on a summary sentence, and then recording on their own papers.
5. Those papers can then serve as study guides for the reading material.

Reciprocal Teaching. This approach, originally developed by Palincsar and Brown (1984, 1985), is one of the best-researched strategies available to teachers. It involves students working together in cooperative groups taking turns designing and asking questions, and leading the group in the process of discussing and working through small portions of the text for comprehension purposes. Research has found that good readers spontaneously use strategies of predicting, questioning, clarifying, and summarizing.

In a reciprocal teaching format, the group is led through this sequential process of reading a short section.

1. *Questioning* about the content read to identify important information in the passage.
2. *Summarizing,* using questions such as "What is this paragraph mostly about? What would be a good title for this passage?"
3. *Clarifying* anything confusing in the reading, using questions such as "Has anyone heard this expression before? What do you think it means?" "Can anyone explain this?"
4. *Predicting* what will happen in the next portion of the reading.

The students proceed in this format, taking turns in the leader role as they read the next portions of the text.

PASS. This reading comprehension strategy by Deshler, Ellis, and Lenz (1996) is a four-step process: preview, ask, summarize, and synthesize. The teacher guides the students through the four steps as described by Sousa (2001b, p. 112):

P *Preview, review, and predict*
Preview by reading the heading and one or two sentences.
Review what you already know about this topic.
Predict what you think the text or story will be about.

A *Ask and answer questions*
Content-focused questions: Who? What? Why? Where? How does this relate to what I already know?
Monitoring questions: Does this make sense? How is this different from what I thought it was going to be?
Problem-solving questions: Do I need to reread part of it? Can I visualize the information? Does it have too many unknown words?

S *Summarize*
Explain what the short passage you read was all about.

S *Synthesize*
Explain how the short passage fits in with the whole passage.
Explain how what you learned fits in with what you knew.

AFTER-READING COMPREHENSION STRATEGIES

These strategies should be utilized to involve the student in deeper thinking and exploration *after* reading the material (Rief, 2003, 2005).

After-Reading Instructional Strategies

Instructional strategies for this stage include

- Using the information to fill out charts and graphic organizers.
- Guiding students and providing activities involving summarizing, analyzing, drawing conclusions, and making inferences.
- Comparing and contrasting with other texts or authors.
- Having deep discussions about the concepts or events in the text or in character analysis.
- Making connections through related writing activities.
- Doing further extension activities related to the theme and content of the reading to apply the learning.

After-Reading Metacognitive Strategies

Research supports the value of metacognitive strategies at the end of the reading process to strengthen comprehension. Strategies such as the following are highly recommended.

Summarizing. This strategy is one of the most important reading comprehension skills. It always involves identifying the main idea. Sometimes the main idea is explicit and easy to find, and other times it is implied or embedded in the passage. Techniques requiring students to stop at points in the reading to paraphrase in their own words or summarize in one or two sentences provide excellent practice building this skill. Students can summarize by

- Responding verbally—for example, telling their partners in one sentence what the paragraph was about.
- Filling out graphic organizers with one or two lines for key information only.
- Outlining.
- Writing a summary sentence or paragraph.
- Composing a heading or title for the passage.
- Responding to prompts like "The main point of this passage was ___________." "Overall, this paragraph was about ______________."

Retelling. Students review the literature through storytelling, time lines, quick writes or quick draws, tape or digital recordings, pocket charts with colored sentence strips, plot charts, or any of the graphic organizers.

Reading Logs. Students can write their feelings, associations, connections, and questions in response to the reading. They may be given specific prompts to guide what is recorded in their logs. For example, "What did you learn?" "How did this make you feel?" "How did this relate to any of your own life experiences?" "What did you like or dislike about the author's style of writing?"

K-W-L-Plus. This variation of K-W-L adds mapping and summarization to the original K-W-L strategy (Carr & Ogle, 1987). The information listed on the chart is organized graphically under categories of topics. Finally, a summary is written based on that organization of ideas. These two tasks incorporate the powerful tools of restructuring text and rewriting to help students process information (Ong, 2000).

Double-Entry Journal. The paper is divided into two columns. Notes are taken in the left column, citing anything of particular interest to the reader—such as quotes, descriptions, or metaphors—along with the page number. In the right-hand column, the reader comments and records personal thoughts, interpretations, connections, and questions triggered by that section of the text.

Metacognitive Journal or Learning Log. The page is divided into two columns. The left column is labeled "What I Learned." The right column is labeled "How I Learned This." This log assists students in thinking about and analyzing their own learning process. The right-hand column can record other things such as "How this Affects Me" or "Why This was Difficult (or Easy) for Me." The key is reflection and analysis of one's own learning.

COGNITIVE READING COMPREHENSION STRATEGIES

Cognitive strategies help a person process and manipulate information to perform tasks (Sousa, 2001a). Following are some cognitive strategies to help students read strategically.

SQ3R. This strategy increases comprehension and retention of textbook material (expository or informational) and comprises the following steps:

- *Survey.* Briefly look through the reading assignment at the titles, chapter headings, illustrations, charts, and graphs. Skim through the assignment and read the chapter summary and any end-of-chapter questions.
- *Question.* Turn the headings and subheadings of the text into questions. For example: *Producing Antibodies* can become: "How do our bodies produce antibodies?" *Organic motor fuels* can become: "What are the different organic motor fuels?"
- *Read.* Read to find the answers to the questions developed above. Identify the main ideas and jot down any questions, notes, or unknown vocabulary.
- *Recite.* At the end of each chapter section, state the gist of what was read. Restating or summarizing into an audiotape or digital recorder is often very effective.
- *Review.* Check recall of important information from the reading. To that end, a study guide of some kind may be created.

SQ4R. In this extension of SQ3R, an additional step is added beginning with the /r/ sound: write. The SQ4R procedure is survey, question, read, recite, *write*, and review. After a brief verbal summary of what the reading passage was about, one must write the answers to the questions (in step 2) and then review.

Question-Answer Relationships (QAR). Students are taught to recognize the types of questions and use strategy in searching for answers of each type (Raphael, 1982). The four different classification of questions are (1) right there, (2) think and search, (3) author and you, and (4) on your own.

1. The answers to "right-there" questions are stated directly in the text and simply require literal comprehension.
2. The answers to "think-and-search" questions are not as explicit and easy to locate, but are found somewhere within the text. Answering these questions requires interpretive or inferential comprehension and "reading between the lines." Finding the main idea of a passage is an example of inferential comprehension.
3. The answers to "author-and-you" questions are not in the text, requiring information that the author has provided combined with what the reader already knows in order to respond. For example, "How would you advise the character, and why?"
4. "On-your-own" questions are more abstract, and the answers cannot be found in the text. These questions require reading "beyond the lines" and involve higher-order thinking skills such as analyzing, evaluating, and creative thinking. Examples include comparing and contrasting or questions such as "What do you think caused ____ to happen?" "What other solution can you think of for that problem?"

The Learning Toolbox. A variety of strategies designed to help middle school students (and secondary students with learning difficulties) are found on the web site of James

Madison University Special Education Department, in the Learning Toolbox. This site offers students, teachers, and parents explicit learning strategies in a number of content areas and study skills: for example, the RAP-Q strategy to help understand the main idea when reading and the SPORE strategy to better understand stories when reading. Each of the strategies utilizes acronyms as a mnemonic to recall steps of the strategy. For example, SPORE is a story web strategy to help identify and understand the *s*etting, *p*roblem, *o*rder of action, *r*esolution, and *e*nd. For more information go to www.jmu.edu and follow the link to Learning Toolbox.

GRAPHIC OUTLINES OR AIDS

Many graphic displays can accompany reading of literature and textbook material to aid comprehension. They help students recognize and organize information in the book and guide critical thinking by creating a graphic representation of the text (Rief, 2003, 2005). They may help organize the main idea with supporting detail, cause and effect, sequence, classification matrix, and so forth. Following are a few examples.

- *Framed Outlines.* Students are given copies of a teacher-prepared outline that contains missing information. As the students read, or later through subsequent discussion, students fill in the missing information. Ideally this technique is modeled to teach the skill on a chart or the overhead or document camera.
- *Storyboards.* Divide a board or piece of paper into sections and have students draw or write story events in sequence in each box or frame.
- *Story Maps.* This graphic displays essential elements of a story: setting, characters, time, place, problem or conflict, actions or happenings, climax, resolution, and theme.
- *Story Frames.* These sentence starters to be completed by students provide a skeleton of the story or chapter. For example, "The setting of this chapter takes place ___________. The character faced a problem when ______________. First he ______________. Next ______________. Then __________________. I predict that in the next chapter ___________________________.
- *Time Lines.* These are used to help visualize chronological text and sequence of events.
- *Plot Charts.* Charts for stories using this format: Somebody . . . wanted . . . but . . . and so . . .
- *Prediction Charts.* Charts that are modified as the story is being read. By referring to the title and illustrations, students make initial predictions. As they read, stop and predict what will happen next. Continue questioning, predicting, and recording. Make clear to students that predictions are best guesses based on the information we have at the time and that good readers are constantly predicting when they are reading.
- *Venn Diagram.* Two overlapping circles are used to display differences and similarities between characters, books, settings, topics, or events.
- *Comparison Chart.* Much like a Venn diagram, but designed as a table with rows and columns, this chart compares and contrasts two or more items, events, concepts, features, characters, or themes.
- *Flow Chart.* Organizes a series of steps, events, or thoughts in logical order, usually with arrows showing the sequence of flow.

- *Cluster Maps or Semantic Maps.* A central concept or main idea is placed in the center of related subtopics, and further details extend from each of the subtopic areas. These are used to categorize or identify related information.
- *Five Ws Chart.* After reading an article or excerpt from a text, the student identifies the five W elements—Who? What? When? Where? Why?—and records that information on the chart. *How* can be added as well.
- *Favorite Part Graph.* The class identifies a number of scenes or parts of the book that are plotted on the graph. Everyone records his or her favorite part on the bar graph.
- *Character Web.* Place the character's name in center of the web, with traits and descriptions stemming from the center.
- *Wanted Posters.* Students create posters listing the identifying characteristics of a character in the book.

TEXT STRUCTURE

As discussed in Chapters Five and Thirteen, awareness and understanding of text structure are very important for enabling readers to comprehend and access the different kinds of text: informational (expository) and narrative (story). Feldman (2000) explains that struggling learners frequently lack a schema to help them get the big ideas and key strategies. Teachers have the task of directly providing these maps or cognitive guides to enable all students access to the critical ideas or strategies in a text or lesson. He makes the following analogy: "Without the appropriate schema (structure or guide for understanding and making sense of new information), trying to understand a story, textbook or classroom lesson is like finding your way through a new town without a map" (p. 45).

Expository or Informational Text Structure

Students need to be taught how to identify the main ideas and supporting details (such as facts, statistics, and examples) in text, to be explicitly shown that the main ideas are generally found in the chapter titles and headings, and that subheadings express the next biggest ideas and points. Learning how to use the glossary, table of contents, index, tables and graphs, as well as the techniques of scanning and skimming to find the answers are important teaching points for helping students learn how to read and comprehend expository material. Teachers in all content areas need to directly teach and provide a good deal of practice for students with the various types of expository text structures, including the patterns of compare-and-contrast, cause-and-effect, classification, sequence, and others.

Narrative Text Structure

Students must be taught *story grammar* or *mapping* to understand the structure of literary text. This concept includes setting, characters, problem or conflict, sequence of major events (actions), climax, resolution or problem solution, and the story theme or moral.

Nancy Fetzer (2006) shares a wonderful strategy for teaching the schema for narrative text. Story structure is taught using a multisensory format incorporating the techniques of chanting, kinesthetic body motions, and illustrating the organization of a story with simple figures or icons. Students receive a copy of a Narrative Text Organization Chart (see Activity 12.2) and learn narrative text structure through modeling and guided practice while referring to the symbols on the chart. The icons represent the story elements in sequence.

Using body motions and chanting, the teacher models and later students accompany the teacher in reciting the explanation of narrative text structure, as provided in Activity 12.3. The physical motions are added as an extra component to help recall the elements being described. For example, to represent the parts of a setting (when and where), point to your wrist and explain to students that you are indicating *when* by pointing to a pretend wristwatch. For *where*, place your hand horizontally above your eyes like you are gazing into the horizon and shielding your eyes from the sun. To indicate a problem or conflict (which is shown on the chart as an X), cross your arms to form a big X when reciting about the conflict. After modeling the text organization with the chart as a reference, repeat with students chanting along with you and following the hand motions you create as well.

ACTIVE READING AND DISCUSSION FORMATS AND ACTIVITIES

A variety of instructional formats is available to encourage interaction and discussion about a text among students. Many such techniques are described in other chapters of this book (Chapters Three, Five, Seven, Eight, Nine, and Ten). The following strategies are also popular in the literacy classroom.

Fishbowl. The class is divided into two circles, one inner and one outer. The inner circle actively engages in discussion about the book (or other topic). The outer circle observes but cannot contribute to the discussion. Their role is to note how well the inner group functioned in critical communication skills: listening to each other's point of view, asking relevant questions, asking for clarification, politely disagreeing, and not interrupting. Roles are then reversed, and the outer circle students are the ones participating in the discussion. Another type of fishbowl strategy is described in Chapter Seven, in the section on making oral language a priority.

Jigsaw. Students are divided into "home" groups, with each group responsible for reading and understanding the same reading selection. Each member is assigned a number (such as one through five) that corresponds to certain sections of the reading assignment. The students with the same number from each home group then meet in their "expert" groups to reread and study their section in depth. Expert groups work together in learning their portion of the material and planning how to teach that information and content to their home group members. Then everyone returns to his or her home group, and each member teaches his or her content to home group peers (Ong, 2000).

Hot Seat. A student volunteers to be on the "hot seat" and represent a particular character from the story. Students ask him or her questions that must be answered in the way the character would answer them. This strategy, described in more depth in Chapter Seven, is also beneficial for helping students with comprehension of text and is a fun after-reading activity.

Activity 12.1

MAPPING WHAT I READ

Comprehension Checkpoint

Student's Name ____________________

Chapter (s) ____________________

Title of Book ____________________

Think of Titles
What title would you give this section/chapter that would help you remember what you read?

Make Predictions
What do you think will happen next?

Draw Mental Pictures
Sketch a picture that will help you remember a main event in this section.

Make Connections

Main Events
What happened in this section?

Activity 12.2

NARRATIVE TEXT ORGANIZATION CHART

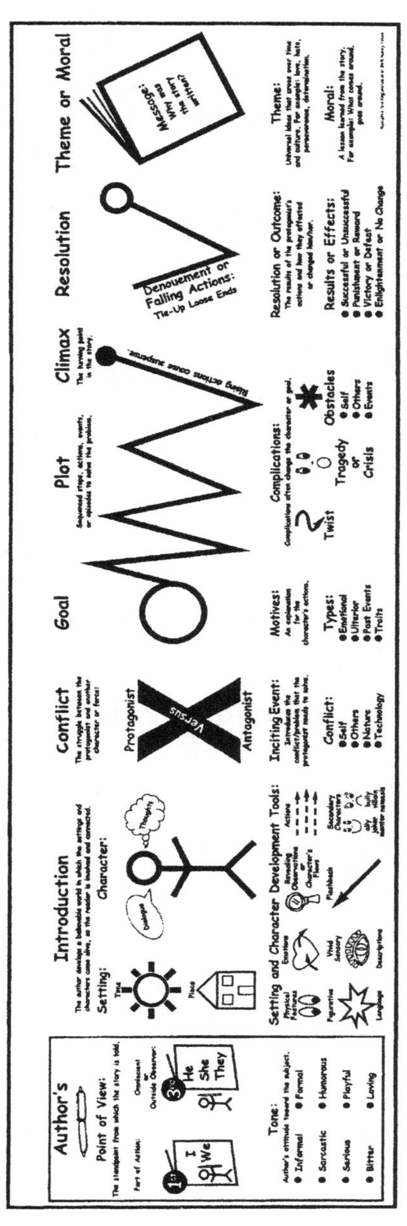

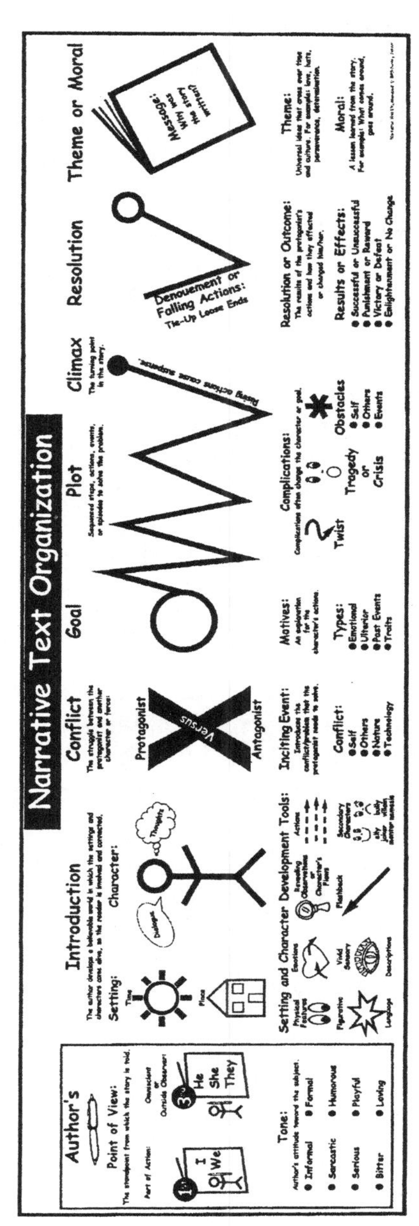

Source: From *Reading Connections: Building High-Level Reading Comprehension Skills and Strategies,* N. Fetzer, 2006, Murrieta, CA, Nancy Fetzer's Literacy Connections. www.nancyfetzer.com. Reprinted with permission.

Activity 12.3

NARRATIVE TEXT ORGANIZATION SCRIPT

Every story has a *setting* and a *character*. The setting tells *when* and *where*. The character drives the action in the story. The author needs to make the setting and character come alive, so that we will want to read the story. In the introduction, the author makes them come alive by using special tools in his toolbox. The author has many tools to use. First, *physical features,* which describe the character and setting. Also, the author uses the *five senses* and *figurative language* to paint a picture of these features. The author must also make the character come alive by revealing the character's *emotions*. Emotions can be internal (inside the character's thoughts) or external (on the outside using dialogue or actions of the character).

Once the author makes the setting and character come alive, then there's a *problem or conflict*. The character can have a problem with himself, another person or people, nature, or technology. Once the character has a problem, then he or she sets a *goal* to figure out how to solve his or her problem. Once the character sets a goal, then he or she goes through a series of steps, actions, episodes, and events to solve the problem. That's called the *plot*.

To make the plot interesting, the author may include *twists, tragedies,* and *obstacles*. A twist is an unexpected direction in the story or the character. For example, the main character's most trusted confidant turns out to be his enemy. A tragedy is when someone is badly hurt or dies. Obstacles are things that get in the way of the character's progress. For example, the character's own fears, or other people (bullies), or nature (a tornado).

The *climax* is the turning point in the story. This is usually the most exciting part in which the outcome is more clear. After the climax is the *resolution*. Was the character successful or unsuccessful in reaching his or her goal? How was the character affected or changed by the events in the story?

The resolution includes the results of the character's actions and how they affected or changed him or her. Also in the resolution are the final actions that tie up loose ends and bring things back to normal again.

Who cares? Why was the story written? What was the author's message? Was the author trying to teach a lesson or trying to communicate universal ideas about people or human nature? The answers to these questions are the *theme* or *moral*.

— *Chapter 13* —

WRITING STRATEGIES, SCAFFOLDS, AND ACCOMMODATIONS

Writing standards and grade-level expectations vary from state to state and district to district. Most students, however, are expected to show similar competencies depending on their grade level in various writing strategies and applications. This requires, for example, being able to write clear, coherent, and focused sentences, paragraphs, and essays with awareness of the audience and purpose; writing with style, using descriptive and figurative language and a variety of sentence structures; and appropriate format and organization for the specific writing genre. Students are also expected to demonstrate grade-level competency in *writing conventions* (grammar, mechanics, punctuation, capitalization, and spelling) and in the *writing process.*

The Kagans (2000) describe common writing process standards for upper elementary and middle school grades as follows:

Grades 3 Through 5

Prewriting. Student uses prewriting strategies to plan written work (brainstorming, story maps and webs, and graphic organizers).

Drafting and Revising. Student uses strategies to draft and revise written work (elaborates ideas, uses paragraphs for separate ideas, and pays attention to word choice, tones, voice and audience).

Editing and Publishing. Student uses strategies to edit written work (grammar, punctuation, and spelling) and to publish work (pays attention to format and integrates pictures, illustrations, charts, and graphs).

Grades 6 Through 8

Prewriting. Student uses a variety of prewriting strategies (brainstorms, collects prior knowledge, makes outlines, and refers to other writing).

Drafting and Revising. Student uses a variety of strategies to draft and revise written work (checks for consistency and continuity, rethinks and rewrites, and elaborates and clarifies).

Editing and Publishing. Student uses a variety of strategies to edit (grammar, punctuation, spelling, and clarity) and to publish work (with a word processor).

Best-practice research for teaching writing to all students—including those with learning disabilities and other struggling writers—identifies the importance of teaching the critical steps in the writing process, explicitly teaching text structures, and providing students a high level of feedback (Russell, Baker, & Edwards, 1999).

THE IMPORTANCE OF MODELING

Explicit teacher modeling of writing strategies, applications, conventions, and processes is a key component of a balanced literacy program. Teacher modeling of grade-level writing skills and standards can take place in whole-group or small-group instruction. During modeled writing, the teacher's demonstration of his or her self-talk is of great value to student writers, particularly those who are weak in applying their own metacognitive skills while writing. Such modeling enables students to listen in and gain insight as the teacher grapples with ideas while planning or drafting, choosing the most descriptive, precise vocabulary, or structuring and organizing detailed sentences to support the topic. Struggling and reluctant writers need many models of good writing presented orally and visually. Modeling also involves providing students with exemplars that highlight what teachers want students to focus on in their writing; for example, authors' use of interesting hooks and leads, powerful verbs and figurative language, and smooth transitions.

GUIDED WRITING

Another important component of a balanced literacy program is guided writing. This is a time for students to receive teacher guidance and feedback while they are working on a writing task and practicing their skills in groups (typically two to three groups). For example, with a guided writing group of students who are to write a summary paragraph, the teacher provides the supports, scaffolding, or on-the-spot teaching needed for that group of writers. This might involve listening in while students in that group are engaged in partner talk—first verbalizing their summary before writing—or guiding them in filling out their own graphic organizers. The teacher may observe and ask questions to ensure that students are first planning appropriately, then utilizing and referring to their prewriting organizational tools while they write. Various strategies or recommendations may be shared with the group through minilessons to advance their skills and quality of writing.

STRATEGIES TO HELP WITH WRITING

The stages of the writing process include *prewriting, drafting, revising, editing,* and *publishing.* Effective teachers are providing explicit instruction of strategies throughout all steps of the process, modeling and guiding students in the production of quality grade-level written work. It is necessary to explicitly teach students the use of any graphic organizers, planning forms, checklists, or other structural tools students are going to be using for the assignment. With any writing assignment, always review the standards that will be addressed through that writing assignment. Discuss and clarify the expectations and criteria for success. Show examples and models whenever possible that highlight the elements that are needed for at-standard grade-level writing. It is very beneficial to create a rubric for writing assignments to guide students in addressing the components necessary for meeting grade-level standards and scoring their written products.

Prewriting

Prewriting is a crucial stage of the writing process, involving the generation, planning, and organization of ideas and deciding "what" and "how" to express ideas before actually beginning to write the first draft. This is a challenge for many students, and struggling writers tend to neglect this important step. Following are some *prewriting* techniques designed to stimulate ideas, topic selection, and effective planning and also to provide much-needed structure, organization, and motivation to write (Rief, 1998, 2003, 2005).

Brainstorming. Sessions are short and focused—no more than three to five minutes. Given a general theme or topic, students call out whatever comes to mind related to that topic while someone records all responses.

Quick Writes. Students have three to four minutes to write down everything they can think of related to a given topic. Model the same uninterrupted writing along with the students at this time.

Writing Topic Folders. Students maintain a folder, card file, or notebook of possible ideas for writing topics. These might include hobbies, places visited, jobs they have done, personal interests, colorful and interesting people they know, pets, special field trips or activities, observations, wonderings, and so forth. The writing folder can also be in the form of a personal collage. Students can use words and pictures cut out of magazines, newspapers, and travel brochures and laminate the folder when done.

Writing Topic Computer File. Students enter on a computer file the same potential writing ideas that might go into a writing topic folder. This may also include digital pictures of people, things, or occasions students want to remember or topics found while exploring sites on the Internet that they find interesting.

Telling Personal Stories. In cooperative groups, students orally respond to prompts by telling personal stories. For example, "Tell about a time you or someone you knew got lost." After the oral telling and sharing of stories in small, cooperative groups, students fill out a graphic organizer, then write a rough draft or outline of the story they told.

Reference Books. Groups of students look through reference books for writing topic ideas—for example, mysteries of nature, music, astronomy, sports, or fashion.

Writing Prompts. The teacher provides a stimulus such as a poem, story, picture, song, or news item to prompt writing. It often helps to offer students a variety of sample topic sentences, story starters, and writing prompts when they are struggling for an idea.

Making an Audio Recording. Some students benefit from first verbalizing their thoughts and what they would like to say before transcribing those ideas onto paper.

Checklists

It is valuable to provide a *prewriting checklist* that lists some specific questions students need to ask themselves at this stage of the writing process. Such self-questioning is an important means of teaching students to apply metacognitive skills and improve their thinking, planning, and writing. When creating a prewriting checklist, teachers may want to select questions such as

- What do I already know about this topic?
- Can I write enough about my selected topic?
- Who is my target audience?
- What is my purpose for writing this (for example, to persuade, inform, or entertain)?
- Which writing genre am I going to use?
- In what style or voice will I write?
- What are some words, ideas, or phrases related to my topic?
- Have I narrowed down my topic?

Prewriting checklists may be divided into specific questions for the beginning, middle, and end of the writing task. For example, for the *beginning* (opening) of a writing assignment

- How will I introduce the subject or topic?
- What kind of hook can I use in my introduction to capture the audience's attention and interest?
- What will be the main idea about my subject?

For the *middle* (body) of the writing assignment

- What interesting details and examples might I use?
- What will be my flow and sequence of ideas?
- Where should I research and gather interesting information to support my topic?

For the *ending* (conclusion) of a writing topic

- What is the message I want to share with readers?
- What would be an interesting or exciting ending?
- How might I tie this to the beginning paragraph and topic statement?

These kinds of questions help the writer think through, plan, and organize prior to drafting. Such questioning can be done independently, but it is also recommended to engage in this questioning process with peers (through partner talk at the prewrite stage) and during guided writing.

Planning Forms and Graphic Organizers

It is highly beneficial to record a plan prior to writing using a thinking or planning form or a graphic organizer of some kind. These are among the most effective ways to help students generate their ideas, as well as formulate and organize their thoughts. Such visual organizers are of particular importance for struggling or reluctant writers who need tools to help plan, structure, and organize their ideas before beginning to write the first draft.

A number of examples of graphic organizers are offered throughout this book. Many resources are also available with graphic organizer templates, including web sites with downloadable graphic organizers for student use, such as http://www.eduplace.com/graphicorganizer (Houghton Mifflin Education Place) and http://www.edhelper.com/teachers/graphic_organizers.htm (EdHelper). Others can be found in some of the recommended web sites in Appendix A. The software program Inspiration,^{TM} available through www.inspiration.com, is another excellent tool for graphically clustering, mapping, organizing, and outlining ideas and concepts during the prewriting stage.

Drafting

Once sufficient time has gone into the prewriting stage of the writing process, students can begin their first draft. They should be using their graphic organizers or other planning tools as their guide and reference as they compose.

As with prewriting, drafting should be modeled. Students benefit from seeing the teacher work through crafting his or her own initial draft while verbalizing the thinking process that takes place while composing. For example, teachers might model the ordering or sequencing of ideas while thinking out loud, "What should I write first, second, and next?" When modeling effective transitions, the teacher might refer to a word wall of various transition words or phrases and ask out loud, "Which words might I use to connect these ideas?" Developing and expanding ideas, adding details in support of the main idea, and incorporating examples or evidence are just a few of the things that teachers may model during the drafting stage. See the section on formats and genres later in this chapter for ideas on drafting specific types of writing.

Written expression requires a great deal of self-monitoring from writers. They need to put themselves in the place of their potential readers and keep asking themselves questions such as

- Is this clear? Does this make sense?
- Do my ideas flow logically?
- Am I using the best choice of words?
- Have I narrowed down my topic?
- How will I transition from this paragraph to the next?
- Am I providing enough details to support each topic?
- Do I need other information or resources?
- Have I left anything important out?

These same questions need to be revisited during the revision process.

Students need feedback when they write their own drafts. This can be provided during guided writing and independent writing time. The feedback can come from the teacher or from peers. While they are writing their drafts, ask a few student volunteers to share with the class what they have written so far. This often helps spark ideas for those students who are struggling to get started or are stuck.

Revising

Many students would prefer to go directly from their first draft to the final draft without revision or editing. Reluctant and struggling writers prefer to avoid the process of rewriting, which can feel overwhelming and tedious to them. However, students need to learn that all good writers make successive revisions to their works before they are ready to publish. As Fletcher and Portalupi (2001) point out, "Revision is a composing tool. Editing involves the surface features of the writing. If students confuse the two, their revisions will be first aid (corrections) instead of the radical surgery that leads to improved writing" (p. 65). "Real revision is a journey, an exploration into the heart of what we are trying to say" (Finn, 1999, p. 37).

Model the revision process, showing students how you go about revising your own writing. Using an overhead or document camera, project a segment of your writing that you wish to revise, and verbalize your thinking process as you toy with different ideas and make a few changes to your current draft. For example, you might model adding dialogue, rewording or restructuring sentences for variety, zooming in on one part and making it more descriptive, or reordering parts of the text. Let students observe how you reshape your writing with your purpose and audience in mind. "Is this clear?" "How can I make this more powerful and exciting?"

Teach students to write on every other line of the paper as they are composing their first draft so that revising and editing is easier (with carets, cross outs, and arrows). They should write in pencil or erasable ink. Their next drafts should be labeled as Draft 2, Draft 3, or by date. Students with access to the computer for their writing will find that making successive drafts is much easier with a word processor. Show examples of this process, with each draft of the document saved and filed by the draft number and date. This makes it easy to locate and also has the advantage of the author not having to worry about losing what has previously been written.

Teach revision techniques and provide students with a revision checklist that includes some of the following (Fletcher & Portalupi, 2001; Education Department of Western Australia, 2004):

- Adding stronger verbs
- Adding sensory details
- Changing the lead or ending
- Adding dialogue
- Narrowing the focus
- Adding sentence variety
- Expanding sentences
- Deleting unnecessary information and ideas that don't belong
- Changing the tense
- Changing the tone
- Changing the point of view
- Changing the sequence or order

It is generally helpful when revising one's writing to hear it read and note what is needed to make the piece sound better. Encourage students to read their work aloud to themselves and make some changes. Then they can read their draft to others. Build in time for students to read their draft to a partner or small group for feedback. They can also take their draft home to work on and read to others at home.

You may wish to prepare questions that your students can use when eliciting feedback from their listeners. For example

- Was anything unclear?
- Was there a part you particularly liked?
- Do you have any suggestions for making this better or more interesting?

Editing

Some proofreading and editing may be done during revision. But it is also important to edit after the revision to catch all the final corrections in grammar, spelling, and mechanics and to polish the piece of work. Editing is also a skill that needs to be modeled, explicitly taught in minilessons, and practiced through guided instruction. Students need to be taught how to access the thesaurus, dictionary, charts, and other tools for checking spelling, finding more precise or descriptive vocabulary words, and so forth.

They should be encouraged to mark words they wish to improve or words that have been overused and to underline or mark the spelling of words they think might be wrong.

For many students, particularly reluctant and struggling writers, this is difficult to do independently. They have great difficulty proofreading their own work and identifying errors in spelling, capitalization, punctuation, or grammar. Allow peers to do this task of proofing and editing together. Some teachers have all students buddy with a partner or work with a writing group. Other teachers assign their strong spellers in the classroom this job, designating them class spelling or editing experts with the job of aiding other students in need of help. Using a computer to write drafts is much easier for many students because of its array of word-processing tools and features, such as the spell-checker, thesaurus, dictionary, and cut and paste.

Publishing

When the finished product is ready to be shared with an audience, the writing process is in its final stage. Whether the final product is in the form of a neatly written or typed paper to be read aloud or posted and displayed for others to read or formatted in a book for a class library, being a published author is a wonderful feeling of accomplishment. An array of fully bound hardcover books ideal for student publication is available from Treetop Publishing at www.barebooks.com. Classrooms have numerous ways to celebrate their authors and showcase their writings with an audience of peers, parents, and others. See Chapter Four for more on publishing and celebrating.

FORMATS AND GENRES

Depending upon their grade and developmental level, students are expected to write in various genres and formats. Following are descriptions of some of these writing genres and their formats.

Paragraphs

There are many kinds of paragraphs: summary, directional or "how-tos," compare and contrast, procedural, descriptive, and narrative. All paragraphs are structured to have a topic sentence, at least three supporting details, and a conclusion. A cohesive paragraph has a clear beginning, middle, and end. Key to becoming a good writer is mastery of paragraph writing. Struggling writers of any age or grade level need direct instruction and a great deal of practice in the skill of paragraph development. This includes how to write a catchy hook; powerful sentences that have variety, descriptive language, and precise word choice; smooth transitions; and an interesting or compelling conclusion. Different paragraph genres regarding, for example, writing about a chocolate chip cookie might include (1) telling how to make the cookie (procedural or directional); (2) telling how the cookie looks, smells, and tastes (descriptive); (3) telling what will happen to the cookie (narrative); (4) convincing others that it is the best kind of cookie or treat (persuasive); (5) comparing or contrasting it to another kind of cookie or dessert.

Powerful Leads and Closings

Writers need to learn how to get their readers' attention and curiosity right at the beginning, hooking in their interest so they will want to keep reading more. There are several ways an author can accomplish this; for example, by asking a rhetorical question, making an emotional statement, or through dialogue or action. As William Zinsser (2001, p. 56) advises, "Your lead must capture the reader immediately and force him to keep reading. It must cajole him with freshness, or novelty, or paradox, or humor, or surprise, or with an unusual idea, or an interesting fact, or a question. Anything will do, as long as it nudges his curiosity and tugs at his sleeve. Next the lead must do some real work. It must provide hard details that tell the reader why the piece was written and why he ought to read it. But don't dwell on the reason. Coax the reader more, keep him inquisitive." Other good leads include a short anecdote, quote, piece of conversation or startling statement (McCarthy, 1998a).

Writing a good conclusion is also a valuable skill. Authors have several means of doing so. For example, the writer might end with humor, a question, a quote or dialogue, or an emotional statement (Fetzer, 2003). The author might also conclude with a surprise or end the piece the way it began, by using a concept, idea, or repetition of phrases from the opening paragraph (Novelli, 2000). When teaching students about strong leads and conclusions, share examples found in text. Show exemplar pieces (via an overhead projector or document camera) of good leads and conclusions. Use models to point out the techniques authors use in their leads to entice their audience to read more and closings that are satisfying and memorable for the reader.

Summaries

A summary can be narrative or expository. To write a summary, students must learn to identify the most important points and be able to illustrate or support those points sufficiently but concisely with significant details. In a *narrative summary,* the first paragraph is the introduction, which includes a hook and identifies the author, title, characters, setting, conflict, goal, and generally the first or beginning episode or event of the story. In the body, the paragraph(s) start with an appropriate transition to tie to the previous paragraph, and include the next main episodes or events sequentially, including the significant supporting details and attempts to solve the problem. The concluding paragraph would have a smooth transition from the previous paragraph and includes the resolution, how the character changed, and the author's message (Fetzer, 2003).

In an *expository summary,* the opening paragraph includes a hook, introductory information stating the author and title, thesis or central idea, and generally the first main idea in support of the topic. A few details (such as examples, facts, illustrations, definitions, statistics, or evidence) in support of the first main idea are provided. Each of the other paragraphs in the body begin with a transition from the preceding paragraph and contain another main idea and supporting details. The concluding paragraph restates the thesis or central idea, and generally an analysis or interpretation of the information is provided.

Teaching students to write a good summary involves modeling and guided instruction. In large- or small-group settings, students should be involved in identifying the main ideas and supporting details in a variety of texts (whether passages or articles). Through modeling and guidance, students should first learn how to structure and organize the key points, cite evidence, and summarize orally. Students will be far more prepared and able to then write their own narrative or expository summaries.

Response to Literature

A response to literature comprises first the summary paragraph(s) of the text and then a response. This can be written in as few as two paragraphs (one summary and one response) or in a five-paragraph essay. Beginning with the narrative summary, the writer must transition to the response paragraph(s). This requires the students to analyze and make interpretations, inferences, and connections.

Letters

It is highly recommended to have students learn letter-writing structures and practice writing this genre through motivating and authentic letter-writing assignments. Give students the opportunity to write to someone they are interested in and to write a letter for a purpose. Use the Celebrity Letter Writing Station described in our book, *How to Reach and Teach All Children in the Inclusive Classroom* (Rief & Heimburge, 2006) to spark interest and enthusiasm.

Narrative

"Narratives are descriptions of events that can be fiction or nonfiction. Usually we think of stories as narratives (realistic fiction, myths, fairy tales, plays, fables, historical fiction, and legends are examples), but biography, a nonfiction genre, can also be considered a narrative" (McCormick, 2003, p. 345). The purpose of a narrative is to tell the reader what happened.

Narratives have a beginning, middle, and end format, with appropriate transitional words (such as *first, before, meanwhile, next, later,* or *at last*) tying the sentences and paragraphs together. Personal narratives relate with observations, memories, and ideas about a memorable event or experience. For example, personal narrative prompts might ask the student to "Describe a time you . . . (learned a valuable lesson, were happy with the choice you made, were frightened or embarrassed)."

Memoirs are a form of personal narrative. "Writing memoir is not just about recording what happened to us, but about exploring the possible significance of an event or important moment" (Finn, 1999, p. 7). "We read and write memoirs to figure out our own experiences and to connect with the experiences and wisdom of others. . . . Unlike biographies, memoirs allow us to get inside the heads of other people, to experience a moment in their lives from their perspective" (Lattimer, 2003, p. 24).

Fictional narratives are any kind of story with use of story grammar and organization. Narratives are well suited for three-paragraph papers (simple beginning, middle, and end of the event), as well as five-paragraph essays (introduction, beginning episode, middle episode, final episode, conclusion), and longer.

Story Grammar

Understanding the components of a story is necessary to explicitly teach student readers and writers. Stein and Glenn (1979) suggested that the following elements be included in story grammar instruction:

Major setting: introducing the protagonist (main character)

Minor setting: describing the time and place of the action

Initiating events: discussing the events that cause the main character to respond

Internal responses: describing the characters' feelings, desires, thoughts, hopes, and goals

Attempt: describing what the main character does to try to achieve the goal

Direct consequences: discussing whether the attempt succeeded or failed and the changes that result from the attempt

Reactions: identifying the main character's thoughts and feelings about the outcome and how other characters are affected by the outcome (Mather & Roberts, 1995)

A well-written narrative requires good *characterization.* Readers must be able to care enough to have empathy for the character and understand his or her personality, attitudes, needs, dreams, struggles, values, feelings, and motivations—basically, to know what makes the character tick. The protagonist is the central character in the story requiring the greatest degree of author effort in characterization. The author must reveal the character's goals, emotions, thoughts, qualities, and flaws. This is done in a variety of ways, such as through dialogue, listening to the character's inner thoughts, or through the protagonist's interactions with the other characters in the story. The character must evolve over the course of the story and have learned something or have been changed in some important way. This character development is a result of what occurs during the events of the story and how he or she dealt with those events.

A good story also needs an interesting *plot.* After hooking in the reader through their emotions or curiosity, the plot takes the reader on a ride of highs and lows, twists and turns. The plot builds up momentum to the climax and has a satisfying ending or resolution. (See Chapter Nine for more about story elements and character studies.)

The Narrative Organizer Chart

The narrative organizer chart in Chapter Twelve is a wonderful teaching strategy and scaffold for students to use in understanding and comprehending narrative text (Fetzer, 2006). The chart is also a helpful tool for students to use and refer to when planning and writing their own stories. Teachers may have students work with partners or small groups in first talking through the elements of their stories at the different stages of the writing process. Using the narrative organizer chart, students can help each other better plan (during prewrite) and clarify their writing (during the drafting and revision stages) while referring to the chart. For example, after drafting their introductions and sharing them with their partner, they can receive feedback from their partners through questions and statements such as

- Are you satisfied that you have enough sensory detail to describe the setting?
- Your main character hasn't come alive to me. I think you need to reveal more about Julia: what she looks like, her emotions, and so on.

Expository Writing

The purpose of expository writing is to inform the reader. It provides an explanation or a report. According to Chapman and King (2003), expository writing may involve giving a step-by-step account or a how-to procedure. Examples of expository writing forms include book reports, how-to guides, recounts of an event, research papers, and news stories. They also include writing messages, invitations, and announcements; writing directions and explanations for a process or procedure; and telling in sequence how to do or make something (McCarthy, 1998b). See Chapters Four, Five, and Twelve for more information about expository text structures and features and accompanying activities.

Two common expository forms of writing required of upper elementary and middle school students are research papers and persuasive letters and essays.

Research Papers

Research papers are formatted to begin with an introductory paragraph that includes a hook and thesis statement. The following paragraphs in the body of the report each state a main idea that illustrates, defines, or supports the thesis. Each paragraph further defines, illustrates, and supports the main idea through examples, facts, statistics, and other evidence. The concluding paragraph restates the topic and its importance and draws a conclusion about the information. See our book *How to Reach and Teach All Children in the Inclusive Classroom* (2nd ed.) (Rief & Heimburge, 2006) for many research strategies, lessons, and activities for use with upper elementary and middle school students.

Persuasive Letters and Essays

Persuasive writing is an important genre in the upper grades. This type of expository writing is conducive to a persuasive letter or a five-paragraph essay format. In Julie's classroom, prior to writing in this genre, students are first exposed to a number of short nonfiction pieces on such topics as school uniforms, see-through backpacks, and soda machines in schools. After discussing the articles at length, students must take a stand on the issue, work in small groups to decide on a position, and present their position to the rest of the class in the effort to sway others to their thinking. Quick writes are then assigned for each issue so that students get a feel for persuasive writing. Julie then does a read-aloud using *Should There Be Zoos?* by Tony Stead and Judy Ballester, and students must write their position on this issue. They then group themselves by their position, chart arguments (for or against the issue), and groups share their ideas and try to persuade others to join their side. Julie also teaches students through minilessons about propaganda techniques such as bandwagons, testimonials, and glittering generality. Students are then assigned to choose their own topic to write about from a list of brainstormed and charted topics such as cafeteria food, homework, illegal immigration, cell phone use while driving, child obesity, gas prices and the oil industry, athlete's salaries, housing costs, and so forth.

A persuasive writing contest was held by California state senator Christine Kehoe that was open to all fifth graders in California. Students were to write a one-page persuasive letter to a school principal, editor of a local newspaper, or senator regarding an issue important to them. Carolyn H.'s fifth-grade class brainstormed issues and talked about them; then students were assigned to write one persuasive letter from each category (addressed to the principal, an editor, and a senator). Students selected their best piece, and it was submitted for the contest. Some of the topics students identified as appropriate issues for a principal included lockers, recess games, and detention. A few of the issues for the editor were the speed limit, housing costs, drunk drivers, homelessness, and a new football stadium. Issues for the senator included pollution, health care, crime, war, border laws, and so forth.

A five-paragraph essay is another format for the persuasive writing genre. See the rubric in Activity 13.1 at the end of this chapter, describing the elements and criteria for writing a strong persuasive essay.

THE USE OF RUBRICS

A rubric is both an instructional and an assessment tool. It contains specific criteria that clearly spells out the expectations for the final product. The rubric describes levels of quality and can be specific to a particular assignment or more generic in nature. Rubrics are typically on a 1 to 4 or 1 to 5 rating scale, with 1 being the lowest level of proficiency (needing improvement) and 4 or 5 being highest performance or superior. Following are some scales from rubrics used in school districts around the country:

4 – Expert (advanced proficient)
3 – Practitioner (proficient)
2 – Apprentice (basic)
1 – Novice (below basic)

4 – Exceeds standard (exemplary)
3 – Meets standard (accomplished)
2 – Approaching standard (developing)
1 – Below standard (beginning)

4 – Consistently demonstrates or conveys . . .
3 – Generally demonstrates or conveys . . .
2 – Somewhat demonstrates or conveys . . .
1 – Rarely demonstrates or conveys . . .

When giving the assignment, provide students with any scoring guide or rubric that will be used to assess the written product when completed. This significantly helps students, particularly those with writing difficulties, with a visual tool for planning, structuring, and self-monitoring their written work. It also helps parents by explaining from the beginning exactly what the teacher expects in the writing assignment and what is considered proficient performance for the grade level.

Model for students how to analyze pieces according to the rubric scoring guide. Share anonymous examples of writing by projecting them on the overhead or document camera and discussing why those writing samples were scored the way they were. Providing models of writing at the various levels of the rubric particularly those that are at standard or above (level 3 and 4) is highly recommended, so students have a good understanding of the criteria that must be met at those levels. Using the rubric when conferencing with students to provide feedback while they are working on a writing project is also very beneficial. For online sources of rubrics, see the RubiStar web site at http://rubistar.4teachers.org.

NOTE TAKING

It is important to teach students the skill of note taking. This involves learning both how to take notes from their textbooks and how to take notes during lectures.

Lecture Notes

According to Bos and Vaughn (1994), on average 55 percent of the time in an elementary classroom is spent with children listening, and by the time students reach secondary level the information load in lectures is so great that note taking becomes necessary to alleviate the memory load. Note taking is not an easy skill, as it involves simultaneously listening and processing the information, determining what is important for recording, and writing that information down quickly. Many students have never been taught how to take notes. By upper elementary and middle school, students should receive explicit instruction in note taking and learn the value of this skill so critical to their school success in the higher grades.

There is a variety of note-taking techniques. The two-column method is commonly used. Students divide their paper into two columns: a wide column on the right (about two-thirds of the paper's width) for recording class notes and a narrow column on the left for key words, terms, main ideas, or questions. Only one side of the paper is used for notes.

Following are recommended strategies for teaching students note-taking skills during lectures (Casbarro, 2003; Bos & Vaughn, 1994):

- Teach students to listen for key words (such as first, second, next), teacher's voice (inflection, volume, and tone), repeated points the teacher makes, and pronouncements such as "This is important to remember."
- Teach students how to use abbreviations, short phrases, and symbols in their note taking.
- When practicing this skill, lecture on a topic that is fairly simple and familiar to students. Use visual aids (pictures and diagrams), as well as examples and nonexamples of the concepts being presented.
- Build in breaks during the lecture for students to work with partners briefly to discuss what they are learning and review their notes together.
- Have students practice reviewing their notes shortly after lecture and ask themselves questions, using the trigger words in the left column.

Nancy Fetzer (2003, 2006) developed a creative lecture note strategy to aid students in comprehension of vocabulary and concepts and use of academic language in their oral and written summaries (see Figure 13.1). As mentioned in Chapter Twelve, the technique is designed

Figure 13.1. Lecture Notes
Source: From *Reading Connections: Building High-Level Reading Comprehension Skills and Strategies,* by N. Fetzer, 2006, Murrieta, CA: Nancy Fetzer's Literacy Connections. wwwnancyfetzer.com. Reprinted with permission.

as a prereading strategy to front-load difficult information in a highly multisensory format. It is also a beneficial strategy for aiding students in written language, particularly in learning how to write powerful summary paragraphs. Following is a description of this procedure.

MULTISENSORY LECTURE NOTE STRATEGY

As a prereading lesson prior to beginning, for example, a social studies or science chapter, the teacher is prepared to introduce the key vocabulary, concepts, and "big ideas" the students will be learning about in the text. The teacher provides background knowledge and summarizes the new information students will be learning while lecturing the class in a highly scaffolded format. The teacher records on the board key information for students to copy in a graphic, easy-to-read format. He or she lectures using "academic language" that students repeat several times in unison or through partner talk, and incorporates hand and body movements (total physical response) to represent some vocabulary and actions.

Information verbally presented is also recorded on the board with simple pictures or icons, bullets with phrases of key points, and vocabulary in bubbles. Vocabulary is introduced in context and placed in a bubble with a drop box connected to the bottom of the bubble or circle. Inside the drop boxes are synonyms, icons, or definitions of the vocabulary word. The students copy this information on a blank piece of paper as directed by the teacher. After teaching and recording a small portion of the information, the teacher stops and models (using academic language) how to summarize the notes on the board.

Next students turn to their buddies and summarize their notes using the similar language they heard their teacher model. The teacher walks around the room and listens in as the students recite from the notes, and provides scaffolds for anyone having difficulty. The teacher continues, sentence by sentence, modeling the language and adding physical motions to provide more meaning to the concepts and vocabulary being taught. Students chant each sentence back while using the hand or body motions as they practice summarizing their notes. This procedure is very valuable for English-language learners and kinesthetic learners and aids with comprehension and recall for all types of learners.

The teacher continues to add more information, stopping periodically to model how to summarize in a cohesive and coherent way (using the physical motions as well). After multiple repetitions reading the notes, students are then asked to turn over their papers and write out in complete sentences the summary that has already been verbalized multiple times (Fetzer, 2006).

Textbook Notes

Taking notes from textbooks is also an important skill for upper-grade students to learn. Teachers should explicitly teach students how to do so. Model and guide students in how to scan and preview the pages of the reading assignment, then read the end-of-chapter or unit questions. Next they should use titles and subchapter headings as an outline, summarize content under each heading in short phrases, reread the end-of-chapter questions looking back at their notes, and add any important information left out the first time around (Heacox, 1991; Casbarro, 2003).

Activity 13.1

PERSUASIVE FIVE-PARAGRAPH ESSAY RUBRIC

Organization and Content

- First paragraph includes a hook to capture reader's attention and interest.
- Thesis statement in first paragraph clearly states writer's position on issue and why reader should agree with writer's point of view.
- Body paragraphs include three main ideas or reasons defending position on issue.
- Each main idea or reason is backed up with supporting details or evidence to defend writer's side of the argument.
- The counterargument or rebuttal on the issue is also given to address reader's concerns.
- A satisfying concluding paragraph restates thesis statement and writer's case for or against the topic.
- Smooth flow and transitions between paragraphs.
- A convincing case is presented for writer's side of the argument.

Scoring Guide

4–Demonstrates seven to eight of the above criteria.

3–Demonstrates five to six of the above criteria.

2–Demonstrates three to four of the above criteria.

1–Demonstrates less than three of the above and/or contains less than five paragraphs

Language Usage, Spelling, Mechanics, and Neatness

- Complete sentences throughout that make sense (no run-ons)
- Descriptive vocabulary and word choice
- A variety of sentence beginnings and lengths
- Correct spelling most of the time
- Correct punctuation most of the time
- Correct use of capitalization most of the time
- Effort made to edit and correct mechanics and spelling errors
- Neat and legible final product

Scoring Guide

4–Demonstrates seven to eight of the above criteria.

3–Demonstrates five to six of the above criteria.

2–Demonstrates three to four of the above criteria.

1–Demonstrates less than three of the above criteria.

— *Chapter 14* —

TEACHING AND ENHANCING LITERACY THROUGH TECHNOLOGY

Teachers have been using technology in the classroom to some degree for over a decade. However, at no previous time have such an array of technological tools and resources been available, accessible, and relatively affordable to make such a positive impact on literacy instruction and student learning. However, there is wide disparity between wealthy school districts and less affluent ones in the use of technologies in the classroom. We hope that more and more teachers throughout the United States who wish to make use of the technologies described in this chapter will be provided the means and training to do so.

Among the conclusions of the National Educational Technology Plan for the U.S. Department of Education (2004)

- There is no dispute over the need for America's students to have the knowledge and competence to compete in an increasingly technology-driven world economy.
- This need demands new models of education facilitated by educational technology.
- In the realm of technology, the educational community is playing catch-up. Industry is far ahead of education, and tech-savvy high school students often are far ahead of their teachers.
- This "digital disconnect" is a major cause of frustration among today's students. Public schools that do not adapt to the technology needs of students risk becoming increasingly irrelevant.

This chapter highlights some of the educational technologies that support and enhance the development of students' reading and writing skills and capabilities. These technologies are beneficial for all students and are particularly important for enabling struggling and reluctant readers and writers to become successful, literate adults. They are powerful learning tools in that they are highly visual in nature and enable multisensory instruction that taps into the learning styles of diverse learners.

There are countless ways teachers can utilize the various technologies to reach and teach students in balanced literacy classrooms. Technology increases the complexity of tasks students can perform and their means of obtaining information, expressing themselves, and demonstrating learning creatively. "By providing students with a variety of media to find, interpret, and present information, as is possible with the use of technology, the power of learning shifts into the hands of the students, enabling them to work with the tools that are best for their own learning" (Wepner, Valmont, & Thurlow, 2000, p. 67).

The International Reading Association's position statement on integrating literacy and technology in the curriculum (2002) says that "the Internet and other forms of information and communication technology (ICT) such as word processors, presentation software, instant messaging, and e-mail are regularly redefining the nature of literacy." In order to become literate adults, our students of the twenty-first century must learn how to read, write, research, access information, and communicate with proficiency using whatever technology is going to be the norm in their future.

PROGRAMS FOR USE IN THE CLASSROOM

Many classrooms as of the mid- to late 1990s have been equipped with one or more desktop computers available for student use. More recently, many schools are seeking ways to provide portable computers in classrooms when possible. Some schools have a class set of laptops or notebook computers stored in a portable cart that can be moved from class to class. Classrooms can share the individual student computers, generally during their writing workshop times, by staggering the days or times of day of the writer's workshop period in different classes. In more affluent schools students often have their own laptops so don't need to share with other students, and in the future it is likely that all students will have their own portable computers.

High-quality software can be used on these computers to supplement the literacy program, enable more individualized instruction, and enhance reading and writing instruction and skill practice. In their efforts to provide intervention to low-performing readers and writers in upper elementary and middle school grades, some schools are using software programs such as SuccessMaker® Enterprise (www.pearsondigital.com), Destination Reading Course III and IV (www.riverdeep.net), Read 180 (www.scholastic.com), and Lexia SOS: Strategies for Older Students (www.lexialearning.com).

Prewriting Software

A popular and user-friendly software program that is very beneficial in the prewriting (planning) process of composition and written expression is Inspiration™ (www.inspiration.com). This application enables students to create their own graphic organizers (concept maps, webs, and flow charts), brainstorm ideas with pictures and words, categorize information visually, and plan and organize ideas prior to writing. Information entered can also be converted to a linear outline view.

Word Processing

Word processing has revolutionized our ability to write with ease and produce professional-looking written documents. There are no technological advances more valuable to us as authors than the user-friendly word processing programs on our computers that enable us to compose, revise, and edit our writing. The ability to cut and paste, spell-check, save drafts of our work, and easily print copies as needed makes the job of writing vastly superior and easier than it was just a decade or so ago. For students, use of computers and word processing has the same benefits. It also frees them from handwriting, which for many children is very tedious and time consuming. Even if drafts are written by hand but final copies are typed and printed from the computer, seeing a neat, easy-to-read copy is satisfying to both student and teacher. Knowing how relatively easy it is at a later stage to revise, reorganize, make changes, replace vocabulary, and correct spelling and grammar enables writers to focus on the content—and likely produce better-quality work. Some of the word processing programs more generally used for upper elementary and middle school students include AppleWorks, Microsoft Word, and ClarisWorks for Kids.

To get the most out of word processing, it is extremely important to learn how to type properly. It is highly recommended to provide training and practice for students in keyboarding skills. Some software programs for learning typing and keyboarding include Type to Learn (Sunburst), Mario Teaches Typing 2 (Brainstorm), JumpStart Typing (Knowledge Adventure), Mavis Beacon Teaches Typing (The Learning Company), UltraKey (Bytes of Learning, Inc.), Typing Instructor Deluxe (Individual Software), and Typing Time (Thomson Learning/South-Western Educational Publishing).

Desktop Publishing

Desktop publishing software enables students to format and lay out text and insert graphics in ways that regular word processing programs cannot match. With such software students can design newspapers, newsletters, and greeting cards and format and publish their writing in creative ways. Some desktop publishing software includes The Print Shop® and PrintMaster® Gold (Broderbund®), and Publish-iT 3.4 (Poster Software). Textease (Softease) is an award-winning word processing and desktop publishing package with multimedia capabilities and is very popular in British schools. Student Writing Center (Riverdeep) is another word processing and easy desktop publishing program.

Multimedia

Various programs have wonderful multimedia capabilities. Clicker 5 (Crick Software) is half talking word processor and the other half a multimedia writing space called a grid. Students compose by clicking images and animations from a grid and dragging them to the word processor. Students can insert text or their own images or work from several grid templates to create video-enhanced books or record their voices to accompany a report (Kennedy, 2006).

PowerPoint, a popular and highly motivating multimedia program, has dramatically improved and changed the way we are able to present information. For those with easy access to an LCD projector or whose rooms are equipped with an interactive whiteboard, PowerPoint is a phenomenally useful teaching tool. PowerPoint presentations use a graphic approach to presenting lessons in the form of slide shows. They are multimedia, integrating sounds, images, movies, and animations within the slide presentation.

Many of this program's features are visually appealing and engaging, such as the wide variety of backgrounds, colors, font types, and text animations. For example, bullets of text can fly in from any side of the slide, spiral into the page, fade in or out, dissolve, or even zoom in or out. Any digitized images and video clips can also be inserted to add to the visual richness of the slides. Web sites for finding images to copy to a slide are available from the Microsoft clip art gallery (http://office.microsoft.com/clipart) and Ask for Kids™ (www.askforkids.com), as well as Yahoo and Google. Go to Sites for Teachers (www.sitesforteachers.com) for links to more clip art resources. Video clips can be inserted into a PowerPoint presentation from Unitedstreaming or other digitized video clips. Slides can be formatted with various transition sounds to gain students' attention, and music and voice recordings can be added as another motivating and engaging sensory dimension to the presentation.

Uses for PowerPoint in Balanced Literacy

PowerPoint can be used to enhance instruction, practice skills, and create exciting, stimulating lessons in reading (fluency, phonics, comprehension, and vocabulary) and writing (spelling, grammar, mechanics, and composition). Some of the possibilities for using PowerPoint in the balanced literacy classroom follow.

- *Flash Card Presentations.* Create flash cards for word recognition and fluency practice. Type individual words or phrases on each slide and have students read aloud, increasing the rate of words flashed from slow to fast. Do repeated readings to build speed and accuracy. Voice recordings with a time delay can help students check themselves during independent practice.
- *Figures of Speech.* Use animated clip art on slides to help students better understand concepts such as personification, like the image of a child doing cartwheels to represent "tumbled" in Figure 14.1.
- *Fluency Practice.* Type a weekly passage on a slide for each guided reading group to practice fluency. The slide is duplicated (one for each student in the group) for their one-minute timings. As one student reads the passage orally, the others in the group silently read the projected slide. Students try to improve their oral rate throughout the week. Print slides for practice at home as well.
- *Linguistic Frames.* Prepare slides with academic language pattern frames that aid comprehension, such as "I predict _____ because ______." "This reminds me of _____." "One explanation is ____." "The evidence for this is ______."

Thoughts **tumbled** through his mind.
Personification

Figure 14.1.

- *Summaries.* After reading a story or portion of text, write a summary on a single slide with student input. Then this summary can be turned into a cloze activity as well, by erasing words for students to fill in, as shown in Figures 14.2 and 14.3.
- *Sound Spelling Cards.* Scan the sound spelling cards that are posted on classroom walls and insert them on PowerPoint slides. Figure 14.4, for example, shows a graphic from the Open Court program of **ar** words.
- *Illustrations of Setting.* Have students find clip art to illustrate the setting on a slide. For example, in *Mrs. Frisby and the Crow* (O'Brien, 2000) students found clip art of a forest, enlarged it to serve as the background, then added cat, owl, crow, and rat characters (see Figure 14.5).
- *Mnemonics.* Enhance recall of words that are tricky to spell by making slides with mnemonics. For example, "O U Lazy Dog" is a mnemonic for remembering the spelling of "could" (see Figure 14.6).

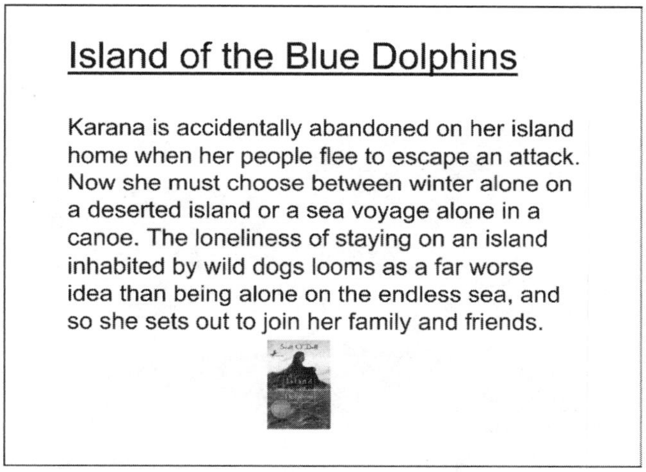

Island of the Blue Dolphins

Karana is accidentally abandoned on her island home when her people flee to escape an attack. Now she must choose between winter alone on a deserted island or a sea voyage alone in a canoe. The loneliness of staying on an island inhabited by wild dogs looms as a far worse idea than being alone on the endless sea, and so she sets out to join her family and friends.

Figure 14.2.

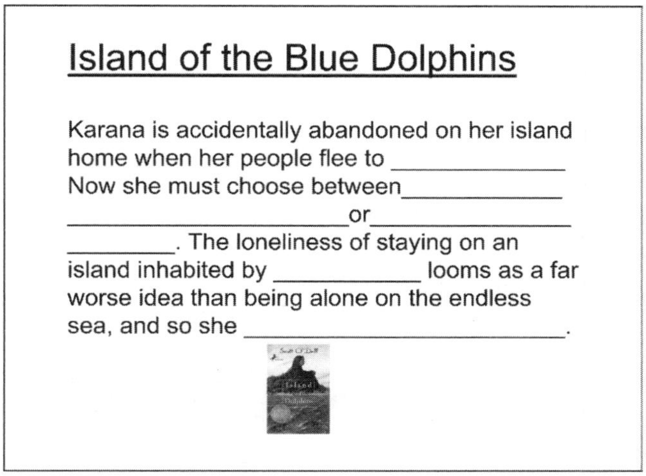

Island of the Blue Dolphins

Karana is accidentally abandoned on her island home when her people flee to _____________ Now she must choose between_____________ ______________________or________________ _________. The loneliness of staying on an island inhabited by ____________ looms as a far worse idea than being alone on the endless sea, and so she ___________________________.

Figure 14.3.

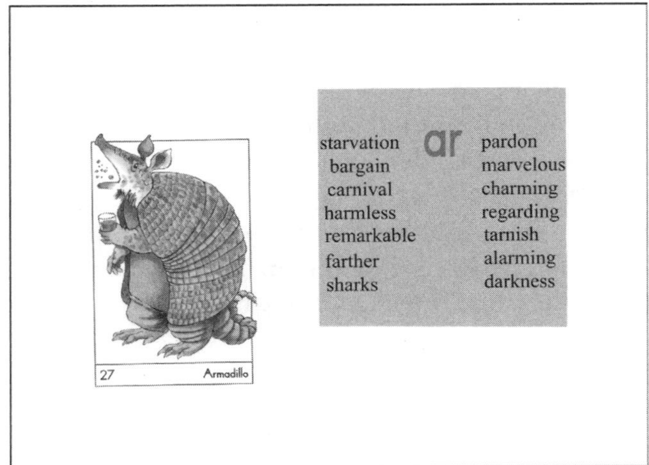

Figure 14.4.

Figure 14.5.

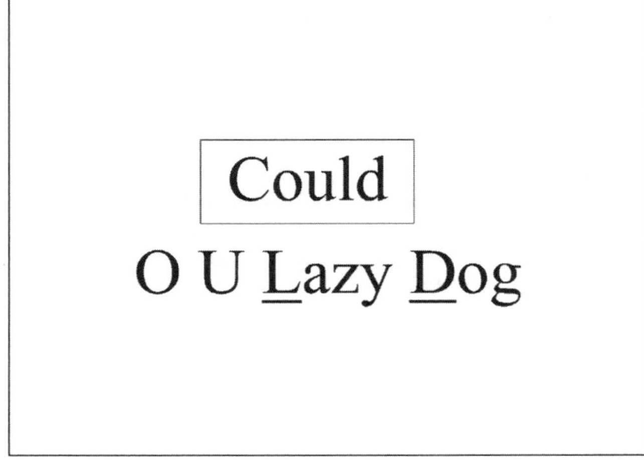

Figure 14.6.

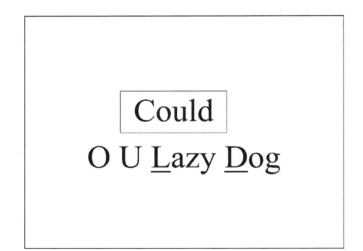

- *Integration of Language Arts and Geography.* Insert a map of the world or United States on a PowerPoint slide. When discussing where a particular event in the news took place or the setting of a story, insert a representative image or one to two words about that location on the map. Other aids to help students remember information and directions such as north, east, south, and west mnemonics can also be inserted, as shown in Figure 14.7.
- *Vocabulary.* Make slides of vocabulary words in context, as in Figure 14.8, and multiple words with the same base, as in Figure 14.9.
- *Weekly Preview.* At the beginning of the week, preview the content that will be taught. Show students a short montage of PowerPoint slides related to the topics you will be covering that week or in that unit.
- *Electronic Portfolios.* Have students create their own PowerPoint presentation showcasing their learning, growth, and achievements by making a slide show that

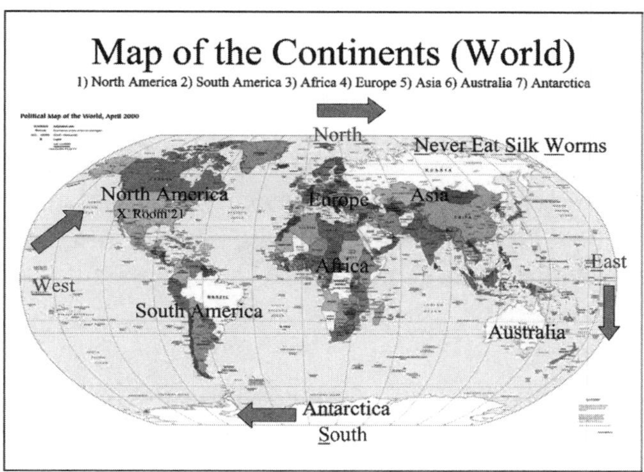

Figure 14.7.

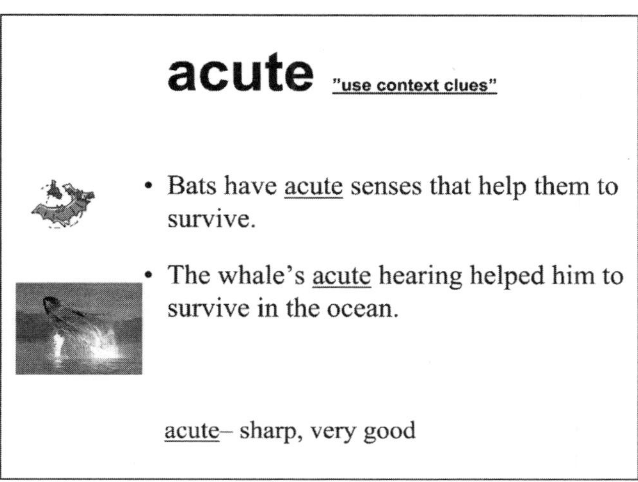

Figure 14.8.

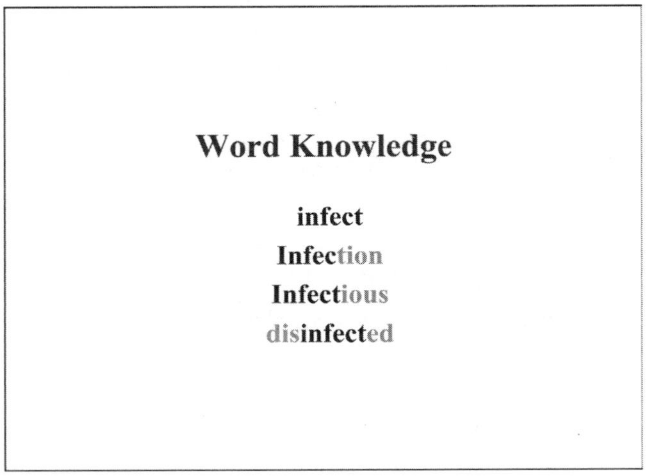

Word Knowledge

infect
Infection
Infectious
disinfected

Figure 14.9.

includes scans of their best written work, digital photos, audio and video clips, and the like.

- *Open House*. Set a PowerPoint presentation to run automatically during an open house. Slides will showcase classroom activities, student work, and accomplishments.
- *Student Presentations*. Provide students the opportunity to develop their own PowerPoint presentations and later present them to their class and others.

PowerPoint Web Sites

The following sites are helpful for learning about the features and uses of PowerPoint in the classroom:

- Internet 4 Classrooms, by Susan Brooks and Bill Byles, at http://www.internet4classrooms.com/on-line_powerpoint.htm.
- PowerPoint in the Classroom, by Act 360 Media Ltd. (Digital Educator Network), at http://www.actden.com/pp.
- Center for Instructional Innovation, Western Washington University, at http://www.ac.wwu.edu/~cii/powerpoint.
- Kent National Grid for Learning, at http://www.kented.org.uk/ngfl/subjects/literacy/powerpoint.
- Electric Teacher, by Cathy Chamberlain, at http://www.electricteacher.com/tutorial3.htm.

AUDIOBOOKS

Audio recordings of books have been available for many years. For general classroom use many teachers use listening centers, which enable students to follow along in a copy of a text while listening to it being read on tape. Audiobooks give students access to books above their reading level that they would not be able to read independently. Students may also use audiobooks for reading practice, developing fluency by reading and rereading text orally along with the fluent reader on the recording.

Children with documented reading disabilities are eligible to receive a wonderful service through Reading for the Blind and Dyslexic (www.rfbd.org). This nonprofit organization is the nation's educational library, serving people who cannot read standard print effectively because of a visual impairment, learning disability, or other physical disability. They lend audiobooks (including all student textbooks) in a broad range of subjects at all educational levels, from kindergarten to postgraduate studies. But in order to access their library, one must be eligible and become a member. Traditionally, Reading for the Blind and Dyslexic (RFB'D) books were provided on four-track cassettes that required a special player. Now textbooks are recorded digitally and are available on CD-ROM through RFB'D's AudioPlus® service. In order to play RFB&D digitally recorded textbooks, the student will need to use specialized CD players or software that installs on standard multimedia PCs. For more information, contact your district's special education department or go to www.rfbd.org.

ELECTRONIC BOOKS (E-BOOKS)

Electronic books (e-books) are texts presented visually and read through the computer or a digital reader. Most incorporate a range of multimedia text enhancements such as graphics and animations, definitions of words, background information and explanations of concepts, and links to related documents to support students' understanding and extend their learning. Many e-books are highly interactive and have embedded speech as well (Anderson-Inman & Horney, 1999; Holum & Gahala, 2001). With interactive electronic books on CD-ROM, text can be read aloud with each word or phrase highlighted as it is read. Students can read the book themselves and ask the computer to identify unfamiliar words or they can read along with the computer to develop their reading fluency. Many programs have reading logs, writing activities, and other interactive activities (Tompkins, 2001).

Electronic books are a wonderful way to provide scaffolded instruction to students and to extend their reading opportunities and learning. As with audiobooks, e-books enable students to access books at higher reading levels than those they can read independently (Cooperman & Cunningham, 2003). It is an excellent way to motivate students to reread text and build fluency, and the highly multisensory format of these books engages children of all learning styles. A number of sources offer electronic books for purchase on CD or via the Internet.

The National Educational Technology Plan recommends that states and districts start moving toward digital content. The plan states: "A perennial problem for schools, teachers and students is that textbooks are increasingly expensive, quickly outdated and physically cumbersome. A move away from reliance on textbooks to the use of multimedia or online information (digital content) offers many advantages, including cost savings, increased efficiency, improved accessibility, and enhancing learning opportunities in a format that engages today's web-savvy students" (U.S. Department of Education, Office of Educational Technology, 2004).

ELECTRONIC MAIL (E-MAIL)

Since the advent of e-mail, it is hard to imagine our past reliance on the postal service for all written correspondence. E-mail has truly revolutionized our lives, allowing us to quickly and easily correspond with people anywhere on the globe. E-mail offers many benefits for students. It is a wonderful way to practice reading and writing for an authentic and important reason: communication with others. The web site ePALS Classroom Exchange® (www.epals.com) connects classrooms around the world. This site maintains the Internet's largest community of collaborative classrooms engaged in cross-cultural exchanges, project sharing, and language learning. In addition to writing to friends and other peers anywhere in the world, students can use e-mail to practice writing with appropriate spelling, grammar, and etiquette to an adult audience. They can write to businesses, organizations, institutions, and their teachers to ask questions or make requests.

THE INTERNET

The Internet—or the World Wide Web—has made it possible for all of us to now have at our fingertips access to a staggering amount of information. By 2003, nearly 100 percent of U.S. public schools had access to the Internet, 95 percent used broadband, and about 93 percent of classrooms were online (Smith, Clark, & Blomeyer, 2005).

The speed and ease of inquiry, researching topics, and gathering information via the Internet has significantly changed our lives and those of our students. There are vast numbers of lessons, learning activities, other curricular material, and resources that teachers can find on the Internet. Many enable interactive, authentic learning experiences that are highly motivating and tap into the learning strengths, styles, and interests of diverse learners. Throughout this book are web sites of interest to educators. For a comprehensive listing of additional web sites (URLs) recommended for a balanced literacy classroom, see Appendix A.

Because the Internet is unregulated, teachers must use precautionary measures such as Internet filtering software to prevent students from accessing inappropriate web sites in the classroom. As Tompkins (2001) points out, when students are conducting research on a topic of study, teachers should preview sites beforehand if possible, mark appropriate sites with bookmarks, or provide a list of URL addresses that students can go to for information, rather than permitting free access.

WebQuest is an inquiry-oriented activity in which most or all of the information used by students is drawn from the Web. The WebQuests are designed to use learners' time well, to focus on using information rather than looking for it, and to support learners' thinking at the levels of analysis, synthesis, and evaluation. The WebQuest model was developed in early 1995 at San Diego State University and has since become very popular among teachers around the country as a vehicle for expanding e-learning experiences for their students. For more information, go to http://webquest.sdsu.edu.

ONLINE INSTRUCTION (E-LEARNING)

In recent years there has been "explosive growth in organized online instruction (e-learning) and 'virtual' schools, making it possible for students at all levels to receive high-quality supplemental or full course of instruction personalized to their needs" (U.S. Department of Education, Office of Educational Technology, 2004). Many of us have by now taken an online course or so for professional development and appreciate the benefits—particularly the flexibility it allows as to when and where to do the course work. Action step 4 of the National Educational Technology Plan (U.S. Department of Education, Office of Educational Technology, 2004) recommends that states, districts, and schools give students access to e-learning and that every teacher should be able to participate in e-learning training. In addition, the plan says that e-learning options to meet No Child Left Behind requirements for highly qualified teachers, supplemental services, and parental choice should be encouraged. Supplemental educational services might include, for example, provision of online tutoring services.

K–12 online learning, which began as a way to expand the curriculum and educational access, is increasingly a tool of educational reform. Although more widespread in post-secondary education, it is becoming a rapidly growing phenomenon in K–12 education (Smith, Clark, & Blomeyer, 2005).

HANDHELD DEVICES

Handheld digital tools such as iPods are being used more frequently now at the university level for enhancing instructional practices. Drexel University in Philadelphia and Georgia College and State University, a liberal arts university in Milledgeville, were among the first to embrace this technology. Now other higher learning institutions are doing so as well. In a history class, for example, course work might be enhanced by having each student download on his or her iPod and listen to music of the time period, audio recordings, historical speeches, video clips, and other multimedia course material. This also frees up class time for deeper discussions and maximizes higher-order thinking during the class period (Georgia College and State University, 2006). Podcasting lectures is becoming quite popular in many universities. This type of technology is likely to be utilized more and more in the coming years in middle and high school education.

VISUAL TECHNOLOGY

According to Burmark (2002), our human brains are wired for images, and research indicates we process visuals sixty thousand times faster than text because we take in all the data from an image simultaneously, whereas we process text in a sequential fashion. Much modern technology can be used to bring images to the classroom.

Digital Cameras

Digital cameras have dramatically changed how we take photographs. Now all of us are able to snap as many pictures as we want and instantly delete or save those we want to keep. We can do our own editing of those pictures, print them from our computers, attach and send others via e-mail, or post them online. They are wonderful tools for the balanced literacy classroom. Students can enhance writing and other projects they are working on by adding pictures and inserting text to go along with those pictures. How wonderful for pen pals who write to one another via e-mail to now be able to share about their lives through digital pictures as well!

Following are some ways to use digital photography to enhance literacy instruction:

- *Sequencing.* Take pictures of steps in an event such as making a smoothie or making a peanut butter and jelly sandwich. Have students put them in order and write about the process, using sequence and order words.
- *Compare and Contrast.* Take pictures of two objects and make a double bubble or Venn diagram of their similarities and differences and write about the comparison.

- *Cause and Effect.* Take before and after pictures and discuss the cause and effect. For example, studying for a test → get good grades.
- *Career Reports.* Have students dress up as what they want to be when they grow up and take pictures of themselves (or of props related to that career) to use for illustrating career reports.
- *Report Illustration.* Superimpose photos of the students standing next to famous landmarks such as the Eiffel Tower or the pyramids to illustrate reports.

For English-language learners and students with language disabilities, the digital camera can be a useful tool to enhance language and vocabulary instruction. For example,

- *Prepositions.* Take pictures of students standing next to, under, on top of, beside, or in front of an object and insert these into a PowerPoint presentation. Students are then required to describe their relationship to the object.
- *Antonyms.* Take pictures depicting antonyms such as wide/narrow, fragile/sturdy, and wild/tame and use these pictures to teach opposites and reinforce vocabulary.
- *Adjectives.* Take photos to depict describing words. For example, take photos showing facial expressions to illustrate what it means to be anxious, joyful, frustrated, elated, disappointed, and so forth.

Digital Video

Digital video (DV) is an ideal format for anyone wanting to use a camcorder (DV camera) to work with video on the PC or the Web. DV camcorders are very engaging and have multiple purposes in the classroom. Learning activities, student presentations, interviews, and any other number of events can be recorded and edited. It is a wonderful way to capture the highlights throughout the year in the balanced literacy classroom and to showcase them to parents and the school community. They are a powerful tool for multimedia presentations, student portfolios, and the like.

Video Streaming

One of the most visual and engaging learning tools for today's classrooms is video streaming. Only a few years old, Unitedstreaming by Discovery Education is a leader in this technology (www.unitedstreaming.com). Unitedstreaming is a standards-based curriculum video-on-demand service that delivers thousands of current K–12 standards-based digital video clips. Videos are available across the curriculum and content areas and are segmented into three- to four-minute portions, each one focusing on an important component from that topic of study.

This technology is a powerful enhancement to the curriculum, and beneficial for all students (including English-language learners, special needs, and gifted students). The videos enable teachers to provide more comprehensible input to supplement text, illustrations, and verbal explanations. On the spot, teachers can show video clips about almost any topic imaginable, all of them suitable for children and the classroom. This is an ideal tool for building background knowledge and introducing students to a topic of study. Unitedstreaming videos can easily be downloaded to hard drives so they are available when needed. Other features are available, such as an image search, online assignment builder, quiz builder, writing prompt builder, audio files, lesson plans, animations, and a calendar feature with video content of events that happened on a particular day, week, or month in history.

BrainPop® also offers hundreds of educational movies for children and is being used in numerous school districts. BrainPop® movies are animated. As with Unitedstreaming, they include a library on a wide range of topics across all subject areas of the curriculum, correlated to state and grade standards (www.brainpop.com).

Following are some suggestions for classroom use of video streaming:

- Use a video clip or movie to activate or build prior knowledge before reading a text to help with comprehension.
- Use to help complete K-W-L charts (see Chapter Twelve).
- Watch a clip as a unit opener or to end a unit.
- View videos with the sound muted and provide your own commentary or ask students to narrate with their own words.
- Embed clips into PowerPoint presentations.
- Start and stop the videos to engage students in discussions.
- Provide questions for students to think about while they watch the video clips.
- Even if there is only one computer in the classroom, a small group of students can watch a video together using a graphic organizer to keep them focused and accountable.
- Students can watch clips as an optional activity at the computer station once they have completed the required assignments. They can learn about topics that are of interest to them.

Document Cameras

A document camera is a wonderful presentation and instructional tool for the classroom, because it engages students' attention and visually enhances instruction. It looks and functions somewhat like an overhead projector, but uses high-resolution video camera for display and allows the user to feed images through multimedia projectors, television sets, or computer screens (Epson Presenters Online, 2006). Document cameras allow text to be projected on a screen without the need for making a transparency. Teachers have the ability to open up a book, magazine, or anything on the table of the document camera and it is projected like an overhead for students to easily see. A document camera can show opaque objects in full color. So any three-dimensional item can be enlarged and projected, enabling students to clearly see the details (such as the writing on a coin). Additional features of a document camera are their capacity to zoom in and out and capture images as you would with a scanner or digital camera, saving them as JPEG files to retrieve later.

Document cameras make on-the-spot instruction possible. At any time, the teacher can clearly show students *anything* without taking the time to prepare transparencies in advance, copy information on a board, or call students up front and close in order to see. They are ideal for demonstrating tasks and strategies, explaining and giving directions, focusing students' attention on items, no matter how small, and providing immediate feedback on students' work.

Document cameras have extraordinary benefits in a balanced literacy classroom. They are perfect tools for modeled reading and writing, guiding students through the reading and writing process, pointing out text features, illustrations, and so forth. They are also perfect tools for displaying, sharing, and responding to students' writing.

Interactive Whiteboards

The interactive whiteboard is a powerful instructional technology for the classroom. It is a touch-sensitive screen that connects to a computer, and the digital projector displays the computer image on the screen. The teacher (or student) simply touches the surface to control the applications and write notes (Knowlton, 2006). All notes or writing on the interactive whiteboard can be saved and printed—a wonderful benefit particularly for students who have difficulty taking notes during class or for students who were absent and missed class instruction. You can use your finger or special pen to write notes on the board with digital ink and draw over any application or web site to highlight key points and brainstorm ideas. The board has a large surface area that students can see easily and use to explore and manipulate computer material by simply touching the surface to select icons, navigate web sites, and move images with a finger as with a mouse.

Flip charts are part of the software that comes with the whiteboards, eliminating the need for easels and paper flip charts for instruction. By linking to web sites or videos, teachers can create interactive learning experiences that take students' interest and learning to an entirely new level (Dewberry & Hitch, 2006).

The interactive whiteboard is very advantageous in the classroom as it easily captures and engages students' focus and attention. It is highly motivating for students to come up to the board to perform a task and actively participate in the lesson. It also increases instructional teaching time, with the teacher controlling the data presented up front at the board with a touch of the screen.

SOUND-FIELD CLASSROOM AMPLIFICATION

Some schools are utilizing a sound-field system in classrooms, such as LightSPEED (by LightSPEED Technologies). The basic purpose is to amplify the teacher's voice evenly throughout the classroom so every student can clearly hear. The teacher wears a wireless microphone that transmits an infrared light to a receiver-amplifier unit. The voice is then played through loudspeakers for the entire class to hear. This amplified voice overcomes background noise, poor room acoustics, and mild hearing loss to make it easier for students to understand and concentrate on what the teacher is saying. Teachers who use this system find benefits in their daily teaching practice such as increased ability to obtain and maintain students' attention and enhance student's focus and concentration when modeling and instructing. There are also other student benefits for the literacy classroom. Children are more attentive and motivated when passing the microphone to each other during whole-group lessons. Students' voices are more audible when sharing. It is a wonderful tool to use during author's chair and reader's chair. English-language learners and students with receptive and expressive language difficulties receive better auditory input, hearing sounds and words more clearly. For more information, go to www.lightspeed-tek.com/education/teachers.html.

MOTIVATING STUDENTS THROUGH TECHNOLOGY AND INTEGRATED LEARNING

San Diego teacher Steve G.'s fifth-grade classroom exemplifies integration of technology with literacy, as well as cross-curricular development of skills and knowledge. Steve's students have the opportunity every spring to participate in the online Stock Market

Game™ program (www.smgww.org), a nonprofit program supported by national and local sponsors for grades 4 through 8. The program's goals for fourth and fifth grades are to reinforce math skills and introduce children to the value of investing and saving for the future. InvestWrite (www.InvestWrite.info) is a companion essay contest produced by the SMG™ program. In classrooms participating in the Stock Market Game, teachers select three of their top essays to submit for the national writing competition.

In Steve's class, students were divided into sixteen groups that were registered to participate in the Stock Market Game using their log-in numbers. During the weeks the game was in play, each group received a hypothetical $100,000 to invest and went online to the SMG web site to trade and follow their stocks on the New York Stock Exchange. This was a very motivating, real-life application of math skills that students very much enjoyed.

The InvestWrite topic for fourth through fifth grade during the spring of 2006 addressed risk tolerance: understanding the difference between volatile and blue chip stocks and identifying the type of risk-tolerant investor the student believed himself or herself to be (high, low, or moderate risk tolerance). The essay prompt also required writers to describe some of the stocks they chose during the SMG™ that matched their risk tolerance and were required to be a maximum of seven hundred words. These essays are judged by the writer's understanding of the subject matter, rationale, and writing style.

Steve's Writer's Workshop Lessons

In preparation, during one class period Steve's class read the background and essay prompt for the contest posted on the InvestWrite web site. This was projected on the document camera for everyone to clearly see as it was discussed and analyzed. Following the prompt, Steve guided the class in generating a rubric for the essay on a chart. It was decided that the essay should have seven paragraphs: an introductory and a concluding paragraph and a five-paragraph body to address the various points within the assignment prompt.

For the next day of Writer's Workshop, Steve typed up copies of the rubric (see Figure 14.10) to distribute to the class using the same student-generated language and content for the rubric.

Checklist	Rubric
Paragraph One	Introduction: This paragraph includes a good lead, introduces the topic, organizes what you're going to do and discusses the risk and high-risk versus blue chip stocks. It ends with a question, transition to the next paragraph or something good.
Paragraph Two	Discuss blue chip vs. high-risk stocks. Give examples.
Paragraph Three	Tell the reader what type of investor you are. Do you like to take a chance with high-risk stock or do you feel safer with blue chip stocks? Are you somewhere in between?
Paragraph Four	Tell the reader a few of the stocks you own and why you bought them. You may wish to mention the EPS (Earnings Per Share) and why you selected these companies.
Paragraph Five	Tell the reader why your stocks match your risk-tolerance.
Paragraph Six	Tell the reader how investing in the stock market *and* understanding risk-tolerance will help you in your life.
Paragraph Seven	Conclusion: Begin with a good lead. Maybe something that ties back to an earlier part of your essay. Mention important points you discussed in the other paragraphs (Briefly). End with something catchy, compelling or something that make the reader think. What can you add that will make the reader remember your essay, after she has read 100 essays?

Figure 14.10.

During whole-class instruction, a PowerPoint slide was projected explaining the initial task of the day.

> *Task: Read the rubric and think about which parts of the essay you think will be easiest to write about and which parts will be most difficult to write about. Highlight in yellow the parts you think will be easy. Highlight in orange the parts that will be hard. Then discuss your choices with a partner.*

Before students began working on this task, Steve first projected a copy of the rubric on the document camera and modeled briefly an example of what he would highlight in yellow and orange, and why. Then, after some time was spent working on this task, a few students shared with the class, projecting their highlighted rubric page with the document camera (see Figure 14.11).

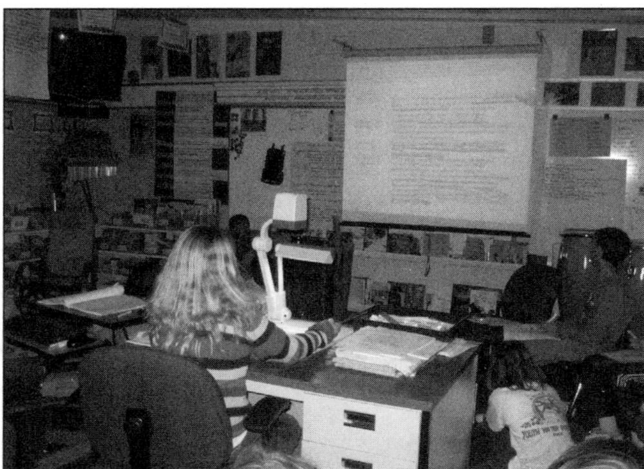

Figure 14.11.

The next part of the Writer's Workshop for that morning was to start drafting their introductory paragraphs, using a good lead to hook the readers' attention and interest. In preparation, Steve had already written his own lead and was ready to model for the students. Using the document camera, he opened his journal to the page of his writing and read it to the class. As he did so, Steve stopped to externalize his thinking process (metacognition) for students to hear:

"This is an idea—I'm not sure I'll use it or not . . ."

> *I stood out of breath, while climbing the steep trail. A thousand feet of nothing below me, and two thousand feet of mountain above. "Why did I do this?" I thought to myself.*

"I need to think about judges reading this. Why is investing in the stock market like climbing a mountain? I want judges to understand that I'm kind of scared. Now I need to transition to let the judges know I have a reason for talking about mountain climbing."

Investing in stocks is a lot like climbing a mountain. Sometimes you're scared, and sometimes you feel safe. Stocks can be scary, too. You take money you earn and give it to someone else to invest in a company. Who knows what will happen with your money?

"Now I'll refer back to my liking to climb mountains and I'll use transition words."

While there are times when I feel scared climbing a mountain, I love the feeling when out of breath I stand atop a snow-covered peak and feel successful.

"Let's look back at the rubric and assignment prompt. I need to get back on topic, introduce the types of stocks, and transition to the next paragraph in an interesting way. But, that's my *lead,* at least for now. Are you ready to give this a try?"

Figure 14.12.

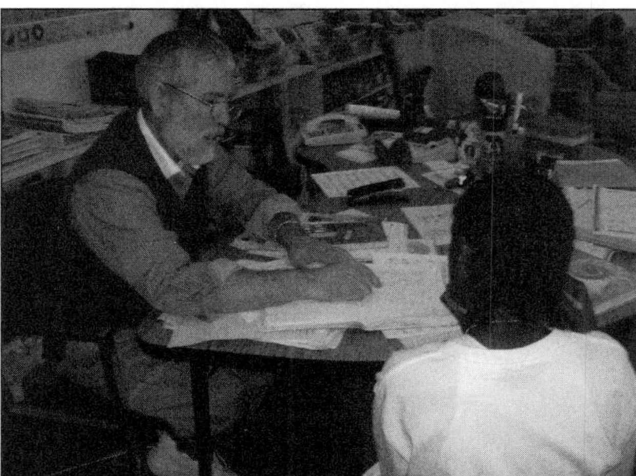

Figure 14.13.

As students were writing, Steve conferred individually with them, listening to their initial ideas and offering feedback (see Figures 14.12 and 14.13). Then the class was called up front and a few students were invited to share what they had written so far. While projecting their writing on the document camera, volunteers read their leads aloud. Classmates had the chance to respond to the writing with their comments and feedback.

The introductory paragraphs students shared were very impressive, incorporating metaphors, analogies, and descriptive language in their leads. The modeling and sharing that was so quickly and easily provided with the aid of technologies contributed significantly to the student engagement, productivity, and the quality of their written work.

ASSISTIVE TECHNOLOGY

According to the Individuals with Disabilities Education Act (2004), an assistive technology device is "any item, piece of equipment, or product system, whether acquired commercially off the shelf, modified, or customized, that is used to increase, maintain, or improve functional capabilities of a child with a disability" (U.S. Department of Education, 2004; Wisconsin Assistive Technology Initiative, 2000). Most of the technologies described earlier such as portable word processors, audiobooks, and concept mapping software would be considered examples of assistive technology when prescribed for use by an individual with disabilities. Many such technologies support struggling readers and writers and enable them to bypass much of their difficulty accessing text or producing written work. This section addresses additional assistive technology for students with reading and writing difficulties.

Portable Word Processors

Inexpensive, lightweight, portable word processors have been used successfully for children with writing disabilities in the general education classroom. Two such popular word processors are AlphaSmart (www.alphasmart.com) and DreamWriter, by Brainium Technologies, now available through ABC School Battery (www.schoolbattery.com). They are primarily used for taking notes, writing assignments, and completing drafts of written work in class. These processors have small screens that show only a few lines of text at a time and are limited in their features and capabilities. Students use them to type and save their work, then later transfer to their home or school desktop computer for expanding, formatting, revising, editing, and so forth.

Word Predictors and Spell-Checkers

Word predictors analyze words as they are written on the computer, then try to predict the words that the student is most likely to want from a dictionary or lexicon of words. As the student types a letter, the program offers a list of the most common words beginning with that letter. If the first letter does not bring up the right word, more choices are offered when a second letter is typed. The writer selects the word with the mouse or keyboard. This enables typing in text with fewer keystrokes (Nisbet, Spooner, Arthur, & Whittaker, 1999). Some programs speak the words from the list out loud to help the writer select the word of choice.

Spell-checkers are also very helpful tools for writers with spelling difficulties. Many of the software programs designed for struggling readers and writers have word prediction and spell-checking with an audio component (Co:Writer,® Write:Outloud,® Textease, Read & Write GOLD, WordQ™, and SpeakQ™). The word choices are read out loud from the computer to make it easier for the user to identify the appropriate word.

Text-to-Speech Software

A number of programs have the capability of reading text out loud from the computer, whether books, text documents, or Internet content. Text-to-speech software shows students text as they hear it read aloud. Some examples include Read & Write GOLD, ClaroRead PLUS, Kurzweil 3000, Read:Out Loud®, and ReadPlease®. Text-to-speech software also reads scanned books and documents.

Scanned Books

Reading for the Blind and Dyslexic (www.rfbd.org) is a service providing audiobooks for students with disabilities, Bookshare (www.bookshare.org) is an online community that offers a repository of scanned books for students who are visually impaired or are otherwise print-disabled. The disabled reader has flexibility in choice of assistive technologies to use for reading the scanned books, whether by listening, enlarging, or reading in Braille.

Speech Recognition Systems

Although such technology has been around for many years, it has only recently become affordable and more user-friendly. Speech recognition systems enable the user to control a computer by speaking to it through a microphone, either entering text or issuing commands to the computer (for example, to load a particular program or to print a document). The earlier systems only used "discrete speech," meaning the user needed to speak one word at a time with pauses between words. Today's programs use "continuous speech," which allows the user to speak in a more natural way (CALL Centre, 2005). Two such software programs with speech recognition are SpeakQ™ and Dragon Naturally Speaking.

Software for Students with Reading and Writing Disabilities

Many different software programs are designed specifically for children and adults with reading and writing disabilities. Following are descriptions of just some of the more popular assistive software for this population of students.

Read & Write GOLD (by TextHelp). This text-to-speech software acts as a personal coach in the form of a floating toolbar, providing literacy support while working within mainstream applications such as word processing, Internet, e-mail, and other programs using text. It allows writers to hear their work as they type and reads aloud from the Internet when the user rolls the mouse over the text.

Kurzweil 3000. This software accesses scanned or web site text, which the software reads aloud while the text is highlighted. Some other features include an audible spell-checker and word prediction.

WordQ™ (by Quillsoft Ltd). This program is used directly along with any standard application, providing word prediction when the writer has trouble spelling or choosing the right word. For editing, highlighted text is read aloud to detect errors.

SpeakQ™ (by Quillsoft Ltd.). This software plugs into WordQ™ and adds simple speech recognition. It has all the benefits of WordQ™, along with the capacity to write by speaking. At any time, the user can choose between typing with the keyboard, using word prediction, or speaking straight into the text.

ClaroRead PLUS (EnableMart). This program has text-to-speech capability and echoes back words and phrases dictated into any text processor or e-mail application. It also scans and converts documents into Microsoft Word text, which can then be read back.

Read:OutLoud SOLO® (by Don Johnston). This text-to-speech program includes a bank of supported reading guides that model comprehension strategies, support research projects, and connect reading with writing.

Write:OutloudSOLO® (by Don Johnston). This talking word processor reads each word out loud as students write, reads any electronic text, and has several other features.

Draft: Builder SOLO™ (by Don Johnston). This software helps students produce a draft by outlining, mapping, and organizing notes they have entered and building a logically sequenced draft. It guides the students through each step of the writing process.

Co:Writer 4000 SOLO™ (by Don Johnston). This talking word prediction program coaches in spelling and grammar. It enables writers to use enriched vocabulary while revising and editing. The eWord Bank and Topic Dictionaries give targeted vocabulary support when writing on any topic and in any genre.

Scanner Pens

The Readingpen® is an assistive reading device designed to provide word support while reading (by Wizcom Tech; www.wizcomtech.com). The pen scans single words or full lines of text in seconds. It reads and spells aloud scanned words, lines of text, definitions, and thesaurus entries with text-to-speech software.

Sources for Assistive Technology

Some of the companies that specialize in assistive software and other technology to enhance skills and to support challenged readers and writers include

Intellitools: www.intellitools.com

Softease: www.softease.com (Textease)

TextHelp: www.texthelp.com (Read & Write GOLD)

Franklin: www.franklin.com (Franklin handheld spell-checkers and other devices)

Quillsoft Ltd.: www.wordq.com and www.quillsoft.com (for WordQ™ and SpeakQ™)

Nuance: www.nuance.com (for Dragon Naturally Speaking)

Kurzweil Educational Systems: www.kurzweiledu.com

ReadPlease: www.readplease.com

Don Johnston: www.donjohnston.com (offering numerous assistive technology products)

EnableMart: www.enablemart.com (ClaroRead PLUS)

— *Appendix A* —

SIXTY RECOMMENDED WEB SITES FOR TEACHERS AND STUDENTS, GRADES 3 THROUGH 8: A WEALTH OF RESOURCES FOR ENHANCING LITERACY

A to Z Teacher Stuff®. http://atozteacherstuff.com. A teacher-created site designed to help teachers find online resources more quickly and easily, with free lesson plans, thematic units, and other resources.

ABC Teach. http://www.abcteach.com. Numerous tools and resources for teachers and students, including over five thousand free printable pages.

Advanced Learning Technologies in Education Consortia, University of Kansas. RubiStar. http://rubistar.4teachers.org. A free tool to help teachers create quality rubrics for project-based learning activities.

ALTEC: Advanced Learning Technologies in Education Consortia. http://www.4teachers.org. Offers free online tools and resources for integrating technology in the curriculum.

Ask for Kids™. http://www.askforkids.com. A fast, easy, and kid-friendly search engine, formerly known as Ask Jeeves for Kids.

Balanced Reading. http://www.balancedreading.com. Research-based resources and information about reading instruction.

Brown, D. K. The Children's Literature Web Guide. http://www.acs.ucalgary.ca/~dkbrown. Internet resources related to books for children and young adults.

Candler, L. Teaching Resources from the Classroom of Laura Candler. http://home.att.net/~teaching/litlessons.htm. Contains numerous literacy lessons, activities, and free reproducibles for upper elementary teachers.

Chamberlain, C. http://oswego.org/staff/cchamber/linkscf/index.cfm. Oswego City School District. Many links to wonderful resources such as themes, WebQuests, and literacy web sites.

Cook, J., & Cook, C. Vocabulary University®. http://www.vocabulary.com. A vocabulary education site, with interactive games, puzzles, and activities at different levels of difficulty.

Edscope. Lesson Plans Page. http://www.lessonplanspage.com. Contains over three thousand free lesson plans for K–12 teachers.

Education Development Center, Inc. Literacy Matters. http://www.literacymatters.org. A site for teachers, parents, and students (middle school and high school) that focuses on adolescent literature, content area literacy, and literacy and technology.

Education World®. http://www.education-world.com. An online resource where educators can find a wealth of lesson plans and research materials.

Gallagher, C. Teaching Heart. http://www.teachingheart.net. A wealth of teaching ideas, lessons, units, activity sheets, and so on for grades K–3.

Hiebert, E. TextProject. http://www.textproject.org. The clearinghouse for the work of Hiebert, one of the nation's foremost researchers on reading education; contains downloadable PowerPoint presentations, articles, and other valuable literacy information.

Houghton Mifflin Company. Education Place. http://www.eduplace.com. Classroom resources for teachers, including several graphic organizers and language arts theme-related activities.

Hurst, C. O., and Otis, R. Carol Hurst's Children's Literature. http://www.carolhurst.com. A collection of reviews of great books for kids, ways to use those books in the classroom, and activities about particular subjects, curriculum areas, themes, and professional topics.

Institute of the Educational Sciences of the U.S. Department of Education. Education Resources Information Center (ERIC). http://www.eric.ed.gov/ERICWebPortal/Home.portal. World's largest Internet-based digital library of education research and information.

International Children's Digital Library. http://www.icdlbooks.org. Titles representing forty-five different cultures.

International Reading Association, National Council of Teachers of English. ReadWrite Think. http://www.readwritethink.org. Providing educators and students access to the highest quality practices and resources in reading and language arts instruction. Contains lessons, standards, web resources, and student materials.

International Reading Association. Reading Online. http://www.readingonline.org. Offers hundreds of articles on a range of topics in reading education.

Jones, R. ReadingQuest: Making Sense in Social Studies. http://www.readingquest.org. A site of strategies for reading, writing, organizing, discussion, and vocabulary strategies in social studies.

KidsKonnect.com®. http://www.kidskonnect.com. A safe Internet gateway for kids created and maintained by educators.

Kidsreads. http://www.kidsreads.com/index.asp. Promotes quality reading through book reviews, related games, author biographies and interviews, book club discussion guides, and more.

Leu, D., & Coiro, J. The Literacy Web. http://www.literacy.uconn.edu. An extensive collection of resources designed to assist classroom teachers in their search for best practices in literacy instruction, including the new literacies of Internet technologies; links to many resources in all major areas of literacy.

Long, J. R. Aesop's Fables Online Collection. http://www.aesopfables.com. Hundreds of Aesop's fables indexed in table format with morals listed and with audio and images.

Lund, D. Southern Utah University. Reading and Literacy Resources for Present and Future Teachers. http://www.suu.edu/faculty/lundd/readingsite/readingresources. Numerous links to literacy and other sites, articles, and resources.

Meadowbrook Press. Giggle Poetry. http://www.gigglepoetry.com. Hundreds of funny poems for children to read and rate.

Meadowbrook Press. Poetry Teachers. http://www.poetryteachers.com. Instructions for how to teach children to write humorous poetry, poetry theater, and poetry activities.

Merriam-Webster. http://www.m-w.com. Merriam-Webster online dictionary that also includes a word of the day, daily crossword, daily buzzword, and other word games.

Nesbitt, K. Poetry 4 Kids: Ken Nesbitt's Children's Poetry Playground. http://www.poetry4kids. com. Funny poems, books, games, contests, lessons, discussion forums, great rhyming dictionary, streaming audio, and more.

Network for Instructional TV. Teachers First. http://www.teachersfirst.com. A collection of K–12 lessons, units, and web resources, selected and reviewed by educators.

Nussbaum, G. MrNussbaum.com. http://www.mrnussbaum.com. An interactive web site with dozens of interactive games, research themes, and activities for K–8, as well as teacher tools.

Pearson Education. FunBrain. http://www.funbrain.com. Provides free educational games and quizzes for students, and resources for teachers and parents.

ProTeacher. http://www.proteacher.com. Provides discussion forums, information, and activities for elementary teachers; thousands of ideas submitted by teachers.

Public Library of Charlotte and Meddenburg County. Story Place. http://www.storyplace.org. A children's digital bilingual library site (Spanish and English), which includes a collection of online texts and activities for elementary students.

Purdue University. Online Writing Lab (OWL). http://owl.english.purdue.edu. Grammar, punctuation, mechanics, and conventions resources, as well as professional writing material and general composition information.

Reading A-Z. Online Reading Program. http://www.readinga-z.com. Provider of affordable, high-quality, Internet-delivered curriculum; thousands of K–6 books and materials to teach and assess guided reading, phonics, fluency, and comprehension.

San Diego County Office of Education, Schools of California Online Resources for Education (SCORE). Cyberguides for Literature. http://www.sdcoe.k12.ca.us/score/cyberguide.html. Offers standards-based guides for many classics and current student novels. Features include teacher guides, lessons, activity banks, standards, and more.

Schlosser, S. E. American Folklore. http://www.americanfolklore.net. Contains retellings of American folktales, Native American myths and legends, tall tales, and ghost stories from every one of the fifty United States.

Schrock, K. Discovery School's Kathy Schrock's Guide for Educators. http://www.school.discovery.com/schrockguide. A categorized list of sites with teaching materials, resources for students, and advice for parents; several links to literacy web sites under literature and language arts.

Screen Actors Guild (SAG) Foundation. Storyline Online. http://www.storylineonline.net. An online streaming video program featuring famous people reading children's books aloud. Each book has accompanying activities and lesson ideas.

Shepard, A. Reader's Theater Editions. http://www.aaronshep.com/rt/RTE.html. Free scripts for reader's theater adapted from stories written by Aaron Shepard and others, aimed mostly at ages 8 through 15.

Sites for Teachers. http://www.sitesforteachers.com. Contains hundreds of educational web sites rated by popularity; includes sites in all content areas and teaching resources such as lesson plans, activities, and clip art.

SmartWriters. http://www.smartwriters.com. Includes interviews with children's writers, writing contest links for young writers, classroom resources for teachers and librarians, and a directory of children's authors and illustrators available for school visits.

Starfall. http://www.starfall.com. A site for free simple downloadable stories such as folk tales, Chinese fables, and Greek myths; stories and illustrations geared more for first and second graders, but would also be beneficial for struggling third-grade readers.

Teacher's Desk. http://www.teachersdesk.org. An excellent collection of activities and resources for teachers of fifth through sixth grades such as paragraph a week (PAW) writing program providing a host of single and multiparagraph writing topics (prompts and scoring guidelines included), over 150 lesson ideas in language arts, numerous activities for guided reading, self-selected reading, and working with words.

TeAchnology™: The Online Teacher Resource. http://www.teach-nology.com/teachers. A web portal that offers a wide variety of free resources intended to bring educators into the world of teaching with technology. It provides links to information on current and best practices in the field of education and a large variety of free classroom materials and support tools.

The Teacher's Corner™. http://www.theteacherscorner.net. Offers primary and intermediate teacher resources, including lesson plans, thematic units, seasonal items, and more.

Texas Education Agency. Teacher Toolbag. http://tea.state.tx.us/tchrtoolbag/CurRes.html. This curriculum resource site contains links to lesson plans, games, activities, and other resources in language arts and other content areas.

TravLang. Word of the Day. http://travlang.com/wordofday. Provides a word of the day in over sixty languages that can be heard as well as shown.

United Nations. The United Nations Cyberschoolbus. http://www.un.org/cyberschoolbus. Global teaching and learning project that offers information in six languages.

Curriculum materials include world data, units on peace making, and ask an ambassador.

U.S. Department of Education. Teacher's Guide to International Collaboration on the Internet. http://www.ed.gov/teachers/how/tech/international/guide.html. Site has links to school projects and organizations that are involved in international education via the Internet.

U.S. National Archives. http://www.archives.gov/education. Gateway to primary sources, activities, and training for educators and students.

Verizon Foundation. MarcoPolo: Internet Content for the Classroom. http://www.marcopolo-education.org. MarcoPolo provides high-quality standards-based educational resources to teachers and students. Includes lessons plans, student materials, reviewed Web resources, and interactives.

Web English Teacher. http://www.webenglishteacher.com. Presents K–12 English and language arts teaching resources such as lesson plans, WebQuests, videos, biography, e-texts, and classroom activities.

Weber, C. Publishing Students. http://www.publishingstudents.com. Contains online student publishing and writing resources, teacher idea exchange, favorite student stories, and competitions.

WETA. Reading Rockets. http://www.readingrockets.org. A national multimedia project that offers research-based and best-practice information on teaching kids to read and helping those who struggle.

WGBH Boston, Sirius Thinking. PBS Kids: Between the Lions. http://pbskids.org/lions. Stories, games, music videos, and songs with various language features, such as Vowel Boot Camp, Sometimes Y, Homophones, and W Trouble.

WritingFix and the Northern Nevada Writing Project. Writing Fix. http://www.writingfix.com. Features interactive writing lessons, activities, tools, games, and so on for building stronger writing skills in writers of any age; wonderful strategies and writing prompts.

— *Appendix B* —

BUILDING COMMUNITY: A TWO-WEEK UNIT OF STUDY

See Chapter One for more information about implementing this unit of study.

Day	Read Aloud	Word Study
1	**Text:** In *The Moon and I:* "Miss Harriet's Room" **Focus:** Introducing the genre of memoir; authors get their ideas from their own personal experiences; using our own life experiences to make connections to the story and the characters. **Discussion:** See detailed lesson plan. **Building Community:** Sharing our favorite memories through discussion helps us to know each other better. **Standards:** Reading 3.0, Listening and Speaking 1.0	**Text:** In *Wham! It's a Poetry Jam:* "Testing New Waters" (use chart or overhead) **Focus:** Words that have more than one meaning can cause confusion in our reading; many words have layers of meaning; different parts of speech. **Discussion:** See detailed lesson plan. **Building Community:** Thinking together helps us unlock the meaning of words. **Standards:** Reading 1.0, 1.1
2	**Text:** In *The Moon and I:* "The First Skateboard in the History of the World" **Focus:** Connecting characters' lives to our own in order to understand and "get into" a story; predicting outcome as you read; review of memoir; focusing on one idea for Writering Workshop **Discussion:** Can you think of an event in your life that was as meaningful as Betsy's? Discuss it with a partner. What made you think that Betsy would go down the hill? When did you realize it? **Building Community:** As we are getting to know each other and building background knowledge about ourselves, focus on one idea about yourself to discuss with a partner. Limit your discussion focus. **Standards:** Reading 3.0, 3.2, 3.3, Listening and Speaking 1.0	**Text:** In *Hey World, Here I Am!:* "Maybe a Fight" **Focus:** Gathering a list of descriptive words about characters to use in future discussions **Discussion:** Set up a word wall: categorize words on separate sheets of paper as you generate lists. Words should be added as children become excited about finding new examples. They can be used as models for Writering Workshop and for future discussion. "Two-faced, bossy, preachy"—are these good descriptive words that mother used? Can you think of other describing words for people and characters you know? **Building Community:** Using a word wall will help us organize our vocabulary for deeper discussion. **Standards:** Reading 1.1

Shared Reading	Listening Speaking
Text: In *Wham! It's a Poetry Jam:* "Testing New Waters" **Focus:** Using our experiences to relate to a poem; making meaning through reading fluently. **Discussion:** See detailed lesson plan. **Building Community:** Taking risks in this classroom depends on each of us feeling valued and respected. We are willing to risk sharing our thoughts and feelings when we feel safe and appreciated. We all need to be good communicators, as both listeners and speakers. **Standards:** Reading 3.1, Listening and Speaking 1.0	**Goal:** To understand conversation and how it helps us make meaning.
Text: In *Hey World, Here I Am!:* "Maybe a Fight" **Focus:** Use of subtle humor to make a point (inference); making predictions from a title; introducing symbolism. **Discussion:** What does the title suggest? Who turned the direction of the fight? What do you think helped to solve the fight? What feelings did the girls have toward each other in the beginning? At the end? What purpose did the teakettle have in this selection? Were you surprised by the mother's remarks? Was this really a fight? Explain your thoughts. What humor did you find in this story? Have you ever had a fight like this before? How did you solve it? **Building Community:** Humor can be a way of settling conflicts. **Standards:** Reading 1.1, 3.0, 3.5	**Establishing Expectations:** Active participation Appropriate body language Keeping focus on the speaker and the speaker's message Looking at the speaker Respect for the ideas of others Sharing the talk time Wait time

Day	Read Aloud	Word Study
3	**Text:** *The Summer My Father Was Ten* **Focus:** Understanding a character's actions and the influence actions have on the plot; making connections **Discussion:** What is "my father's" dilemma? How does he deal with it? Why was it not easy to approach Mr. Bellavista about his apology? Have you ever had a similar situation? How did you resolve it? **Building Community:** We need to get to know someone before we judge him or her. **Standards:** Reading 3.0, 3.2, 3.3	**Text:** Excerpt from *The Summer My Father Was Ten*—"And so that's what he did . . . over their heads before letting them fly." **Focus:** Listening to the words that an author uses to move a scene along in time and space. **Discussion:** How does the author create the scene in our minds? How does he make us think that we are actually there? How does he speed up the action so we can feel the power and chaos of the scene? **Building Community:** Good pieces of literature will provide models for our own writing. **Standards:** Reading 3.7
4	**Text:** *The Royal Bee* **Focus:** Building background knowledge; making inferences from illustrations about unfamiliar settings **Discussion:** How do we gain meaning from a book if we do not have a lot of background knowledge? How can we build background knowledge from the illustrations and words? What can you infer about living in Korea? In what ways do you relate to the main character? **Building Community:** Each of us is privileged to be able to read and write. We can all become stronger readers and writers in this classroom this year. By being active and engaged learners, we will deepen our reading and writing skills. **Standards:** Reading 3.0, 3.3	**Text:** *The Royal Bee* **Focus:** Unlocking the meaning of foreign words; using strategies to help you remember meaning of words; using context clues to figure out meaning of words that we are unfamiliar with **Discussion:** Korean words help us make meaning of the story (such as *yangban* and *sangmin*). Why is it important that we understand the meaning of these words in the story? **Building Community:** We will not know how to correctly pronounce some words unless one of our classmates knows the language. We use our knowledge of the English language to approximate the pronunciation. We should show respect for other people's languages. **Standards:** Reading 1.0, 3.7

Shared Reading	Listening Speaking
Text: In *Hey World, Here I Am!:* "Five Dollars" **Focus:** Comparing and contrasting characters' feelings and actions **Discussion:** How do you think Kate is feeling about her actions? Give evidence for your thinking. Do you think her mom knows or cares about the money? Explain your thoughts. What part of her actions gives you insight into Kate's character? How are "my father's" and Kate's situations similar? **Building Community:** Sometimes the decisions that we make are made impulsively without thinking. Doing the right thing and taking responsibility for our actions builds character. **Standards:** Reading 3.3 **Text:** *The Royal Bee:* "What does winning the Royal Bee mean to you?" (one copy of each boy's speech for each student) **Focus:** Evaluating the words and behavior of a character; reading "between the lines" for deeper meaning **Discussion:** If you were the judge of these two speeches, whose would you choose? Why did you make that decision? What words or ideas swayed your thinking? Do you think the judges in the story made the right decision? What can you infer about the characters from their speeches? **Building Community:** Hard work pays off with big rewards. The way we express ourselves in words helps others know our thoughts and opinions. We need to listen carefully to each other so that we can learn from each other and appreciate other thoughts and opinions. **Standards:** Reading 3.6, 3.7	**Throughout the unit and the school year, students will learn about and engage in:** Adding to and expanding Developing conversation skills and responding to each other Learning to disagree Questioning for deeper understanding Responding to the talk Supporting answers with evidence and holding students accountable to staying with the text

DAY	READ ALOUD	WORD STUDY
5	**Text:** *The Armadillo from Amarillo* **Focus:** Sorting out fiction and nonfiction; sorting out important information that is embedded in a story; determining importance of information **Discussion:** Why did the author choose this format to tell us about our world? What elements of the story would be true? What elements of the story are fictionalized? Why did the author use postcards? How did they help you gain meaning about the text? Why did the author use an armadillo and an eagle to take us on a journey? **Building Community:** We can all develop friendships and help each other on our journey through fifth grade. **Standards:** Reading 2.1, 2.3	**Text:** *The Armadillo from Amarillo* **Focus:** Searching for specialized words within a nonfiction narrative; building geographical background knowledge through vocabulary ("prairie," "continent," "planet," and the like) **Building Community:** Many of us have lived and traveled in different states and countries. This adds to our diversity and gives us ideas for deeper discussion. Building background knowledge from our own class's life experiences brings us closer together. **Standards:** Reading 1.0
6	**Text:** *Anastasia Krupnik* (pages 17–27) **Focus:** Distinguishing physical characteristics of main characters; inferring what someone looks like from words **Discussion:** What do we know about Anastasia, her parents, and Mrs. Westvessel from the narrator and from the characters themselves? Do we have a clear picture of what they look like? How are you feeling about Mrs. Westvessel at this point? Do you think Anastasia is exaggerating? **Building Community:** Writing down your thoughts in a journal is a good outlet for responding to your likes and dislikes. You can say a lot without hurting others' feelings. **Standards:** Reading 3.3	**Text:** Various **Focus:** Creating a list of physical characteristics of book characters and people we know **Discussion:** What are some of our own characteristics? Have each child design a chart with his or her own physical characteristics and personality traits. **Building Community:** Thinking about ourselves helps us problem-solve about new characters we meet. **Standards:** Reading 1.2

Shared Reading	Listening Speaking
Text: In *The Armadillo from Amarillo:* Author's Note (an individual copy for each child) **Focus:** Reading for specific information; using special features of nonfiction to clarify meaning of the text; circling key words; using sticky notes **Discussion:** What additional information did we find out about armadillos in the Author's Note? How did this help with our understanding of the story? Why did the author include these sections in his book? **Building Community:** Knowing where we fit in the scheme of our own classroom environment makes us feel more comfortable and gives us a sense of direction. Each of us has a special place in this classroom. **Standards:** Reading 2.5	
Text: *Anastasia Krupnik* (pages 17–18) **Focus:** Finding evidence about characters within the text **Discussion:** What does Anastasia look like? Look for the evidence. Reread this section and highlight physical traits that you recognize in Anastasia, her parents, and Mrs. Westvessel (provide highlighters and make a chart of Anastasia's personal traits and physical characteristics). **Building Community:** We all look and act different; it is our differences that strengthen our thinking. **Standards:** Reading 3.0, 3.3	**Goal:** To understand conversation and how it helps us make meaning

Day	Read Aloud	Word Study
7	**Text:** *Anastasia Krupnik* (pages 27–38) **Focus:** Refining our thoughts about characters as the plot evolves; finding evidence within the story about character traits **Discussion:** As you got further into the story, how did your feelings about the character change? Were you prepared for the type of behavior that Mrs. Westvessel demonstrated? Do you think Mrs. Westvessel was fair giving Anastasia an F? If you put in a lot of effort, should you get a bad grade? How do you think Anastasia felt about Mrs. Westvessel's evaluation of her poem? **Building Community:** Each person needs to feel appreciated for his or her strengths and supported in his or her challenges. **Standards:** Reading 3.2, 3.3	**Text:** Various **Discussion:** Generate a list of personality traits found in characters we have met in this unit. Look for more sophisticated words using a thesaurus. Use adjectives that sound like your own voice that you use in your own speaking. For example, "nice" becomes "agreeable," "pleasing," or "enjoyable." Find more sophisticated words for "good," "bad," "sad," and "friendly." **Building Community:** Use the word wall for common words as we dig deeper into characters in our discussion and writing. **Standards:** Reading 1.0, 1.1
8	**Text:** In *Hey World, Here I Am!:* "Mr. Entwhistle" **Focus:** Using inference to understand a character's actions; introducing point of view **Discussion:** Was Kate being disrespectful? What makes you think that? Was Mr. Entwhistle correct in his assessment of Kate's behavior? Why do you think he was so "charged up"? In your opinion, did he overreact? Was Kate correct in not fighting back? How did her behavior influence Mr. Entwhistle's decision not to send her to the office? Would you have done the same thing or reacted differently? How do we grow from making a mistake? **Building Community:** We all make mistakes. Making mistakes helps us grow as individuals. How can we help others when they make a mistake? **Standards:** Reading 3.3	**Text:** In *Hey World, Here I Am!:* "Mr. Entwhistle" **Focus:** Action words that powerfully move the plot along **Discussion:** Gather words from the story that give the reader an effective picture of the author's intent of the action ("blasted," "glanced," and so on). How do they make the story more interesting? How do they keep us actively reading? **Building Community:** Using the right words to communicate exactly what you feel and think will help others form a clearer mental picture of what you mean. Use more sophisticated words to convey your thoughts. **Standards:** Reading 3.7

Shared Reading	Listening Speaking
Text: *Anastasia Krupnik:* Enlargement of text of the three students' poems **Focus:** Making a judgment about character's skills and thoughts; evaluating a character's thinking and actions **Discussion:** Read through each of the poems. If you were the teacher, which poem would you give the highest grade? Why? Can you tell who put in the most work? What was Mrs. Westvessel's main complaint about Anastasia's poem? Should she have been reprimanded the way she was in front of the other kids? How was she helped through her feelings? **Building Community:** Listening to directions is important in order to do our assignments correctly. How do we offer constructive criticism without hurting someone's feelings? **Standards:** Reading 3.7	**Establishing Expectations:** Active participation Appropriate body language Keeping focus on the speaker and the speaker's message Looking at the speaker Respect for the ideas of others Sharing the talk time Wait time
Text: In *Hey World, Here I Am!:* "Growing Pains" **Focus:** Understanding and evaluating a character's moods **Discussion:** Is mother justified in taking out her anger on Kate? Have you ever been treated in the same way? What would you do in a situation like this? Do you think Kate was really lazy, self-centered, and had a room that was a pigsty? **Building Community:** Sometimes we take things out on the people around us. Usually this has nothing to do with them, but is because of something that has happened at home or outside of school. People need space and time to deal with their anger. We all have bad days. Being a friend can help others get through their feelings. **Standards:** Reading 3.3	**Throughout the unit and the school year, students will learn about and engage in:** Adding to and expanding Developing conversation skills and responding to each other Learning to disagree Questioning for deeper understanding Responding to the talk Supporting answers with evidence and holding students accountable to staying with the text

DAY	READ ALOUD	WORD STUDY
9	**Text:** *Bud, Not Buddy* **Focus:** Using inference to make meaning; using inference to determine characters' feelings **Discussion:** What emotions is Buddy feeling? How does it feel when someone has gone through your things? How did Buddy react? What does he remember about his mother? How does he feel toward his mother in this section of the book? Why do you think that? How would you feel? Do you think Buddy will be safe on the rest of his journey? What makes you think that way? **Building Community:** What is special about your name? We all need to respect one another and our possessions. **Standards:** Reading 3.0, 3.3	**Text:** In *Wham! It's A Poetry Jam*: "I Am" and "Blue Prints" **Focus:** Recognizing rhyming words in poetry; finding the poet's message; having fun with the sounds of rhyming words; introduction to a rhyming dictionary **Discussion:** Why do poets use rhyme? Why don't all poems rhyme? **Building Community:** Enjoying the sound of words by reading poetry together. **Standards:** Reading 3.0, 3.4, Listening and Speaking 1.6
10	**Text:** *Nothing Ever Happens on 90th Street* **Focus:** Problem-and-solution; inferring an author's message (theme: friendship, being a good neighbor, and cooperation) **Discussion:** What problem did the characters face in this story? How was the problem solved? What big idea was the author trying to give the reader? Why do you think that way? What makes up a good story? What story elements were used to create the girl's story? Keep a theme chart to help us remember the big ideas of stories. **Writing Workshop Connection:** Which of the elements of a good story did you learn from this book? How does adding detail make our stories better? How can we become better writers? **Building Community:** How can we make learning happen in this classroom? What is the outcome of cooperation in this classroom? **Standards:** Reading 3.2, 3.4	**Text:** *Nothing Ever Happens on 90th Street* **Discussion:** Many words that we have in the English language are derived from other languages. Does anyone speak French in our classroom? How can we tell that these words are derived from the French language? Are there any rules of pronunciation that you can deduce from these French words? French words from this story: *mousse, plie, fedora, limousine, promenade, gourmet, filets,* and *bouquet.* **Building Community:** Recognizing the words that come from other languages makes us feel that the world is a smaller place. **Standards:** Reading 1.1, 1.2

SHARED READING	LISTENING SPEAKING
Text: In *Wham! It's a Poetry Jam:* "I Am" and "Blue Prints" **Focus:** Exploring theme in poetry **Discussion:** How long does a poem have to be? Can a poet send a message in sixteen words? Is there a common theme in these poems? Discuss it with your partner. What would you like us to know about you? What are some things that you wonder about yourself and what you might become? **Building Community:** Knowing who we are helps us build better working teams for learning. **Standards:** Reading 3.4	
Text: In *Wham! It's a Poetry Jam:* "Who's Boss" **Focus:** Reading for fluency and enjoyment; reading with expression and appropriate pacing; making choices about how to read a poem **Discussion:** What makes these two poems fit together so nicely? How will you choose to chunk the poem into parts? What is the value of dividing the poem up into parts? **Building Community:** working together cooperatively makes learning seem easier and more fun. **Standards:** Reading 1.1, 3.3, Listening and Speaking 1.6	

REFERENCES

Anastasia Krupnik, by L. Lowry. New York: Random House, 1979.

The Armadillo from Amarillo, by L. Cherry. San Diego, CA: Harcourt Brace, 1994.

"Blue Prints." In *Wham! It's a Poetry Jam*, by S. Holbrook. New York: Boyds Mills Press, 2002.

Bud, Not Buddy, by C. Curtis. New York: Random House, 1999.

"The First Skateboard in the History of the World." In *The Moon and I*, by B. Byars. New York: Simon and Schuster, 1991.

"Five Dollars," by J. Little, in *Hey World, Here I Am!* Toronto: Harper Trophy, 1986.

"Growing Pains," by J. Little, in *Hey World, Here I Am!* Toronto: Harper Trophy, 1986.

"I Am." In*Wham! It's a Poetry Jam*, by S. Holbrook. New York: Boyd Mills Press, 2002.

"Maybe a Fight," by J. Little, in *Hey World, Here I Am!* Toronto: Harper Trophy, 1986.

"Miss Harriet's Room." In *The Moon and I*, by B. Byars. New York: Simon and Schuster, 1991.

"Mr. Entwhistle," by J. Little, in *Hey World, Here I Am!* Toronto: Harper Trophy, 1986.

Nothing Ever Happens on 90th Street, by R. Schotter. *New York*: Orchard Paperbacks, 1997.

The Royal Bee, by F. and G. Park. Honedale, PA: Boyds Mills Press, 2000.

The Summer My Father Was Ten, by P. Brisson. New York: Boyds Mills Press, 1998.

"Testing New Waters." In *Wham! It's a Poetry Jam*, by S. Holbrook. New York: Boyds Mills Press, 2002.

"Who's Boss." In *Wham! It's a Poetry Jam*, by S. Holbrook. New York: Boyds Mills Press, 2002.

REFERENCES

Aliki. (1998). *Marianthe's story: Painted words and spoken memories.* New York: Greenwillow Books.

Allen, J. (1999). *Words, words, words: Teaching vocabulary in grades 4–12.* York, ME: Stenhouse.

Allington, R. (2006). *What really matters for struggling readers: Designing research-based programs.* (2nd ed.) Boston: Pearson Education.

Anderson, C. (2000). *How's it going?* Portsmouth, NH: Heinnemann.

Anderson-Inman, L., & Horney, M. A. (1999, April). *Electronic books: Reading and studying with supportive resources.* International Reading Association, Reading Online. Retrieved October 2, 2006, from http://www.readingonline.org/electronic/ebook/index.html.

Armbruster, B. B., Lehr, F., & Osborn, J. (2001, September). *Put reading first: The research building blocks for teaching children to read.* National Institute for Literacy. Retrieved November 1, 2006, from http://www.nifl.gov/partnershipforreading/publications/reading_first1.html.

Armstrong, W. (1969). *Sounder.* New York: Scholastic.

Atwell, N. (1987). *In the middle: Writing, reading, and learning with adolescents.* Portsmouth, NH: Heinemann.

Avi. (1979). *Night journeys.*New York: Pantheon.

Avi. (1980). *Encounter at Easton.* New York: Pantheon.

Avi. (1984). *The fighting ground.* New York: Trophy.

Avi. (1986). *Wolf rider.* New York: Atheneum.

Avi. (1990). *The true confessions of Charlotte Doyle.* New York: Avon Books.

Avi. (1992). *Windcatcher.* New York: HarperTrophy.

Avi. (1995). *Poppy.* New York: HarperCollins.

Avi. (1999). *Ragweed.* New York: HarperCollins.

Avi. (2000). *Ereth's birthday.* New York: HarperTrophy.

Avi. (2001). *The secret school.* New York: Harcourt.

Babbitt, N. (1975). *Tuck everlasting*. New York: Farrar, Straus and Giroux.

Baker, L., & Brown, A. L. (1984). Metacognitive skills in reading. In P. D. Pearson (Ed.), *Handbook of reading research* (pp. 353–394). New York: Longman.

Base, G. (1993). *Anamalia*. New York: Abrams.

Bear, D. R., Invernizzi, M., Templeton, S., & Johnston, F. (2004). *Words their way*. (3rd ed.) Upper Saddle River, NJ: Pearson Education.

Beaver, J. (2002). *Developmental reading assessment*. Glenview, IL: Celebration.

Bender, W. N. (2002). *Differentiating instruction for students with learning disabilities*. Thousand Oaks, CA: Corwin Press & Council for Exceptional Children.

Bender, W. N., & Larkin, M. J. (2003). *Reading strategies for elementary students with learning difficulties*. Thousand Oaks, CA: Corwin Press.

Benson, V. (2002). Shifting paradigms and pedagogy with nonfiction: A call to arms for survival in the 21st century. *New England Reading Association Journal*, *38*(2), 1–6.

Berger, M., & Berger, G. (2000). *What do sharks eat for dinner?* New York: Scholastic.

Bos, C., & Vaughn, S. (1994). *Strategies for teaching students with learning and behavior problems*. (3rd ed.) Boston: Allyn & Bacon.

Brozo, W. (2004). It's okay to read, even if other kids don't: Learning about and from boys in a middle school book club. *The California Reader*, *38*(2), 4–12.

Bunting, E. (1995). *Smoky night*. New York: Harcourt Brace.

Burchers, S., Burchers, M., & Burchers, B. (1998). *Vocabulary cartoons*™. Punta Gorda, FL: New Monics Books.

Burmark, L. (2002). *Visual literacy: Learn to see, see to learn*. Alexandria, VA: Association for Supervision & Curriculum Development.

Byars, B. (1991). *The moon and I*. New York: Simon & Schuster.

Byrd, R., & Weitzman, M. (1994). Predictors of early grade retention among children in the United States. *Pediatrics*, *93*, 481–487.

Calkins, L. M. (1994). *The art of teaching writing*. (2nd ed.) Portsmouth, NH: Heinemann.

Gardiner, J. R.(1996).*Stone fox*.New York:Trophy.

Calkins, L. M. (2001). *The art of teaching reading*. New York: Addison-Wesley Educational.

CALL Centre (2005, January). *Communication aids for language and learning (CALL) information sheet 15: Speech recognition systems*. Edinburgh, Scotland: University of Edinburgh. Retrieved August 10, 2006, from http://callcentre.education.ed.ac.wk/downloads/speech_recognition/introduction.pdf.

Carr, E., & Ogle, D. (1987). K-W-L plus: A strategy for comprehension and summarization. *Journal of Reading*, *30*, 626–631.

Carter, B., & Abrahamson, R. (1990). *Nonfiction for young adults: From delight to wisdom*. Phoenix, AZ: Oryx Press.

Casbarro, J. (2003). *Test anxiety and what you can do about it*. Port Chester, NY: Dude.

Caswell, L. J., & Duke, N. K. (1998). Non-narrative as a catalyst for literacy development. *Language Arts*, *75*(2), 108–117.

Chapman, C., & King, R. (2003). *Differentiated instructional strategies for writing in the content areas*. Thousand Oaks, CA: Corwin Press.

Cherry, L. (1992). *A river ran wild.* San Diego, CA: Harcourt.

Cherry, L. (1994). *The Armadillo from Amarillo.* San Diego, CA: Harcourt Brace.

Clement, A. (1999). *Frindle.* New York: Harper Collins.

Cobb, V. (1994). *Science experiments you can eat.* New York: HarperCollins.

Colfer, E. (2004). *Artemis Fowl.* New York: HarperCollins.

Cooper, F. (2004). *Jump! From the life of Michael Jordan.* New York: Philomel.

Cooper, J. D. (1993). *Literacy: Helping children construct meaning* (2nd ed.). Boston: Houghton Mifflin.

Cooperman, N., & Cunningham, A. (2003, May). Balanced literacy and technology. *Teaching Matters.* Retrieved March 18, 2006, from http://backend.teachingmatters.org/files/whitepaper.pdf.

Creech, S. (1994). *Walk two moons.* New York: HarperCollins.

Culham, R. (2003). *6 + 1 traits of writing.* Portland, OR: Northwest Regional Educational Laboratory.

Cunningham, P. M., & Hall, D. P. (1997). *Making more big words: Grades 3–6.* Torrance, CA: Good Apple/Frank Schaffer.

Cunningham, P. M., & Hall, D. P. (1998). *Month-by-month phonics for upper grades.* Greensboro, NC: Carson-Dellosa.

Currie, P. S., & Wadlington, E. M. (2000). *The source for learning disabilities.* East Moline, IL: LinguiSystems.

Curtis, C. (1999). *Bud, not Buddy.* New York: Random House Children's Books.

Cushman, K. (1996). *The ballad of Lucy Whipple.* New York: Clarion.

Dahl, R. (1964). *Charlie and the chocolate factory.* New York: Puffin Books.

Dahl, R. (1988). *Matilda.* New York: Penguin Books.

Daniels, H. (2002). *Literature circles: Voice and choice in book clubs and reading groups.* Portland, ME: Stenhouse.

Daniels, H. (1994). *Literature circles: Voice and choice in the student-centered classroom.* Portland, ME: Stenhouse.

DeGross, M. (1994). *Donovan's word jar.* New York: HarperCollins.

Deshler, D. D., Ellis, E. S., & Lenz, B. K. (1996). *Teaching adolescents with learning disabilities: Strategies and methods.* Denver, CO: Love Publishing.

Dewberry, L., & Hitch, B. (2006, February). Creating multi-sensory classrooms. *Discovery Education,* pp. 22–23.

DiCamillo, K. (2000). *Because of Winn-Dixie.* New York: Candlewick Press.

DiCamillo, K. (2003). *Tales of Despereaux.* New York: Candlewick Press.

Donahue, P., Finnegan, R., Lutkus, A., Allen, M., & Campbell, J. (2001, April). *The nation's report card: Fourth-grade reading 2000.* National Center for Education Statistics, p. 40. Retrieved October 15, 2006, from http://nces.ed.gov/nationsreportcard/pubs/main2000/2001499.asp.

Donahue, P., Voelkl, K., Campbell, J., & Mazzeo, J. (1999). *NAEP reading report card for the nation and states.* Washington, DC: National Center for Education Statistics.

Duey, K., & Bale, K. A. *Survival Series.* New York: Aladdin Books.

Duke, N. K. (2000). 3.6 minutes per day: The scarcity of informational texts in first grade. *Reading Research Quarterly, 35*(2), 295–318.

Education Department of Western Australia. (2004). *First steps: Writing development continuum.* Salem, MA: STEPS Professional Development and Consulting.

Epson Presenters Online. (2006). *Put more power in your next presentation: Use a document camera.* Retrieved October 15, 2006, from http://www.presentersonline.com/technology/tools/documentcamera.shtml.

Feldman, K. (2000, March 21). *Ensuring all students learn to read well: Linking research to practice in effective reading programs* [Handbook]. Santa Rosa, CA: Sonoma County SELPA. Retrieved October 15, 2006, from www.sonoma.k12.ca.us.

Feldman, K. (2001, November). *Supporting struggling secondary readers: Decoding, fluency and comprehension—what works?* CEC Annual California State Conference.

Fetzer, N. (2003). *Writing connections: From oral language to written text.* Murrieta, CA: Nancy Fetzer's Literacy Connections.

Fetzer, N. (2006). *Reading connections: Building high-level reading comprehension skills and strategies.* Murrieta, CA: Nancy Fetzer's Literacy Connections.

Fielding, L., & Pearson, P. D. (1994). Reading comprehension: What works. *Educational Leadership, 51*(5), 62–68.

Finn, P. (1999). *Teaching memoir writing.* New York: Scholastic Professional Books.

First Steps. *Reading: Resource book 1994* (pp. 123–136). Melbourne, Australia: Longman & Education Department of Western Australia.

Fisher, L., Fetzer, N., & Rief, S. (1999). *Successful classrooms: Effective teaching strategies for raising achievement in reading and writing* [video]. San Diego, Calif.: Educational Resource Specialists. (Available at www.sandrarief.com.)

Fisher, D., Flood, J., Lapp, D., & Frey, N. (2004). Interactive read alouds: Is there a common set of implementation practices? *The Reading Teacher, 58,* 8–17.

Fleischman, P. (1985). *I am Phoenix.* New York: HarperCollins.

Fleischman, P. (1988). *Joyful noise.* New York: HarperCollins.

Fleischman, P. (1997). *Seedfolks.* New York: Harper-Collins.

Fleischman, S. (1995). *The thirteenth floor.* New York: Bantam Doubleday Dell.

Fletcher, R., & Portalupi, J. (2001). *Writing workshop: The essential guide.* Portsmouth, NH: Heinemann.

Florian, D. (1986). *Mammalabilia.* Orlando, FL: Harcourt.

Florian, D. (1987). *In the swim.* Orlando, FL: Harcourt.

Florian, D. (1989). *Lizards, frogs, and polliwogs.* Orlando, FL: Harcourt.

Florian, D. (1998). *Insectlopedia.* Orlando, FL: Harcourt.

Fountas, I. C., & Pinnell, G. (1996). *Guided reading: Good first teaching for all children.* Portsmouth, NH: Heinemann.

Fountas, I. C., & Pinnell, G. (2001). *Guiding readers and writers (grades 3–6).* Portsmouth, NH: Heinemann.

Fox, P. (1973). *The slave dancer.* New York: Random House.

Frank, M. (1995). *If you're trying to teach kids how to write, you've gotta have this book.* Nashville, TN: Incentive.

Frey, N., & Fisher, D. (2006). *Language arts workshop.* Upper Saddle River, NJ: Pearson Education.

Fry, E. (2000). *Skimming and scanning (middle level).* Blacklick, OH: Glencoe/McGraw-Hill.

Funke, C. (2005). *The thief lord.* New York: Random House.

Ganske, K. (2000). *Word journeys: Assessment-guided phonics, spelling, and vocabulary instruction.* New York: Guilford Press.

Gardiner, J. R. (1996). *Stone fox.* New York: Trophy.

Gardner, H. (1983). *Frames of mind: The theory of multiple intelligences.* New York: Basic Books.

Gavelek, J. R. (1986). The social context of literacy and schooling: A developmental perspective. In T. E. Rapael (Ed.), The concepts of school-based literacy, pp. 3–26. New York: Random House.

George, J. (1959). *My side of the mountain.* New York: Puffin Books.

Georgia College and State University. (2006). Apple +iPods GCSU. Retrieved October 7, 2006, from http://ipod.gcsu.edu/GCSU.

Gibbons, G. (1993). *Caves and caverns.* New York: Voyager Books.

Gibbons, G. (1997). *The moon book.* New York: Scholastic.

Glassman, J., & Einhorn, K. (2004). *100 vocabulary words kids need to know by 5th grade.* New York: Scholastic.

Golenbook, P. (1990). *Teammates.* Orlando, FL: Harcourt.

Graham, S., & Harris, K. (2000, Fall). *Preventing writing difficulties.* Nashville, TN: CASL News, Vanderbilt University. www.vanderbiltedu/CASL/reports.html.

Graham, S., Harris, K., and Larsen, L. (2001). *Prevention and intervention of writing difficulties for students with learning disabilities.* LDOnline. Retrieved October 31, 2006, from http:// www.ldonline.org/article/6213.

Griffiths, M. (Director). (1990). *A cry in the wild* [Film].

Grow, G. O. (1996). *Serving the strategic reader: Reader response theory and its implications for the teaching of writing.* Expanded version of a paper presented to the Qualitative Division of the Association for Educators in Journalism and Mass Communication, Atlanta, GA, August 1994. Retrieved May 15, 2006, from http:// www.longleaf.net/ggrow.

Guthrie, J. T., & Humenick, N. M. (2004). Motivating students to read: Evidence for classroom practices that increase motivation and achievement. In P. McCardle & V. Chhabra (Eds.), *The voice of evidence in reading research* (pp. 329–354). Baltimore: Paul Brookes.

Hall, S., & Moats, L. C. (1999). *Straight talk about reading: How parents can make a difference in the early years.* Chicago: Contemporary Books.

Harris, A. J., & Sipay, E. R. (1990). *How to increase reading ability.* (8th ed.) New York: Longman.

Harvey, S. (1998). *Nonfiction matters: Reading, writing, and research in grades 3–8.* York, ME: Stenhouse.

Harvey, S., & Goudvis, A. (2000). *Strategies that work: Teaching comprehension to enhance understanding.* York, Maine: Stenhouse.

Heacox, D. (1991). *Up from underachievement*. Minneapolis: Free Spirit Publishing.

Head, M. H., & Readence, J. E. (1986). Anticipation guides: Meaning through prediction. In E. K. Dishner, T. W. Bean, J. E. Redadence, & D. W. Moore (Eds.), *Reading in the content areas*. (2nd ed.) (pp. 229–234). Dubuque, IA: Kendall/Hunt.

Hepler, S. (1998). Nonfiction books for children: New directions, new challenges. In R. A. Bamford, & J. V. Kristo (Eds.), *Making facts come alive: Choosing quality nonfiction literature K-8* (pp. 3–17). Norwood, MA: Christopher-Gordon.

Hindley, J. (1997). *How your body works*. Fairfield, IA: Henderson.

Holbrook, S. (2002). *Wham! It's a poetry jam*. New York: Boyds Mills Press.

Holdaway. (1979). *The foundations of literacy*. Sydney, Australia: Ashton Scholastic.

Holum, A., & Gahala, J. (2001, October). *Critical issue: Using technology to enhance literacy instruction*. Naperville, IL: Learning Point Associates™, North Central Regional Educational Laboratory (NCREL). Retrieved March 15, 2006, from www.ncrel.org/sdrs/areas/issues/content/cntareas/reading/li300.htm.

Honig, B. (1999). Reading the right way. In *CORE reading research anthology*. Novato, CA: Arena Press & Consortium on Reading Excellence.

How Would You Survive in . . . ? (series). London: Franklin Watts.

Hoyt, L., Mooney, M., & Parkes, B. (2003). *Exploring informational texts*. Portsmouth, NH: Heinemann.

Individuals with Disabilities Education Act of 2004, 20 U.S.C. § 1401. *Definitions*.

International Dyslexia Association. (2000, May). *Just the facts: Dyslexia basics*. Baltimore, MD: International Dyslexia Association.

International Reading Association. (2002). *Integrating literacy and technology in the curriculum: A position statement of the International Reading Association*. Newark, DE: Author. Retrieved online from http://www.reading.org/downloads/positions/ps1048_technology.pdf.

Invernizzi, M. A., & Worthy, M. J. (1989). An orthographic-specific comparison of spelling errors of learning disabled and normal children across four grade levels of spelling achievement. *Reading Psychology*, *10*, 173–188.

Jones, S. (2003, Spring). Accommodations for students with handwriting problems. *The Resource*, *18*(1), 6–12. Available at www.dyslexia-ca.org.

Kagan, S., Kagan, M., & Kagan, L. (2000). *Reaching standards through cooperative learning: English/language arts*. Port Chester, NY: National Professional Resources.

Kamma, A. (2001). *If you were at the first Thanksgiving*. New York: Scholastic.

Kemper, D., Sebranek, P., & Nathan, R. (1995). *Writers express*. Wilmington, MA: Write Source®.

Kennedy, K. (2006, October). *Clicker 5*. Retrieved October 18, 2006, from http://www.techlearning.com/shared/printableArticle.jhtml?articleID=193200384.

Kinsella, K. (2005, February 26). *Narrowing the 4–12 achievement gap: The pivotal role of robust school-wide academic vocabulary development*. Keynote presentation at California Association of Resource Specialists (CARS+) annual convention inSan Jose, CA.

Knowlton, N. (2006). *Products for learning—Smart solutions for K-12: SMART technologies manual*. Retrieved October 16, 2006, from www.smarttech.com.

Kristo, J., & Bamford, R. (2004). *Nonfiction in focus.* New York: Scholastic.

Krull, K. (1996). *Wilma unlimited.* San Diego, CA: Harcourt Brace.

Kurtus, R. (2001). *Overcoming the fear of speaking to groups.* www.school-for-champions.com/speaking/fear.htm.

Laskowski, L. (1996). *Overcoming speaking anxiety in meetings and presentations.* Retrieved November 15, 2006, from LJL Seminars http://wwwljlseminars.com/anxiety.htm.

Lattimer, H. (2003). *Thinking through genre.* Portland, ME: Stenhouse.

Lester, J. (1968). *To be a slave.* New York: Scholastic.

Levine, M. (2001). *The kids' address book.* New York: Perigee.

Levitin, S., & Robinson, C. (1970). *Journey to America.* New York: Scholastic.

Lewis, C. S. (1950). *The chronicles of Narnia: The lion, the witch and the wardrobe.* New York: HarperCollins.

Little, J. (1986). *Hey world, here I am!* Toronto, Canada. Harper Trophy.

London, J. (1903). *Call of the wild.* New York: Simon & Schuster.

Lowry, L. (1979). *Anastasia Krupnik.* New York: Bantam.

Lowry, L. (1989). *Number the stars.* New York: Bantam Doubleday Dell.

Lyon, G. R. (1998, April 28). *Overview of reading and literacy initiatives.* [Statement of G. Reid Lyon]. Bethesda, MD: National Institute of Child Health and Human Development.

MacLachlan, P. (1998). *It's fine to be nine.* New York: Scholastic.

Marten, C. (2003). *Word crafting.* Portsmouth, NH: Heinemann.

Martin, J. B. (1998). *Snowflake Bentley.* Boston: Houghton Mifflin.

Marzano, R. J. (2004). *Building background knowledge for academic achievement.* Alexandria, VA: Association for Supervision and Curriculum Development.

Marzano, R. J., & Pickering, D. J. (2005). *Building academic vocabulary.* Alexandria, VA: Association for Supervision & Curriculum Development.

Mather, N., & Roberts, R. (1995). *Informal assessment and instruction in written language.* Hoboken, NJ: Wiley.

McCarthy, T. (1998a). *Persuasive writing (grades 4–8).* New York: Scholastic Professional Books.

McCarthy, T. (1998b). *Expository writing (grades 4–8).* New York: Scholastic Professional Books.

McCormick, S. (2003). *Instructing students who have literacy problems.* (4th ed.) Upper Saddle River, NJ: Pearson Education.

McFann, J. (2004, August). Boys and books. *Reading Today, 22*(1), 20–21.

Mercer, C. D., & Mercer, A. R. (1993). *Teaching students with learning problems.* (4th ed.) New York: Macmillan.

Meyer, M., & Felton, R. (1999). Repeated reading to enhance fluency: Old approaches and new directions. *Annals of Dyslexia, 49,* 283–306.

Moats, L. (1995). *Spelling: Development, disability, and instruction.* Baltimore, MD: York Press.

Moats, L. (2001, March). When older kids can't read. *Educational Leadership, 58,* 6.

Mooney, M. (2001). *Text forms and features.* New York: Richard C. Owen.

Moss, B. (2004). Teaching expository text structures. *The Reading Teacher, 57*(8), 710–718.

Nagy, W. E., & Anderson, R. C. (1984). How many words are there in printed school English? *Reading Research Quarterly, 19,* 304–330.

National Center for Education Statistics. (2000). *Trends in educational equity for girls and women.* Washington, DC: U.S. Department of Education.

National Center for Education Statistics. (2006). *Indicator 12: Reading performance of students in grades 4 and 8.* Retrieved October 30, 2006, from http://nces.ed.gov/programs/coe/2006/section2/indicator12.asp.

National Communication Association. (2007). *Speaking, listening, and media literacy standards for K through 12 education.* Retrieved April 25, 2007, from http://www.natcom.org/Instruction/k-12/K12Stds.htm.

National Geographic School Publishing. (2007). *Program goals.* Retrieved April 25, 2007, from http://www.ngschoolpub.org/c/2Kcsk2LCF.BzA/Pages/rwwgoals.web.

National Institute of Child Health and Human Development (NICHD). (2000, April). *Report of the national reading panel: An evidence-based assessment of the scientific research literature on reading and its implications for reading instruction.* NICHD, National Institutes of Health.

National Reading Panel. (2000, April). *Teaching children to read: An evidence-based assessment of the scientific research literature on reading and its implications for reading instruction.* Washington, DC: National Institute of Child Health and Human Development. Available at www.nationalreadingpanel.org.

Nisbet, P. D., Spooner, R.W.S., Arthur, E., Whittaker, P. (1999). Supportive writing technology. In P. D. Nisbet (Ed.), *Teaching literacy using technology* (pp. 63–73). Retrieved July 15, 2006, from http://callcentre.education.ed.ac.uk/downloads/swbook/swbook8.pdf.

Novelli, J. (2000). *Teaching story writing.* New York: Scholastic Professional Books.

O'Brien, R. C. (2000). Mrs. Frisby and the cow. From C. Bereiter, M. Adams, et al. (Eds.), *Mrs. Frisby and the rats of NIMH: SRA Open Court reading book 4.* Columbus, OH: SRA.

O'Dell, S. (1969). *Island of the blue dolphins.* Boston: Houghton Mifflin.

O'Dell, S. (1970). *Sing down the moon.* New York: Bantam Doubleday Dell.

O'Dell, S. (1977). *The black pearl.* New York: Dell.

O'Dell, S. (1980). *Sarah Bishop.* New York: Scholastic.

Ogle, D. M. (1986). K-W-L: A teaching model that develops active reading of expository text. *The Reading Teacher, 39,* 564–570.

Ong, F. (2000). *Strategic teaching and learning: Standards-based instruction to promote content literacy in grades four through twelve.* Sacramento, CA: California Department of Education.

Palincsar, A., & Brown, A. (1984). Reciprocal teaching of comprehension fostering and comprehension monitoring activities. *Cognition and Instruction, 1*(2), 117–175.

Palincsar, A., & Brown, A. (1985). Reciprocal teaching: Activities to promote reading with your mind. In T. L. Harris & E. J. Cooper (Eds.), *Reading, thinking, and concept development: Strategies for the classroom.* New York: College Board.

Pappas, C. C. (1991). Fostering full access to literacy by including information books. *Language Arts, 68,* 449–462.

Paris, S. G. (1986). Teaching children to guide their reading and learning. In T. E. Raphael (Ed.), *The contexts of school-based literacy* (pp. 115–130). New York: Random House.

Paterson, K. (1978). *Bridge to Terabithia.* New York: HarperCollins.

Paterson, K. (1978). *The great Gilly Hopkins.* New York: Harper Trophy.

Paulsen, G. (1996). *Brian's winter.* New York: Delacorte.

Paulsen, G. (1987). *Hatchet.* New York: Puffin Books.

Paulsen, G. (1991). *The river.* New York: Dell Publishing.

Pearson, E. (2002). *Ordinary Mary's extraordinary deed.* Layton, UT: Gibbs Smith.

Pearson, P. D., & Fielding, L. (1991). Comprehension instruction. In R. Barr, M. L. Kamil, P. Mosenthal, & P. D. Pearson (Eds.), *Handbook of reading research.* (Vol. 2, pp. 815–860). White Plains, NY: Longman.

Philbrick, R. (1993). *Freak the mighty.* New York: Scholastic.

Pike, K., & Mumper, J. *Nonfiction and other informational texts come alive.* Boston: Pearson Education.

Pinnell, G. S., & Fountas, I. C. (1998). *Word matters: Teaching phonics and spelling in the reading/writing classroom.* Portsmouth, NH: Heinemann.

Piven, J., & Borgenicht, D. (1999). *The worst-case scenario survival handbook.* San Francisco: Chronicle Books.

Piven, J., & Borgenicht, D. (2002). *The worst-case scenario survival handbook: Holidays.* San Francisco: Chronicle Books.

Pratt, K. J. (1992). *A walk in the rainforest.* Nevada City, CA: Dawn.

Prelutsky, J. (1984). *The new kid on the block.* New York: Greenwillow Books.

Prelutsky, J. (1990). *Something big has been here.* New York: Greenwillow Books.

Prelutsky, J. (1996). *A pizza the size of the sun.* New York: Greenwillow Books.

Public Broadcasting Service. (2002). *Misunderstood minds. Writing basics, difficulties, responses.* Boston: WGBH Educational Foundation. Available at http://www.pbs.org/wgbh/misunderstoodminds.

Raphael, T. (1982). Questioning-answering strategies for children. *The Reading Teacher, 37,* 377–382.

Raphael, T., Goatley, V. J., McMahon, S. I., and Woodman, D. A. (1995). Promoting meaningful conversations in student book clubs. In N. Roser & M. Martinez (Eds.), *Book talk and beyond: Children and teachers respond to literature* (pp. 66–68). Newark, DE: International Reading Association.

Raphael, T. E., & McMahon, S. I. (1994, October). Book club: An alternative framework for reading instruction. *The Reading Teacher, 48*(2), 102–116.

Reiss, J. (1973). *The upstairs room.* New York: Harper Trophy.

Resnick, L. (1995). From aptitude to effort: A new foundation for our schools. *Daedalus, 124*(4), 55–62.

Rhodes, L. K., & Dudley-Marling, C. (1988). *Readers and writers with a difference: A holistic approach to teaching learning disabled and remedial students.* Portsmouth, NH: Heinemann.

Richmond, V. P., & McCroskey, J. C. (1995a). *Communication: Apprehension, avoidance, and effectiveness.* Scottsdale, AZ: Gorsuch Scarisbrick.

Richmond, V. P., & McCroskey, J. C. (1995b). *Nonverbal behavior in interpersonal relations.* (3rd ed.) Needham Heights, MA: Allyn & Bacon.

Ridpath, I. (1993). *The children's giant atlas of the universe*. Melbourne, Australia: Hamlyn Children's Books.

Rief, S. (1998). *The ADD/ADHD checklist: An easy reference for parents and teachers*. San Francisco: Jossey-Bass.

Rief, S. (2003). *The ADHD book of lists*. San Francisco: Jossey-Bass.

Rief, S. (2005). *How to reach and teach children with ADD/ADHD*. (2nd ed.) San Francisco: Jossey-Bass.

Rief, S., & Heimburge, J. (2006). *How to reach and teach all children in the inclusive classroom*. (2nd ed.) San Francisco: Jossey-Bass.

Rosenberg, G. (2000, July 24). Some schools are fighting poor acoustics with microphones and amplifiers. *eSchool News*. Retrieved December 2, 2006, from http://www.eschoolnews.org/news/showStory.cfm?ArticleID=1344.

Routman, R. (2003). *Reading essentials*. Portsmouth, NH: Heinemann.

Routman, R. (1996). *Literacy at the crossroads*. Portsmouth, NH: Heinemann.

Rowling, J. K. *Harry Potter* (series). New York: Scholastic Press.

Russell, G., Baker, S., & Edwards, L. (1999, December). *Teaching expressive writing to students with learning disabilities*. ERIC Clearinghouse on Disabilities and Gifted Children, Council for Exceptional Children. Retrieved July 30, 2006, from www.ldonline.org/article/6201.

Ryan, P. M. (2000). *Esperanza rising*. New York: Scholastic.

Sacher, L. (1998). *Holes*. New York: Random House.

Sanacore, J. (1991). Expository and narrative text: Balancing young children's reading experiences. *Childhood Education*, *67*, 211–214.

Say, A. (1994). *Grandfather's journey*. Boston: Houghton Mifflin.

Schaefer, L. (2001). *Teaching young writers strategies that work*. New York: Scholastic.

Schwab Learning. (2002). *Educator's guide to learning differences*. San Francisco, CA: Author. Available at www.schwablearning.org.

Scieszka, J. (2005). *Guys write for guys read*. New York: Viking Juvenile.

Silverstein, S. (1991). *A light in the attic*. New York: HarperCollins.

Simon, S. (1989). *Storms*. New York: HarperCollins.

Simon, S. (1996). *Wildfires*. New York: Harper Collins.

Smith, M. W., & Wilhelm, J. D. (2002). *Reading don't fix no chevys*. Portsmouth, NH: Heinemann.

Smith, R., Clark, T., & Blomeyer, R. (2005, November). *A synthesis of new research on K–12 online learning*. Naperville, IL: North Central Regional Educational Laboratory, Learning Point Associates™. Retrieved October 14, 2006, from http://www.ncrel.org/tech/synthesis.

Snicket, L. *A series of unfortunate events* (series). New York: HarperCollins.

Snow, C. E., Burns, S. M., & Griffin, P. (Eds.) (1998). *Preventing reading difficulties in young children*. Washington, DC: National Research Council, National Academy Press.

Sousa, D. A. (2001a). *How the brain learns*. (2nd ed.) Thousand Oaks, CA: Corwin Press.

Sousa, D. A. (2001b). *How the special needs brain learns*. Thousand Oaks, CA: Corwin Press.

Spandel, V. (2004). *Creating young writers: Using the six traits to enrich writing process in primary classrooms.* Boston: Allyn & Bacon.

Speare, E. (1959). *Witch of blackbird pond.* New York: Bantam Doubleday Dell.

Speare, E. (1983). *Sign of the beaver.* New York: Bantam Doubleday Dell.

Spinelli, J. (1990). *Maniac McGee.* New York: Little Brown.

Stanovich, K. E., & West, R. F. (1989). Exposure to print and orthographic processing. *Reading Research Quarterly, 24,* 402–433.

Stauffer, P. G. (1975). *Directing the reading-thinking process.* New York: HarperCollins.

Stead, T. (2002). *Should there be zoos? A persuasive text.* New York: Mondo.

Stead, T., & Ballester, J. (2000). *Should there be zoos? A persuasive text.* New York: Mondo.

Stein, N., & Glenn, C. G. (1979). An analysis of story comprehension in elementary school children. In R. O.Freedle (Ed.), *New directions in discourse processes* (Vol. 2, pp. 53–120). Norwood, NJ: Ablex.

Stock, G. (2004). *Kids' book of questions.* New York: Workman Press.

Storm, R. *Survival Guides* (series). New York: Scholastic.

Swanson, P. N., & DeLaPaz, S. (1998). Teaching effective comprehension strategies to students with learning and reading disabilities. *Intervention in School and Clinic, 33,* 209–218.

Szymusiah, K., & Sibbersoni, F. (2001). *Beyond leveled books.* Portland, ME: Stenhouse.

Taylor, T. (1969). *The cay.* New York: Avon Books.

Taylor, T. (1993). *Timothy of the cay.* New York: Avon Books.

Terban, M. (1982). *Eight ate: A feast of homonym riddles.* New York: Clarion Books.

Thaler, M. (1997). *The librarian from the black lagoon.* New York: Jared D. Lee Studio.

Tolan, S. (2002). *Surviving the Applewhites.* New York: HarperCollins.

Tompkins, G. E. (2001). *Literacy for the 21st century: A balanced approach.* (2nd ed.) Upper Saddle River, NJ: Merrill/Prentice Hall.

Torgeson, J. (2003, November). *Closing the gap through intensive instruction: New hope from research.* Keynote address at the International Dyslexia Association 54th Annual Conference, San Diego, CA.

Townend, J., & Turner, M. (2000). *Dyslexia in practice: A guide for teachers.* New York: Kluwer Academic/Plenum.

Traugh, S. *Voices of America.* Cypress, CA: Creative Teaching Press.

Tyre, P. (2006, January 30). The trouble with boys. *Newsweek,* pp. 44–52.

U.S. Department of Education, Office of Educational Technology. (2004). *Conclusions. In Toward a new golden age in American education: How the internet, the law and today's students are revolutionizing expectations.* Retrieved October 8, 2006, from http://www.ed.gov/about/offices/list/os/technology/plan/2004.

Vangelisti, A. & Daly, J. (1989). Correlates of speaking skills in the United States: A national assessment. *Communication Education,* 38, 123–143.

Vacca, H. L., Vacca, R. T., Grove, M. K., Burkey L., Lenhart, L. A., & Keon, C. (2003). *Reading and learning to read.* (5th ed.) Boston: Allyn & Bacon.

Van Allsburg, C. (1968). *The polar express.* Boston: Houghton Mifflin.

Van Allsburg, C. (1979). *The garden of Abdul Gasazi*. Boston: Houghton Mifflin.

Van Allsburg, C. (1981). *Jumanji*. Boston: Houghton Mifflin.

Van Allsburg, C. (1982). *Ben's dream*. Boston: Houghton Mifflin.

Van Allsburg, C. (1983). *The wreck of the Zephyr*. Boston: Houghton Mifflin.

Van Allsburg, C. (1984). *The mysteries of Harris Burdick*. Boston: Houghton Mifflin.

Van Allsburg, C. (1987). *The Z was zapped*. Boston: Houghton Mifflin.

Van Allsburg, C. (1990). *Just a dream*. Boston: Houghton Mifflin.

Van Allsburg, C. (1991). *The wretched stone*. Boston: Houghton Mifflin.

Van Allsburg, C. (1992). *The widow's broom*. Boston: Houghton Mifflin.

Van Allsburg, C. (1993). *The sweetest fig*. Boston: Houghton Mifflin.

Wagstaff, J. M. (1999). *Teaching reading and writing with word walls*. New York: Scholastic Professional Books.

Weiner, S. (1994). Four first graders' descriptions of how they spell. *Elementary School Journal*, *94*, 315–332.

Wepner, S., Valmont, W., & Thurlow, R. (2000). *Linking literacy and technology*. Newark, DE: International Reading Association.

Whaley, C. (2002). Meeting the diverse needs of children through storytelling: Supporting language learning. *Young Children*, *57*(2), 31–34.

White, E. B. (1952). *Charlotte's web*. New York: HarperCollins.

Williams, V. B. (1983). *A chair for my mother*. New York: Mulberry Books.

Wisconsin Assistive Technology Initiative. (2000, December). *Showcasing assistive technology in Wisconsin schools*. Oshkosh: Wisconsin Assistive Technology Initiative.

Wolf, M. (2006a). *Common questions about fluency*. Retrieved December 4, 2006, from http://content.scholastic.com/browse/article.jsp?id=4470.

Wolf, M. (2006b). *What is fluency? Fluency development: As the bird learns to fly*. Research Paper, Vol. 1. Retrieved December 2, 2006, from http://content.scholastic.com/content/collateral_resources/pdf/w/WhatIsFluency.pdf.

Wren, S. (2003a, August). *Developing research-based resources for the balanced reading teacher: Science to the rescue*. Retrieved October 30, 2006, from www.balancedreading.com.

Wren, S. (2003b, August). *Developing research-based resources for the balanced reading teacher: Older struggling readers*. Retrieved October 30, 2006, from www.balancedreading.com.

Wren, S. (2003c). *Developing research-based resources for the balanced reading teacher: Vocabulary*. Retrieved November 1, 2006, from http://www.balancedreading.com/vocabulary.html.

Wright, R. (Director). (1987). *I Am Joe's heart* [Film] Santa Monica, CA: Pyramid Films.

Yolen, J. (1990). *The devils's arithmetic*. New York: Puffin Books.

Yolen, J. (1992). *Letting swift river go*. Boston: Little Brown.

Zinsser, W. (2001). *On writing well*. (6th ed.) New York: HarperCollins.

Zutell, J. (1998). Word sorting: A developmental spelling approach to word study for delayed readers. *Reading and Writing Quarterly*, *14*, 219–238.

NAME INDEX

R

S

T

V

W

Y

Z

SUBJECT INDEX

D

I

Q

R

S

U

V

W

Y

Z

Other Books of Interest

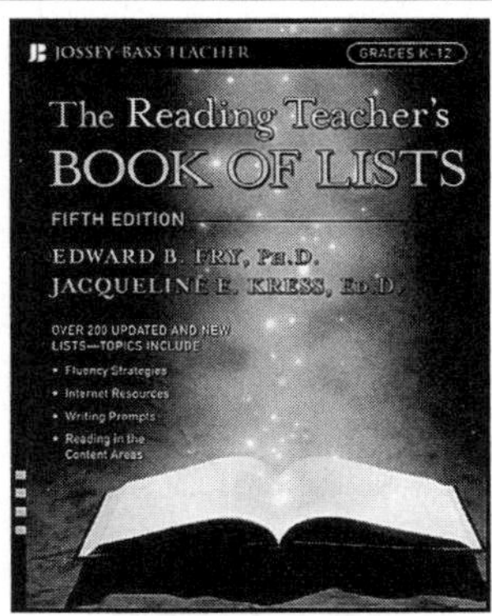

The Reading Teacher's Book of Lists

Fifth Edition

Edward B. Fry and Jacqueline E. Kress

Paper ISBN: 978-0-7879-8257-7

www.josseybass.com

"*The Reading Teacher's Book of Lists* should be on the bookshelf of every reading teacher in the English-speaking world! It is a tremendous resource that I have used over and over again throughout my career. The fifth edition is the best yet! It has more useful information than any of the previous editions. You can be assured that I will make good use of Dr. Fry and Dr. Kress's classic book."—**Timothy Rasinski, Ph.D., professor of education, Kent State University**

Written for anyone who teaches reading, *The Reading Teacher's Book of Lists* is the thoroughly revised edition of the best-selling foundational reading reference book. This classic resource is filled with 218 up-to-date lists that teachers can use to develop instructional materials and plan lessons that might otherwise take years and much effort to acquire. The book is organized into eighteen sections that are brimming with practical examples, key words, teaching ideas, and activities that can be used as-is or adapted to meet the students' needs. It covers everything from Greek and Latin roots to teacher's correction marks, word plays, prefixes, oxymorons, vocabulary, and more.

This revised fifth edition contains a complete overhaul of teaching methods sections and includes new sections on electronic resources, new literacies, building fluency, and reading in content areas. It is an essential resource with endless uses.

Edward B. Fry, Ph.D. (Laguna Beach, CA) is a professor emeritus of education at Rutgers University (New Brunswick, NJ). At Rutgers, Dr. Fry was the director of the Reading Center and taught graduate and undergraduate courses in reading, curriculum, and other educational subjects. A respected author and speaker, he has also written *The Vocabulary Teacher's Book of Lists* for Jossey-Bass (ISBN 0787971014). Dr. Fry is internationally renowned for his Readability Graph, which is used by teachers, publishers, and others to judge the reading difficulty of books and other materials.

Jacqueline E. Kress, Ed.D. (Elizabeth, NJ) is dean of education at New York Institute of Technology. She has designed numerous educational programs, including programs for at-risk students, students with special needs, and standards-based K–12 and college-level curricula. Dr. Kress is also the author of *The ESL Teacher's Book of Lists* for Jossey-Bass.

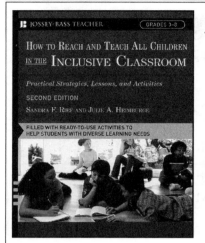

Also by Sandra F. Rief

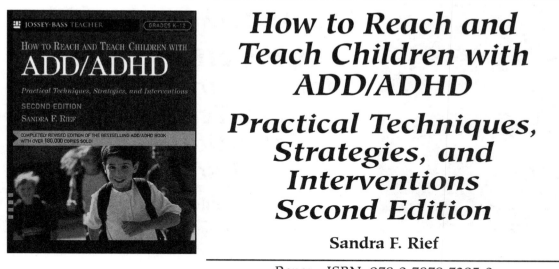

How to Reach and Teach Children with ADD/ADHD

Practical Techniques, Strategies, and Interventions Second Edition

Sandra F. Rief

Paper ISBN: 978-0-7879-7295-0

www.josseybass.com

"For over a decade, *How to Reach and Teach Children with ADD/ADHD* has been the most definitive and user-friendly guide for teachers and parents eager to help children with ADHD succeed in school, home, and life overall. Now updated with the latest research from the last ten years, this book outstrips even the original. . . . [It] is hands-on, well-organized, extremely readable, and full of the . . . practical advice that only comes from someone who has been there (and continues to be there!) helping teachers, parents, children, and youth struggling with ADHD. I especially like the focus on different ages, school settings, and subjects. My highest recommendation for this book, and my greatest praise for Sandra making this invaluable resource available!"—**Peter S. Jensen, M.D., director, Center for the Advancement of Children's Mental Health and Ruane Professor of Child Psychiatry at Columbia University**

How to Reach and Teach Children with ADD/ADHD is filled with practical strategies and techniques to improve the academic, behavioral, and social performance of students with ADHD. For over a decade, this best-selling book has served as a resource for teachers, school professionals, parents, and clinicians. It is easy to read, includes the most current research-based information about ADHD, and outlines effective treatments.

Sandra Rief offers myriad real-life case studies, interviews, and student intervention plans for children with ADD/ADHD. This invaluable resource includes proven suggestions for:

- Engaging students' attention and active participation
- Keeping students on-task and productive
- Preventing and managing behavioral problems in the classroom
- Differentiating instruction and addressing students' diverse learning styles
- Building a partnership with parents
- And much more!

With enhanced content in many areas, the second edition of this highly successful book is designed to serve as a guide for school personnel trying to make a difference in the lives of children who have been diagnosed with ADD/ADHD.

Also by Sandra F. Rief

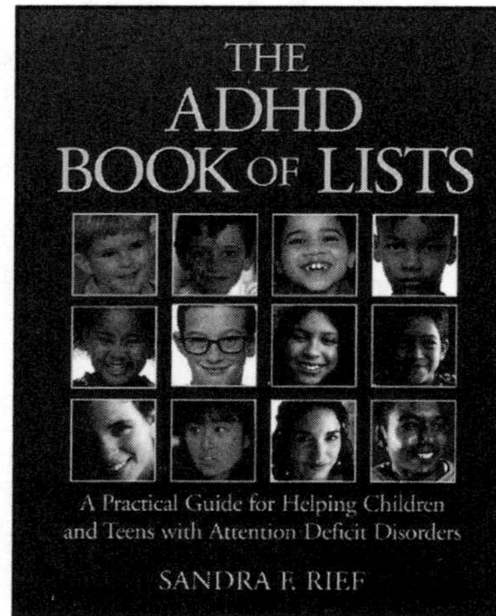

The ADHD Book of Lists

A Practical Guide for Helping Children and Teens with Attention Deficit Disorders

Sandra F. Rief

Paper ISBN: 978-0-7879-6591-4

www.josseybass.com

"If you are looking for information, tips, strategies, interventions, references, and tools to help your child or student with ADHD, Sandra Rief's book has it all in an easy-to-read, comprehensive encyclopedia of practical information for parents and educators. As an in-service provider, I am always looking for the right source of information, and this is the book I have been waiting for!"— **Beth A. Kaplanek, RN, BSN, advocate, parent of an ADHD child, and former national president of CHADD**

"Look no more— this is it! This book is the consummate resource for finding everything you want to know about ADHD— from diagnosis to intervention. Valuable for both parents and professionals."— **Ginger E. Gates, Ph.D., NCSP, LSSP, school psychologist and professional development trainer, Houston, Texas**

The ADHD Book of Lists is a comprehensive, reliable source of answers, practical strategies, and tools written in a convenient list format. Created for teachers (K–12), parents, school psychologists, medical and mental health professionals, counselors, and other school personnel, this important resource contains the most current information about Attention Deficit/Hyperactivity Disorder (ADHD). It is filled with the strategies, supports, and interventions that have been found to be the most effective in minimizing the problems and optimizing the success of children and teens with ADHD. The book contains a wealth of information to guide in the management of ADHD in school and at home. In addition, *The ADHD Book of Lists*' easy-to-use 8-1/2-by-11-inch lay-flat format is filled with reproducible checklists, forms, tools, and resources.

A companion video by Sandra F. Rief is also available for purchase. *ADHD & LD: Powerful Teaching Strategies and Accommodations* (ISBN: 978-0-7879-7472-5) provides a thorough, non-technical introduction to ADD and ADHD, with hundreds of practical instructional and behavioral strategies tested in diverse elementary and middle school classrooms. It is an excellent supplement to the *ADHD Book of Lists.*